SIXTH EDITION

STUDENT STUDY GUIDE

to accompany

INTERMEDIATE ACCOUNTING

DONALD E. KIESO Ph.D., C.P.A.

Northern Illinois University
DeKalb, Illinois

JERRY J. WEYGANDT Ph.D., C.P.A.

University of Wisconsin
Madison, Wisconsin

Prepared by

RAYMOND J. CLAY, JR.

North Texas State University
Denton, Texas

WILEY

JOHN WILEY AND SONS
New York   Chichester   Brisbane
Toronto   Singapore

ISBN 0-471-61932-9

Printed in the United States of America

10 9 8 7 6 5 4 3 2

CONTENTS

Note to Students

NOTE TO STUDENTS

This Study Guide is provided as an aid to your study of *Intermediate Accounting*, by Donald E. Kieso and Jerry J. Weygandt. If used wisely, it can supplement and reinforce your understanding of the concepts and techniques presented in the textbook. **Never rely on the Study Guide as a substitute for a thorough reading of the textbook material.** This Study Guide merely highlights the in-depth presentation in the textbook.

An approach that combines use of the Study Guide and textbook material is suggested below.

1. Read the textbook presentation of the chapter.
2. Read the chapter review paragraphs in the Study Guide.
3. Answer the questions and review exercises appearing at the end of the chapter review paragraphs and compare your answers with those found at the end of each chapter. The extent of your success in answering these questions and exercises will indicate your understanding of the chapter. If you were unsuccessful in answering a large percentage of these questions correctly, you should read the textbook again.
4. Work the problems assigned from the textbook.

Solutions to the review questions and exercises are found at the end of each chapter. In addition to identifying the correct answer to each true-false and multiple choice question, an explanation is provided indicating why the answer is false and why a particular alternative (for multiple choice questions) is correct. This approach is designed to aid you in gaining a complete understanding of the material in each chapter.

When preparing for examinations, the Study Guide material may be used to determine your recall of the information presented in specific chapters. Once you have identified those subject areas in need of further review, return to the textbook material for a complete discussion of the subject matter involved. Remember, the Study Guide merely highlights the textbook material; it cannot be relied upon as a comprehensive treatment of a subject area.

In the study of accounting, there is no substitute for hard work and a desire to learn. A proper attitude and a willingness to work will go a long way toward ensuring your success in intermediate accounting.

The following supplemental items are also available from your bookstore, or the publisher, for use in conjunction with this Study Guide and with the textbook, *Intermediate Accounting*, Sixth Edition.

Practice Set (Rockford Corporation). The accounting practice set for the sixth edition has been revised with the assistance of Professor John C. Borke of the University of Wisconsin-Platteville and is designed to be used at or near the beginning of intermediate accounting. The practice set provides material that can be assigned in conjunction with Chapter 3, "A Review of the Accounting Process." With this sixth edition we provide an alternative set of instructions so that the instructor has the choice of two sets of data to assign. The practice set has been designed as a student review and update of the accounting cycle and the preparation of financial statements that are covered in the traditional first-year principles of financial accounting. Completion of this practice set requires the student to (1) analyze transactions, (2) journalize transactions, (3) post to the general ledger and to subsidiary ledgers, (4) prepare year-end adjusting entries, (5) use a 10-column work sheet, (6) prepare financial statements, and (7) close the accounts. The Rockford Corporation Practice Set is estimated to take between 12 and 16 hours to work. A Solutions Manual is available free for instructors.

Computerized Practice Set. A disk and accompanying documentation to run the Rockford Corporation Practice Set (described above) on microcomputer has been prepared by James Perkins. This practice set runs on IBM-PC and Apple microcomputers. For any adoption of the practice set wherein the students buy the Rockford Corporation Practice Set Workbook, John Wiley & Sons will provide one master disk with documentation to the department for their use on microcomputers. The Solutions Manual is the same one that accompanies the manual practice set described above.

Working Papers I and II. Working Papers I is provided for all problems in Chapters 1 through 14. These working papers are partially filled in with company names, numerous headings, and some preliminary data. Working Papers II provides similar partial information for Chapters 14 through 27. The Working papers save students time, standardize the solutions format, and facilitate rapid reviews by the instructor.

Solving Intermediate Accounting Problems Using SuperCalc3 and Solving Intermediate Accounting Problems Using Lotus 1-2-3. Two new supplements with this sixth edition have been prepared by David R. Koeppen, University of Wisconsin-La Crosse. Each consists of a workbook plus disk that contains intermediate accounting problems formatted on templates to run on Lotus 1-2-3 or SuperCalc3. The SuperCalc3 package includes the spreadsheet programs themselves; the instructor or the department must have access to Lotus 1-2-3 in order to use the Lotus package. Both packages are set up so that the student purchases them for use as the instructor wishes. The templates include problems covering time value of money, notes receivable, retail inventory method, dollar-value LIFO, exchange of used assets, depreciation, bonds payable, percent of completion method, pensions, lease amortization, and many others.

Cases in Financial Accounting. This casebook, prepared by David E. Mielke of Marquette University, consists of 250 cases relating to 23 chapters in the Kieso/Weygandt text with a variety of formats, solutions approaches, and degrees of difficulty. These cases can be used as a supplement in intermediate accounting, as the primary text for an advanced accounting seminar or issues course, as well as for masters' students or business executives.

1

The environment of financial accounting and the development of accounting standards

Chapter Synopsis

Chapter 1 describes the environment that has influenced both the development and use of the financial accounting process. The chapter traces the development of financial accounting standards, focusing on the groups that have had or currently have the responsibility for developing such standards. Certain groups other than those with direct responsibility for developing financial accounting standards have significantly influenced the standard-setting process. These various pressure groups are also discussed in Chapter 1.

Chapter Review

1. The **purpose of accounting** is to provide quantitative financial information about an economic entity to persons interested in the activities of that entity. The focus of this text is on the subset of the accounting discipline known as **financial accounting**. This subset is concerned with the accumulation of financial information for the purpose of developing **general-purpose financial statements** that report an entity's financial position, results of operations, and changes in financial position. The generalized format of these financial statements makes them useful both to individuals within the enterprise and to those outside of it.

2. Modern financial accounting practices are influenced by the environment within which the economic enterprise must operate. As that environment changes, financial accounting practices must change so that the reporting process remains relevant. Modern financial accounting is the product of many influences and conditions. Five of the more significant influences and conditions are: (a) **accounting exists in a world of scarce means and resources; (b) accounting is influenced by society's current legal and ethical concepts of property and other rights; (c) economic activity is conducted by separately identifiable business units; (d) owners often entrust the custodianship of and control over property to managers;** and (e) **accounting**

provides measures of the changes in economic resources, economic obligations, and residual interests of a business enterprise.

3. Accounting is a system that feeds back information to organizations and individuals that they can use to reshape their environment. It provides information for the reevaluation of social, political, and economic objectives as well as the relative costs and benefits of alternative means of achieving these objectives. Thus, accounting information has a direct impact on the transfer of resources among entities and individuals.

4. **Statement of Financial Accounting Concepts (SFAC) No. 1,** "Objectives of Financial Reporting by Business Enterprises," represents an attempt by the **Financial Accounting Standards Board (FASB)** to establish a foundation upon which financial accounting and reporting standards will be based. According to **SFAC No. 1,** the objectives of financial reporting are to provide information (a) that is useful in investment and credit decisions, (b) that is useful in assessing cash flow prospects, and (c) about enterprise resources, claims to those resources, and changes in those resources.

5. As has been noted, accounting is influenced by its environment, and that environment is influenced simultaneously by accounting. The financial statements that result from the accounting process are based upon **accounting standards or principles** developed by the accounting profession. The accounting profession has attempted to provide a **body of accounting theory and practice** that is generally accepted and universally applied. This body of accounting theory and practice serves to promote **uniformity** and **comparability** in the preparation and analysis of **general-purpose financial statements.**

6. The accounting profession has developed a common set of accounting concepts, standards, and procedures known as **generally accepted accounting principles (GAAP).** These principles serve as a general guide to the accounting practitioner in accumulating and

reporting the financial information of a business enterprise. Although the adoption of some generally accepted accounting principles has caused controversy among accountants as well as members of the financial community, a majority of the members in each group recognize the ultimate benefit an accepted set of accounting principles can bring to the financial reporting process.

7. The GAAP in use at this time in the United States are primarily a result of the accounting profession's efforts during the past 60 years. Prior to that time accounting practices were relatively unsophisticated owing to the lack of extensive economic development in the United States. The **American Institute of Certified Public Accountants (AICPA),** the national professional organization of practicing Certified Public Accountants (CPA's), has been a catalyst in the development of GAAP in the United States. Although the responsibility for setting accounting standards now rests with the FASB, other organizations can and do influence the standards-setting process. The more significant of these organizations are the following:

(a) **Securities and Exchange Commission (SEC),**
(b) **American Accounting Association (AAA),**
(c) **Financial Executives Institute (FEI),** and
(d) **National Association of Accountants (NAA).**

8. The first group appointed by the AICPA to address the issue of uniformity in accounting practice was the **Committee on Accounting Procedure (CAP).** This group served the accounting profession from 1939 to 1959. During that period they issued 51 **Accounting Research Bulletins (ARBs)** that narrowed the wide range of alternative accounting practices then in existence. Even though the work of the Committee on Accounting Procedure was a valuable aid to accounting practitioners, the authority for their pronouncements rested solely on general acceptance by the accounting profession.

9. In 1959, the AICPA created the **Accounting Principles Board (APB)** and a new **Accounting Research Division.** The charge of this group was: (a) to establish basic postulates, (b) to formulate a set of broad principles, (c) to set up rules to guide the application of principles in specific situations, and (d) to base the entire program on research. The APB was designated as the AICPA's sole authority for public pronouncements on accounting principles. Their pronouncements, known as **APB Opinions, (or APBOs),** were intended to be based mainly on research studies and supported by reasoning. The APB Opinions constituted GAAP until superseded by subsequent pronouncements of the body designated by the accounting profession to issue such pronouncements. Although the AICPA recognized other sources as providing substantial authoritative support for accounting practices, the burden for justifying a departure from GAAP rests with the reporting member.

10. The APB operated in a somewhat hostile environment for 13 years. Early in its existence it was criticized for overreacting to certain issues. A committee, known as the **Study Group on Establishment of Accounting principles (Wheat Committee),** was set up to study the APB and recommend changes in its structure and operation. The result of the Study Group's findings was the demise of the APB and the creation of the Financial Accounting Standards Board (FASB). The FASB represents the current rule-making body within the accounting profession, and its pronouncements represent GAAP.

11. The FASB issues **Statements of Financial Accounting Standards** and **Interpretations** of those Statements. Both the Standards and the Interpretations are considered GAAP and must be followed in practice in the same manner as APBs. The FASB also issues **Statements of Financial Accounting Concepts (SFAC)** and **Technical Bulletins.** The SFAC represent and attempt to move away from the problem-by-problem approach to standard setting that has been characteristic of the accounting profession. The Concept Statements are intended to form a cohesive set of interrelated concepts, a body of theory, or conceptual framework, that will serve as a tool for solving existing and emerging problems in a consistent, sound manner. Unlike FASB Statements, the Concept Statements do not establish GAAP. Technical Bulletins provide answers to specific questions related to the application and implementation of FASB Statement or Interpretations, APBOs, and ARB. Technical Bulletins do not alter GAAP; they merely provide guidance on questions related to existing GAAP.

12. The **SEC** takes a great deal of interest in the standards developed by the accounting profession. The SEC is a regulator agency of the federal government that monitors the activities of corporate enterprises whose stock is publicly held. The SEC requires each corporate entity under its jurisdiction to **file a set of annual audited financial statements.** Historically, the SEC has supported the development of accounting standards by the private sector. The SEC confronts financial accounting and reporting practices of U.S. businesses on a daily basis and frequently identifies emerging problems for the FASB Exposure Drafts, and provides the FASB with counsel and advice on request.

13. Certain of the professional groups and agencies have influenced accounting theory and the development of accounting standards. These groups include: The **American Accounting Association (AAA),** the **National Association of Accountants (NAA),** the **Financial Executives Institute (FEI),** the **Internal Revenue Service (IRS),** and the **Cost Accounting Standards Board (CASB).** These groups influence the standard-setting process because of their expressed interest in

accounting, their extensive use of the reports generated by the accounting process, or both.

14. Even though the FASB has assumed primary responsibility for the development of accounting and reporting standards, the AICPA has remained quite active in making known its views on major issues. Through its **Accounting Standards Executive Committee (AcSEC)** the AICPA responds to pronouncements of both the FASB and SEC. The AcSEC also informs the FASB of financial reporting problems that are emerging in practice through the development of **issue papers.** Issue papers identify the problem, suggest alternative treatments, and recommend preferred solutions. The AICPA's **Auditing Standards Board** remains the leader in the development of auditing standards and other issues related to the practice of public accounting.

15. Generally accepted accounting principles (GAAP) are those that have **substantial authoritative support.** Accounting principles that have substantial authoritative support are those found in FASB Statements and Interpretations, APB Opinions (APBOs) and Interpretations, and CAP Accounting Research Bulletins, (ARBs). If an accounting transaction is not covered in any of these documents, the accountant may look to other authoritative accounting literature for guidance.

16. Although accounting standards are developed by using careful logic and empirical findings, a certain amount of pressure and influence is brought to bear by groups interested in or affected by accounting standards. The sources of influence are numerous, but the most intense and continuous pressure comes from governmental agencies, financial analysts, bankers, industry associations, clients of CPAs, individual companies, academicians, and public opinion. The FASB does not exist in a vacuum, and politics and special-interest pressures remain a part of the standard-setting process.

REVIEW QUESTIONS

True-False

Indicate whether each of the following is true (T) or false (F) in the space provided.

_____ 1. The purpose of accounting is to provide quantitative financial information about an economic entity to persons interested in the activities of that entity.

_____ 2. Financial accounting is the process that culminates in the preparation of financial reports that are relative to the enterprise as a whole and that are used by parties both internal and external to the enterprise.

_____ 3. The environment of accounting is unaffected by social-economic-political-legal conditions, restraints, and influences that vary from time to time.

_____ 4. The principal role of accounting is to furnish investors and lenders information that is useful in assessing the prospective risks and returns associated with an investment.

_____ 5. Accounting is responsible for providing standards that insure accurate financial information that cannot be manipulated or improperly reported.

_____ 6. Accounting provides measures of the changes in economic resources, economic obligations, and residual interests of a business enterprise as a basis for comparison and evaluation.

_____ 7. One of the objectives of financial reporting is to provide information that is useful in assessing cash flow prospects of the entity being reported on.

_____ 8. The difference between generally accepted accounting principles (GAAP) and specifically accepted accounting principles concerns the degree of authority each possesses.

_____ 9. The American Institute of Certified Public Accountants (AICPA) is the national professional organization of practicing Certified Public Accountants (CPAs)

_____ 10. The authority behind the accounting pronouncements issued by the FASB comes from the SEC.

_____ 11. The Accounting Principles Board (APB) replaced the Committee on Accounting Procedure (CAP) and was designated as the AICPA's sole authority for public pronouncements on accounting principles.

_____ 12. The difference between Accounting Research Bulletins (ARBs) and Accounting Principles Board Opinions (APBOs) is that ARBs deal with accounting theory and the APBOs deal with accounting practice.

_____ 13. Generally accepted accounting principles (GAAP) are defined, in part, as those principles that have substantial authoritative support.

_____ 14. The major purpose of the ABP during its 13-year existence was to develop a single set of accounting standards useful to all business entities.

_____ 15. The Accounting Principles Board (APB) was replaced in 1973 by the Financial Accounting Standards Board (FASB), which now is responsible for setting accounting standards.

_____ 16. All those who serve on the FASB must be Certified Public Accountants.

_____ 17. FASB Interpretations represent modifications or extensions of existing FASB Standards and have the same authority as Standards.

_____ 18. FASB Technical Bulletins are designed to provide guidance on the implementation or application of FASB Statements or Interpretations.

_____ 19. The Securities and Exchange Commission (SEC) sets accounting standards for companies that do work for the government.

_____ 20. A major role of the Accounting Standards Executive Committee (AcSEC) is to inform the FASB of financial reporting problems that are developing in practice.

SOLUTIONS TO REVIEW QUESTIONS

True-False

1. (T)

2. (T)

3. (F) Accounting standards are as much a product of political action as they are of careful logic or empirical findings. Standard-setting is part of the real world and, as such, cannot escape politics and political pressure. Also, accounting objectives and practices are not the same today as they were in the past because accounting theory has evolved to meet changing demands and influences.

4. (T)

5. (F) Accounting standards are designed to act as a general guide in developing financial information about an economic entity. Such standards can always be misinterpreted or intentionally violated, thus producing unreliable financial information.

6. (T)

7. (T)

8. (F) The term "specifically accepted accounting principles" has no meaning in accounting.

9. (T)

10. (F) The authority for pronouncements of standard-setting bodies in accounting can be traced to the *Code of Professional Ethics* of the AICPA. Rule 203 of the *Code* prohibits a member of the AICPA from expressing an opinion that financial statements conform with GAAP if those statements contain a material departure from an accounting principle promulgated by the FASB, the APB, or the CAP.

11. (T)

12. (F) Both ARB and APBO represent authoritative pronouncements designed to establish principles of accounting. The Major difference is that ARB were issued by the Committee on Accounting Procedure (CAP) and APBO were issued by the Accounting Principles Board.

13. (T)

14. (F) The major purposes of the APB were (a) to advance the written expression of accounting principles, (b) to determine appropriate practices, and (c) to narrow the areas of difference and inconsistency in practice.

15. (T)

16. (F) At the present time it is not necessary to be a PA to be a member of the FASB.

17. (T)

18. (T)

19. (F) The SEC is empowered to administer the 1933 and 1934 Securities Acts. The SEC was given broad powers to prescribe the accounting practices and standards to be employed by companies that issue securities to the public or are listed on a stock exchange.

20. (T)

2

Conceptual framework underlying financial accounting

Chapter Synopsis

Chapter 2 outlines the development of a conceptual framework for financial accounting and reporting by the FASB. The entire conceptual framework is affected by the environmental aspects discussed in Chapter 1. It is composed of basic objectives, fundamental concepts, and operational guidelines. These notions are discussed in Chapter 2 and should enhance your understanding of the topics covered in intermediate accounting.

Chapter Review

1. A **conceptual framework** is a coherent system of interrelated objects and fundamentals that can lead to consistent standards and that prescribes the nature, function, and limits of financial accounting and financial statements. The benefits its development will generate can be characterized as follows: (a) the FASB should be able to issue more useful and consistent standards in the future; (b) new practice problems should be solved more rapidly by reference to an existing framework; (c) financial statement users should gain a better understanding of and confidence in the financial reporting process; and (d) a company's financial statements should be more easily comparable.

2. The FASB recognized the need, early in its existence, for a conceptual framework upon which a consistent set of financial accounting standards could be based. As an initial step in addressing this need, the FASB issued a massive three-point discussion memorandum entitled *Conceptual Framework for Financial Accounting and Reporting: Elements of Financial Statements and Their Measurements*. This document set forth the major issues considered necessary to establish a basic framework for resolving financial reporting controversies.

3. Since publication of the initial discussion memorandum, the FASB has issued four Statements of Financial Accounting Concepts (SFAC) that relate to financial reporting. They are listed and described briefly below:

SFAC No. 1. "Objectives of Financial Reporting by Business Enterprises" presents the goals and purposes of accounting.

SFAC No. 2. "Qualitative Characteristics of Accounting Information" examines the characteristics that make accounting information useful.

SFAC No. 3. "Elements of Financial Statements of Business Enterprises" defines the broad classifications of items found in financial statements.

SFAC No. 5. "Recognition and Measurement in Financial Statements of Business Enterprises," sets forth fundamental recognition criteria and guidance on what information should be formally incorporated into financial statements and when.

SFAC No. 6. "Elements of Financial Statements," replaces *SFAC No. 3*, "Elements of Financial Statements of Business Enterprises," expanding its scope to include not-for-profit organizations.

4. *SFAC No.1* describes the objectives of financial reporting as the presentation of information that is useful (a) in making investment and credit decisions, (b) in assessing cash flow prospects, and (c) in learning about enterprise resources, claims to those resources, and changes in them. *SFAC No.2* identifies the primary and secondary qualitative characteristics of accounting information that distinguish better (more useful) information from inferior (less useful) information for decision-making purposes. The **primary qualities** that make accounting information useful for decision making are **relevance** and **reliability**. The **secondary qualities** identified are **comparability** and **consistency**. Each of these qualities is defined below:

Relevance. Accounting information is relevant if it is capable of making a difference in a decision.

Reliability. Accounting information is reliable to the extent that users can depend on it to represent the economic conditions or events that it purports to represent.

Comparability. Accounting information that has been measured and reported in a similar manner for different enterprises is considered comparable.

Consistency. Accounting information is consistent when an entity applies the same accounting treatment from period to period to similar accountable events.

5. Knowledge of the specific meaning of certain **basic elements** is essential for an understanding of financial accounting. However, the specific meanings that accountants attach to these basic elements sometimes differ from their meanings in a nonaccounting context. Ten basic elements that are most directly related to measuring the performance and financial status of an enterprise are formally defined in *SFAC No. 6*. These elements, as defined below, are further discussed and interpreted throughout the text.

Assets. Probable future economic benefits obtained or controlled by a particular entity as a result of past transactions or events.

Liabilities. Probable future sacrifices of economic benefits that arise from present obligations of a particular entity to transfer assets or provide services to other entities in the future as a result of past transactions or events.

Equity. Residual interest in the assets of an entity that remains after deducting its liabilities. In a business enterprise, the equity is the ownership interest.

Investment by Owners. Increases in net assets of a particular enterprise that result from transfers to it from other entities of something of value to obtain or increase ownership interests (or equity) in it. Assets are most commonly received as investment by owners, but that which is received may include services or satisfaction or conversion of liabilities of the enterprise.

Distribution to Owners. Decreases in net assets of a particular enterprise that result from transferring assets, rendering services, or incurring liabilities by the enterprise to owners. Distributions to owners decrease ownership interests (or equity) in an enterprise.

Comprehensive Income. Change in equity (net assets) of an entity during a period from transactions and other events and circumstances involving nonowner sources. It includes all changes in equity during a period, except those resulting from investments by owners and distribution to owners.

Revenues. Inflows or other enhancement of assets of an entity or settlement of liabilities (or a combination of both) during a period as a result of delivering or producing goods, rendering services, or other activities that constitute the entity's ongoing major or central operations.

Expenses. Outflows or other using up of assets or incurrences of liabilities (or a combination of both) during a period as a result of delivering or producing goods, rendering services, or carrying out other activities that constitute the entity's ongoing major or central operations.

Gains. Increases in equity (net assets) from peripheral or incidental transactions of an entity and from all other transactions and other events and circumstances that affect the entity during a period, except those that result from revenues or investments by owners.

Losses. Decreases in equity (net assets) from peripheral or incidental transactions of an entity from all other transactions and other events and circumstances that affect the entity during a period, except those that result from expenses or distributions to owners.

6. In the practice of financial accounting, certain basic assumptions are important to an understanding of the manner in which data are presented. The following four basic assumptions underlie the financial accounting structure.:

Economic Entity Assumption. The economic activities of an entity can be accumulated and reported in a manner that assumes the entity is separate and distinct from its owners or other business units.

Going-Concern Assumption. In the absence of contrary information, a business entity is assumed to remain in existence for an indeterminate period of time. The current relevance of the historical cost principle is dependent on the going-concern assumption.

Monetary Unit Assumption. In the United States, economic activities of an entity are measured and reported in dollars. These dollars are assumed to remain relatively stable over the years in terms of purchasing power. In essence, this assumption disregards any inflation or deflation in the economy in which the entity operates.

Periodicity Assumption. The life of an economic entity can be divided into artificial time periods for the purpose of providing periodic reports on the economic activities of the entity.

As you progress through the remaining chapters in the text, the reasoning behind these assumptions should become more apparent.

7. Certain **basic principles** are followed by accountants in recording the transactions of a business entity. These principles relate basically to how assets, liabilities, revenues, and expenses are to be **identified, measured,** and **reported.** The following is a brief review of the basic principles considered in Chapter 2 of the text:

Historical Cost Principle. Acquisition cost is the most objective and verifiable basis upon which to account for assets and liabilities of a business enterprise. Cost has been found to be more definite and determinable than other suggested valuation methods.

Revenue Recognition Principle. Revenue is recognized when the earning process is virtually complete and an exchange transaction has occurred. Generally, this takes place when a sale to another individual or independent entity has been confirmed. Confirmation is usually accomplished by a transfer of ownership in an exchange transaction. Certain variations in the revenue recognition principle include: the **percentage-of-completion** approach, the **end-of-production** recognition, and the recognition upon **receipt of cash.**

Matching Principle. Accountants attempt to match the revenues earned during a fiscal period with the expense incurred in earning those revenues. Use of **accrual accounting procedures** assists the accountant in allocating revenues and expenses properly among the fiscal periods that compose the life of a business enterprise.

Full Disclosure Principle. In the preparation of financial statements, the accountant should include sufficient information to permit the knowledgeable reader to make an informed judgment about the financial condition of the enterprise in question.

8. Although accounting theory is based upon certain assumptions and the application of basic principles, there are some exceptions to these assumptions. These exceptions, often called constraints, sometimes justify departures from basic accounting theory. The constraints presented in Chapter 2 are the following:

Cost-Benefit Relationship. This constraint relates to the notion that the benefit to be derived from having certain accounting information should exceed the cost of providing that information. The difficulty in cost-benefit analysis is that the costs and especially the benefits are not always evident or measurable.

Materiality. In the application of basic accounting theory, an amount may be considered less important because of its size in comparison with revenues and expenses, assets and liabilities, or net income. Deciding when an amount is material in relation to other amounts is a matter of judgment and professional expertise.

Industry Practices. Basic accounting theory may not apply with equal relevance to every industry that accounting must serve. The fair presentation of financial position and results of operations for a particular industry may require a departure from basic accounting theory because of the peculiar nature of an event or practice common only to that industry.

Conservatism. When in doubt, an accountant should choose a solution that will be least likely to overstate assets and income. The conservatism should be applied only when doubt exists. An intentional understatement of assets or income is not acceptable accounting.

9. The basic theory outlined in Chapter 2 is critical for a thorough understanding of the financial accounting process. In subsequent chapters many problem areas are examined that build upon and expand the framework developed in Chapter 2. One's ability to grasp and apply the information related to those problem areas is greatly aided by a familiarity with this framework.

REVIEW QUESTIONS

True-False

Indicate whether each of the following is true (T) or false (F) in the space provided.

_____ 1. The principles of accounting are unlike the principles of the natural sciences and mathematics because they cannot be derived from or proved by the laws of nature, and they are not viewed as fundamental truths or axioms.

_____ 2. A conceptual framework is a coherent system of interrelated objectives and fundamentals that can lead to consistent standards and that prescribes the nature, function, and limits of financial accounting and financial statements.

_____ 3. A conceptual framework underlying financial accounting is necessary because future accounting practice problems can be solved by reference to the conceptual framework and a formal standard-setting body will not be necessary.

_____ 4. Use of a sound conceptual framework in the development of accounting principles will make financial statements of all entities comparable because alternative accounting methods for similar transactions will be eliminated.

_____ 5. *Statement of Financial Accounting Concepts No.1*, issued by the FASB, indicates that financial reporting should provide information useful for investment and credit decisions for readers with a reasonable understanding of business rather than for naive or totally unsophisticated investors.

_____ 6. Accounting theory is developed without consideration of the environment within which it exists.

____ 7. Relevance and reliability are the two primary qualities that make accounting information useful for decision making.

____ 8. Adherence to the concept of consistency requires that the same accounting principles be applied to similar transactions for a minimum of five years before any change in principle is adopted.

____ 9. The fact that equity represents an ownership interest and a residual claim against the net assets of an enterprise means that in the event of liquidation, creditors have a priority over owners in the distribution of assets.

____ 10. The economic entity assumption is useful only when the entity referred to is a profit-seeking business enterprise.

____ 11. The going-concern assumption is generally applicable in most business situations unless liquidation appears imminent.

____ 12. Adherence to the monetary unit assumption in accounting is difficult to defend in light of current economic trends in the United States.

____ 13. The periodicity assumption is a result of the demands of various financial statement user groups for timely reporting of financial information.

____ 14. If Company A wishes to acquire an asset owned by Company B, the historical cost principle would require Company A to record the asset at the original cost to Company B.

____ 15. Generally, confirmation by a sale to independent interests is used to indicate the point at which revenue is recognized.

____ 16. Recognition of revenue when cash is collected is appropriate only when it is impossible to establish the revenue figure at the time of sale because of the uncertainty of collection.

____ 17. Under the matching principle, it is possible to have an expense reported on the income statement in one period and the cash payment for that expense reported in another period.

____ 18. Consistent application of generally accepted accounting principles (GAAP) will eliminate any large variations in reported net income between accounting periods.

____ 19. When an amount is determined by the accountant to be immaterial in relation to other amounts reported in the financial statements, that amount may be deleted from the financial statements.

____ 20. The conservatism convention allows for the reporting of financial information in any manner the accountant desires when there is doubt surrounding a particular issue.

Multiple Choice

____ 1. Which of the following is not a benefit associated with the FASB Conceptual Framework Project?
   A. A conceptual framework should increase financial statement users' understanding of and confidence in financial reporting.
   B. Practical problems should be more quickly solvable by reference to an existing conceptual framework.
   C. A coherent set of accounting standards and rules should result.
   D. Business entities will need far less assistance from accountants because the financial reporting process will be quite easy to apply.

____ 2. When determining whether financial information should or should not be presented, the overriding criterion to be applied relates to:
   A. the cost of providing the information.
   B. the ease with which the information can be obtained.
   C. its usefulness for decision-making purposes.
   D. whether or not it is required by GAAP.

____ 3. In accounting an economic entity may be defined as:
   A. a business enterprise.
   B. an individual.
   C. a division within a business enterprise.
   D. all of the above.

____ 4. Which of the following basic accounting assumptions is threatened by the existence of severe inflation in the economy?
   A. Monetary unit assumption.
   B. Periodicity assumption.
   C. Going-concern assumption.
   D. Economic entity assumption.

____ 5. The major objective of the consistency principle is to:
   A. provide timely financial information for statement users.
   B. promote comparability between financial statements of different accounting periods.
   C. match the appropriate revenues and expenses in a given accounting period.
   D. be sure the same information is disclosed in each accounting period.

____ 6. If accounting information is verifiable, representationally faithful, and neutral, it can be considered:
  A. relevant.
  B. timely.
  C. comparable.
  D. reliable.

____ 7. Comprehensive income as characterized in *SFAC No.6* includes all changes in equity during a period except:
  A. sale of assets other than inventory.
  B. those resulting from investments by or distribution to owners.
  C. sales to a particular entity where ultimate payment by the entity is doubtful.
  D. those resulting from revenue generated by a totally owned subsidy.

____ 8. Under the revenue recognition principle, revenue is generally recognized when the earning process is virtually complete and:
  A. exchange transaction has occurred.
  B. the merchandise has been ordered.
  C. all expenses have been identified.
  D. the accounting process is virtually complete.

____ 9. In complying with the full disclosure principle, an accountant must determine the amount of disclosure necessary. How much disclosure is enough?
  A. Information sufficient for a person without any knowledge of accounting to understand the statements.
  B. All information that might be of interest to an owner of a business enterprise.
  C. Information that is of sufficient importance to influence the judgment and decisions of an informed user.
  D. Information sufficient to permit most persons coming in contact with the statements to reach an accurate decision about the financial condition of the enterprise.

____ 10. Which of the following best describes the concept of constraints as related to the application of basic accounting principles?
  A. They represent areas where GAAP never apply.
  B. They refer only to unimportant or inconsequential items.
  C. They allow for misstatement in the financial position of an enterprise when the amounts are questionable or the accountant is unable to resolve doubt.
  D. They represent exceptions to the practical application of basic accounting theory.

SOLUTIONS TO REVIEW QUESTIONS

True-False

1. (T)

2. (T)

3. (F) Development of a conceptual framework will not provide a solution to all future accounting problems, nor will it eliminate the need for a formal standard-setting body. However, a soundly developed conceptual framework should enable the FASB to issue more useful and consistent standards resulting in easier solutions to emerging practical problems.

4. (F) Use of a sound conceptual framework will not eliminate alternative accounting methods for similar transactions. However, a sound conceptual framework should allow practitioners to dismiss certain alternatives quickly and focus on a logical and acceptable treatment.

5. (T)

6. (F) The environment within which any discipline exists plays an integral role in shaping the theory of that discipline. The purpose of accounting is to serve the business environment through the issuance of timely and relevant financial information. To present such information, accounting theory must be developed with consideration being given to the business environment.

7. (T)

8. (F) Consistency means that a company applies the same methods to similar accounting transactions from period to period. It does not mean that companies cannot switch from one method to another.

Companies can change to a new method that is considered preferable to the old method as long as financial statement users are made aware to the change.

9. (T)

10. (F) The economic entity assumption holds that the activity of a business entity can be kept separate and distinct from its owners and any other business unit. This assumption has nothing to do with the nature of the business organization.

11. (T)

12. (T)

13. (T)

14. (F) The historical cost principle requires that assets be accounted for on the basis of acquisition cost. Whatever it costs a particular entity to acquire an asset is that entity's acquisition cost.

15. (T)

16. (T)

17. (T)

18. (F) Net income is based upon the volume of revenue and expense transactions. If sales volume increases significantly, net income could increase without any change in the accounting principles employed.

19. (F) Because an item is deemed to be immaterial does not justify its deletion from financial statements. If an amount is so small that it is quite unimportant when compared with other items, application of a particular standard may be considered of less importance.

20. (F) The conservatism convention states that, when in doubt, the accountant should choose the solution that will be least likely to overstate assets and income.

Multiple Choice

1. (D) The financial reporting process will always require the expertise of a person trained in accounting. The development of a conceptual framework will aid the accountant because new and emerging practical problems should be more quickly solvable by reference to an existing framework. Alternatives A, B, and C are benefits of the Conceptual Framework Project.

2. (C) The usefulness of information for decision-making purposes is the overriding criterion when considering the presentation of financial information. The cost and difficulty (A and B) are not relevant considerations for information considered essential for an understanding of the financial statements. An item could be required by GAAP but because of unusual circumstances the accountant could withhold the information if he or she believed disclosure would cause the financial statements to be misleading.

3. (D) All of the alternatives (A, B, and C) are economic entities for accounting purposes.

4. (A) The monetary unit assumption holds that the unit of measure--the dollar--remains reasonably stable. Severe inflation would cause this assumption to lose its relevance.

5. (B) Comparability between financial statements presumes consistent application of GAAP.

6. (D) To be reliable, accounting information must possess three key characteristics: verifiability, representational faithfulness, and neutrality.

7. (B) Comprehensive income, as defined in *SFAC No.6*, includes net income and all other changes in equity, exclusive of owners' investments and distributions. Items A, C, and D fit into this broad definition.

8. (A) Revenue is generally recognized when (a) the earning process is virtually complete and (b) and exchange transaction has occurred.

9. (C) In deciding what information to report, accountants follow the general practice of providing information that is of sufficient importance to influence the judgment and decisions of an informed user. Alternatives A and D are wrong because they do not assume an informed user. Alternative B would result in disclosing a significant amount of extraneous information.

10. (D) Constraints represent exceptions to the practical application of basic accounting theory. The two overriding constraints that provide for such exceptions are (a) the cost-benefit relationship and (b) materiality.

3

A review of the accounting process

Chapter Synopsis

Chapter 3 presents a concise yet thorough review of the accounting process. The basic elements of the accounting process are identified and explained, and the way in which these elements are combined in completing the accounting cycle is described.

Chapter Review

1. The accounting process can be described as a set of procedures used in **identifying, recording, classifying,** and **interpreting** information related to the transactions and other events of a business enterprise. To understand the accounting process, one must be aware of the basic terminology employed in the process. The basic terminology includes: **events, transactions, real accounts, nominal accounts, ledger, journal, posting, trial balance, adjusting entries, financial statements,** and **closing entries.** These terms refer to the various activities that make up the **accounting cycle.** As we review the steps in the accounting cycle, the individual terms will be defined.

2. The first step in the accounting cycle is **analysis of transactions and selected other events.** The purpose of this analysis is to determine which events represent transactions that should be recorded. Two criteria must be met before an event can be considered a transaction and included in the accounting process. The event must be capable of being **objectively measured in financial terms** and it must **affect the financial position** of the enterprise.

3. Events can be classified as **external** or **internal.** External events are those between the enterprise and other entities, whereas internal events relate to transactions totally within the enterprise being accounted for. Of the two, internal events are the more difficult to isolate and record.

4. Once an event has been identified as a transaction, it must be recorded in the accounts. **Double-entry accounting** refers to the process used in recording transactions. The terms **debit** and **credit** are used in the accounting process to indicate the effect a transaction has on account balances. Also, the debit side of any account

is the left side; the right side is the credit side. Assets and expenses are increased by debits and decreased by credits. Liabilities, owners' equity, and revenues are decreased by debits and increased by credits.

5. Transactions are initially recorded in **a journal,** sometimes referred to as **the book of original entry.** A **general journal** is merely a chronological listing of transactions expressed in terms of debits and credits to particular accounts. No distinction is made in a general journal concerning the type of transaction involved. In addition to a general journal, **specialized journals** are used to accumulate transactions possessing common characteristics. Special journals benefit the accounting process by summarizing similar transactions such as sales on account, thus reducing the efforts associated with the posting process. A complete discussion of special journals is found in **Appendix 3B, Specialized Journals and Methods of Processing Accounting Data.**

6. The second step in the accounting cycle involves transferring amounts entered in the journal to the **general ledger.** The ledger is a book that usually contains a separate page for each account. Transferring amounts from a journal to the ledger is called **posting.** Transactions recorded in a general journal must be posted individually, whereas entries made in specialized journals are generally posted by columnar total.

7. The general ledger contains information related to the balance of accounts included therein. Many of the accounts listed in a general ledger are known as **controlling accounts.** Controlling accounts such as accounts receivable and accounts payable represent an accumulation of many individual customer or creditor balances. A detailed listing of the individual account balances is maintained in a **subsidiary ledger.** The use of subsidiary ledgers frees the general ledger from details concerning numerous individual balances.

8. The third step in the accounting cycle is the preparation of a **trial balance.** A trial balance is a list of all open accounts in the general ledger and their balances. An entity may prepare a trial balance at any time in the accounting cycle. A trial balance prepared after posting has been completed serves to check the mechanical accuracy of the posting process and provides a listing of accounts to be used in preparing financial statements.

9. Preparation of **adjusting journal entries** is the fourth step in the accounting cycle. Adjusting entries are entries made at the end of an accounting period to bring all accounts up to date on an accrual accounting basis so that correct financial statements can be prepared. One common characteristic of all adjusting entries is that they affect at least **one real account** (asset, liability, or equity account) and **one nominal account** (revenue or expense account). Adjusting entries can be classified as: **prepaid expenses, unearned revenues, accrued liabilities, accrued assets,** and **estimated items**.

10. Prepaid expenses and unearned revenues refer to situations where cash has been paid or received but the corresponding expense or revenue will not be recognized until a future period. Accrued liabilities and accrued assets are expenses and revenues recognized in the current period for which the corresponding payment or receipt of cash is to occur in a future period. Estimated items are expenses such as bad debts and depreciation whose amounts are a function of unknown future events or developments.

11. After adjusting entries are recorded and posted, and **adjusted trial balance** is prepared. This trial balance serves as a basis for the preparation of the financial statements discussed in the next two chapters. Preparation of the adjusted trial balance and financial statements represents steps 5 and 6 in the accounting cycle.

12. When inventory records are maintained on other than a perpetual basis, an adjustment is usually needed to reflect the difference between the beginning and ending inventory. This **year-end inventory adjustment** eliminates all nominal accounts related to the purchase of inventory by transferring them to Cost of Goods Sold. The adjustment also eliminates the beginning inventory amount and establishes the amount of ending inventory to be included on the balance sheet.

13. After financial statements have been prepared, nominal (revenues and expenses) accounts should be reduced to zero in preparation for recording the transactions of the next period. This **closing process** requires recording and posting of closing entries. All nominal accounts are reduced to zero by closing them through the **Income Summary** account. The net balance in the Income Summary account after closing is equal to net income or net loss for the period. The net income or net loss for the period is transferred to owners' equity by closing the Income Summary account to Retained Earnings.

14. A third trial balance may be prepared after the closing entries are recorded and posted. This **postclosing trial balance** shows that equal debits and credits have been posted properly to the Income Summary.

15. Preparation and posting of **reversing entries** is the final step in the accounting cycle. The entries subject to reversal are the adjusting entries for accrued assets, accrued liabilities, and prepaid items initially entered in expense or income accounts.

16. In summary, the steps in the accounting cycle performed in every fiscal period are as follows:
   a. Enter the transactions of the period in appropriate journals.
   b. Post from the journals to the ledger.
   c. Take a trial balance (first trial balance).
   d. Prepare adjusting journal entries and post them to the ledger.
   e. Take a trial balance after adjusting (second trial balance).
   f. Prepare the financial statements from the second trial balance.
   g. Prepare closing journal entries and post them to the ledger.
   h. Take a postclosing trial balance (third trial balance).
   i. Prepare reversing entries and post them to the ledger. (Optional step)

17. The method used to process accounting information does not alter the steps in the accounting cycle. When sophisticated electronic data processing (EDP) systems are used, the accounting records may change in appearance, but the steps performed are the same as those in a manual system.

18. A multicolumn (8, 10, 12, etc.) **work sheet** serves as an aid to the accountant in adjusting the account balances and preparing the financial statements. The work sheet provides an orderly format for the accumulation of information necessary for preparation of financial statements. Use of a work sheet does not replace any financial statements, nor does it alter any of the steps in the accounting cycle.

19. **Appendix 3A, Cash Basis Accounting Versus Accrual Basis Accounting**, is presented at the conclusion of Chapter 3 for the purpose of demonstrating the difference between cash basis and accrual basis accounting. Under the **strict cash basis of accounting**, revenue is recognized only when cash is received, and expenses are recorded only when cash is paid. The accrual basis of accounting recognizes revenue when it is earned and expenses when incurred without regard to the time of receipt or payment of cash.

REVIEW QUESTIONS AND EXERCISES

True-False

Indicate whether each of the following is true (T) or false (F) in the space provided.

_____ 1. Events that can be measured and that directly affect the financial statements of an entity should be recorded by the entity.

_____ 2. An example of an internal event would be a flood that destroyed a portion of an entity's inventory.

_____ 3. In general, debits refer to increases in account balances, and credits refer to decreases.

_____ 4. Double-entry accounting is the process that leads to the basic equality in accounting expressed by the formula: assets = liabilities + owners' equity.

_____ 5. A general journal may be used by any entity in recording its transactions, whereas special journals may be used only by entities whose transactions meet certain requirements.

_____ 6. If an entity fails to post one of its journal entries to its general ledger, the trial balance will not show an equal amount of debit and credit balance accounts.

_____ 7. One purpose of a trial balance is to prove that debits and credits of an equal amount are in the general ledger.

_____ 8. Adjusting entries are used to correct errors that occur during the posting process.

_____ 9. Adjusting entries result from compliance with the accrual system of accounting.

_____ 10. An adjustment for wages expense, earned but unpaid at year end, is an example of an accrued liability.

_____ 11. Proper matching of revenues and expenses requires that bad debts be recorded as an expense of the period in which the sale was made.

_____ 12. When inventory records are maintained using a periodic inventory system, a purchases account is used and the inventory is unchanged during the period.

_____ 13. The computation of Cost of Goods Sold under a periodic inventory system has the characteristics of both an adjusting entry and a closing entry.

_____ 14. The Income Summary account used during the closing process is shown in the owners' equity section of the balance sheet.

_____ 15. It is not necessary to post the closing entries to the ledger accounts because new revenue and expense accounts will be opened in the subsequent accounting period.

_____ 16. Because each accrued item involves either a later receipt of cash for income or a later disbursement of cash for expense, a reversing entry is made to offset part of the credit to income or part of the debit to expense.

_____ 17. A work sheet completed through the adjusted trial balance column provides the information needed for preparation of the financial statements without reference to the ledger or other records.

_____ 18. An adjusted trial balance that shows equal debit and credit columnar totals proves the accuracy of the adjusting entries.

_____ 19. Reversing entries are made at the end of the accounting cycle to correct errors in the original recording of transactions.

_____ 20. In general, all adjusting entries for prepaid items for which the original amount was entered in a revenue or expense account and for all accrued items should be reversed.

Multiple Choice

Select the best answer for each of the following items and enter the corresponding letter in the space provided.

_____ 1. During the first year of Ken Co.'s operations, all purchases were recorded as assets. Store supplies in the amount of $6,540 were purchased. Actual year-end store supplies inventory amounted to $2,150. The adjusting entry for store supplies will:
   A. increase net income $4,390.
   B. increase expenses by $4,390
   C. decrease store supplies by $6,540.
   D. debit accounts payable for $2,150.

_____ 2. A reversing entry should never be made for an adjusting entry that:
   A. accrues unrecorded revenue
   B. adjusts expired costs from an asset account to an expense account.
   C. accrues unrecorded expenses.
   D. adjusts unexpired costs from an expense account to an asset account.

_____ 3. A trial balance taken at year end showed Ken Co.'s debit total exceeding the credit total by $6,300. This discrepancy was probably caused by:
   A. the balance of $47,000 in accounts receivable being entered in the trial balance as $40,700.
   B. an error in adding the Sales Journal.
   C. the balance of $700 in the Office Equipment account being entered as a debit of $7,000
   D. a net loss of $6,300.

_____ 4. Which of the following journal entries is appropriate when a company receives payment in advance for goods or services?

A. Debit cash and credit an expense account.
B. Credit cash and debit a revenue account.
C. Debit cash and credit a liability account or a revenue account.
D. Credit cash and debit a liability or revenue account.

_____ 5. The work sheet for Jeff Co. consisted of eight pairs of debit and credit columns. The dollar amount of one item appeared in both the credit column of the income statement and the debit column of the balance sheet section. That item is:
A. net income for the period.
B. beginning inventory.
C. cost of goods sold.
D. ending inventory.

_____ 6. The difference between the accounting process and the accounting cycle is:
A. the accounting process results in the preparation of financial statements, whereas the accounting cycle is concerned with recording business transactions.
B. the accounting cycle represents the steps taken to accomplish the accounting process.
C. the accounting process represents the steps taken to accomplish the accounting cycle.
D. merely semantic, because both concepts refer to the same thing.

_____ 7. Which of the following statements best describes the purpose of closing entries?
A. To facilitate posting and taking a trial balance.
B. To determine the amount of net income or net loss for the period.
C. To reduce the balances of revenue and expense accounts to zero so that they may be used to accumulate the revenues and expenses of the next period.
D. To complete the record of various transactions that were started in a prior period.

_____ 8. An adjusting entry should never include:
A. a debit to expense and a credit to a liability.
B. a debit to expense and a credit to revenue.
C. a debit to a liability and a credit to revenue.
D. a debit to revenue and a credit to a liability.

_____ 9. If expenses are greater than revenues, the Income Summary account will be closed by a debit to:

A. Income Summary and a credit to Cash.
B. Income Summary and a credit to Retained Earnings.
C. Cash and a credit to Income Summary.
D. Retained Earnings and a credit to Income Summary.

_____ 10. The accounting equation (A = L + OE) must remain in balance:
A. throughout each step in the accounting cycle.
B. only when journal entries are recorded.
C. only at the time the trial balance is prepared.
D. only when formal financial statements are prepared.

Review Exercises

1. The accounts listed below have been taken from Ken Co.'s general ledger as of December 31, 1990. The accounts all have normal balances. This is the end of Ken Co.'s first year of operations. Prepare the trial balance, income statement, and balance sheet for Ken Co. You must also determine sales for the year.

Cash	$ 34,000
Buildings (net)	210,000
Note Payable	72,000
Salary Expense	19,000
Inventory	36,000
Accounts Payable	60,000
Common Stock	185,000
Accounts Receivable	48,000
Sales	_____
Notes Receivable	22,000
Bonds payable	75,000
Rent Expense	15,000
Land	125,000
Cost of Goods Sold	165,000
Tax Expense	20,000
Tax Payable	31,000

2. The following changes occurred in the account balances of Joan's Corporation during 1990.

Accounts Increasing	Amount
Cash	$50,000
Inventory	30,000
Building	25,000
Capital Stock	30,000
Additional Paid-in Capital	10,000

Accounts Decreasing	Amount
Accounts Receivable	$10,000
Accounts Payable	20,000

From the changes above determine the amount of net income or net loss for 1990. The accounts shown above represent all the balance sheet accounts for Joan's Corporation with the exception of Retained Earnings. No dividends were declared during 1990.

3. The following data relate to the accounts of Jeff Company. Prepare the necessary adjusting journal entries indicated by each item for the year ended December 31, 1990.

A. A three-year insurance policy was purchased on March 1, 1990. The $360 insurance premium was fully paid on that date and a debit to prepaid insurance was recorded.

B. Unpaid salaries at year end amount to $650.

C. Service revenue was credited for $816 on May 1, 1990. The amount represents a one-year advance payment for services to be performed by Jeff Company through April 30, 1990.

D. The Office Supplies account shows a balance of $1,250 on December 31, 1990. A physical count of the supplies on hand at this date reveals a total of $480 available.

E. Jeff Company holds bonds of another corporation that pay interest at a rate of $900 per year. These bonds were purchased on August 1, 1990, and the first interest payment will be received on August 1, 1990.

4. The postclosing trial balance of the John Allen Company at January 1, 1990 is shown below.

Account No.	Account	Debit	Credit
101	Cash	$46,000	
102	Investment in Bonds	50,000	
103	Accounts Receivable	28,000	
104	Allowance for Doubtful Accounts		900
105	Interest receivable		
106	Inventory (periodic)*	24,000	
107	Building (15-year, $3,000 salvage)	45,000	
108	Accumulated Depreciation-Building		12,000
109	Delivery Truck (5-year life, $3,000 salvage)	18,000	
110	Accumulated Depreciation-Delivery Truck		6,000
200	Accounts Payable		18,000
201	Notes Payable		29,000
202	Wages Payable		
203	Income Taxes Payable		5,000
300	Common Stock, Par Value $1.00		85,000
301	Retained Earnings		55,100
400	Sales		
401	Interest Revenue		
500	Operating Expenses		
501	Wages Expense		
502	Depreciation Expense-Building		
503	Depreciation Expense-Trucks		
504	Bad Debt Expense		
505	Purchases		
506	Income Tax Expense		
		$211,000	$211,000

*Ending Inventory (12/31/90) $26,000.

The following transactions took place during 1990.

1. Collected: Accounts Receivable, $25,000; Interest on Bonds, $5,000; Cash Sales, $80,000.
2. Paid: Accounts Payable, $15,000; Notes Payable, $21,000; Income Taxes Payable, $5,000; Operating Expenses, $37,000.
3. Made sales on account, $85,000.
4. Purchased inventory, $32,000, of which $16,000 was purchased on account. (Assume periodic inventory.)
5. On June 30, 1990, purchased a second delivery truck for $15,000, paying cash. The truck has a useful life of 10 years and a salvage value of $3,000.

Required

A. Journalize each of the transactions above of the John Allen Company. Some items required more than one journal entry.

B. Post the entries to appropriate accounts. (You should set up a T account for each account noted on the trial balance.)

C. Prepare a trial balance after posting the journal entries and enter the amounts on a 10-column work sheet like the one shown in the text. Enter all the accounts shown on the original trial balance.

D. Enter the following adjustments on the work sheet: (a) Accrued wages at year end total $700; (b) Bad debt expense is estimated at 1% of credit sales; (c) Record straight-line depreciation on the building and trucks; (d) Accrued interest on the investments in bonds is $1,500; (e) Income tax expense for 1990 is $21,065. The tax is not due until 1991.

E. Complete the income statement and balance sheet columns of the work sheet.

F. Prepare closing journal entries.

SOLUTIONS TO REVIEW QUESTIONS AND EXERCISES

True-False

1. (T)

2. (F) This statement characterizes an external event rather than an internal event. Internal events occur within an entity, whereas external events involve interaction between an entity and its environment.

3. (F) Debits can be increases or decreases in account balances, depending on the account involved. Debits increase asset and expense accounts; they decrease liability, owner equity, and revenue accounts. Credits result in the opposite effect on account balances.

4. (T)

5. (F) Special journals can be used by any entity for any groups of transactions possessing common characteristics. See **Appendix 3A** for a complete discussion of special journals.

6. (F) Failure to post one journal entry to the general ledger will misstate the debit and credit side of a trial balance by the same amount. Thus, the trial balance will show an equal amount of debits and credits.

7. (T)

8. (F) Adjusting entries are necessary to achieve a proper matching of revenues and expenses in the determination of net income for the current period and to achieve an accurate statement of the assets and equities existing at the end of the period. If errors are made in the posting process, they are corrected by means of correcting entries, not adjusting entries.

9. (T)

10. (T)

11. (T)

12. (T)

13. (T)

14. (F) The income summary account is a clearing account through which all revenue and expense accounts are closed at the end of an accounting period. Once the revenue and expense accounts have been closed, any balance existing in the income summary account is closed to retain earnings. Thus, the income summary account never appears on a financial statement.

15. (F) Failure to post closing entries to the general ledger will leave a balance in revenue and expense accounts from a previous period and the retained earnings account will be misstated.

16. (T)

17. (T)

18. (F) An adjusted trial balance that shows equal debit and credit columnar totals proves nothing more than the fact that each adjusting entry contained an equal amount of debits and credits. Adjusting entries could have included the wrong total dollar amount or an inappropriate account could have been debited or credited. Mistakes such as these would still produce an adjusted trial balance that shows equal debit and credit columnar totals.

19. (F) Reversing entries are made to simplify the recording of a subsequent transaction related to an adjusting entry. When an entry is reversed, the related subsequent transaction can be recorded as if the adjusting entry had never been recorded. Reversing entries have nothing to do with the correction of errors.

20. (T)

Multiple Choice

1. (B) Purchased.........................$6,540
   Year-end inventory 2,150
   Used during year..............$4,390

Adjusting entry:	Supplies Expense	4,390	
	Store Supplies		4,390

2. (B) The adjusting entry shown in the solution to multiple-choice question 1 above is an example of an adjusting entry that adjusts expired costs from an asset to an expense account. To reverse such an entry would increase the Store Supplies account. This is obviously inappropriate because the only way to increase Store Supplies is to purchase additional supplies. The other three alternatives represent appropriate candidates for reversing entries.

3. (C) Recorded amount.............$7,000
   Actual balance.................. 700
   Excess debit total $6,300

4. (C) An advance payment for goods or services requires a debit to cash, but the corresponding credit can be made to a liability or a revenue account. When the goods or services are delivered to the customer, consideration of the account credited in the original entry will dictate the manner in which this event is reflected in the accounts.

5. (D) Ending inventory is the only account that affects the income statement and the balance sheet in the manner indicated. Ending inventory reduced Cost of Goods Sold in the income statement columns (credit) and is an asset (debit) on the balance sheet.

6. (B) The basic procedures normally used to ensure that the effects of transactions and selected other events are recorded correctly and transmitted to the user are often called the steps in the accounting cycle. The accounting process encompasses all the steps in the accounting cycle.

7. (C) Closing entries represent the formal process by which all nominal accounts (revenue and expense) are reduced to zero and the net income or net loss is determined and transferred to owners' equity. Even though the amount of net income or net loss is determined through the closing process (alternative B), this is not the primary purpose of closing entries.

8. (B) All adjusting entries include one balance sheet account (asset or liability) and one income statement account (revenue or expense). Thus, all alternatives other than alternative B represent possible adjusting entry descriptions.

9. (D) If expenses are greater than revenues, then the Income Summary account will have a debit balance after closing entries have been made. Thus, to close the Income Summary account the journal entry would include a debit to Retained Earnings and a credit to Income Summary.

10. (A) If the accounting equation is out of balance at any time during the accounting cycle, then an error has been made.

Review Exercises

1.

Ken Co.
Trial Balance
December 31, 1990

Cash	$34,000	
Accounts Receivable	48,000	
Notes Receivable	22,000	
Inventory...	36,000	
Building	210,000	
Land..	125,000	
Accounts Payable		$ 60,000
Notes Payable		72,000
Taxes Payable		31,000
Bonds Payable		75,000
Common Stock..		185,000
Sales..		271,000
Cost of Goods Sold..	165,000	
Rent Expense	15,000	
Salary Expense..	19,000	
Tax Expense...	20,000	
....	$694,000	$694,000

Ken Co.
Statement of Income
Year Ended December 31, 1990

Sales..		$271,000
Cost of Goods Sold..		165,000
Gross Profit on Sales		$106,000
Rent Expense	$ 15,000	
Salary Expense..	19,000	
Tax Expense...	20,000	
Total Expenses..		54,000
Net Income..		$52,000

Ken Co.
Balance Sheet
December 31, 1990
Assets

Current Assets:			
Cash	$ 34,000		
Accounts Receivable	48,000		
Notes Receivable	22,000		
Inventory...	36,000		
Total Current Assets		$140,000	
Fixed Assets:			
Building	$210,000		
Land...	125,000		
Total Fixed Assets		335,000	
Total Assents			$475,000

Liabilities and Stockholders' Equity

Current Liabilities:

Accounts Payable	$60,000		
Notes Payable	72,000		
Taxes Payable	31,000		
Total Current Liabilities		$163,000	
Long-term Liabilities:			
Bond Payable		75,000	238,000
Stockholders' Equity:			
Common Stock		185,000	
		52,000	237,000
Retained Earnings			
Total Liabilities and Stockholders' Equity			$475,000

2. Net change in assets:

Cash		$50,000	
Accounts Receivable	(10,000)		
Inventory	30,000		
Building	25,000		
Net Change			$95,000

Less net change in liabilities and owners' equity:

Accounts Payable	($20,000)		
Capital Stock	30,000		
Additional Paid-in Capital	10,000		
Net Change			20,000
Net Income for 1990 (Change in Retained Earnings)			$75,000

3.	A.	Insurance Expense	100	
		Prepaid Insurance		100
	B.	Salaries Expense	650	
		Salaries Payable		650
	C.	Service Revenue	272	
		Unearned Service Revenue		272
	D.	Supplies Expense	770	
		Office Supplies		770
	E.	Interest Receivable	375	
		Interest Income		375

4.	A.	Item 1:	Cash	25,000	
			Accounts Receivable		25,000
			Cash	5,000	
			Interest Revenue		5,000
			Cash	80,000	
			Sales		80,000
		Item 2:	Accounts Payable	15,000	
			Cash		15,000
			Notes Payable	21,000	
			Cash		21,000
			Income Taxes Payable	5,000	
			Cash		5,000
			Operating Expenses	37,000	
			Cash		37,000
		Item 3:	Accounts Receivable	85,000	
			Sales		85,000

Item 4:	Purchases	32,000	
	Cash		16,000
	Accounts Payable		16,000
Item 5:	Delivery Truck	15,000	
	Cash		15,000

B.

Cash
	46,000	15,000	(2)	
(1)	25,000	21,000	(2)	
(1)	5,000	5,000	(2)	
(1)	80,000	37,000	(2)	
		16,000	(4)	
		15,000	(5)	

Investments In Bonds
50,000	

Accounts Receivable
	28,000	25,000	(1)
(3)	85,000		

Allowance for Doubtful Accounts
	900

Interest Receivable

Inventory
24,000	

Building

Accumulated Depreciation--Bldg
	12,000

Delivery Trucks
18,000	
15,000	

Accumulated Depreciation-Trucks
	6,000

Accounts Payable
(2)	15,000	18,000	
		16,000	(4)

Notes Payable
(2)	21,000	29,000	

Wages Payable

Income Taxes Payable
5,000	5,000

Common Stock
	85,000

Retained Earnings	
	55,100

Sales		
	80,000	(1)
	85,000	(3)

Interest Revenue		
	5,000	(1)

	Operating Expenses	
(2)	37,000	

Wages Expense	

Depreciation Expense--Bldg	

Depreciation Expense--Trucks	

Bad Debts Expense	

	Purchases	
(4)	32,000	

Income Tax Expense	

C. D. E.

John Allen Company
Ten-Column Work Sheet
December 31, 1990

No.	Account	Trial Balance Dr.	Trial Balance Cr.	Adjustments Dr.	Adjustments Cr.	Adjusted Trial Balance Dr.	Adjusted Trial Balance Cr.	Income Statement Dr.	Income Statement Cr.	Balance Sheet Dr.	Balance Sheet Cr.
101	Cash	47,000				47,000				47,000	
102	Investments in Bonds	50,000				50,000				50,000	
103	Accounts Receivable	88,000				88,000				88,000	
104	Allowance for Doubtful Accounts		900		(b) 850		1,750				1,750
105	Interest Receivable			(d) 1,500		1,500				1,500	
106	Inventory	24,000				24,000		24,000			
107	Building	45,000				45,000				45,000	
108	Accumulated Depreciation--Bldg		12,000		(c) 3,000		15,000				15,000
109	Delivery Trucks	33,000				33,000				33,000	
110	Accumulated Depreciation--Trucks		6,000		(c) 3,600		9,600				9,600
200	Accounts Payable		19,000				19,000				19,000
201	Notes Payable		8,000				8,000				8,000
202	Wages Payable				(a) 700		700				700
203	Income Taxes Payable				(e) 21,065		21,065				21,065
300	Common Stock		85,000				85,100				85,100
301	Retained Earnings		55,100				55,100				55,100
400	Sales		165,000				165,000		165,000		
401	Interest Revenue		5,000		(d) 1,500		6,500		6,500		
500	Operating Expense	37,000				37,000		37,000			
501	Wages Expense			(a) 700		700		700			
502	Depreciation Expense--Bldg			(c) 3,000		3,000		3,000			
503	Depreciation Expense--Trucks			(c) 3,600		3,600		3,600			
504	Bad Debts Expense			(b) 850		850		850			
505	Purchases	32,000				32,000		32,000			
506	Income Tax Expense			(e) 21,065		21,065		21,065			
		$356,000	$356,000	$31,315	$31,315	$386,715	$386,715	122,215	197,500	290,500	
	Inventory, 12/31/90								26,000	26,000	
								122,215	197,500		75,285
	Net Income							75,285			
								$197,500	$197,500	$290,500	$290,500

F. Inventory (12/31)   26,000
    Cost of Goods Sold   30,000
        Inventory (1/1)   24,000
        Purchases   32,000
            (To record ending inventory and determine cost of goods sold)
    Interest Revenue   6,500
    Sales   165,000
        Cost of Goods Sold   30,000
        Operating Expenses   37,000
        Wages Expense   700
        Depreciation Expense--Bldg   3,000
        Depreciation Expense--Trucks   3,600
        Bad Debts Expense   850
        Income Tax Expense   21,065
        Income Summary   75,285
            (To close revenues and expenses to income summary)
    Income Summary   75,285
        Retained Earnings   75,285
            (To close income summary to retained earnings)

4

Statement of income and
retained earnings

Chapter Synopsis

Chapter 4 presents a detailed discussion of the concepts and techniques that underlie the preparation of the Income Statement and Statement of Retained Earnings. The requirements for adequate presentation of reported net income are described and illustrated throughout the chapter.

Chapter Review

1. The income statement measures the success of business operations for a given period of time. This statement assists the business community in determining investment value, credit worthiness, and income success of a particular business enterprise. The income statement is an important financial statement because it provides investors and creditors with information that helps them predict the **amount, timing,** and **uncertainty** of future cash flows. Through use of the income statement, investors and creditors are able to (a) evaluate the past performance of an enterprise and (b) determine the risk of achieving particular cash flows.

2. The data accountants use in measuring an entity's net income must be susceptible to objective quantification. This approach has been criticized by economists for failing to include any of the qualitative benefits that the economists include in their definitions of income. Accountants are aware that income often includes qualitative benefits. However, these qualitative benefits have been discarded by accountants in reporting net income because of the difficulty involved in their measurement.

3. Net income can be measured by the **capital maintenance approach** or the **transaction approach**. The capital maintenance approach measures net income by computing the change in net assets for the period, adjusted for any additional investment made during the period. The transaction approach measures the basic transactions that occur during a period and summarizes them in an income statement. Although both approaches measure the change in net assets resulting from income, the transaction approach is superior because of the

additional information it provides about the elements of income. The major elements of net income, as described in Chapter 2, are: **revenues, expenses, gains,** and **losses.**

4. The income statement may be presented in the **single-step format** or the **multiple-step format**. Single-step income statements derive their name from the fact that total costs and expenses are subtracted from total revenues in a "single step" to arrive at net income. Income taxes are shown as a separate last item on a single-step statement. The multiple-step format separates results achieved by regular operations of the entity from those obtained by nonoperating activities. Expenses are also classified by function such as cost of sales, selling, and administration. The multiple-step format provides more information to financial statement users than does the single-step format; however, both are found in actual practice.

5. An income statement is composed of various sections that relate to different aspects of the earning process. The seven sections identified in the chapter are: an **operating section, nonoperating section, income taxes, discontinued operations, extraordinary items, cumulative effect of a change in accounting principle,** and **earnings per share.** The data included in some sections are further classified, making the income statement more informative.

6. For the most part, accountants tend to agree on the composition of items included on the income statement. However, certain unusual items have stirred controversy in regard to the effect they should have on the presentation of net income. Some accountants favor an **all-inclusive approach** that reports the unusual items directly in the income statement. Those who support the **current operating approach** to income measurement believe that the unusual items should be closed directly to retained earnings (not included in computing net income). The accounting profession currently favors the all-inclusive approach to income measurement over the current operating approach because of its treatment of these unusual items. Also, *APB Opinion No. 9* adopted the all-inclusive concept and requires application of this approach in practice with a few exceptions.

7. **Extraordinary items** are defined as material items that are **unusual in nature** and **occur infrequently**. Both characteristics must exist for an item to be classified as an extraordinary item on the income statement. Only in rare situations will an event or transaction occur that clearly meets both criteria and thus gives rise to an extraordinary gain or loss. If an event or transaction meets both tests, it is shown net of taxes in a separate section of the income statement just above net income.

8. Material gains and losses that are **either** unusual or occur infrequently, **but not both**, are excluded from the extraordinary item classification. These items are presented with the normal, recurring revenues, costs, and expenses. If material, these items are disclosed separately; if immaterial, they may be combined with other items in the statement.

9. *FASB Statement 16* established the criteria for an item to be accounted for as a **prior period adjustment**. Basically the following two items shall be accounted for and reported as prior period adjustments: (a) correction of an error in the financial statements of a prior period and (b) adjustments that result from realization of income tax benefits of preacquisition operating loss carry forwards of purchased subsidiaries. When one of these two items is encountered by an entity it is charged or credited (net of tax) to the opening balance of retained earnings and, thus excluded from the determination of net income for the current period.

10. Adjustments resulting from the use of estimates in accounting are not prior period adjustments. Such adjustment are used in the determination of income for the current period and future periods and should not be charged or credited directly to Retained Earnings.

11. A **change in accounting principle** results when an entity adopts a new GAAP that is different from the one previously used. When this type of change is made, the income statement for the year in which the change occurred will include retroactive treatment of the cumulative effect of the change. The effect of the change (net of tax) should be disclosed as a separate item on the income statement following extraordinary items.

12. When an entity decides to **dispose of a segment** of its business, certain classification and disclosure requirements must be met. The income statement should include a separate category before extraordinary items for the gain or loss from the disposal. Also, any operating results generated by the segment that has been or will be disposed of are separated from the results of continuing operations and reported along with the gain or loss on disposal.

13. **Intraperiod tax allocation** is the process of relating the income tax effect of an unusual item to that item when it appears on the income statement. Income tax expense related to **continuing operations** is shown on the income statement at its appropriately computed amount. All other items included in the determination of net income should be shown net of their related tax effect. The tax amount may be disclosed in the income statement or in a footnote. Prior period adjustments should also be shown net of tax when reported in the retained earnings statement.

14. In general, **earnings per share** represents the ratio of income to outstanding shares of common stock. This ratio must be disclosed on the face of the income statement. It is considered by many financial statement users to be the most significant statistic presented in the financial statement. The presentation of earnings per share should include per share data for (a) income from continuing operations, (b) net income before extraordinary items and cumulative effect of accounting changes, and (c) cumulative effect of changes in accounting principles, when such items are included in the determination of net income. Reporting per share amounts for gain or loss on discontinued operations and gain or loss on extraordinary items is optional.

15. In the past, standards involving the measurement and reporting of income were developed on an ad hoc, piecemeal basis over time, often in response to practical problems that demanded immediate solutions. As the conceptual framework progresses, future standards in this area should flow from an integrated set of soundly developed concepts and criteria. Income, as characterized in the conceptual framework concepts statements, is now referred to as **comprehensive income**. This is an all-inclusive concept of income under which all changes in net assets would be reported a part of income.

16. The **statement of retained earnings** serves to reconcile the balance of the retained earnings account from the beginning to the end of the year. The important information communicated by the statement of retained earnings includes: prior period adjustments, the relationship of dividend distributions to net income for the period, and any transfers to and from retained earnings. Some accountants believe that the statements of income and retained earnings are so closely related that they present both statements in one combined report. The advantage of a **combined statement of income and retained earnings** is that all items affecting income are shown in one statement. However, critics contend that the combined statement tends to bury the net income figure in the body of the statement.

17. **Appendix 4A, Accounting for Discontinued Operations,** discusses the more technical aspects of how gains and losses related to discontinued operations are computed, along with related reporting issues.

REVIEW QUESTIONS

True-False

Indicate whether each of the following is true (T) or false (F) in the space provided.

_____ 1. Accountants and economists have traditionally been consistent in their approach to the measurement of income.

_____ 2. Use of the single-step income statement format is predominant in business reporting today.

_____ 3. The multiple-step income statement recognizes a separation of operating transactions from nonoperating transactions and matches costs and expenses with related revenues.

_____ 4. The advocates of the current operating performance concept include extraordinary items in the calculation of net income.

_____ 5. Extraordinary items are events and transactions that are distinguished by their unusual nature and the infrequency of their occurrence.

_____ 6. Adjustments that grow out of the use of estimates in accounting are not classified as prior period adjustments.

_____ 7. A change in accounting principle is considered appropriate only when a clearly preferable accounting principle is adopted.

_____ 8. Intraperiod tax allocation causes a reduction in income tax expense for the period in which it is used.

_____ 9. Because of the inherent dangers of focusing attention on earnings per share by itself, the accounting profession concluded that this ratio should be disclosed on the face of the income statement.

_____ 10. The statement of retained earnings provides a reconciliation of the retained earnings account from the beginning of the year to the end of the year.

_____ 11. The presentation of earnings per share is affected by the existence of prior period adjustments.

_____ 12. The statement of retained earnings shows the total change in stockholders' equity for a specified period.

_____ 13. From a bank loan officer's point of view, the single-step income statement is preferable to the multiple-step income statement.

_____ 14. An example of an extraordinary loss, reported as a separate item in the income statement, is a large write-down of accounts receivable caused by the unexpected bankruptcy of a major customer.

_____ 15. A prior period adjustment results from the correction of an error in the financial statements of a prior period discovered subsequent to their issuance.

_____ 16. Prior period adjustments should be charged or credited to the opening balance of retained earnings and, thus, excluded from the determination of net income for the current period.

_____ 17. A manufacturer of computer hardware who sells all computer manufacturing facilities located in foreign countries can record the transaction as a disposal of a segment.

_____ 18. The combined statement of income and retained earnings has been criticized by some on the grounds that net income for the year is buried in the body of the statement.

_____ 19. The effect on net income of adopting a new accounting principle should be disclosed as a separate item following extraordinary items in the income statement.

_____ 20. The results of operations of a segment that has been or will be disposed of need not be separated from the results of continuing operations as long as the gain or loss from the disposal is shown separately.

Multiple Choice

Select the best answer for each of the following items and enter the corresponding letter in the space provided.

_____ 1. The concept that reports extraordinary items in the income statement is called:
A. single-step income statement.
B. prior period adjustment.
C. current operating concept.
D all-inclusive concept.

_____ 2. Earnings per share should always be shown separately for:
A. net income and gross margin.
B. net income and pretax income.
C. income before extraordinary items.
D. extraordinary items and prior period adjustments.

_____ 3. An income statement shows "income before income taxes and extraordinary items" in the amount of $685,000. The income taxes payable for the year are $360,000, including $120,000 that is applicable to an extraordinary gain. Thus, the "income before extraordinary items" is:
   A. $445,000.
   B. $205,000.
   C. $465,000.
   D. $225,000.

_____ 4. In general, the basic difference between the concepts of revenues and gains concerns:
   A. the materiality of the item being considered.
   B. whether the event giving rise to the item relates to the typical activity of the enterprise.
   C. whether the item is taxable in the current year.
   D. the effect on total assets of the enterprise.

_____ 5. Which of the following asset disposals would qualify as a disposal of a segment?
   A. Phasing out of a product line or class of service.
   B. Changes occasioned by a technological improvement.
   C. Sale by an auto parts manufacturer of one of its five parts-manufacturing subsidiaries.
   D. Sale by a transportation company of its bus operations but not its airline operations.

_____ 6. The occurrence that most likely would have no effect on 1990 net income is the:
   A. sale in 1990 of an office building contributed by a stockholder in 1950.
   B. collection in 1990 of a dividend from an investment.
   C. correction of an error in the financial statements of a prior period discovered subsequent to their issuance.
   D. stock purchased in 1982 deemed worthless in 1990.

_____ 7. The income statement reveals:
   A. resources and equities of a firm at a point in time.
   B. resources and equities of a firm for a period of time.
   C. net earnings (net income) of a firm at a point in time.
   D. net earnings (net income) of a firm for a period of time.

_____ 8. Which of the following should not be reported on the income statement as an extraordinary item?
   A. The write-off of major assets as a result of new environmental laws prohibiting their use.
   B. The write-off of a large receivable resulting from a customer's bankruptcy proceedings.
   C. A large loss as a result of an earthquake.
   D. Expropriation of assets by a foreign government.

_____ 9. As defined by the FASB, comprehensive income is the increase in the amount of net assets resulting from:
   A. transactions and other events and circumstances occurring during a period of time.
   B. the sale of any item owned or controlled by an enterprise.
   C. an exchange of goods between two entities resulting in favorable benefits to both.
   D. an exchange of goods between two entities resulting in favorable benefits to the one recording income.

_____ 10. When a company changes from one GAAP to another GAAP, the income statement for the year of change:
   A. will normally not be affected, as this event is taken directly to Retained Earnings.
   B. should include only footnote disclosure so readers will be aware of the change.
   C. should include the cumulative effect, based on a retroactive computation, disclosed as a separate-line item.
   D. should include the effect of the change related to the current year only and be disclosed as a separate line item.

Review Exercises

1. Complete the following tabulation by filling in the missing amounts.

	1989	1990	1991
Sales	46,800		78,000
Beginning Inventory		14,200	16,400
Purchases (Net)	20,050	50,200	
Ending Inventory	14,200		18,600
Cost of Goods Sold		48,000	
Gross Margin of Profit	10,800	14,400	18,000
Operating Expenses			6,000
Income Before Taxes	8,800		
Tax Expense (40%)		2,560	
Net Income (Net Loss)		3,840	

2. Use the following data for Muller Corporation, a retail store, to develop an income statement for the year ending December 31, 1990:

Sales	$90,000
Extraordinary loss due to hurricane	5,000
Income tax saving on extraordinary loss	(1,100)
Cost of goods sold	55,000
Interest expense	1,000
Selling expenses	11,000
Income tax expense on operations	4,400
General and administrative expenses	3,000
Shares of capital stock outstanding, 10,000	

3. For each of the items listed below, describe (a) the criteria used to identify the item and (b) its placement on the financial statements. Assume that each item is material.
    A. Extraordinary items.
    B. Material gains or losses, not considered extraordinary items.
    C. Prior period adjustments.
    D. Changes in estimates.
    E. Changes in principle.
    F. Discontinued operations.

4. The following accounts are taken from the adjusted trial balance of Marlene Peterson Company as of December 31, 1990.

Common Stock (100,000 shares)	$ 300,000	Purchases	$ 485,600
Transportation-in	12,600	Sales Returns	15,900
Rent Revenue	28,500	Purchase Discounts	12,100
Administrative Expense (Total)	145,800	Gain on Sale of Land	18,300
Merchandise Inventory (12/31)	117,500	Selling Expense (Total)	186,800
Sales Discounts	9,500	Merchandise Inventory (1/1)	96,200
Bond Interest Expense	14,300	Retained Earnings (1/1)	226,900
Sales	1,265,000	Dividend Income	17,700

The gain on the sale of the land is not an extraordinary item. All income is taxed at a uniform rate of 42% except for the gain on the sale of the land, which is taxed at 25%.

Required

Prepare a multiple-step income statement for Marlene Peterson Company for the year ended December 31, 1990.

SOLUTIONS TO REVIEW QUESTIONS AND EXERCISES

True-False

1. (F) Economists have often criticized accountants for their definition of income because accountants do not include many items that contribute to the general growth and well-being of an enterprise. However, if an item is not susceptible to being quantified with any degree of reliability, it cannot be included in the accountant's concept of income.

2. (T)

3. (T)

4. (F) Advocates of the current operating performance concept argue that the net income figure should show only the regular recurring earnings of the business based on its normal operations. Extraordinary items are financial gains or losses that are not expected to recur frequently and would not be considered as recurring in the normal operating process of the business.

5. (T)

6. (T)

7. (T)

8. (F) Intraperiod tax allocation is a method designed to relate the income tax expense of the fiscal period to the items that affect the amount of the tax provision. Use of this method does not affect the income tax expense for the period, merely the manner in which the income tax expense is presented.

9. (T)

10. (T)

11. (F) Because prior period adjustments are carried directly to retained earnings, the presentation of earnings per share, which is included in the income statement, is unaffected.

12. (F) The statement of retained earnings presents a reconciliation of the balance of the retained earnings account from the beginning to the end of the year. This statement does not include information about the other accounts that appear in an entity's equity section.

13. (F) The multiple-step income statement allows a user the opportunity to observe numerous relationships among revenue and expense data. Thus, it is more suitable for use by a bank loan officer than is the single-step income statement.

14. (F) To be classified as an extraordinary item, an event must (a) be unusual in nature and (b) occur infrequently. The write-off of a large account receivable due to the unexpected bankruptcy of a major customer is an event that is neither unusual nor infrequent. Any business that extends credit to a customer risks loss due to the insolvency of the customer.

15. (T)

16. (T)

17. (F) To qualify as a disposal of a segment, the entity must completely divest itself of operations in a particular line of business. The entity depicted in this question is still in the computer business, so the sale of the foreign manufacturing facilities does not qualify as a disposal of a segment.

18. (T)

19. (T)

20. (F) According to generally accepted accounting principles, the assets, results of operations, and activities of a segment of a business must be clearly distinguishable from the other assets, results of operations, and activities of the entity to qualify for discontinued operations treatment.

Multiple Choice

1. (D) The all-inclusive concept of income holds that any gain or loss experienced by a concern, whether directly or indirectly related to operations contributes to its long-run profitability and should be included in the computation of net income.

2. (C) Earnings per share must be disclosed on the face of the income statement. In addition to net income per share, per share amounts should be shown for income from contributing operations, income before extraordinary items and cumulative effect of accounting changes, and cumulative effect of changes in accounting principles. Reporting per share amounts for gain or loss on discontinued operations and gain or loss on extraordinary items is optional.

3. (A)

Income before tax and extraordinary item	$685,000
Income tax ($360,000 - $120,000)	240,000
Income before extraordinary item	$445,000

4. (B) Revenues represent inflows from activities that constitute the entity's ongoing major or central operations. Gains, on the other hand, represent increases in equity from peripheral or incidental transactions of an entity. The concepts of materiality (A) or taxability (C) have nothing to do with distinguishing revenues from gains.

5. (D) The only disposal that qualifies as a disposal of a segment is the disposal by the transportation company of its entire bus operations. This company remains in the transportation business, but an entire segment of the business has been terminated. Items (A), (B), and (C) are specific examples of asset disposals that do not qualify as disposals of a segment.

6. (C) Prior period adjustments should be charged or credited to the opening balance of retained earnings and, thus, excluded from the determination of net income. Two distinct circumstances give rise to prior period adjustments: (a) correction of an error in the financial statements of a prior period and (b) adjustments that result from realization of income tax benefits of preacquisition operating loss carry-forwards of purchased subsidiaries.

7. (D) The income statement is defined as the financial statement of a business entity that reveals net earnings for a period of time.

8. (B) The criteria for treating an item as extraordinary are: (a) the item must be unusual in nature and (b) its occurrence should not reasonably be expected to recur in the foreseeable future. Alternatives (A), (C), and (D) clearly meet the two criteria. Alternative (B) is not unusual in the business world, and it is always possible that such an event could recur.

9. (A) Comprehensive income is an all-inclusive concept of income under which all changes in net assets (except transactions with owners) are reported as part of income. Alternatives (B), (C), and (D) do not totally define the concept of comprehensive income.

10. (C) The effect on net income of a change from one GAAP to another should be disclosed as a separate item following extraordinary items in the income statement. These types of change are recognized by including in the income statement of the current year the cumulative effect (net of tax), based on a retroactive computation, of changing to a new accounting principle.

Review Exercises

	1989	1990	1991
1. Sales	46,800	**62,400**	78,000
Beginning Inventory	**30,150**	14,200	16,400
Purchases (Net)	20,050	50,200	**62,200**
Ending Inventory	14,200	**16,400**	18,600
Cost of Goods Sold	**36,000**	48,000	**60,000**
Gross Margin of Profit	10,800	14,400	18,000
Operating Expenses	**2,000**	**8,000**	**6,000**
Income Before Taxes	8,800	**6,400**	**12,000**
Tax Expense (40%)	**3,520**	2,560	**4,800**
Net Income (Net Loss)	**5,280**	3,840	**7,200**

2.

Muller Corporation
Income Statement
Year Ending December 31, 1990

Revenues:			
Sales...		$90,000	
Cost of goods sold		55,000	
Gross margin			$35,000
Expenses: Operating			
Selling expenses		$11,000	
General and administrative..		3,000	
Total operating expenses...................................			14,000
Income for operations			21,000
Financial expenses:			
Interest expense			1,000
Pretax income..			20,000
Income taxes on operations...			4,400
Income before extraordinary items			15,600
Extraordinary items:			
Loss due to hurricane...		5,000	
Less: Income taxes saved		1,100	3,900
Net income...			$11,700
Earnings per share:			
Income before extraordinary items ($15,600 ÷ 10,000)...........................			$1.56
Extraordinary items (3,900 ÷ 10,000)...........................			(.39)
Net income (11,700 ÷ 10,000)...........................			1.17

3.

Item	Criteria	Placement
A. Extraordinary items	Unusual *and* nonrecurring.	Separate section in the income statement labeled "extraordinary items."
B. Material gains or losses not considered extraordinary	Unusual *or* infrequent, but not both. Typical of the customary business activity.	Separate section in the income statement above income before extraordinary items.
C. Prior period adjustments	Corrections of errors in previously issued financial statement of a prior period, or income tax benefits of preacquisition operating loss carry-forwards of purchased subsidiaries.	Direct adjustment to the beginning balance of retained earnings.
D. Changes in estimates	Normal, recurring corrections or adjustments to estimate.	Change in income statement only in the account affected.
E. Changes in principle	Change from one GAAP to another.	Cumulative effect of the adjustment is reflected in the income statement as a separate item following extraordinary items.
F. Discontinued operations	Disposal of a segment of a business constituting a separate line of business or a class of customer.	Separate section in the income statement after continuing operations but before extraordinary items.

4.

Marlene Peterson Company
Income Statement
For the Year Ended December 31, 1990

Sales

Sales			$1,265,000
Less: Sales discounts		$ 9,500	
Sales returns		15,900	25,400
Net sales			1,239,600

Cost of Goods Sold

Merchandise inventory 1/1		96,200	
Purchases	$485,600		
Less purchase discounts	12,100		
Net purchases	473,500		
Transportation-in	12,600	$486,100	
Merchandise available for sale		582,300	
Less merchandise inventory 12/31		117,500	
Cost of goods sold			464,800
Gross profit on sales			774,800

Operating Expenses

Selling Expenses	186,800	
Administrative Expenses	145,800	332,600
Income from operations		442,200

Other Revenues and Gains

Rent revenue	28,500	
Dividend income	17,700	
Gain on sale of land	18,300	64,500
		506,700

Other Expenses and Losses

Bond interest expense	14,300
Income before taxes	492,400
Income taxes ($474,100 x .42 + $18,300 x .25)	203,697
Net income for the year	$288,703
Earnings per share ($288,703 ÷ 100,000)	$2.89

5

Balance sheet and statement of cash flows

Chapter Synopsis

Chapter 5 presents a detailed discussion of the concepts and techniques that underlie the preparation and analysis of the balance sheet. Along with the mechanics of preparation, acceptable disclosure requirements are examined and illustrated. A brief introduction to the statement of cash flows is also presented. This explanation serves as a foundation for the more comprehensive discussion of this subject presented in Chapter 24.

Chapter Review

1. For many years financial statement users generally considered the income statement to be superior to the balance sheet as a basis for judging the economic well-being of an enterprise. However, the balance sheet can be a very useful financial statement. If a balance sheet is examined carefully, users can gain a considerable amount of information related to **enterprise liquidity** and **financial flexibility**. Enterprise liquidity is generally related to the amount of time that is expected to elapse until an asset is realized or otherwise converted into cash or until a liability has to be paid. Financial flexibility is the ability of an enterprise to take effective action to alter the amounts and timing of cash flow so that it can respond to unexpected needs and opportunities.

2. Criticism of the balance sheet has revolved around the limitations of the information presented therein. These limitations include: (a) failure to reflect current value information, (b) the extensive use of estimates, and (c) failure to include items of financial value that cannot be recorded objectively.

3. The **major classifications** used in the balance sheet are **assets, liabilities, and owners' equity**. These items were defined in the discussion presented in Chapter 2. To provide the financial statement reader with additional information, these major classifications are divided into several **subclassifications**. Assets are further classified as **current** or **noncurrent**, with the noncurrent divided among long-term investments; property, plant, and equipment; intangible assets; and other assets. Liabilities are classified as **current** or **noncurrent**. Owners' equity includes capital stock, additional paid-in capital, and retained earnings.

4. **Current assets** are cash and other assets that are expected to be realized in cash, sold, or consumed either in one year or in the operating cycle, whichever is longer. Current assets are presented in the balance sheet in the order of their liquidity and normally include cash, marketable securities, receivables, inventories, and prepaid expenses.

5. **Current liabilities** are the obligations that are reasonably expected to be liquidated either through the use of current assets or the creation of other current liabilities. Items normally shown in the current liabilities section of the balance sheet include notes and accounts payable, advances received from customers, current maturities of long-term debt, taxes payable, and accrued liabilities. Obligations due to be paid during the next year may be excluded from the current liability section if the item is expected to be refinanced through long-term debt or the item will be paid out of non-current assets.

6. Items classified as **long-term investments** in the asset section of the balance sheet include security holdings, tangible assets not currently used in operations, and special fund balances. Management acquires the assets with the intention of holding them for an extended period of time.

7. **Property, plant, and equipment** are physical properties of a durable nature that are used in the operations of the enterprise. Examples include land, buildings, machinery, furniture, tools, and wasting resources. **Intangible assets** lack physical substance; however, their benefit lies in the rights they convey to the holder. Examples include patents, copyrights, franchises, goodwill, trademarks, trade names, and secret processes. The cost of tangible assets, other than land and wasting resources, is charged to income through a process known as **depreciation**. The process for charging the cost of intangible assets to income is known as **amortization**.

8. **Long-term liabilities** are obligations whose settlement date extends beyond the normal operating cycle or one year, whichever is longer. Examples include bonds payable, notes payable, lease obligations, and pension obligations. Generally, the disclosure requirements for long-term liabilities are quite substantial as a result of various covenants and restrictions included for the protection of the lenders. Long-term liabilities that

mature during the next operating cycle are classified as current liabilities if their liquidation requires use of current assets.

9. The **owners' equity section** of the balance sheet includes information related to capital stock, additional paid-in capital, and retained earnings. Preparation of the owners' equity section should be approached with caution because of the various restrictions imposed by state corporation laws, liability agreements, and voluntary actions of the board of directors.

10. Supplemental information related to **contingencies, valuation methods, contractual situations, and postbalance sheet disclosure** provide for elaboration or qualification of items listed in the balance sheet.

11. **Contingencies** are uncertain occurrences that may have a material effect on financial position. Contingencies are normally disclosed in footnotes to the financial statements, and can represent a possible gain or a possible loss. **Gain contingencies** are rarely disclosed unless the probabilities are quite high that they will materialize. **Loss contingencies** are the subject matter addressed in *FASB Statement No. 5*. These items should be disclosed in a footnote to the financial statements, unless at the date of the financial statements it is **probable** that a liability has been incurred **and** the amount of loss can be **reasonably estimated**. If **both** conditions are met, the loss should be charged to income and a corresponding liability should be recorded.

12. Although financial statements are dated to coincide with the end of the accounting period, several weeks, and sometimes months, elapse before they are actually issued. If significant events that occur between the date of the statements and their issuance date are not disclosed, the statements could prove to be misleading. The two types of **post balance sheet events** are: (a) those that provide evidence of conditions that existed at the balance sheet date and (b) those that arose subsequent to the balance sheet date but prior to its issuance. The first type requires an adjustment, but it would require disclosure if in the judgment of the preparer failure to disclose would make the financial statements misleading.

13. Effective communication of the information required to be disclosed in financial statements is an important consideration. Accountants have developed certain methods that have proven useful in disclosing pertinent information. These methods are **parenthetical explanations, footnotes, supporting schedules, and cross reference and contra items.**

14. Two common arrangements followed in the presentation of the balance sheet are the **account form** and the **report form.** The former lists assets on the left side and liabilities and owners' equity on the right side. The latter shows liabilities and owners' equity directly below the assets.

15. The **statement of changes in financial position** is useful in gaining an understanding of the **significant financing and investing activities** of a business entity. Although the balance sheet, income statement, and statement of retained earnings contain information about the financing and investing activities of an entity, such activities are difficult to isolate and interpret from an analysis of these statement. Thus, the statement of change in financial position presents, in one document, and analysis of the resource (funds) inflow and outflow experienced by an entity during the preceding year.

16. *SFAC No. 5* recommended preparation of a statement that reports cash flows. Basically, a statement that provides a better predictor of future cash flows and enhances the user's evaluation of liquidity and financial flexibility. With the issuance of **FASB Statement No. 95, "Statement of Cash Flows,"** presentation of the statement of changes in financial position has been replaced by the **statement of cash flows.** The primary purpose of the statement of cash flows is to provide relevant information about the cash receipts and cash payments of an enterprise during a period. The statement's value lies in its ability to assist users in better understanding an entity's liquidity, solvency, and financial flexibility. To that end, the statement of cash flows reports **(a)** the cash effects during a period of an enterprises' operations, **(b)** its investing activities, **(c)** its financing activities, and **(d)** the net increase or decrease in cash during the period. Chapter 24 is devoted entirely to a presentation of the statement of cash flows including information on preparation, presentation, content, and use of the statement.

REVIEW QUESTIONS AND EXERCISES

True - False

Indicate whether each of the following is true (T) or false (F) in the space provided.

_____ 1. The balance sheet reflects a corporation's results of operations for a specified period of time.

_____ 2. The three general classes of items included in the balance sheet are assets, liabilities, and owners' equity.

____ 3. If cash is restricted for purposes other than the liquidation of current obligations, it should not be classified as a current asset.

____ 4. Current assets are any assets expected to be sold within one year or the operating cycle, whichever is longer.

____ 5. The generally accepted method used in accounting for short-term investments is referred to as: "cost or market, whichever is lower."

____ 6. Proper presentation of inventories for a manufacturing concern includes disclosure of the basis of valuation, the method of pricing, and the stage of completion.

____ 7. Current liabilities are the obligations that are reasonably expected to be liquidated either by creation of other current liabilities or through the use of current assets.

____ 8. Price level adjusted information should be disclosed in the balance sheet whenever the inflation rate is above 10%.

____ 9. The use of an other-asset section varies widely in practice. It should be restricted to unusual items that are different from assets included elsewhere.

____ 10. Long-term liabilities are obligations that are not reasonably expected to be liquidated within one year or the normal operating cycle, whichever is longer.

____ 11. The stockholders' equity accounts used by a corporation are the same as those used in accounting for a partnership or proprietorship.

____ 12. Contracts and negotiations of significance, in addition to contingencies, are disclosed in footnotes to the financial statements.

____ 13. The AICPA has recommended that the word "reserve" be used only to describe an appropriation of retained earnings.

____ 14. A contingent liability and an estimated liability are treated in the same manner for financial statement reporting purposes.

____ 15. According to the conceptual framework project, individual balance sheet items should be separately reported and classified in sufficient detail to permit users to assess the amounts timing, and uncertainty of future cash flows.

____ 16. When the balance sheet is prepared using the report form, a special section is included that presents a narrative explanation of the balance sheet classifications.

____ 17. The primary purpose of the statement of cash flows is to provide relevant information about the cash receipts and cash payments of an enterprise during a period.

____ 18. Determination of cash flows from operating activities requires predicting the amount of cash the entity will collect from customers who purchase the entity's product on account.

____ 19. The sale of 12,000 shares of its common stock by Xerax Company for $22,000 cash would be classified as an investing activity due to the increased investment by company shareholders.

____ 20. The statement of cash flows replaces the statement of changes in financial position as a required basic financial statement.

Multiple Choice

Select the best answer for each of the following items and enter the corresponding letter in space provided.

____ 1. Which of the following is not a current asset?
   A. Prepaid property taxes that relate to the next operating period.
   B. The cash surrender value of a life insurance policy carried by a corporation on its president.
   C. Marketable securities purchased as a temporary investment of cash.
   D. Installment notes receivable due over 15 months in accordance with normal trade practices.

____ 2. If $1,240 cash and a $4,760 note are given in exchange for a delivery truck to be used in a business:
   A. assets and liabilities will change by the same amount.
   B. owners' equity will be increased.
   C. assets will increase and liabilities decrease.
   D. assets and liabilities will increase but by different amounts.

____ 3. Which of the following items should never be included in the current section of the balance sheet?
   A. Receivable from a customer outstanding for more than a year.
   B. Deferred income taxes resulting from interperiod tax allocation.
   C. Three-year premium for fire insurance on plant and equipment.
   D. A pension fund.

____ 4. Which of the following balance sheet classification would normally require the greatest amount of supplementary disclosure?
A. Current assets.
B. Current liabilities.
C. Plant assets.
D. Long-term liabilities.

____ 5. One criticism not normally aimed at a balance sheet prepared using current accounting and reporting standards is:
A. failure to reflect current value information.
B. the extensive use of separate classifications.
C. an extensive use of estimates.
D. failure to include items of financial value that cannot be recorded objectively.

____ 6. According to FASB Statement No. 5, the estimated loss from a loss contingency should be recorded in the accounts if information available prior to issuance of the financial statements indicates that it is:
A. probable that a liability was incurred and the amount of loss is reasonably estimated.
B. probably that a liability was incurred or the amount of loss is reasonably estimated.
C. reasonably possible that a loss will result.
D. probably that a liability will result.

____ 7. One of the main reasons for separating liabilities into current and long-term is:
A. to provide decision makers with information regarding currently maturing debts.
B. to separate large and small debts.
C. to separate capital into its component parts.
D. to separate total equity into its two basic parts.

____ 8. Which of the following contingencies should be accrued?
A. Notes receivable discounted.
B. Accommodation endorsements on customer notes.
C. Additional compensation for past services that may be payable on a dispute not being arbitrated.
D. Estimated claims under a service warranty on new products sold.

____ 9. The basis used to classify assets as current or noncurrent is the period of time it normally takes to convert:
A. inventory into cash or 12 months, whichever is longer
B. inventory into cash or 12 months, whichever is shorter.
C. accounts receivable into cash or 12 months, whichever is longer.
D. accounts receivable into cash or 12 months, whichever is shorter.

____ 10. Which of the following would not be considered a basic source of information useful in preparing a statement of cash flows?
A. Selected transaction data.
B. Comparative balance.
C. An analysis of sales by territory
D. The current income statement.

Review Exercises

1. Bright Corporation had a balance in accounts receivable on September 1, 1990, of $33,000. All sales are made on account. During September the corporation collected $30,800 from customers, and at the end of September the accountants receivable totaled $27,500. The sales for September must have been $_____.

2. On December 31, 1990, the total assets of Ace, Inc. were $91,000, and liabilities were $48,000. Ace, Inc. began business January 1, 1986, and had an average net income of $16,000 per year. Total dividends paid for the five-year period were $63,850. Ace, Inc.'s current owners' equity balance as of December 31, 1990 is $_____, and the original investment was $_____.

3.   Indicate the most preferred balance sheet classification of each item in Group B by inserting the appropriate letter from Group A in the space provided.

Group A	Group B
A. Current assets	_____ 1. Cash fund for plant expansion
B. Property, plant, and equipment	_____ 2. Preferred stock
C. Long-term investments	_____ 3. Franchise
D. Intangible assets	_____ 4. Accrued interest on customers' notes
E. Other assets	_____ 5. Dividend payable in cash
F. Current Liabilities	_____ 6. Premium on common stock
G. Long-term liabilities	_____ 7. Non fund reserve for possible inventory loss
H. Capital stock	_____ 8. Advances to suppliers
I. Additional paid-in capital	_____ 9. Accrued employee wages
J. Unappropriated retained earnings	_____ 10. Unexpired insurance
K. Appropriated retained earnings	_____ 11. Ten-year bonds issued to finance plant acquisition
L. Footnote disclosure	_____ 12. Land
M. Not shown on balance sheet	_____ 13. Uncertain outcome of a pending lawsuit
	_____ 14. Undistributed portion of current year's net income
	_____ 15. Accumulated depreciation
	_____ 16. Stock dividend distributable
	_____ 17. Discount on bonds payable
	_____ 18. Sinking fund for bond retirement
	_____ 19. Patent
	_____ 20. Purchase commitment (3 years)

4.   The following accounts appeared on the trial balance of Luttmer Company at December 31, 1990.   All accounts have normal balances.

Notes Payable	$ 64,000	Accounts Receivable	$ 172,800
Accumulated Depreciation - Bldg.	261,000	Prepaid Expenses	18,750
Supplies on Hand	12,6000	Customers' Deposits	1,250
Accrued Salaries and Wages	11,400	Common Stock***	375,000
Securities at Cost*	93,700	Unappropriated Retained Earnings	?
Cash 56,750		Inventories (average cost)	526,750
Bonds Payable Due 1/1/97	400,000	Land at Cost	155,000
Allowance for Doubtful Accts.	2,600	Marketable Securities (cost)	24,400
Franchise	64,300	Accrued Interest on Notes	
Notes Receivable	46,000	Payable	650
Income Taxes Payable	52,000	Buildings at Cost	642,000
Preferred Stock**	250,000	Accounts Payable	136,650
Appropriated Retained Earnings	98,000	Additional Paid-in Capital	54,600

   *Market value, $106,500 - to be held at least 5 years.
  **8% cumulative; $10 par value; 25,000 shares authorized and outstanding.
 ***$1 par value; 400,000 shares authorized; 375,000 shares issued and outstanding.

Required
Prepared a classified balance sheet for Luttmer Company at December 31, 1990, using the report form presentation.

SOLUTIONS TO REVIEW QUESTIONS AND EXERCISES

True - False

1. (F) The balance sheet reflects a corporation's financial position for a point in time. This accounts for the heading on a balance sheet, which states, in part, "As of December 31, 19X1.

2. (T)

3. (T)

4. (F) Current assets are cash and other assets that are expected to be converted into cash, sold, or consumed either in one year or in the operating cycle, whichever is longer.

5. (T)

6. (T)

7. (T)

8. (F) Historical cost is the basis used to report assets and liabilities on the balance sheet. Price-level adjusted information may be disclosed by an entity as a supplement to the historical cost data. However, there is no accounting requirement to disclose price-level adjusted information when changes in the inflation rate occur.

9. (T)

10. (T)

11. (F) A partnership or proprietorship used individual capital accounts for each owner in the owners' equity section of the balance sheet. A corporation's owners' equity section shows capital stock accounts representing ownership and a retained earnings account that reflects undistributed earnings of the corporation.

12. (T)

13. (T)

14. (F) In most instances, an estimated liability meets the criteria for recording in the accounts (an asset has been impaired and the amount can be reasonably estimated). An item that is considered to be a contingent liability does not meet one or both of the criteria necessary for recording it in the accounts. Thus, contingent liabilities are generally disclosed by means of a balance sheet footnote.

15. (T)

16. (F) A balance sheet presented in the report form lists the liabilities an stockholders' equity directly below the assets and on the same page. A narrative description of classification sections is not included.

17. (T)

18. (F) Cash flow from operating activities refers to the amount of cash inflow and cash outflow which result from the activities an entity enters into for the purpose of generating net income. Because an income statement is prepared on an accrual basis, it includes revenues earned and expenses incurred in earning revenues without regard for the receipt or payment of cash. To compute cash flow from operating activities you must add to or deduct from net income those items in the income statement which did not generate or require the use of cash.

19. (F) When an entity sells its stock for cash it is considered to have entered into a transaction designed to aid in financing the entity's operation. Thus, this transaction would be classified as a financing activity on Xerax Company's statement of cash flows. Investing activities refer to those activities designed to utilize cash to acquire debt and equity investments of other companies (bonds and stocks) as well as property, plant, and equipment.

20. (T)

Multiple Choice

1. (B)   Generally, the rule is that if an asset is to be turned into cash or is to be used to pay a current liability within a year or the operating cycle, whichever is longer, it is classified as current. The cash surrender value of a life insurance policy is not expected to be turned into cash or used to pay a current liability. This item is normally shown in the long-term investments section of the balance sheet.

2. (A)   This transaction causes assets to increase by $4,760. the asset account truck increases by $6,000 (the purchase price), but assets also decrease by $1,240 due to the cash payment. Liabilities increase by $4,760 as a result of the issuance of the note.

3. (D)   A pension fund is an investment made by a company for the retirement benefits of its employees. These funds will not be converted to cash for use in the business nor will they be used to liquidate current liabilities. The other three alternatives (A, B, and C) include items that, although somewhat unusual, could be classified as current.

4. (D)   Long-term liabilities normally require the greatest amount of supplementary disclosure. This is because the terms of all long-term liability agreements, including maturity date or dates, rate of interest, nature of obligation, and any security pledged to support the debt, should be disclosed. The other classifications do require supplementary disclosure, but rarely is it as extensive as that required for long-term liabilities.

5. (B)   The balance sheet is criticized for its failure to reflect current value (A), the extensive use of estimates in its preparation (C), and its failure to include items of financial value that cannot be measured objectively (D). The balance sheet is rarely, if ever, criticized for its division of items into separate classifications.

6. (A)   Loss contingencies result when it is probable that an asset has been impaired or a liability has been incurred and the amount of the loss can be reasonably estimated. Both conditions must be satisfied before a liability can be recorded in the accounts.

7. (A)   Alternative (B) is incorrect because dividing liabilities between current and long-term has nothing to do with the amount of the debt. Alternative (C) is incorrect because the term "capital" is not a correct term to use in describing debt. Alternative (D) is incorrect because total equity includes both debt and owners' equity.

8. (D)   A loss contingency should be accrued if it is probable that a liability has been incurred and the amount can be reasonably estimated. In the case of estimated claims under a service warranty, some of the products covered by the warranty will require repair work resulting in a liability. Also, the company providing the warranty normally has experience with previous years' warranty claims so that an amount can be reasonably estimated. The other alternatives (A,B, and C) fail to satisfy one or both of the required criteria.

9. (A)   The criteria used to classify items as current assets are their ability to be turned into cash or to be used for paying a current liability within a year or the operating cycle, whichever is longer. The operating cycle is defined as the time it takes to convert inventory into cash.

10. (C)   A statement of cash flows deals with gross inflows and outflows of cash. An analysis of sales by territory would generate no information about the cash flow from the sales.

Review Exercises

1.
Beginning Receivable balance	$33,000
Ending Receivable balance	27,5000
Net change	($5,500)
Collection during September	$30,800
Less decrease in Receivables	5,500
September Sales	$25,300

2. December 31, 1990:

    Assets   = Liabilities + Owners' Equity
    $91,000 = $48,000   + $43,000

Original Investment::

12-31-90 Owners' Equity		$43,000
Net Income 1-1-86--12-31-90 (16,000 x 5)	$80,000	
Less Dividends Paid	63,850	
Increase in Owners' Equity from Operations		16,150
Original Investment		$26,850

3.
1.	(C)	11.	(G)
2.	(H)	12.	(B)
3.	(D)	13.	(L)
4.	(A)	14.	(J)
5.	(F)	15.	(B)
6.	(I)	16.	(H)
7.	(K)	17.	(G)
8.	(A)	18.	(C)
9.	(F)	19.	(D)
10.	(A)	20.	(L) or (M)

Luttmer Company
Balance Sheet
December 31, 1990

Assets

Current Assets

Cash		$56,750	
Marketable securities at cost		24,400	
Accounts receivable	$172,800		
Less allowance for doubtful accounts	2,600	170,200	
Notes receivable		46,000	
Inventories at average cost		526,750	
Supplies on hand		12,600	
Prepaid expenses		18,750	
Total current assets			$855,450

Long-term investments

Securities at cost (market value $106,500	93,800

Property, plant, and equipment

Land at cost		155,00	
Building at cost	642,000		
Less accumulated depreciation	261,000	381,000	
Total property, plant and equipment			536,000

Luttmer Company
Balance Sheet
December 31, 1990

Intangible assets

Franchise		64,300
Total assets...		$1,549,550

Liabilities and Stockholders' Equity

Current liabilities

Notes payable...	$64,000	
Accounts payable	136,650	
Accrued interest on notes payable...	650	
Income taxes payable	52,000	
Accrued salaries and wages...	11,400	
Customers' deposits	1,250	
Total current liabilities		$265,950

Long-term debt

Bonds payable - due 1/1/97		400,000
Total liabilities		665,950

Stockholders' equity

Preferred stock, 8% cumulative, $10 par value, 25,000			
shares authorized and outstanding		$250,000	
Common stock, $1 par value, 400,000 shares authorized,			
375,000 shares issued and outstanding		375,000	
Additional paid-in-capital..		54,600	
Earnings retained in the business			
Appropriated	98,000		
Unappropriated...	106,000	204,000	
Total stockholders' equity...			883,600
Total liabilities and stockholders' equity			$1,549,550

6

Accounting and the time value of money

Chapter Synopsis

Chapter 6 discusses the essentials of compound interest, annuities and present value. These techniques are being used in many areas of financial reporting where the relative values of cash inflows and outflows are measured and analyzed. The material presented in Chapter 6 will provide a sufficient background for application of these techniques to topics presented in subsequent chapters.

Chapter Review

1. **Compound interest, annuity,** and **present value** techniques can be applied to many of the items found in financial statements. In accounting, these techniques can be used to measure the relative values of cash inflows and outflows, evaluate alternative investment opportunities, and determine periodic payments necessary to meet future obligations. Some of the accounting items to which these techniques may be applied are: (a) **notes receivable and payable,** (b) **leases,** (c) **amortization of premiums and discounts,** (d) **pensions,** (e) **capital assets,** (f) **sinking funds,** (g) **business combinations,** (h) **depreciation,** and (i) **installment contracts.**

2. **Interest** is the cost of borrowing money. It is normally stated as a percentage of the amount borrowed (principal) calculated on a yearly basis. For example, an entity may borrow $5,000 from a bank at 7% interest. The yearly interest on this loan is $350. If the loan is repaid in six months, the interest due would be 1/2 of $350, or $175. Were the loan to be outstanding for two years, the interest would amount to $700. This type of interest computation is known as **simple interest** because the interest is computed on the amount of the principal only. The formula for simple interest can be expressed as **P x i x n** where **P** is the principal, **i** is the rate of interest for one period, and **n** number of periods.

3. Selecting an interest rate that is appropriate for a particular financial situation is not an easy task. This is because an interest rate generally has three components: (a) pure rate of interest, (b) credit risk rate of interest, and (c) expected inflation rate of interest. Combining these concepts into the selection of an appropriate interest rate for a company or investor is an important factor in presenting relevant and reliable accounting information

4. **Compound interest** is the process of computing interest on the principal plus any interest previously earned. Referring to the example in (2) above, if the loan was for two years with interest compounded annually, the second year's interest would be $374.50 (principal plus first year's interest multiplied by 7%). Compound interest is most common in business situations where large amounts of capital are financed over long periods of time. Simple interest is applied mainly to short term investments and debts due in one year or less. How often interest is compounded can make a substantial difference in the level of return achieved. When the compounding frequency is greater than once a year, the effective interest rate will always be greater than the state rate.

5. In discussing compound interest, the term **period** is used in place of **years** because interest may be compounded daily, weekly, monthly, and so on. Thus, to convert the **annual interest rate** to the **compounding period interest rate**, divide the annual interest rate by the number of compounding periods in a year. Also, the number of periods over which interest will be compounded is calculated by multiplying the number of years involved by the number of compounding periods in a year.

6. Certain concepts are fundamental to all compound interest problems. These concepts are:
   a. **Rate of Interest.** The annual rate that must be adjusted to reflect the length of the compounding period if less than one year.
   b. **Number of Periods.** The number of compounding periods (a period may be equal to or less than a year).
   c. **Future Amount.** The value at a future date of a given sum or sums invested assuming compound interest.
   d. **Present Value.** The value now (present time) of a future sum or sums discounted assuming compound interest.

7. The remaining chapter review paragraphs pertain to **present values** and **future amounts.** The text material

covers the following six major time values of money concepts:

    a.   Future amount of a single sum.
    b.   Present value of a single sum.
    c.   Future amount of an ordinary annuity.
    d.   Present value of an ordinary annuity.
    e.   Future amount of an annuity due.
    f.   Present value of an annuity due.

8.   Single-sum problems generally fall into one of two categories. The first category consists of problems that require the computation of the **unknown future amount** of a known single sum of money that is invested now for a certain number of periods at a certain interest rate. The second category consists of problems that require the computation of the **unknown present value** of a known single sum of money in the future that is discounted for a certain number of periods at a certain interest rate.

9.   The concept of **present value** is described as the amount that must be invested now to produce a known future value. This is the opposite of the compound interest discussion in which the present value was known and the future value was determined. An example of the type of question addressed by the present value method is: What amount must be invested today at 6% interest compounded annually to accumulate $5,000 at the end of 10 years? In this question the present value method is used to determine the initial dollar amount to be invested. The present value method can also be used to determine the initial dollar amount to be invested. The present value method can also be used to determine the **number of years** or the **interest rate** when the other facts are known.

10.   An **annuity** is a series of equal periodic payments or receipts called **rents**. An annuity requires that the rents be paid or received at equal time intervals, and that compound interest be applied. The **future amount of an annuity** is the sum (future value) of all the rents (payments or receipts) plus the accumulated compound interest on them. If the rents occur at the end of each time period, the annuity is known as **an ordinary annuity.** If rents occur at the beginning of each time period, it as an **annuity due.** Thus, in determining the a amount of an annuity for a given set of facts, there will be one less interest period for an ordinary annuity than for an annuity due.

11.   Compound interest tables have been developed to aid in the computation of present values and annuities. Examples of the four types of compound interest tables discussed in Chapter 6 are presented at the end of the chapter and on pages 50 to 59 in this study guide. Careful analysis of the problem to which compound interest tables will be applied is necessary to determine the appropriate procedures to follow.

12.   The **present value of an annuity** is a sum of money invested today at compound interest that will provide for a series of equal withdrawals for a specified number of future periods. If the annuity is an **ordinary annuity**, the initial sum of money is invested at the beginning of the first period and withdrawals are made at the end of each period. If the annuity, is an **annuity due,** the initial sum of money is invested at the end of the first period and withdrawals are made at the beginning of each subsequent period. Thus, the first rent withdrawn in an annuity due occurs on the day after the initial sum of money is invested. When computing the present value of an annuity, for a given set of facts, there will be one less discount period for an annuity due than for an ordinary annuity.

13.   A **deferred annuity** is an annuity in which two or more periods must pass, after it has been arranged, before the rents will begin. For example, an ordinary annuity of 10 annual rents deferred five years means that no rents will occur during the first five years, and that the first of the 10 rents will occur at the end of the sixth year. An annuity due of 10 annual rents deferred five years means that no rents will occur during the first five years, and that the first of the 10 rents will occur at the beginning of the sixth year. The fact that an annuity is a deferred annuity affects the computation of the present value. However, the **future amount of a deferred annuity** is the same as the amount of an annuity not deferred because there is no accumulation or investment on which interest may accrue.

14.   The following is a summary of the contents of the four types of compound interest tables discussed in the chapter.

"Future amount of 1" table. Contains the amounts to which 1 will accumulate if deposited now at a specified rate and left for a specified number of periods.

"Present value of 1" table. Contains the amount that must deposited now at a specified rate of interest to amount to 1 at the end of a specified number of periods.

"Future amount of ordinary annuity of 1" table. Contains the amount to which periodic rents of 1 will accumulate if the rents are invested at a specified rate of interest and are continued for a specified number of periods. (This table may also be used as a basis for converting to the amount of an annuity due of 1.)

"Present value of an ordinary annuity of 1" table. Contains the amounts that must be deposited now at a specified rate of interest to permit withdrawals of 1 at regular periodic intervals for the specified number of periods. (This table may also be used as a basis for converting to the present value of an annuity due of 1.)

Demonstration Problems

1. Compute the future amount of 10 periodic payments of $5,000 each made at the beginning of each period and compounded at 12%.

   Solution:

   This is the amount of an annuity due of $5,000 a period for 10 periods at 12%.

   First, find the amount of an ordinary annuity of $5,000 a period for 11
   periods at 12% from Table 6-3 and multiply that amount by $5,000:

20.5645 x $5000	$103,272.90
Second, deduct the last payment	5,000.00
The result is the amount of an annuity due of $5,000	
a period for 10 periods at 12%	$98,272.90

2. Compute the present value of 14 receipts of $800 each received at the beginning of each period, discounted at 10% compound interest.

   Solution

   This is the present value of an annuity due of 14 $800 payments for 13 periods at 10%.

   First, find the present value of an ordinary annuity of 13 $800 payments
   for 13 periods at 10% from Table 6-4 and multiply that amount by $800:

7.10336 x $800	$5,682.69
Second, add one additional receipt	800.00
The result is the present value of an annuity due to	
14 $800 payments for 13 periods at 10%	$6,482,69

3. How much must be invested at the end of each year to accumulate a fund of $50,000 at the end of 10 years, if the fund earns 9% interest, compounded annually?

   Solution:

Known final amount (a)	$50,000
Divide (a) by the amount of an ordinary annuity of $1 for 10 years at 9% (Table 6-3)	15.19293
The result is the periodic rent that would accumulate $50,000 at the end of	
10 years at 9% interest	$3,291

REVIEW QUESTIONS AND EXERCISES

True - False

Indicate whether each of the following is true (T) or false (F) in the space provided.

___ 1. Present value techniques can be used in valuing receivables and payables that carry no stated interest rate.

___ 2. The amount of interest on a $1,000, 6%, 6-month note is the same as the amount of interest on a $1,000, 3%, 1-year note.

___ 3. In the formula for compound interest, the number of periods refers to the number of months an obligation will be outstanding.

___ 4. The major difference between compound interest and simple interest lies in the fact that compound interest is computed twice each year, whereas simple interest is computed only once.

___ 5. The growth in principal is the same under both compound and simple interest if only one time period is involved.

___ 6. If interest is compounded quarterly and the annual interest rate is 8%, the compounding period interest rate is 4%.

___ 7. Present value is the amount that must be invested now to produce a known future amount.

___ 8. An annuity requires that periodic rents always be the same even though the interval between the rents may vary.

____ 9. An annuity is classified as an ordinary annuity if the rents occur at the end of the period; it is classified as an annuity due if the rents occur at the beginning of the period.

____ 10. The ordinary annuity table may be used to compute the periodic rents when the desired future amount of the annuity is not known.

____ 11. Periodic interest earnings under an ordinary annuity will always be lower by one period's interest than the interest earned by an annuity due.

____ 12. The present value of an ordinary annuity is the present value of series of rents to be made at equal intervals in the future.

____ 13. The number of rents exceeds the number of discount periods under the present value of an ordinary annuity.

____ 14. The future amount of a deferred annuity is normally greater than the future amount of an annuity not deferred.

____ 15. The valuation of a sum as of an earlier date involves a determination of present value; the valuation of a sum as of a later date involves a determination of an amount.

Review Exercises

1. Listed below are a series of questions. These questions can be answered using the methods presented in Chapter 6. You are to match each question with the method most conveniently used in providing a solution. The methods are listed below on the right.

Questions

____ 1. How much will I receive if I invest $1,000 for 1 year at 5%?

____ 2. How much should I deposit at the end of each 6-month period to accumulate $20,000 when I graduate in 4 years assuming that I can earn an annual rate of 10% compounded semiannually?

____ 3. What rate of interest must I earn on an investment of $60,000 to be able to withdraw $9,000 at the beginning of each year for the next 10 years?

____ 4. What amount should I invest now at 12% to provide 5 payments of $5,000 at the end of each year, starting 3 years from now?

____ 5. How many years will it take to accumulate $20,000 if I invest $1,845 at 10%?

____ 6. If I invest $3,000 at 8%, with interest computed on the principal plus undistributed interest how much will I have at the end of 10 years (annual compounding?)

____ 7. If I have $15,000 in a bank earning 6% interest compounded annually, how much can I withdraw at the end of each year for the next 8 years?

____ 8. At what annually compounded interest rate must I invest $25,331 to provide $50,000 at the end of 6 years?

____ 9. How much should Joan deposit on each birthday beginning on her twentieth birthday to accumulate $50,000 on her 50th birthday, assuming that she can earn 12% interest compounded annually (no deposit on fiftieth birthday)?

____ 10. How much should my employer set aside now, assuming that he can earn 8% interest compounded annually, so I can withdraw $10,000 at the end of each year for the next 10 years?

Method

A. Simple Interest
B. Compounded Interest
C. Present Value
D. Future Amount of an Ordinary Annuity
E. Future Amount of an Annuity Due
F. Present Value of an Ordinary Annuity
G. Present Value of an Annuity Due
H. Present Value of a Deferred Annuity

2. Compute the answer to each of the 10 items listed in question 1.

TABLE 6 - 1 FUTURE AMOUNT OF 1

$$a = (1 + i)^n$$

(n) Periods	2%	2-1/2%	3%	4%	5%	6%
1	1.02000	1.02500	1.03000	1.04000	1.05000	1.06000
2	1.04040	1.05063	1.06090	1.08160	1.10250	1.12360
3	1.06121	1.07689	1.09273	1.12486	1.15763	1.19102
4	1.08243	1.10381	1.12551	1.16986	1.21551	1.26248
5	1.10408	1.13141	1.15927	1.21665	1.27628	1.33823
6	1.12616	1.15969	1.19405	1.26532	1.34010	1.41852
7	1.14869	1.18869	1.22987	1.31593	1.40710	1.50363
8	1.17166	1.21840	1.26677	1.36857	1.47746	1.59385
9	1.19509	1.24886	1.30477	1.42331	1.55133	1.68948
10	1.21899	1.28008	1.34392	1.48024	1.62889	1.79085
11	1.24337	1.31209	1.38423	1.53945	1.71034	1.89830
12	1.26824	1.34489	1.42576	1.60103	1.79586	2.01220
13	1.29361	1.37851	1.46853	1.66507	1.88565	2.13293
14	1.31948	1.41297	1.51259	1.73168	1.97993	2.26090
15	1.34587	1.44830	1.55797	1.80094	2.07893	2.39656
16	1.37279	1.48451	1.60471	1.87298	2.18287	2.54035
17	1.40024	1.52162	1.65285	1.94790	2.29202	2.69277
18	1.42825	1.55966	1.70243	2.02582	2.40662	2.85434
19	1.45681	1.59865	1.75351	2.10685	2.52695	3.02560
20	1.48595	1.63862	1.80611	2.19112	2.65330	3.20714
21	1.51567	1.67958	1.86029	2.27877	2.78596	3.39956
22	1.54598	1.72157	1.91610	2.36992	2.92526	3.60354
23	1.57690	1.76461	1.97359	2.46472	3.07152	3.81975
24	1.60844	1.80873	2.03279	2.56330	3.22510	4.04893
25	1.64061	1.85394	2.09378	2.66584	3.38635	4.29187
26	1.67342	1.90029	2.15659	2.77247	3.55567	4.54938
27	1.70689	1.94780	2.22129	2.88337	3.73346	4.82235
28	1.74102	1.99650	2.28793	2.99870	3.92013	5.11169
29	1.77584	2.04641	2.35657	3.11865	4.11614	5.41839
30	1.81136	2.09757	2.42726	3.24340	4.32194	5.74349
31	1.84759	2.15001	2.50008	3.37313	4.53804	6.08810
32	1.88454	2.20376	2.57508	3.50806	4.76494	6.45339
33	1.92223	2.25885	2.65234	3.64838	5.00319	6.84059
34	1.96068	2.31532	2.73191	3.79432	5.25335	7.25103
35	1.99989	2.37321	2.81386	3.94609	5.51602	7.68609
36	2.03989	2.43254	2.89828	4.10393	5.79182	8.14725
37	2.08069	2.49335	2.98523	4.26809	6.08141	8.63609
38	2.12230	2.55568	3.07478	4.43881	6.38548	9.15425
39	2.16474	2.61957	3.16703	4.61637	6.70475	9.70351
40	2.20804	2.68506	3.26204	4.80102	7.03999	10.28572

8%	9%	10%	12%	15%	(n) Periods
1.08000	1.09000	1.10000	1.12000	1.15000	1
1.16640	1.18810	1.21000	1.25440	1.32250	2
1.25971	1.29503	1.33100	1.40493	1.52088	3
1.36049	1.41158	1.46410	1.57352	1.74901	4
1.46933	1.53862	1.61051	1.76234	2.01136	5
1.58687	1.67710	1.77156	1.97382	2.31306	6
1.71382	1.82804	1.94872	2.21068	2.66002	7
1.85093	1.99256	2.14359	2.47596	3.05902	8
1.99900	2.17189	2.35795	2.77308	3.51788	9
2.15892	2.36736	2.59374	3.10585	4.04556	10
2.33164	2.58043	2.85312	3.47855	4.65239	11
2.51817	2.81267	3.13843	3.89598	5.35025	12
2.71962	3.06581	3.45227	4.36349	6.15279	13
2.93719	3.34173	3.79750	4.88711	7.07571	14
3.17217	3.64248	4.17725	5.47357	8.13706	15
3.42594	3.97031	4.59497	6.13039	9.35762	16
3.70002	4.32763	5.05447	6.86604	10.76162	17
3.99602	4.71712	5.55992	7.68997	12.37545	18
4.31570	5.14166	6.11591	8.61276	14.23177	19
4.66096	5.60441	6.72750	9.64629	16.36654	20
5.03383	6.10881	7.40025	10.80385	18.82152	21
5.43654	6.65860	8.14028	12.10031	21.64475	22
5.87146	7.25787	8.95430	13.55235	24.89146	23
6.34118	7.91108	9.84973	15.17863	28.62518	24
6.84847	8.62308	10.83471	17.00000	32.91895	25
7.39635	9.39916	11.91818	19.04007	37.85680	26
7.98806	10.24508	13.10999	21.32488	43.53532	27
8.62711	11.16714	14.42099	23.88387	50.06561	28
9.31727	12.17218	15.86309	26.74993	57.57545	29
10.06266	13.26768	17.44940	29.95992	66.21177	30
10.86767	14.46177	19.19434	33.55511	76.14354	31
11.73708	15.76333	21.11378	37.58173	87.56507	32
12.67605	17.18203	23.22515	42.09153	100.69983	33
13.69013	18.72841	25.54767	47.14252	115.80480	34
14.78534	20.41397	28.10244	52.79962	133.17552	35
15.96817	22.25123	30.91268	59.13557	153.15185	36
17.24563	24.25384	34.00395	66.23184	176.12463	37
18.62528	26.43668	37.40434	74.17966	202.54332	38
20.11530	28.81598	41.14479	83.08122	232.92482	39
21.72452	31.40942	45.25926	93.05097	267.86355	40

TABLE 6 - 2 PRESENT VALUE OF 1

$$p^n = \frac{1}{(1+i)^n} = (1+i)^{-n}$$

(n) Periods	2%	2-1/2%	3%	4%	5%	6%
1	.98039	.97561	.97087	.96154	.95238	.94340
2	.96117	.95181	.94260	.92456	.90703	.89000
3	.94232	.92860	.91514	.88900	.86384	.83962
4	.92385	.90595	.88849	.85480	.82270	.79209
5	.90573	.88385	.86261	.82193	.78353	.74726
6	.88797	.86230	.83748	.79031	.74622	.70496
7	.87056	.84127	.81309	.75992	.71068	.66506
8	.85349	.82075	.78941	.73069	.67684	.62741
9	.83676	.80073	.76642	.70259	.64461	.59190
10	.82035	.78120	.74409	.67556	.61391	.55839
11	.80462	.76214	.72242	.64958	.58468	.52679
12	.78849	.74356	.70138	.62460	.55684	.49697
13	.77303	.72542	.68095	.60057	.53032	.46884
14	.75788	.70773	.66112	.57748	.50507	.44230
15	.74301	.69047	.64186	.55526	.48102	.41727
16	.72845	.67362	.62317	.53391	.45811	.39365
17	.71416	.65720	.60502	.51337	.43630	.37136
18	.70016	.64117	.58739	.49363	.41552	.35034
19	.68643	.62553	.57029	.47464	.39573	.33051
20	.67297	.61027	.55368	.45639	.37689	.31180
21	.65978	.59539	.53755	.43883	.35894	.29416
22	.64684	.58086	.52189	.42196	.34185	.27751
23	.63416	.56670	.50669	.40573	.32557	.26180
24	.62172	.55288	.49193	.39012	.31007	.24698
25	.60593	.53939	.47761	.37512	.29530	.23300
26	.59758	.52623	.46369	.36069	.28124	.21981
27	.58586	.51340	.45019	.34682	.26785	.20737
28	.57437	.50088	.43708	.33348	.25509	.19563
29	.56311	.48866	.42435	.32065	.24295	.18456
30	.55207	.47674	.41199	.30832	.23138	.17411
31	.54125	.46511	.39999	.29646	.22036	.16425
32	.53063	.45377	.38834	.28506	.20987	.15496
33	.52023	.44270	.37703	.27409	.19987	.14619
34	.51003	.43191	.36604	.26355	.19035	.13791
35	.50003	.42137	.35538	.25342	.18129	.13011
36	.49022	.41109	.34503	.24367	.17266	.12274
37	.48061	.40107	.33498	.23430	.16444	.11579
38	.47119	.39128	.32523	.22529	.15661	.10924
39	.46195	.38174	.31575	.21662	.14915	.10306
40	.45289	.37243	.30656	.20829	.14205	.09722

8%	9%	10%	12%	15%	(n) Periods
.92593	.91743	.90909	.89286	.86957	1
.85734	.84168	.82645	.79719	.75614	2
.79383	.77218	.75132	.71178	.65752	3
.73503	.70843	.68301	.63552	.57175	4
.68058	.64993	.62092	.56743	.49718	5
.63017	.59627	.56447	.50663	.43233	6
.58349	.54703	.51316	.45235	.37594	7
.54027	.50187	.46651	.40388	.32690	8
.50025	.46043	.42410	.36061	.28426	9
.46319	.42241	.38554	.32197	.24719	10
.42888	.38753	.35049	.28748	.21494	11
.39711	.35554	.31863	.25668	.18691	12
.36770	.32618	.28966	.22917	.16253	13
.34046	.29925	.26333	.20462	.14133	14
.31524	.27454	.23939	.18270	.12289	15
.29189	.25187	.21763	.16312	.10687	16
.27027	.23107	.19785	.14564	.09293	17
.25025	.21199	.17986	.13004	.08081	18
.23171	.19449	.16351	.11611	.07027	19
.21455	.17843	.14864	.10367	.06110	20
.19866	.16370	.13513	.09256	.05313	21
.18394	.15018	.12285	.08264	.04620	22
.17032	.13778	.11168	.07379	.04017	23
.15770	.12641	.10153	.06588	.03493	24
.14602	.11597	.09230	.05882	.03038	25
.13520	.10639	.08391	.05252	.02642	26
.12519	.09761	.07628	.04689	.02297	27
.11591	.08955	.06934	.04187	.01997	28
.10733	.08216	.06304	.03738	.01737	29
.09938	.07537	.05731	.03338	.01510	30
.09202	.06915	.05210	.02980	.01313	31
.08520	.06344	.04736	.02661	.01142	32
.07889	.05820	.04306	.02376	.00993	33
.07305	.05340	.03914	.02121	.00864	34
.06763	.04899	.03558	.01894	.00751	35
.06262	.04494	.03235	.01691	.00653	36
.05799	.04123	.02941	.01510	.00568	37
.05396	.03783	.02674	.01348	.00494	38
.04971	.03470	.02430	.01204	.00429	39
.04603	.03184	.02210	.01075	.00373	40

TABLE 6 - 3 FUTURE AMOUNT OF AN ORDINARY ANNUITY OF 1

$$A_{\overline{n}|i} = \frac{(1+i)^n - 1}{i}$$

(n) Periods	2%	2-1/2%	3%	4%	5%	6%
1	1.00000	1.00000	1.00000	1.00000	1.00000	1.00000
2	2.02000	2.02500	2.03000	2.04000	2.05000	2.06000
3	3.06040	3.07563	3.09090	3.12160	3.15250	3.18360
4	4.12161	4.15252	4.18363	4.24646	4.31013	4.37462
5	5.20404	5.25633	5.30914	5.41632	5.52563	5.63709
6	6.30812	6.38774	6.46841	6.63298	6.80191	6.97532
7	7.43428	7.54743	7.66246	7.89829	8.14201	8.39384
8	8.58297	8.73612	8.89234	9.21423	9.54911	9.89747
9	9.75463	9.95452	10.15911	10.58280	11.02656	11.49132
10	10.94972	11.20338	11.46338	12.00611	12.57789	13.18079
11	12.16872	12.48347	12.80780	13.48635	14.20679	14.97164
12	13.41209	13.79555	14.19203	15.02581	15.91713	16.86994
13	14.68033	15.14044	15.61779	16.62684	17.71298	18.88214
14	15.97394	16.51895	17.08632	18.29191	19.59863	21.01507
15	17.29342	17.93193	18.59891	20.02359	21.57856	23.27597
16	18.63929	19.38022	20.15688	21.82453	23.65749	25.67253
17	20.01207	20.86473	21.76159	23.69751	25.84037	28.21288
18	21.41231	22.38635	23.41444	25.64541	28.13238	30.90565
19	22.84056	23.94601	25.11687	27.67123	30.53900	33.75999
20	24.29737	25.54466	26.87037	29.77808	33.06595	36.78559
21	25.78332	27.18327	28.67649	31.96920	35.71925	39.99273
22	27.29898	28.86286	30.53678	34.24797	38.50521	43.39229
23	28.84496	30.58443	32.45288	36.61789	41.43048	46.99583
24	30.42186	32.34904	34.42647	39.08260	44.50200	50.81558
25	32.03030	34.15776	36.45926	41.64591	47.72710	54.86451
26	33.67091	36.01171	38.55304	44.31174	51.11345	59.15638
27	35.34432	37.91200	40.70963	47.08421	54.66913	63.70577
28	37.05121	39.85980	42.93092	49.96758	58.40258	68.52811
29	38.79223	41.85630	45.21885	52.96629	62.32271	73.63980
30	40.56808	43.90270	47.57542	56.08494	66.43885	79.05819
31	42.37944	46.00027	50.00268	59.32834	70.76079	84.80168
32	44.22703	48.15028	52.50276	62.70147	75.29883	90.88978
33	46.11157	50.35403	55.07784	66.20953	80.06377	97.34316
34	48.03380	52.61289	57.73018	69.85791	85.06696	104.18376
35	49.99448	54.92821	60.46208	73.65222	90.32031	111.43478
36	51.99437	57.30141	63.27594	77.59831	95.83632	119.12087
37	54.03425	59.73395	66.17422	81.70225	101.62814	127.26812
38	56.11494	62.22730	69.15945	85.97034	107.70955	135.90421
39	58.23724	64.78298	72.23423	90.40915	114.09502	145.05846
40	60.40198	67.40255	75.40126	95.02552	120.79977	154.76197

8%	9%	10%	12%	15%	(n) Periods
1.00000	1.00000	1.00000	1.00000	1.00000	1
2.08000	2.09000	2.10000	2.12000	2.15000	2
3.24640	3.27810	3.31000	3.37440	3.47250	3
4.50611	4.57313	4.64100	4.77933	4.99338	4
5.86660	5.98471	6.10510	6.35285	6.74238	5
7.33592	7.52334	7.71561	8.11519	8.75374	6
8.92280	9.20044	9.48717	10.08901	11.06680	7
10.63663	11.02847	11.43589	12.29969	13.72682	8
12.48756	13.02104	13.57948	14.77566	16.78584	9
14.48656	15.19293	15.93743	17.54874	20.30372	10
16.64549	17.56029	18.53117	20.65458	24.34928	11
18.97713	20.14072	21.38428	24.13313	29.00167	12
21.49530	22.95339	24.52271	28.02911	34.35192	13
24.21492	26.01919	27.97498	32.39260	40.50471	14
27.15211	29.36092	31.77248	37.27972	47.58041	15
30.32428	33.00340	35.94973	42.75328	55.71747	16
33.75023	36.97371	40.54470	48.88367	65.07509	17
37.45024	41.30134	45.59917	55.74972	75.83636	18
41.44626	46.01846	51.15909	63.43968	88.21181	19
45.76196	51.16012	57.27500	72.05244	102.44358	20
50.42292	56.76453	64.00250	81.69874	118.81012	21
55.45676	62.87334	71.40275	92.50258	137.63164	22
60.89330	69.53194	79.54302	104.60289	159.27638	23
66.76476	76.78981	88.49733	118.15524	184.16784	24
73.10594	84.70090	98.34706	133.33387	212.79302	25
79.95442	93.32398	109.18177	150.33393	245.71197	26
87.35077	102.72314	121.09994	169.37401	283.56877	27
95.33883	112.96822	134.20994	190.69889	327.10408	28
103.96594	124.13536	148.63093	214.58275	377.16969	29
113.28231	136.30754	164.49402	241.33268	434.74515	30
123.34587	149.57522	181.94343	271.29261	500.95692	31
134.21354	164.03699	201.13777	304.84772	577.10046	32
145.95062	179.80032	222.25154	342.42945	644.66553	33
158.62667	196.98234	245.47670	384.52098	765.36535	34
172.31680	215.71076	271.02437	431.66350	881.17016	35
187.10215	236.12472	299.12681	484.46312	1014.34568	36
203.07032	258.37595	330.03949	543.59869	1167.49753	37
220.31595	282.62978	364.04343	609.83053	1342.62216	38
238.94122	309.06646	401.44778	684.01020	1546.16549	39
259.05652	337.88245	442.59256	767.09142	1779.09031	40

TABLE 6 - 4 PRESENT VALUE OF AN ORDINARY ANNUITY OF 1

$$P_{\overline{n}|_i} = \frac{1 - \dfrac{1}{(1+i)^n}}{i} = \frac{1 - v^n}{i}$$

(n) Periods	2%	2-1/2%	3%	4%	5%	6%
1	.98039	.97561	.97087	.96154	.95238	.94340
2	1.94156	1.92742	1.91347	1.88609	1.85941	1.83339
3	2.88388	2.85602	2.82861	2.77509	2.72325	2.67301
4	3.80773	3.76197	3.71710	3.62990	3.54595	3.46511
5	4.71346	4.64583	4.57971	4.45182	4.32948	4.21236
6	5.60143	5.50813	5.41719	5.24214	5.07569	4.91732
7	6.47199	6.34939	6.23028	6.00205	5.78637	5.58238
8	7.32548	7.17014	7.01969	6.73274	6.46321	6.20979
9	8.16224	7.97087	7.78611	7.43533	7.10782	6.80169
10	8.98259	8.75206	8.53020	8.11090	7.72173	7.36009
11	9.78685	9.51421	9.25262	8.76048	8.30641	7.88687
12	10.57534	10.25776	9.95400	9.38507	8.86325	8.38384
13	11.34837	10.98319	10.63496	9.98565	9.39357	8.85268
14	12.10625	11.69091	11.29607	10.56312	9.89864	9.29498
15	12.84926	12.38138	11.93794	11.11839	10.37966	9.71225
16	13.57771	13.05500	12.56110	11.65230	10.83777	10.10590
17	14.29187	13.71220	13.16612	12.16567	11.27407	10.47726
18	14.99203	14.35336	13.75351	12.65930	11.68959	10.82760
19	15.67846	14.97889	14.32380	13.13394	12.08532	11.15812
20	16.35143	15.58916	14.87747	13.59033	12.46221	11.46992
21	17.01121	16.18455	15.41502	14.02916	12.82115	11.76408
22	17.65805	16.76541	15.93692	14.45112	13.16300	12.04158
23	18.29220	17.33211	16.44361	14.85684	13.48857	12.30338
24	18.91393	17.88499	16.93554	15.24696	13.79864	12.55036
25	19.52346	18.42438	17.41315	15.62208	14.09394	12.78336
26	20.12104	18.95061	17.87684	15.98277	14.37519	13.00317
27	20.70690	19.46401	18.32703	16.32959	14.64303	13.21053
28	21.28127	19.96489	18.76411	16.66306	14.89813	13.40616
29	21.84438	20.45355	19.18845	16.98371	15.14107	13.59072
30	22.39646	20.93029	19.60044	17.29203	15.37245	13.76483
31	22.93770	21.39541	20.00043	17.58849	15.59281	13.92909
32	23.46833	21.84918	20.38877	17.87355	15.80268	14.08404
33	23.98856	22.29188	20.76579	18.14765	16.00255	14.23023
34	24.49859	22.72379	21.13184	18.41120	16.19290	14.36814
35	24.99862	23.14516	21.48722	18.66461	16.37419	14.49825
36	25.48884	23.55625	21.83225	18.90828	16.54685	14.62099
37	25.96945	23.95732	22.16724	19.14258	16.71129	14.73678
38	26.44064	24.34860	22.49246	19.36786	16.86789	14.84602
39	26.90259	24.73034	22.80822	19.58448	17.01704	14.94907
40	27.35548	25.10278	23.11477	19.79277	17.15909	15.04630

8%	9%	10%	12%	15%	(n) Periods
.92593	.91743	.90909	.89286	.86957	1
1.78326	1.75911	1.73554	1.69005	1.62571	2
2.57710	2.53130	2.48685	2.40183	2.28323	3
3.31213	3.23972	3.16986	3.03735	2.85498	4
3.99271	3.88965	3.79079	3.60478	3.35216	5
4.62288	4.48592	4.35526	4.11141	3.78448	6
5.20637	5.03295	4.86842	4.56376	4.16042	7
5.74664	5.53482	5.33493	4.96764	4.48732	8
6.24689	5.99525	5.75902	5.32825	4.77158	9
6.71008	6.41766	6.14457	5.65022	5.01877	10
7.13896	6.80519	6.49506	5.93770	5.23371	11
7.53608	7.16073	6.81369	6.19437	5.42062	12
7.90378	7.48690	7.10336	6.42355	5.58315	13
8.24424	7.78615	7.36669	6.62817	5.72448	14
8.55948	8.06069	7.60608	6.81086	5.84737	15
8.85137	8.31256	7.82371	6.97399	5.95424	16
9.12164	8.54363	8.02155	7.11963	6.04716	17
9.37189	8.75563	8.20141	7.24967	6.12797	18
9.60360	8.95012	7.36492	7.36578	6.19823	19
9.81815	9.12855	8.51356	7.46944	6.25933	20
10.01680	9.29224	8.64869	7.56200	6.31246	21
10.20074	9.44243	8.77154	7.64465	6.35866	22
10.37106	9.58021	8.88322	7.71843	6.39884	23
10.52876	9.70661	8.98474	7.78432	6.43377	24
10.67478	9.82258	9.07704	7.84314	6.46415	25
10.80998	9.92897	9.16095	7.89566	6.49056	26
10.93516	10.02658	9.23722	7.94255	6.51353	27
11.05108	10.11613	9.30657	7.98442	6.53351	28
11.15841	10.19828	9.36961	8.02181	6.55088	29
11.25778	10.27365	9.42691	8.05518	6.56598	30
11.34980	10.34280	9.47901	8.08499	6.57911	31
11.43500	10.40624	9.52638	8.11159	6.59053	32
11.51389	10.46444	9.56943	8.13535	6.60046	33
11.58693	10.51784	9.60858	8.15656	6.60910	34
11.65457	10.56682	9.64416	8.17550	6.61661	35
11.71719	10.61176	9.67651	8.19241	6.62314	36
11.77518	10.65299	9.70592	8.20751	6.62882	37
11.82887	10.69082	9.73265	8.22099	6.63375	38
11.87858	10.72552	9.75697	8.23303	6.63805	39
11.92461	10.75736	9.77905	8.24378	6.64178	40

TABLE 6 - 5 PRESENT VALUE OF AN ANNUITY DUE OF 1

$$P_{\overline{n}|i} = 1 + \frac{1-\frac{1}{(1+i)^{n-1}}}{i} = (1+i)\left(\frac{1-v^n}{i}\right) = (1+i)\left(a_{\overline{n}|i}\right)$$

(n) Periods	2%	2-1/2%	3%	4%	5%	6%
1	1.00000	1.00000	1.00000	1.00000	1.00000	1.00000
2	1.98039	1.97561	1.97087	1.96154	1.95238	1.94340
3	2.94156	2.92742	2.91347	2.88609	2.85941	2.83339
4	3.88388	3.85602	3.82861	3.77509	3.72325	3.67301
5	4.80773	4.76197	4.71710	4.62990	4.54595	4.46511
6	5.71346	5.64583	5.57971	5.45182	5.32948	5.21236
7	6.60143	6.50813	6.41719	6.24214	6.07569	5.91732
8	7.47199	7.34939	7.23028	7.00205	6.78637	6.58238
9	8.32548	8.17014	8.01969	7.73274	7.46321	7.20979
10	9.16224	8.97087	8.78611	8.43533	8.10782	7.80169
11	9.98259	9.75206	9.53020	9.11090	8.72173	8.36009
12	10.78685	10.51421	10.25262	9.76048	9.30641	8.88687
13	11.57534	11.25776	10.95400	10.38507	9.86325	9.38384
14	12.34837	11.98319	11.63496	10.98565	10.39357	9.85268
15	13.10625	12.69091	12.29607	11.56312	10.89864	10.29498
16	13.84926	13.38138	12.93794	12.11839	11.37966	10.71225
17	14.57771	14.05500	13.56110	12.65230	11.83777	11.10590
18	15.29187	14.71220	14.16612	13.16567	12.27407	11.47726
19	15.99203	15.35336	14.75351	13.65930	12.68959	11.82760
20	16.67846	15.97889	15.32380	14.13394	13.08532	12.15812
21	17.35143	16.58916	15.87747	14.59033	13.46221	12.46992
22	18.01121	17.18455	16.41502	15.02916	13.82115	12.76408
23	18.65805	17.76541	16.93692	15.45112	14.16300	13.04158
24	19.29220	18.33211	17.44361	15.85684	14.48857	13.30338
25	19.91393	18.88499	17.93554	16.24696	14.79864	13.55036
26	20.52346	19.42438	18.41315	16.62208	15.09394	13.78336
27	21.12104	19.95061	18.87684	16.98277	15.37519	14.00317
28	21.70690	20.46401	19.32703	17.32959	15.64303	14.21053
29	22.28127	20.96489	19.76411	17.66306	15.89813	14.40616
30	22.84438	21.45355	20.18845	17.98371	16.14107	14.59072
31	23.39646	21.93029	20.60044	18.29203	16.37245	14.76483
32	23.93770	22.39541	21.00043	18.58849	16.59281	14.92909
33	24.46833	22.84918	21.38877	18.87355	16.80268	15.08404
34	24.98856	23.29188	21.76579	19.14765	17.00255	15.23023
35	25.49859	23.72379	22.13184	19.41120	17.19290	15.36814
36	25.99862	24.14516	22.48722	19.66461	17.37419	15.49825
37	26.48884	24.55625	22.83225	19.90828	17.54685	15.62099
38	26.96945	24.95732	23.16724	20.14258	17.71129	15.73678
39	27.44064	25.34860	23.49246	20.36786	17.86789	15.84602
40	27.90259	25.73034	23.80822	20.58448	18.01704	15.94907

8%	9%	10%	12%	15%	(n) Periods
1.00000	1.00000	1.00000	1.00000	1.00000	1
1.92593	1.91743	1.90909	1.89286	1.86957	2
2.78326	2.75911	2.73554	2.69005	2.62571	3
3.57710	3.53130	3.48685	3.40183	3.28323	4
4.31213	4.23972	4.16986	4.03735	3.85498	5
4.99271	4.88965	4.79079	4.60478	4.35216	6
5.62288	5.48592	5.35526	5.11141	4.78448	7
6.20637	6.03295	5.86842	5.56376	5.16042	8
6.74664	6.53482	6.33493	5.96764	5.48732	9
7.24689	6.99525	6.75902	6.32825	5.77158	10
7.71008	7.41766	7.14457	6.65022	6.01877	11
8.13896	7.80519	7.49506	6.93770	6.23371	12
8.53608	8.16073	7.81369	7.19437	6.42062	13
8.90378	8.48690	8.10336	7.42355	6.58315	14
9.24424	8.78615	8.36669	7.62817	6.72448	15
9.55948	9.06069	8.60608	7.81086	6.84737	16
9.85137	9.31256	8.82371	7.97399	6.95424	17
10.12164	9.54363	9.02155	8.11963	7.04716	18
10.37189	9.75563	9.20141	8.24967	7.12797	19
10.60360	9.95012	9.36492	8.36578	7.19823	20
10.81815	10.12855	9.51356	8.46944	7.25933	21
11.01680	10.29224	9.64869	8.56200	7.31246	22
11.20074	10.44243	9.77154	8.64465	7.35866	23
11.37106	10.58021	9.88322	8.71843	7.39884	24
11.52876	10.70661	9.98474	8.78432	7.43377	25
11.67478	10.82258	10.07704	8.84314	7.46415	26
11.80998	10.92897	10.16095	8.89566	7.49056	27
11.93518	11.02658	10.23722	8.94255	7.51353	28
12.05108	11.11613	10.30657	8.98442	7.53351	29
12.15841	11.19828	10.36961	9.02181	7.55088	30
12.25778	11.27365	10.42691	9.05518	7.56598	31
12.34980	11.34280	10.47901	9.08499	7.57911	32
12.43500	11.40624	10.52638	9.11159	7.59053	33
12.51389	11.46444	10.56943	9.13535	7.60046	34
12.58693	11.51784	10.60858	9.15656	7.60910	35
12.65457	11.56682	10.64416	9.17550	7.61661	36
12.71719	11.61176	10.67651	9.19241	7.62314	37
12.77518	11.65299	10.70592	9.20751	7.62882	38
12.82887	11.69082	10.73265	9.22099	7.63375	39
12.87858	11.72552	10.75697	9.23303	7.63805	40

SOLUTIONS TO REVIEW QUESTIONS AND EXERCISES

True - False

1. (T)
2. (T)
3. (F)   In the formula for compound interest the number of periods refers to the number of time interest is compounded. Interest is generally expressed in terms of an annual rate, however, in many business circumstances, the compounding period is less than a year (daily, monthly, quarterly, semiannually, etc.). In such circumstances the annual interest rate must be converted to correspond to the length of the period. This is done by dividing the annual rate by the number of compounding periods per year.
4. (F)   Simple interest is the term used to describe interest that is computed on the amount of the principal only. Compound interest is the term used to describe interest that is compounded on principal and on any interest earned that has not been paid or withdrawn.
5. (T)
6. (F)   In this case the compounding interest rate is 2% rather than 4%. This is computed by dividing the annual rate (8%) by the number of compounding periods per year (4).
7. (T)
8. (F)   An annuity requires that (a) the periodic payments or receipts (called rents) always be the same, (b) the interval between such rents always be the same, and (c) the interest be compounded once each interval.
9. (T)
10. (F)   If the desired future amount of an annuity is not known, the periodic rents cannot be computed because the tables cannot be used to solve problems with two unknowns.
11. (T)
12. (T)
13. (F)   The present value of an ordinary annuity is the present value of a series of equal rents to be withdrawn at equal intervals in the future.
14. (F)   Because there is no accumulation or investment on which interest may accrue, the future amount of a deferred annuity is the same as the future amount of an annuity not deferred.
15. (T)

Review Exercise

1. 1. (A)   6.   (B)
    2. (D)   7.   (F)
    3. (G)   8.   (C)
    4. (H)   9.   (E)
    5. (C)   10.   (F)

2. 1. $1,000 x 1.05 = $1,050

    2. $20,000 ÷ 9.54911 = $2,094.43 (From Table 6-3, 5% for 8 periods.)

    3. $60,000 ÷ $9,000 = 6.666 + 1 = 7.6666 (From Table 6-5, the interest
        rate is between 8% and 9%.)

    4. a. Each periodic rent $5,000
        b. Present value of an ordinary annuity of 1 for total
           periods (8) involved [number of rents (5) plus number
           of deferred periods (3)] at 12% 4.96764
        c. Less: Present value of an ordinary annuity of 1 for
           the number of deferred periods (3) at 12% 2.40183
        d. Difference (times the rents).. x 2.56581
        e. Present value of 5 rents of $5,000 .... $12,829.05

    5. 20,000 ÷ $1,845 = 10.84010)From Table 6-1, in the 10% column
        the number 10.84010 corresponds to 25 years; thus 25 years is the appropriate period.

    6. $30,000 x 2.15892 = $6,476.76 (From Table 6-1, 8% for 10 years).

    7. $15,000 ÷ 6.20979 = $2,415.54 (From Table 6-4)

    8. $25,331 ÷ $50,000 = .50662 (From Table 6-2, this amount is found
        for 6 years at 12% interest.)

    9. Future amount of an ordinary annuity of 1 for 31 years at 12%.............................. 271.29261
        Deduct one rent 1.00000
        Future amount of an annuity due for 30 years at 12%.. 270.29261

        $50,000 ÷ 270.29261 = $184.98

    10. $10,000 x 6.71008 = $67,100.80 (From Table 6-4).

7

Cash and receivables

Chapter Synopsis

Chapter 7 focuses on two of the primary liquid assets of a business enterprise. The techniques for proper management and control of these assets are presented in the chapter along with the related issue of accountability.

Chapter Review

1. **Cash** consists of coin, currency, bank deposits, and negotiable instruments such as money orders, checks, and bank drafts. Cash that has been designated for some specific use, other than for payment of currently maturing obligations, is segregated from the general cash account. This amount may be classified as a current asset if it will be disbursed within one year or the operating cycle, whichever is longer. Otherwise, the amount should be shown as a noncurrent asset.

2. It is common practice for an enterprise to have any agreement with a bank concerning credit and borrowing arrangements. When such an agreement exists, the bank usually requires the enterprise to maintain a minimum cash balance on deposit. This minimum balance is known as a **compensating balance**. Compensating balances that result in legally restricted deposits must be separately classified in the balance sheet. The nature of the borrowing arrangement determines whether the compensating balance is classified as a current asset or a noncurrent asset.

3. Control over the handling of cash and cash transactions is an important consideration for any business enterprise. Cash is the most liquid asset held by an enterprise and is the asset most easily converted to personal use by officers or employees. Numerous control procedures for cash transactions are discussed in other accounting courses, but two more commonly used procedures are presented in the text. These are: the **imprest petty cash systems** and **bank reconciliation**.

4. Two general forms of bank reconciliation are in common use. One form is the **bank to books** reconciliation. This begins with the bank balance; then, by adding or subtracting various reconciling items, it works to the book balance. The other form is described as the **reconciliation of bank and book balances to corrected cash balance**. This form is composed of two separate sections that begin with the bank balance and book balance, respectively. Reconciling items that apply to the bank balance are added and subtracted to arrive at the corrected cash balance. Likewise, reconciling items that apply to the book balance are added and subtracted to arrive at the same corrected cash balance. The corrected cash balance is the amount that should be shown on the balance sheet at the reconciliation date.

5. Proper cash management involves the problem of liquidity versus profitability. In terms of liquidity, management attempts to provide an ample amount of cash to meet all its obligations as they mature. However, when the focus is on profitability, management attempts to make maximum use of cash by purchasing revenue-producing assets. Thus, the problem concerns the identification of an optimum cash position, one that will permit prompt payment of maturing obligations and provide for maximum investment in revenue-producing assets. In most instances some trade-off between liquidity and profitability must be made.

6. **Short-term receivables** are defined as claims held against others for money, goods, or services collectible within a year or the operating cycle, whichever is longer. Receivables may generally be classified as **trade** or **nontrade**. Trade receivables (accounts receivable) are the most significant receivables an enterprise possesses. They result from the credit sale of goods and services to customers in the normal operations of the business. Nontrade receivables arise from a variety of transactions and can be written promises either to pay or to deliver. They are generally classified and reported as separate items in the balance sheet when they are material in amount.

7. The proper amount to record for a receivable is dependent upon (a) the face value of the receivable, (b) the probability of future collection, and (c) the length of time the receivable will be outstanding. The face value of a receivable will be outstanding. The face value of a receivable is affected by certain **discounts, returns,** and **allowances** that must be considered in accounting for receivables at the time of sale or collection.

8. Two types of discounts that must be considered in determining the value of receivables are **trade discounts** and **cash discounts**. Trade discounts represent reductions from the list or catalog prices of merchandise. they are often used to avoid frequent changes in catalogs

or to quote different prices for different quantities purchased. Cash discounts (also called sales discounts) are offered as an inducement for prompt payment and are communicated in terms that read 2/10, n/30 (2% discount if paid within 10 days of the purchase or invoice data, otherwise the gross amount is due in 30 days).

9. It is highly unlikely that a company that extends credit to its customers will be successful in collecting all of its receivables. Thus, some method must be adopted to account for receivables that ultimately prove to be uncollectible. The two methods currently used are: the **direct write-off method** and the **allowance method**. Under the direct write-off method, the receivable account is reduced and an expense is recorded when a specific account it determined to be uncollectible. The direct-write off method is theoretically deficient because it usually does not match costs and revenues of the period, nor does it result in receivables being stated at estimated realizable value on the balance sheet.

10. Use of the allowance method requires a year-end estimate of expected uncollectible accounts based upon credit sales or outstanding receivables. The estimate is recorded by debiting an expense and crediting an allowance account in the period in which the sale is recorded.

11. Advocates of the allowance method contend that its use provides for a proper matching of revenues and expenses as well as reflecting a proper carrying value for accounts receivable at the end of the period. When the allowance method is used, the estimated amount of uncollectible accounts is normally based upon a percentage of sales or outstanding receivables. The **percentage-of-sales method** attempts to match costs with revenues, and is frequently referred to as the income statement approach. The **percentage-of-outstanding-receivables approach** provides a reasonably accurate estimate of the net realizable value of receivables shown on the balance sheet. This approach is commonly referred to as the balance sheet approach.

12. The method used to determine the amount of bad debts expense each year affects the amount of expense recorded. Under the percentage-of-sales method, the amount recorded as bad debts expense is the amount determined by multiplying the estimated percentage times the credit sales. However, under the outstanding-receivables approach, the ending balance in the allowance account must be considered in arriving at bad debts expense for the year.

13. Companies wishing to avoid the 30- to 60-day collection period for accounts receivables can generate cash immediately by either **assigning**, or **factoring**, their accounts receivable. Assignment is a borrowing-type arrangement in which assigned accounts receivable are pledged as security for the loan received. Factoring of

accounts receivable is an outright sale of the receivables to a finance company or bank.

14. The assignment of accounts receivable can be a **general assignment** or a **specific assignment**. In a general assignment, all accounts receivable serve as collateral for the note. Thus, new receivables can be substituted for the ones collected. In a specific assignment, an agreement is reached between the borrower and lender concerning (a) who is to receive the collections, (b) the finance charges, (c) the specific accounts that serve as security, and (d) notification or nonnotification of debtors. The accounts assigned in a specific assignments should be transferred to a special ledger control account, and assignment should be clearly noted in the subsidiary ledger.

15. When accounts receivable are factored (sold), the factoring arrangement can be **with recourse** or **without recourse**. If receivables are factored on a with recourse basis, the seller guarantees payment to the factor in the event the debtor does not make payment. When a factor buys receivables without recourse, the factor assumes the risk of collectibility and absorbs any credit losses. Receivables that are factored with recourse should be accounted for an reported as a collateralized loan unless the following three conditions are met: (a) transferor surrenders control of the future economic benefits of the receivables, (b) transferor's obligation under the recourse provisions can be reasonably estimated, and (c) transferee cannot require the transferor to repurchase the receivables. If these conditions are met, the with recourse arrangement should be account for as a sale.

16. The major differences between trade accounts receivables and **trade notes receivables** are (a) notes represent a formal promise to pay and (b) notes bear an interest element because of the time value of money. Notes are classified as interest-bearing or noninterest bearing. **Interest-bearing notes** have a stated rate of interest, whereas **noninterest-bearing notes** include the interest as part of their face amount instead of stating it explicitly. Notes receivable are recorded at the present value of the future cash inflows. Determination of the present value can be complicated, particularly when a noninterest-bearing note or a note bearing an unreasonable interest rate is involved.

17. Long-term notes receivable should be recorded and reported at the present value of the cash expected to be collected. When the interest stated on an interest-bearing note is equal to the effective (market) rate of interest, the note sells at face value. When the stated rate is different from the market rate, the cash exchanged (present value) is different from the face value of the note. The difference between the face value and the cash exchanged, either a discount or a premium, is then recorded and amortized over the life of the note to approximate the effective interest rate. The discount or

premium is shown on the balance sheet as a direct deduction from or addition to the face of the note.

18. Whenever the face amount of a note does not reasonably represent the present value of the consideration given or received in the exchange, the accountant must evaluate the entire arrangement to record properly the exchange and the subsequent interest. Notes receivable are sometimes issued with no interest rate stated or at a stated rate that is unreasonable. In such instances the present value of the note is measured by the cash proceeds to the borrower or fair value of the property, goods, or services rendered. The difference between the face amount of the note and the cash proceeds or fair value of the property represents the total amount of interest during the life of the note. If the fair value of the property, goods, or services rendered is not determinable, estimation of the present value requires use of an **imputed interest rate**. The choice of a rate may be affected specifically by the credit standing of the issuer, restrictive covenants, collateral, payment, and the existing prime interest rate. Determination of the imputed interest rate is made when the note is received; any subsequent changes in prevailing interest rates are ignored.

19. Generating cash receipts from a note receivable before maturing can be accomplished by **discounting the note** at a bank. In most instances, the company discounting the note guarantees payment of the note to the bank at maturity. Thus, a company discounting notes receivable under such an arrangement must disclose a contingent liability in its financial statements. This contingency is normally recognized in the accounts by crediting the account Notes Receivable Discounted when the entry is made for the discounting of the note.

20. Accounting for a discounted note receivable involves the following six steps: (a) determine the maturity value of the note (face value plus total interest), (b) compute the discount (maturity value times the bank discount rate times the period of time the bank will hold the note), (c) determine the proceeds (maturity value minus the bank discount), (d) compute the book value of the note (face value plus the interest accrued to the date of discounting), (e) determine any interest revenue or expense (proceeds minus the book value), and (f) record the journal entry. The journal entry includes the following accounts:

Cash (proceeds)
Interest expense (if book value exceeds proceeds)

> Interest revenue (if proceeds exceed book value)
> Notes receivable discounted (face value of note)
> Interest receivable (any accrued interest)

21. The presentation of receivables in the balance sheet includes the following considerations: (a) segregate the different receivables that an enterprise possesses, if material; (b) insure that the valuation accounts are appropriately offset against the proper receivable accounts: (c) determine that receivables classified in the current asset section will be converted into cash within the year or the operating cycle, whichever is longer; (d) disclose any loss contingencies that exists on the receivables; and (e) disclose any receivables assigned or pledged as collateral.

22. Appendix 7A presents a description of a four-column bank reconciliation. This type of reconciliation is most often used by auditors in connection with their examination of any entity's financial statements. Appendix 7B includes a comprehensive illustration of transfers or receivables. The accounting for without recourse and with recourse transfers are both illustrated.

Demonstration Problems

1. The following information applies to the cash account of the Tom LeStarge Aviation Corporation as of August 31.

Balance per company books	$7,165.84
Bank service charge for August..	25.00
Note collected for the company by the bank	1,200.00
August outstanding checks...	1,822.17
NSF* check returned with August bank statement	328.45
Balance per August bank statement...	8,438.56
Interest on the note collected by the bank	54.00
Receipts recorded on August 31 and sent to the bank on that day	1,450.00

* Not sufficient funds.

Required:

A.   Prepare a bank reconcilation for LeStarge Aviation Corporation at August 31 that shows the correct cash balance as of that date.

B.   Prepare any necessary journal entries.

Solution:

A.

LeStarge Aviation Corporation
Bank Reconciliation
August 31

Book balance	$7,165.84		Bank Balance	$8,438.56
Add:			Add:	
Note collected	1,200.00		Deposit in transit	1,450.00
Interest on note	54.00			9,888.56
	8,419.84			
Less:				
Service charge	25.00		Less:	
NSF check	328.45	353.45	Outstanding checks	1,822.17
Correct cash balance		$8,066.39		$8,066.39

B.

Miscellaneous expense	25.00	
Accounts receivable	328.45	
Cash		373.45
Cash	1,254.00	
Notes receivable		1,200.00
Interest income		54.00

2. The following account balances appeared on the trail balance of Carol Company at 12/31:

	Dr.	Cr.
Accounts Receivable	$88,500	
Allowance for Doubtful Accounts		2,065
Sales		452,600
Sales Returns	3,200	

Required:

What amount would be debited to Allowance for Doubtful Accounts if they company records bad debts expense based on:
- a. 2% of net sales
- b. 8% of accounts receivable

Solution:

a.	Net sales ([$452,600 - $3,200] x .02) $8,988	$8,988
	(The current balance in the "Allowance account is not considered. Thus, the "Allowance" account would have a balance of $11,053 ($8,988 + $2,065) after the entry)	
b.	$88,500 x .08	$7,080
	Less current "Allowance" balance	2,065
	Entry amount	$5,015

3. On December 31, 1988, Michael Construction Company accepted a promissory note from Virginia Enterprises for services rendered. The note has a face value of $475,000, is due December 31, 1995, and pays interest annually at a stated rate of 3%. Because their face value of the note and services are not readily determinable, the parties agree that a 9% interest rate should be imputed as appropriate in the circumstances.

Required:

Compute the present value of the note and the discount.

Solution:

Face value of the note		$475,000
Present value of $475,000 due in 7 years at 9%:		
$475,000 x .54703 (Table 6-2)	$259,839	
Present value of $14,250 payable annually for 7 years at 9%:		
$14,250 x 5.03295 (Table 6-4)	71,719	
Present value of the note		331,558
Discount		$143,442

REVIEW QUESTIONS AND EXERCISES

True-False

Indicate whether each of the following is true (T) or false (F) in the space provided.

____ 1. Bond sinking fund cash should not be classified as a current asset because its use is restricted.

____ 2. Because the bank has the legal right to demand notice before withdrawal, savings accounts usually are not classified on a entity's balance sheet as cash.

____ 3. Legally restricted deposits held as compensating balances against short-term borrowing arrangements should be stated separately among the cash and cash items in current assets.

____ 4. The replenishment of the petty cash fund under an imprest system requires a debit to the Petty Cash account for the amount of the replenishment.

____ 5. A bank reconciliation is an integral part of the system of internal control over cash.

____ 6. Of the two bank reconciliation formats used by a business entity, the more widely used form reconciles both the bank balance and the book balance to a correct cash balance.

____ 7. When preparing a bank reconciliation for the purpose of arriving at a correct cash balance, NSF (not sufficient funds) checks are subtracted from the balance per books.

8. When a sale and the related receivable are initially recorded at the gross amount, sales discounts will be recognized in the accounts only when payment is received within the discount period.

9. The direct write-off method used in recording uncollectible accounts receivable allows the expense associated with bad debts always to be recorded in the accounting period in which the sale was made.

10. Because the collectibility of receivables is considered a loss contingency, the allowance method for recording bad debts is appropriate only in situations where it is probable that an asset has been impaired and that the amount of the loss can be reasonably estimated.

11. It is improper to offset assets and liabilities in the balance sheet, except where a right of offset exists.

12. The inclusion in the income statement of all returns and allowances made during the period is not acceptable accounting practice as some of the returns and allowances resulted from sales of a prior period and, thus, the matching concept is violated.

13. A trade receivable due two years hence should never be classified as a current asset.

14. Factoring is the term used to describe the pledging of receivables as collateral for a loan.

15. If receivables are sold with recourse, the seller guarantees payment to the purchaser in the event the debtor does not pay.

16. An imputed interest rate on a note receivable is the rate used by a bank when the note is discounted.

17. The credit balance in Unamortized Discount on Notes Receivable should be classified on the balance sheet as a deferred credit.

18. A discounted note receivable is an example of a loss of contingency.

19. The present value of a note is measured by the fair value of the property, goods, or services exchanged for the note or by an amount that reasonably approximates the market value of the note.

20. The essence of a transfer of receivables in a borrowing transaction is that the transferor retains the same risks of collectibility on the receivables after the transaction that it had before the transaction.

Multiple Choice

Select the best answer for each of the following items and enter the corresponding letter in the space provided.

1. Which of the following is properly classified as cash?
   A. Customer's postdated checks on hand.
   B. Certificates of deposit.
   C. Savings accounts.
   D. Bond sinking fund cash.

2. On a balance sheet, what is the preferable presentation of notes or accounts receivable from officers, employees, or affiliated companies?
   A. As trade notes an accounts receivable if they otherwise qualify as current assets.
   B. As assets but separated from other receivables.
   C. As offsets to capital.
   D. By means of notes or footnotes.

3. The advantage of relating a company's bad debt expense to its accounts receivable is that this approach:
   A. gives a reasonably correct measure of receivables in the balance sheet.
   B. relates bad debt expense to the period of sale.
   C. is the only generally accepted method of valuing accounts receivable.
   D. makes estimates of uncollectible accounts unnecessary.

4. When preparing a bank reconciliation for the purpose of arriving at the correct cash balance:
   A. outstanding checks can be added to the balance per books.
   B. NSF checks should be deducted from the balance per books.
   C. deposits in transit are deducted from the balance per bank.
   D. notes collected by the bank should be added to the balance per bank.

5. Which of the following statements is untrue regarding uncollectible accounts receivable?
   A. The direct write-off method records the bad debt in the year that it is determined that a specific receivable cannot be collected.
   B. The allowance method is based on the assumption that the percentage of receivables that will not be collected can be predicted from past experiences, present market conditions, and an analysis of outstanding balances.

C. The direct write-off method will provide for a proper matching of costs with revenues of the period when the average monthly accounts receivable balance is consistent throughout the year.

D. An uncollectible account receivable is a loss of revenue that requires--through proper entry in the account--a decrease in the asset accounts receivable and a related decrease in income and stock-holder's equity.

_____ 6. Alpha Corporation uses the allowance method of accounting for uncollectible accounts. During 1990 Alpha had charges to Bad Debts Expense of $20,000 and wrote off as uncol-lectible, accounts receivable totaling $16,000. These transactions decreased working capital by:
A. $20,000.
B. $16,000.
C. $ 4,000.
D. $ 0.

_____ 7. Gary sold land to Cates for $100,000 cash and a noninterest-bearing note with a face amount of $400,000. The fair value of the land at the date of sale was $450,000. Gary should value the note receivable at:
A. $450,000.
B. $400,000.
C. $350,000.
D. $500,000.

_____ 8. The balance in the Notes Receivable Dis-counted account represents:
A. a current liability.
B. an addition to the Notes Receivable account.
C. a current asset.
D. a loss contingency.

_____ 9. Hughes Company discounted a $1,000, 60-day, 6% note receivable dated July 1, 1990, at its own bank. The note was dis-counted on July 16, 1990, at a bank discount rate of 8%, based on the maturity value of the note. The proceeds of the note to Hughes Company would be:
A. $1,000.00.
B. $ 999.00.
C. $1,010.00.
D. $ 990.00.

_____ 10. Lisa Company's records show a cash balance of $3,600 at January 31, 1990. A bank reconciliation revealed that on January 31, outstanding checks totaled $500 and a deposit in transit amounted to $200. On the basis of this information, the January 31, 1990 balance per bank statement was:
A. $4,100.
B. $3,300.
C. $3,600.
D. $3,900.

Review Exercises

1. You are asked to prepare a bank reconciliation for Smith Company as of October 31, 1990. By placing the appropriate letter in the space provided, indicate whether the following items should be:
A. added to the balance per bank statement
B. deducted from the balance per bank statement.
C. added to the balance per books.
D. deducted from the balance per books.
E. omitted from the bank reconciliation because the bank amount and the book amount are already in agreement with respect to this item.

_____ 1. Outstanding checks of Smith Company as of October 31, 1990; the checks were written in October 1990.

_____ 2. Outstanding checks of Smith Company as of October 31, 1990; the checks were written in September 1990.

_____ 3. A check of Smythe Company had been charged by the bank against the account of Smith Company.

_____ 4. A certified check by Smith Company, dated October 10, 1990, that is outstanding as of October 31.

_____ 5. Bank service charges for October.

_____ 6. Discovered that check No. 101 (one of the cancelled checks included with the bank statement) had been made ou to Blue Company (a creditor) for $100. Smith Company had recorded the check in its Cash Payments Journal in the amount of $1,000.

_____ 7. Smith Company understated the amount of a customer's check in its Cash Receipts Journal. The check was received and deposited by Smith in October.

2. A trial balance for Finnegan Company shows the following balances at December 31:

	Debit	Credit
Accounts Receivable	$120,000	
Allowance for Doubtful Accounts		$ 200
Sales		360,000
Sales Discounts	10,000	

Prepare the adjusting entry necessary at December 31 to provide for estimated uncollectibles under each of the following independent assumptions.

A. Finnegan Company uses the percentage of sales method of accounting for uncollectible accounts. Company experience indicates that 1% of net sales will prove uncollectible.

B. Finnegan bases its estimate of uncollectible accounts on an aging of accounts receivable. The aging at December 31 indicates uncollectible accounts of $4,000.

3. Prepare the journal entries necessary to record the following transactions of Bazzetta Company during 1988.

August 14	--	Sold merchandise on account to Bob Company for $10,000.
September 5	--	Received a $10,000, 6%, 60-day note dated September 5 from Bob Company for sale made on August 14.
September 25	--	Discounted the note receivable from Bob Company at M.J. State Bank at an 8% discount rate. (Bazzetta Company uses a Notes Receivable Discounted account.)
November 5	--	Received notification from M.J. State Bank that Bob Company had defaulted on its note dated September 5. Paid M.J. State Bank the amount due.

4. Snyder Company agreed to loan Denise Glass Corporation $400,000. Denise Glass Corporation gave a noninterest bearing note due in 4 years and also promised to provide Snyder Company with glass products at a special discount price. (A 12% interest rate is an appropriate rate for both companies.)

Required:

A. Prepare the journal entry Snyder Company would make to record this transaction.

B. Prepare an amortization schedule for the note using the effective interest method.

SOLUTIONS TO REVIEW QUESTIONS AND EXERCISES

True-False

1. (T)

2. (F) Banks rarely exercise the right to demand notice before withdrawal of funds from a savings account. Thus, these funds are normally classified as cash for financial reporting purposes.

3. (T)

4. (F) Entries are made to the Petty Cash account only to increase or decrease the size of the fund. When the petty cash fund is replenished, various expense accounts are debited and the cash account is credited.

6. (T)

7. (T)

8. (T)

9. (F) The direct write-off method does not always match costs with revenues of the period. This is because receivables recorded late in one year might be written off in a subsequent year under the direct write-off method.

10. (T)

11. (T)

12. (F) Including all returns and allowances in the current period's income statement is an acceptable accounting practice justified on the basis of practicality and immateriality.

13. (F)   The rule about classification of current assets is that the item is classified as a current asset if it will be converted into cash within one year or the operating cycle, whichever is longer. Thus, if a company had an operating cycle of two years or longer, the trade receivable due in two years would be classified as a current asset.

14. (F)   Factoring is the sale of accounts receivable to factors. Factors are finance companies or banks that buy receivables from businesses for a fee and then collect remittances directly from the customer.

15. (T)

16. (F)   The process of interest-rate approximation is called imputation, and the resulting interest rate is called an imputed interest rate.

17. (F)   Unamortized discounts and premiums on notes receivable are classified along with the note. Discounts are deducted from notes receivable and premiums are added to notes receivable when shown on the balance sheet.

18. (T)

19. (T)

20. (T)

Multple Choice

1. (C)   A customer's postdated check is most appropriately classified as a receivable. Certificates of deposit provide investors with an opportunity to earn high rates of interest and should be classified as temporary investments rather than cash. Bond sinking fund cash is restricted and is classified either in the current asset or in the long-term asset section, depending on the date of disbursement. A savings account is the only item listed that is properly classified as cash.

2. (B)   Receivables from officers, employers, or affiliated companies are nontrade receivables. Such receivables are generally classified and reported as separate items in the balance sheet when they are material in amount.

3. (A)   The objective of relating bad debts expense to accounts receivable is to report receivables in the balance sheet at net realizable value. Relating bad debts to accounts receivable is a balance sheet approach. The other commonly used approach to the determination of bad debts expense is to take a percentage of credit sales for the period.

4. (B)   When preparing a bank reconciliation for the purpose of arriving at a correct cash balance, NSF (not sufficient funds) checks should be deducted from the balance per books. This is because these checks were added to the book balance when received; however, as the maker is unable to pay the check, the cash book balance would be overstated if the amounts were not deducted. The other alternatives reflect the opposite treatment each would receive on a bank reconciliation designed to arrive a a corrected cash balance.

5. (C)   The major problem with the direct write-off method is that it does not match costs with revenues of the period nor does it result in receivables being stated at estimated net realizable value on the balance sheet. The other three alternatives reflect accurate statements about uncollectible accounts receivable.

6. (A)   The entry to record bad debts expense includes a credit to the Allowance for Doubtful Accounts account. Working capital is reduced by the credit to the account because it is a contra account to the current asset accounts receivable. The subsequent entry to write off $16,000 of accounts deemed uncollectible does not affect working capital because the net amount of accounts receivable (total receivables less the allowance) is unchanged. For example:

	Before Write-off	After Write-off
Accounts Receivable	$120,000	$104,000
Allowance	30,000	14,000
Net	$ 90,000	$ 90,000

7. (C) The note should be valued at the fair value of the asset received. If the land has a fair value of $450,000 and $100,000 in cash is given, then the note is valued at $350,000. The additional $50,000 ($400,000 - $350,000) is an interest factor or discount that should be amortized over the life of the note.

8. (D) Because the entity discounting the note is contingently liable for payment of the note should the maker default, this is considered a loss contingency.

9. (B)
Face value of note	$1,000.00
Plus interest ($1,000 x .06 x 1/6)	10.00
Maturity value	$1,010.00
Less discount ($1,010 x .08 x 1/9)	10.00
Proceeds	$ 999.90

10. (D)
Balance per books	$3,600
Outstanding checks	500
	4,100
Deposit in transit	200
Balance per bank	$3,900

Review Exercises

1.
1.	(B)	5.	(D)
2.	(B)	6.	(C)
3.	(A)	7.	(C)
4.	(E)		

2.
A.	Bad Debts Expense	$3,500*	
	Allowance for Doubtful Accounts.		$3,500

*.01 (360,000-10,000)= 3,500

B.	Bad Debts Expense	$3,800*	
	Allowance for Doubtful Accounts		$3,800

*4,000-200= 3,800

3.
August 14	Accounts Receivable	10,000.00	
	Sales		10,000.00
September 5	Notes Receivable	10,000.00	
	Accounts Receivable		10,000.00
September 25	Cash	10,010.22*	
	Notes Receivable Discounted		10,000.00
	Interest Revenue		10.22

$$*\text{Maturity value} = 10,000 + \left(10,000 \times \tfrac{6}{100} \times \tfrac{60}{360}\right) = 10,100.00$$

$$\text{Proceeds} = 10,100 - \left(10,100 \times \tfrac{8}{100} \times \tfrac{40}{360}\right) = 10,010.22$$

November 5	Defaulted Notes Receivable	10,100	
	Cash		10,100
	Notes Receivable Discounted	10,000	
	Notes Receivable		10,000

4.   A.   Deferred Charge 145,792
          Notes Receivable... 400,000
              Cash   400,000
              Discount on Notes..   145,792

          Calculation of discount:
              Amount of loan $400,000
              Face amount of note.. $400,000
              P.V.* of 1 at 12%, 4 years 63552
              Present value of the note...   254,208
              Discount... $145,792

     *Present value.

B.	Year	Cash Interest	Effective Interest	Discount Amortized	Unamortized Discount	Note Present Value
					$145,792	$254,208
	1	$0	$ 30,505	$ 30,505	115,287	$284,713
	2	0	34,166	34,166	81,121	318,879
	3	0	38,265	28,265	42,856	357,144
	4	0	42,856	42,856	0	400,000
			$145,792	$145,792		

     *Rounded by $1.

8

Valuation of inventories: a cost basis approach

Chapter Synopsis

Inventories are of particular significance to merchandising and manufacturing companies because they affect both the balance sheet and the income statement. Chapter 8 initiates the discussion of the basic issues involved in recording, valuing, and reporting items classified as inventories. This discussion is concluded in Chapter 9.

Chapter Review

1. Inventories are asset items held for sale in the ordinary course of business or goods that will be used or consumed in the production of goods to be sold. **Merchandise inventory** refers to the goods held for resale by trading concern. The inventory of **a manufacturing firm** is composed of three separate items: **raw materials, work in process,** and **finished goods.**

2. Inventory **planning** and **control** is of vital importance to the success of a trading or manufacturing enterprise. If an excessive amount of inventory is accumulated, there is the danger of loss owing to obsolescence. If the supply of inventory is inadequate, the potential for lost sales exists. This dilemma makes inventory an asset to which management must devote a great deal of attention.

3. A **perpetual inventory system** provides a means for generating up-to-date records related to inventory quantities. Under this inventory system, data are available at any time relative to the quantity of material or type of merchandise on hand. A perpetual inventory system can be implemented through the use of a detailed subsidiary ledger supporting the general ledger control account. Alternatively, a perpetual system can be maintained independent of the general ledger by a separate record outside the double-entry system.

4. Reconciliation between the recorded inventory amount and the actual amount of inventory on hand is normally performed at least once a year. This is called a **physical inventory** and involves counting all inventory items and comparing the amount counted with the amount shown in the detailed inventory records. Any errors in the records are corrected to agree with the physical count.

5. The **cost of goods sold** during any accounting period is defined as all the **goods available for sale** during the period less any unsold goods on hand at the end of the period **(ending inventory).** The process of computing cost of goods sold is complicated by the determination of (a) the goods to be included in inventory, (b) the costs to be included in inventory, and (c) the cost flow assumption to be used.

6. Normally, goods are included in inventory when they are received from the supplier. However, at the end of the period, proper accounting requires that all goods to which the company has legal title be included in ending inventory. Goods in transit at the end of the period, shipped **f.o.b. shipping point,** should be included in the buyers' ending inventory. If goods are shipped **f.o.b. destination,** they belong to the seller until actually received by the buyer. Inventory held on **consignment** belongs to the consignee's inventory.

7. In actual practice a few exceptions exist regarding the general rule that inventory is recorded by the company that has legal title to the merchandise. These exceptions are known as **special sale agreements.** Three of the more common special sale agreements are (a) sales with buy-back agreement, (b) sales with high rates of return, and (c) installment sales.

8. Errors in recording inventory can affect the balance sheet, the income statement, or both, because inventory is used in the preparation of both financial statements. For example, the failure to include certain inventory items in a year-end physical inventory count would result in the following items being overstated (O) or understated (U): ending inventory (U); working capital (U); cost of goods sold (O); an gross profit.

9. Inventories are recorded at cost when acquired. Cost in terms of inventory acquisition includes all expenditure necessary in acquiring the goods and converting them to a saleable condition. *FASB Statement No. 34*, "Capitalization of Interest Cost," allows for the capitalization of Interest cost associated with the acquisition of an asset when a significant period of time will be required to get the asset ready for its intended use. A "significant period of time" means one year or more. In

the case of inventory, once it is ready for sale, interest capitalization should end.

10. **Product costs** are those costs that "attach" to the inventory and are considered to be a part of the total inventory valuation. Selling expenses and general and administrative expenses are not considered to be directly related to the acquisition or production of goods and, therefore, are not considered to be a part of the inventories. These costs are **period costs** rather than product costs, (a) **variable costing**, often called **direct costing**, and (b) **absorption costing**, also called **full costing**. Variable costing, where all manufacturing costs are classified as fixed or variable costs, is used by management for internal analysis and decision making. Under absorption costing all manufacturing costs, whether fixed, variable, direct, or indirect are included in the cost of inventory.

11. Although **purchase discounts** are sometimes recorded as revenue, they are most appropriately treated as a reduction in the purchase price of inventory. When purchases are recorded net of discounts, failure to pay within the discount period results in the treatment of lost discounts as a financial expense.

12. In a manufacturing firm, the cost of work in process and finished goods is composed of raw material, direct labor, and manufacturing overhead costs. Thus, the **cost of goods manufactured** for a manufacturing firm is analogous to the **cost of merchandise purchased** for a trading concern. A manufacturing firm prepares a separate statement to determine the cost of goods manufactured. This amount is used on the income statement arriving at cost of goods sold.

13. Determining the specific cost of inventory items that have been sold as well as those remaining in ending inventory is sometimes a difficult process. Thus, the consistent use of a **cost flow assumption**, other than specific identification, is often required in accounting for inventories. Inventory cost flow assumptions include **first-in, first-out (FIFO); last-in, first-out (LIFO); dollar-value LIFO; average cost; base stock; and standard costs**. It should be remembered that these assumptions relate to the flow of costs and **not** the physical flow of inventory items.

14. Use of the **FIFO inventory method** assumes that the oldest inventory costs are the first costs recorded for goods manufactured or sold. Under this method, the cost flow assumption tends to approximate the normal physical flow of goods. A major advantage of the FIFO method is that the ending inventory is stated in terms of an approximate current cost figure. However, because FIFO tends to reflect current costs on the balance sheet, a basic disadvantage of this method is that current costs are not matched against current revenues on the income statement.

15. Use of the **LIFO inventory method** assumes that the most recent inventory costs are the first costs recorded for goods manufactured or sold. When inventory records are kept on a **period basis**, the ending inventory would be priced by using the total units as a basis of computation, disregarding the exact dates of purchases. The calculation of ending inventory and cost of sales changes somewhat when the LIFO method is used in connection with **perpetual inventory records**.

16. When the LIFO inventory method is used, many companies combine inventory items into natural groups or **pools.** Each pool is assumed to be one unit for the purpose of costing the inventory. Any increment above beginning inventory is normally identified as a new inventory layer and priced at the average cost of goods purchased during the year. When the inventory is decreased, the most recently added inventory layer is the first layer eliminated (last-in, first-out). The **pooled approach** reduces record keeping and, accordingly, the cost of utilizing the LIFO inventory method.

17. Use of the pooled approach can result in problems for companies that often change the mix of their products, materials, and production methods. To overcome these problems, the **dollar-value LIFO method** has been developed. The important feature of the dollar-value LIFO method is that increases and decreases in a pool are determined and measured in terms of total dollar value, not the physical quantity of the goods as is done in the traditional LIFO pool approach.

18. In computing inventory under the dollar-value LIFO method, the ending inventory is first priced at the most current cost. Current cost is then restated to prices prevailing when LIFO was adopted. This is accomplished by using a **price index.** A new inventory layer is formed when the ending inventory, stated in base-year costs, exceeds the base-year costs of beginning inventory. Increases are priced at current cost. If the ending inventory, stated at base-year costs, is less than beginning inventory, the decrease is subtracted from the most recently added layer. A price index for the current year is computed by dividing **Ending Inventory for the Period at Current-Year Costs** by **Ending Inventory for the Period at Base-Year Costs.** The dollar-value method is a more practical way of valuing a complex, multiple-item inventory than the traditional LIFO method.

19. Proponents of the LIFO method advocate its use on the basis of its (a) proper matching of recent costs with current revenue, (b) tax benefits, (c) improved cash flow, and (d) future earnings hedge. Those opposed the the LIFO method claim that it (a) lowers reported earnings, (b) reports outdated costs on the balance sheet, (c) is contrary to normal physical flow, (d) fails to measure real income, (e) creates involuntary liquidation problems, and (f) invites poor buying habits.

20. The primary objectives of financial reporting of inventories are to provide (a) information useful in investment and credit decisions, (b) information that is useful in assessing cash flow prospects, and (c) information about enterprise resources, claims to these resources, and changes in them. The inventory valuation method that leads to the accomplishment of these objectives should be the one selected. The variety of inventory methods that exist have been devised to assist in accurate computation of net income rather than to permit manipulation of reported net income. Thus, it is suggested that once an inventory method is selected, it should be applied consistently thereafter. However, if a change should subsequently be made, it should be clearly explained and the effects disclosed in the financial statements.

REVIEW QUESTIONS AND EXERCISES

True - False

Indicate whether each of the following is true (T) or false (F) in the space provided.

_____ 1. In the determination of cost of goods sold, cost of goods manufactured is to a manufacturing concern what cost of goods purchased is to a merchandising concern.

_____ 2. A physical inventory should be taken at least annually, even when a perpetual inventory system is used.

_____ 3. Cost of goods sold is the excess of the cost of goods available for sale during the period over the cost of the goods on hand at the end of the period.

_____ 4. When goods are shipped f.o.b. shipping point, title passes only when the seller receives full payment for the merchandise.

_____ 5. Goods held on consignment should be included in the consignee's inventory reported on the balance sheet.

_____ 6. An understatement of the ending inventory will cause cost of goods sold to be understated and net income to be overstated for that period.

_____ 7. Variable costing, which excludes fixed manufacturing costs from inventory, is not an acceptable accounting practice for general-purpose financial statements.

_____ 8. A major argument in favor of the FIFO method if inventory costing is that current costs are matched against current revenues.

_____ 9. The ending inventory under a FIFO periodic inventory system will be the same as under a FIFO perpetual inventory system.

_____ 10. If LIFO is used for tax purposes, it must also be used for financial reporting purposes.

_____ 11. LIFO comes closer than FIFO to stating inventory on the balance sheet at current costs.

_____ 12. A manufacturing concern that uses a standard cost system predetermines the unit costs for material, labor, and manufacturing overhead.

_____ 13. Period costs and product costs are both inventoriable costs that relate to manufactured rather than purchased inventory.

_____ 14. Under absorption costing, all manufacturing costs, variable and fixed, direct and indirect, incurred in the factory or production process attach to the product and are included in the cost of inventory.

_____ 15. The use of a Purchase Discounts Lost account indicates that purchases are being recorded not of purchase discounts.

_____ 16. When a company selects a cost flow assumption (FIFO, LIFO, average cost, etc.), it must be consistent with the actual physical movement of goods through the company.

_____ 17. Under dollar-value LIFO, there will never be a layer for a particular year unless the quantity of inventory increased during that year.

_____ 18. All companies using the dollar-value LIFO method are required to use the same price index.

_____ 19. In a period of rising prices, LIFO yields a larger cost of good sold than does FIFO.

_____ 20. A change in inventory methods requires that the change be explained and its effect be disclosed in the financial statements.

Multiple Choice

Select the best answer for each of the following items and enter the corresponding letter in the space provided.

_____ 1. Which of the following inventory methods comes closest to stating inventory at replacement cost?
A. FIFO.
B. LIFO.
C. Weighted-average.
D. Base stock.

_____ 2. Which of the following is not considered to be an inventoriable cost under variable costing?
A. Raw materials.
B. Direct labor.

    C. Variable factory overhead.

    D. Fixed factory overhead.

____ 3. The use of LIFO under a perpetual inventory system (units and costs):

    A. may yield a higher inventory valuation than LIFO under a periodic inventory system when prices are steadily falling.

    B. may yield a higher inventory valuation than LIFO under a periodic inventory system when prices are steadily rising.

    C. always yields the same inventory valuation as LIFO under a periodic inventory system.

    D. can never yield the same inventory valuation as LIFO under a periodic inventory system.

____ 4. The failure to record a purchase of merchandise on account even though the goods are properly included in the physical inventory results in:

    A. an overstatement of assets and net income.

    B. an understatement of assets and net income.

    C. an understatement of cost of goods sold and liabilities and an overstatement of assets.

    D. an understatement of liabilities and an overstatement of owners' equity.

____ 5. The use of a Purchase Descounts Lost account implies that the recorded cost of a purchased inventory item is its:

    A. invoice price.

    B. invoice price plus the purchase discount price.

    C. invoice price less the purchase discount allowable, whether or not taken.

    D. invoice price less the purchase discount allowable, whether or not taken.

____ 6. Which of the following represents a departure from the historical cost basis of valuing inventories.

    A. Dollar-value LIFO.

    B. Specific identification.

    C. Replacement cost.

    D. Absorption costing.

____ 7. Green Company has been using the LIFO inventory method for 10 years. Its inventory at the end of year 10 was $30,000, but it would have been $40,000 if FIFO had been used. Accordingly, if FIFO had been used, Green Company's income before income taxes would have been:

    A. $10,000 larger over the 10-year period.

    B. $10,000 smaller over the 10-year period.

    C. $10,000 larger in year 10.

    D. $10,000 smaller in year 10.

____ 8. The purchase of inventory items on account using the perpetual inventory method:

    A. decreases working capital and the current ratio.

    B. has no effect on working capital but decreases the current ratio.

    C. has no effect on the current ratio but decreases working capital.

    D. has no effect on working capital or the current ratio.

____ 9. The dollar-value inventory method is an improvement over the traditional LIFO pool approach because:

    A. the mathematical computations are greatly simplified.

    B. it is easier to apply where few inventory items are employed and little change in product mix is anticipated.

    C. increases and decreases in a pool are determined and measured in terms of total dollar value rather than the physical quantity of the goods in the inventory pool.

    D. dissimilar items of inventory can be grouped to form pools under the dollar-value LIFO method.

____ 10. The acquisition cost of a heavily used raw material changes frequently. The inventory amount of this material at year end will be the same if perpetual records (units and costs) are kept as it would be under a periodic inventory method only if the inventory amount is computed under the:

    A. weighted-average method.

    B. first-in, first-out method.

    C. last-in, first-out method.

    D. direct costing method.

Review Exercises

1. Buick Pei Company's records show the following information related to one of its products:

May 1	Balanced on hand	300 units @ $5
May 12	Purchased	600 units @ $6
May 30	Purchased	100 units @ $7

Buick Pei Company uses a periodic inventory system. Assuming that 600 units were sold during May, compute the May 31 inventory and the cost of goods sold during May 31 under each of the following inventory methods:

		May 31 Inventory	Cost of Goods Sold
A.	FIFO	_____	_____
B.	LIFO	_____	_____
C.	Weighted-average	_____	_____

2. An examination of the records of Major Company revealed that goods costing $1,000 were received on December, 31, 1990. The purchase invoice for these goods was not received until January 4, 1991, at which time the purchase and related liability were recorded. Major Company incorrectly excluded the cost of the goods from its December 31, 1990, inventory. Indicate whether the following financial statement items were understated (U), overstated (O), or not misstated (N) for the years 1990 and 1991.

	1990	1991
Purchases	_____	_____
Inventory, December 31	_____	_____
Cost of goods sold	_____	_____
Net income	_____	_____
Assets	_____	_____
Liabilities	_____	_____
Retained earnings	_____	_____

3. Stewart Company manufactures a single product. On December 31, 1990, Stewart adopted the dollar-value LIFO inventory method. The inventory on that date using the dollar-value LIFO inventory method was $50,000. Inventory data are as follows:

Year	Inventory at Respective Year-End Cost Prices	Price Index at Year End
1988	$50,000	100
1989	73,500	105
1990	71,500	110

Compute the inventory at December 31, 1991 and 1992 using the dollar-value LIFO method.

4. UPC purchased merchandise inventory costing $24,000 with credit terms of 2/10, net 30. Eight days after the purchase, UPC paid one-half of the outstanding obligation. The remaining amount was paid 30 days after the date of purchase. Prepare the journal entries UPC would make for the purchase and the two subsequent payments using:
A. the gross method.
B. the net method.

SOLUTIONS TO REVIEW QUESTIONS AND EXERCISES

True - False

1. (T)
2. (T)
3. (T)
4. (F) When goods are shipped f.o.b. shipping point, title passes to the buyer when the seller delivers the goods to the common carrier who acts as an agent for the buyer.
5. (F) Goods held on consignment by a consignee remain the property of the consignor until the goods are sold. Thus, goods on consignment are properly included in the consignor's inventory rather than the inventory of the consignee.
6. (F) An understatement in ending inventory results in an overstatement of cost of good sold and a corresponding understatement of net income.
7. (T)

8. (F) Under the FIFO method of inventory costing, the first costs into the inventory account that are the oldest costs matched against the current revenue. Thus, current costs are not matched against current revenue under the FIFO inventory method.

9. (T)

10. (T)

11. (F) LIFO is an inventory valuation method that emphasizes the recording of current costs on the income statement. Under LIFO the most recent inventory costs are charged against revenue, thus the older inventory costs are shown on the balance sheet.

12. (T)

13. (F) Purchase costs are those costs that "attach" to the inventory (whether purchased or manufactured) and are considered to be a part of the total inventory valuation. Period costs are not considered to be directly related to the acquisition or production of goods and therefore are not considered to be a part of the inventories.

14. (T)

15. (T)

16. (F) A company can select any cost flow assumption regardless of the physical flow of its goods.

17. (T)

18. (F) The index used in dollar-value LIFO computations is an index computed using the following formula:

$$\frac{\text{Ending inventory for the period at current cost}}{\text{Ending inventory for the period at base-year cost}} = \text{Price index for current year}$$

19. (T)

20. (T)

Multiple Choice

1. (A) Because the oldest costs in inventory are charged against income under the FIFO inventory method, the inventory valuation shown on the balance sheet represents the most recent inventory costs. Thus, FIFO comes closest to stating inventory at replacement costs when compared to the other three methods listed.

2. (D) Under variable costing, only costs that vary directly with the volume of production are charged to products as manufacturing takes place. Fixed costs are not viewed as costs of the products being manufactured. Alternative (D) represents the only fixed cost listed.

3. (B) In a period of steadily rising prices, LIFO under a periodic inventory system will find the highest inventory cost being charged against revenue. Under the same set of circumstances, the use of LIFO under a perpetual inventory system (units and costs) might find inventory purchases made subsequent to the final sale. If such is the case, the perpetual method would yield a higher ending inventory valuation.

4. (D) The failure to record the purchases understates liabilities because the payable was not recorded. The fact that the amount of the purchase was properly included in the physical inventory but omitted from goods available for sale causes cost of goods sold to be understated. This understatement of cost of goods sold causes net income to be overstated resulting in an overstatement of owner's equity.

5. (D) The Purchase Discounts Lost account arises when the purchase of inventory is recorded net of the allowable discount and the purchaser does not pay within the discount period.

6. (C) Replacement cost is a future valuation concept and represents a departure from the historical cost basis of valuing inventories.

7. (A) The greater ending inventory would result in cost of goods sold being $10,000 less than reported under the LIFO method. The smaller cost of goods sold would result in a larger net income, larger by $10,000.

8. (B) The purchase of inventory on account increases both current assets (inventory) and current liabilities (accounts payable) by the same amount. This results in no change in working capital. However, if current assets and current liabilities are both increased by the same amount, the current ratio will decrease.

9. (C) The dollar-value LIFO method not only allows increases and decreases in a pool to be determined and measured in terms of total dollar value, but also two additional advantages are noted. First, a broader range of goods may be included in a dollar-value LIFO pool than in a regular pool. Second, in a dollar-value LIFO pool, replacement is permitted if it is similar as to type of material, or similarity in use or interchangeability.

10. (B) Whether inventory is priced under the periodic or perpetual method, the ending inventory valuation and cost of goods sold will be the same as long as the FIFO cost flow assumption is used.

Review Exercises

1.

		May 31 Inventory	Cost of Goods Sold
A.	FIFO	$2,500	$3,300
B.	LIFO	2,100	3,700
C.	Weighted-average	2,320	3,480

2.

	1990	1991
Purchase	U	O
Inventory, December 31	U	N
Cost of goods sold	N	N
Net income	N	N
Assets	U	N
Liabilities	U	N
Retained earnings	N	N

3.

December 31, 1991 inventory at 1991 prices	$73,500
December 31, 1991, inventory at base-year prices ($73,500 ÷ 1.05)	70,000
January 1, 1991 inventory at base-year prices	50,000
1991 inventory increase at base-year prices	20,000
1991 inventory increase at 1991 prices ($20,000 x 1.05)	21,000

December 31, 1991 inventory:

Layer	Base-Year Prices	Price Index	Dollar-Value Lifo
1988	$50,000	100	$50,000
1989	20,000	105	21,000
	$70,000		$71,000

December 31, 1992 inventory at 1992 prices	$71,500
December 31, 1992 inventory at base-year prices ($71,500 ÷ 1.10)	65,000
January 1, 1992 inventory at base-year prices	70,000
1992 inventory decrease at base-year prices	5,000
1992 inventory decreases at prices in existence when most recent layer was added (1992) $5,000 x 1.05	5,250

December 31, 1992 inventory:

Layer	Base-Year Prices	Price Index	Dollar-Value Lifo
1988	$50,000	100	$50,000
1989	15,000	105	15,750
	$65,000		$65,750

4A. PURCHASE:

Purchases	24,000	
Accounts Payable		24,000
PAYMENTS:		
(1) Accounts Payable	12,000	
Purchase Discounts		240
Cash		11,760
(2) Accounts Payable	12,000	
Cash		12,000

4B. PURCHASE:

Purchases	23,520	
Accounts Payable		23,520
PAYMENTS:		
(1) Accounts Payable	11,760	
Cash		11,760
(2) Accounts payable	11,760	
Purchase Discounts Lost	240	
Cash		12,000

9

Inventories: additional valuation problems

Chapter Synopsis

Chapter 9 concludes the discussion of inventories by addressing certain unique valuation problems not covered in Chapter 8. Chapter 9 also includes a description of the development and use of various estimation techniques used to value ending inventory without a physical count.

Chapter Review

1. When the **future revenue** associated with inventory is below its **original cost,** the inventory should be written down to reflect this loss. Thus, the historical cost principle is abandoned when the future utility (revenue-producing ability) of the asset is no longer as great as its original cost. This is known as the **lower of cost or market (LCM)** method of valuing inventory and is accepted accounting practice.

2. The term "market" in lower of cost or market generally refers to the **replacement cost** of an inventory item. However, market value should not exceed **net realizable value (NRV)**, nor should it be less than **net realizable value less a normal markup.** These are known as the **upper** (ceiling) and **lower** (floor) limits of market. Market is defined as replacement cost if such cost falls between the upper and lower limits. Should replacement cost be above the upper limit, market would be defined as net realizable value. If replacement cost falls below the lower limit, market is defined as net realizable value less a normal markup.

3. For example, consider the following illustration.

Inventory - sales value	$800
Less: Cost to complete and sell	200
Net realizable value (NRV)	600
Less: Normal markup	100
NRV less normal markup	$500

To arrive at the final inventory valuation, **market value** must be determined and then compared to **cost.** Market value is determined by comparing replacement cost of the inventory with the upper and lower limits. If replacement cost of the inventory in the example is $550, then $550 is compared to cost in determining lower of cost or market because replacement cost falls between the upper ($600) and lower ($500) limits. If replacement cost of the

inventory is $650, it would exceed the upper limit; thus the upper limit ($600) would be compared to cost in determining lower of cost or market. Similarly, if replacement cost of the inventory is $450, it would be lower than the lower limit and thus the lower limit ($500) would be compared to cost in determining lower of cost or market.

4. When application of the lower of cost or market rule results in a decline in the value of inventory, it is preferable to show the loss as a separate-line item on the income statement. The **loss due to market decline of inventory** may be recorded by a direct reduction in inventory or a contra asset account may be established.

5. The cost or market rule may be applied on an individual-item basis or to the total of the inventory. The individual-item approach is preferred by many companies because tax rules require its use where practical, and it produces the most conservative balance sheet valuation. When inventory is written down to market, this new basis is considered to be the cost basis for future periods. A subsequent rise in the market value of inventory previously written down should not be recognized.

6. **Purchase commitments** represent contracts for the purchase of inventory at a specified price in a future period. If the contract price is in excess of the market price and it is expected that losses will occur when the purchase is effected, the loss should be recognized in the period during which the market decline took place.

7. Recording inventory at selling price less estimated cost to complete and sell is acceptable in certain instances. To be accorded this treatment, the item should (a) have a controlled market with a fixed price applicable to all quantities and (b) have relatively insignificant disposal costs. Certain minerals sold in a government-controlled market and agricultural products that are marketable at fixed prices provide examples of inventory items carried at selling price.

8. When a group of varying inventory items is purchased for a lump sum price, a problem exists relative to the cost per item. The **relative sales value method** apportions the total cost to individual items on the basis of the selling price of each item.

9. The **gross profit method** is used to estimate the amount of ending inventory. Its use is **not** appropriate for financial reporting purposes; however, it can serve a useful purpose when an approximation of ending inventory is needed. Such approximations are sometimes required by auditors or when inventory and inventory records are destroyed by fire or some other catastrophe. The gross profit method should never be used as a substitute for a yearly physical inventory unless the inventory has been destroyed.

10. The **retail inventory method** is an inventory estimation technique based upon an observable pattern between cost and sales price that exists in most retail concerns. This method requires that a record be kept of (a) the total cost of goods purchased, (b) the total retail value of the goods available for sale, and (c) the sales for the period.

11. Basically, the retail method requires the computation of the **cost to retail ratio** of inventory available for sale. This ratio is computed by dividing the **cost** of the goods available for sale by the **retail value** (selling price) of goods available for sale. Once the ratio is determined, total sales for the period are deducted from the retail value of inventory available for sale. The resulting amount represents ending inventory priced at retail. When this amount is multiplied by the cost to retail ratio, an approximation of the cost of ending inventory results. Use of this method eliminates the need for a physical count of inventory each time an income statement is prepared. However, physical counts are made at least yearly to determine the accuracy of the records and to avoid overstatements due to theft, loss, and breakage.

12. An understanding of this terminology common to the retail method is necessary for accurate application. Those terms and their definitions are shown below:

Original Retail Price. The price at which the item was originally marked for sale.

Markup. An increase above the original retail price.

Markup Cancellation. A decrease in the selling price of an item that had been previously marked up above the original retail price. A markup cancellation will never reduce the selling price below the original retail price.

Markdowns. A decrease below the original retail price.

Markdown Cancellation. An increase in the selling price that follows a markdown. A markdown cancellation will never increase the selling price above the original retail price.

13. When the cost to retail ratio is computed after net markups (markups less markup cancellations) have been added, the retail inventory method approximates lower of cost or market. This is known as the **conventional retail inventory method.** If both net markups and net markdowns are included before the cost to retail ratio is computed, the retail inventory method approximates cost.

14. Many accountants suggest a LIFO assumption be adopted for use with the application of the retail inventory method. Use of LIFO in connection with the retail inventory method is thought to result in a better matching of costs and revenues. The application of **LIFO retail** is made under two assumptions (a) **stable prices**, and (b) **fluctuating prices.** Because the LIFO method is a cost method, not a cost or market approach, both the markups and markdowns must be considered in obtaining the proper cost to retail percentage. Beginning inventory is excluded from the computation of the cost to retail percentage because of the layer effect that results from the use of the LIFO method.

15. If changes in the price level occur, the effect of such changes must be eliminated when using the LIFO retail method. If an enterprise wishes to change from conventional retail to LIFO retail, the beginning inventory must be restated to conform with the LIFO assumption. In effecting the change, the inventory of the prior period must be recomputed on the LIFO basis. This amount than serves as the beginning inventory for the LIFO retail method applied in the current period.

16. The retail inventory method becomes more complicated when such items as **freight-in, purchase returns and allowances,** and **purchase discounts** are involved. In essence, the treatment of the items affecting the cost column of the retail inventory approach follows the computation of cost of goods available for sale. Other items that require careful consideration include **transfers-in, normal shortages, abnormal shortages,** and **employee discounts.** The retail inventory method is widely used **(a)** to permit the computation of net income without a physical count of inventory, **(b)** as a control measure in determining inventory shortages, **(c)** in regulating quantities of inventory on hand, and **(d)** as a basis for information needed for insurance purposes.

17. Inventories normally represent one of the most significant assets held by a business entity. Therefore, the accounting profession has mandated certain disclosure requirements related to inventories. Some of the disclosure requirements include: the composition of the inventory, the inventory financing, the inventory costing methods employed, and whether costing methods have been consistently applied. Currently, there is a great deal of interest in the effects of inflation on inventory holdings.

18. **Appendix 9-A, Special LIFO Reporting Problems,** discusses (a) initial adoption of LIFO, (b) LIFO reserves, and (c) interim reporting problems.

Demonstration Problems

1. Determine the lower of cost or market inventory valuation on the basis of the following facts: quantity, 1,500 units; cost per unit, $4.45; replacement cost, $4.40; selling price, $5.75; cost to complete and sell, $.65; normal profit, $1.00.

Solution:

Upper Limit:	Selling price	$5.75	
	Less cost to complete and sell	.65	
	Net realizable value (upper limit)		$5.10
Lower Limit:	Net realizable value (NRV)	$5.10	
	Less normal profit	1.00	
	NRV less profit (lower limit)		$4.10

Decision rule: 1.   If replacement cost is *between* the upper ($5.10) and lower ($4.10) limits, compare replacement cost to cost in deciding on the lower of cost or market. In the problem above, replacement cost ($4.40) is between the upper and lower limits, so it would be compared to cost ($4.45) and inventory would be valued at the lower ($4.40) of these two numbers.

2.   If replacement cost *exceeds* the upper limit, then the upper limit is used to compare to cost in determining LCM.

3.   If replacement cost is *lower* than the lower limit, then the lower limit is used to compare to cost in determining LCM.

2. Compute the approximate ending inventory for the Fox Department Store assuming: beginning inventory (cost), $85,000; purchases (cost), $226,000; sales at selling price, $345,000; average gross rate on selling prices is 38%.

Solution:

Beginning inventory		$85,000
Purchases		226,000
Goods available		311,000
Sales	$345,000	
Less gross profit	131,000*	
Sales at cost		213,900
Approximate ending inventory		$97,100

*(38% x $345,000)

REVIEW QUESTIONS AND EXERCISES

True-False

Indicate whether each of the following is true (T) or false (F) in the space provided.

_____ 1. Inventory should be written down to market when its revenue-producing ability is no longer as great as its cost.

_____ 2. As used in the lower of cost or market rule, market should not exceed net realizable value.

_____ 3. Net realizable value is the estimated selling price in the normal course of business less the normal profit margin.

_____ 4. It is acceptable practice to write down inventory to market when market is lower than cost, but it is not acceptable to write up inventory to market when market is higher than cost.

_____ 5. The loss resulting from the write-down of inventory to market normally should be shown in the income statement as an extraordinary item.

_____ 6. When inventory is written down to market, this new basis is considered to be the cost basis for future periods.

_____ 7. Under the lower of cost or market rule, the income statement may show a larger net income in future periods than would be justified if the inventory were carried forward at cost.

_____ 8. Under the lower cost of market rule, an item of inventory should not be valued at an amount in excess of net realizable value.

_____ 9. The application of the lower of cost or market rule to the inventory as a whole would yield a more conservative inventory value than would application of the rule to each individual item.

_____ 10. The account Accrued Loss on Purchase Commitments should be included in the stockholders' equity section of the balance sheet.

_____ 11. The recognition of inventories at selling price less cost of disposal means that income is usually recognized before the goods are transferred to an outside party.

_____ 12. Standard costs, as used by a manufacturing firm that employs a standard cost system, are determined on the basis of the costs that should be incurred per unit of finished goods when the plant is operating at normal capacity.

_____ 13. The allocation of a lump sum cost among the individual units on the basis of relative sales value assumes that each individual unit should show the same dollar amount of profit.

_____ 14. Gross margin is the excess of selling price over cost.

_____ 15. The gross margin expressed as a percentage of cost is normally less than the gross margin expressed as a percentage of sales.

_____ 16. The use of the gross profit method for interim reports does not preclude the need for a physical inventory to be taken at least annually.

_____ 17. The conventional retail method includes net markdowns but excludes net markups in the computation of the cost to retail percentage.

_____ 18. The inclusion of both net markups and net markdowns in the computation of the cost to retail percentage yields an inventory valuation that approximates cost.

_____ 19. The retail method assumes that the mix of the ending inventory is the same as the mix of the total goods available for sale.

_____ 20. A major assumption of the LIFO retail method is that the markups and markdowns apply only to the goods purchased during the current period, **not** to the beginning inventory.

Multiple Choice

Select the best answer for each of the following items and enter the corresponding letter in the space provided.

_____ 1. Item X has an original cost of $15 and a replacement cost of $12. The cost of completion and disposal is $2. If item X has a net realizable value of $16 and a normal profit margin of $5, its inventory value should be:
A. $15.
B. $12.
C. $16.
D. $11.

_____ 2. Let A equal the reported inventory value if the lower of cost or market rule is applied to individual items of inventory; B equals the reported inventory value if the lower of cost or market rule is applied to the inventory as a whole. Which of the following best describes the relationship between A and B?
A. A will always be equal to B.
B. A will always be equal to or less than B.
C. A will always be equal to or greater than B.
D. A can never be equal to B.

____ 3. Under the lower of cost or market rule, market will be replacement cost except when replacement cost is:
   A. higher than cost.
   B. less than net realizable value.
   C. less than net realizable value less a normal profit margin.
   D. less than cost.

____ 4. The fact that it is accepted practice to recognize decreases in the value of inventory prior to the point of sale, but not increases, is an illustration of which one of the following accounting concepts?
   A. Objectivity.
   B. Conservatism.
   C. Materiality.
   D. Consistency.

____ 5. Which of the following is not a basic assumption of the gross profit method?
   A. The beginning inventory plus the purchases equal total goods to be accounted for.
   B. Goods not sold must be on hand.
   C. If the sales, reduced to the cost basis, are deducted from the sum of the opening inventory plus purchases, the result is the amount of inventory on hand.
   D. The total amount of purchases and the total amount of sales remain relatively unchanged from the comparable previous period.

____ 6. On January 31, fire destroyed the entire inventory of Tensor Company. The following data are available:

Sales for January	$60,000
Inventory, January 1	10,000
Purchases for January	55,000
Markup on cost	25%

The amount of the loss is estimated to be:
   A. $17,000.
   B. $20,000.
   C. $15,000.
   D. $16,250.

____ 7. To determine an inventory valuation that approximates lower of average cost or market using the retail method, the computation of the cost to retail percentage should:
   A. include markups but not markdowns.
   B. include markups and markdowns.
   C. include markdowns but not markups.
   D. exclude markups but not markdowns.

____ 8. The retail method has been used by a retail department store during its first year of operations. As of the end of the year, compare (a) the markdowns with (b) the markdown cancellations:
   A. a will be equal to b.
   B. a will be less than or equal to b.
   C. a will be greater than or equal to b.
   D. a cannot be equal to b.

____ 9. Goldstein Co., a specialty clothing store, uses the retail inventory method. The following relates to 1988 operations:

Inventory, January 1, 1990, at cost	$14,200
Inventory, January 1, 1990 at sales price	20,100
Purchases in 1990 at cost	32,600
Purchases in 1990 at sales price	50,000
Additional markups on normal sales price	1,900
Sales (including $4,200 of items that were marked down from $6,400)	60,000

The cost of the December 31, 1990 inventory determined by the conventional retail method is:
   A. $9,800.
   B. $6,370.
   C. $6,743.
   D. $6,543.

____ 10. One of the basic assumptions of the conventional retail method is that:
   A. net markups apply to the goods sold.
   B. net markdowns apply to the total goods available for sale.
   C. net markdowns apply only to the goods sold.
   D. the cost to retail percentage is unchanged from that of prior years.

Review Exercises

1. You are given the following information regarding four inventory items:

	Inventory Items			
	A	**B**	**C**	**D**
Cost	$62	$41	$46	$85
Replacement cost	48	42	40	80
Net realizable value	59	47	42	78
Normal profit martin	8	4	4	5

In the space provided, indicate the inventory value for each item in accordance with the lower of cost or market rule.

A_____   B_____   C_____   D_____

2. Neeley Company uses the gross profit method to estimate monthly inventory balances. During recent months gross profit has averaged 30% of net sales. The following data for January are obtained from the ledger:

Inventory, January 1	$ 30,000
Purchases	100,000
Purchase returns	2,000
Freight-in	3,000
Sales	120,000
Sales returns	4,000

Compute the January 31 inventory.

3. The following information for the month of April is available from the records of Suzanne Department Store:

	At Cost	At Retail
Inventory, April 1	$ 8,400	$12,000
Purchases	48,810	80,000
Freight-in	2,000	
Additional markups		4,300
Markup cancellations		800
Markdowns		6,600
Markdowns cancellations		200
Sales		72,600

Compute the April 30 inventory at the lower of approximate cost or market using the conventional retail method.

4. The following information pertains to the records of the Jim Hale Company.

	Cost	Retail
Beginning inventory	$46,000	$65,000
Net purchases	374,000	535,000
Markups		35,000
Markup cancellations		10,000
Markdowns		26,000
Markdown cancellations		16,000
Net sales		520,000

Compute the ending inventory under each of the following methods.

A. Conventional retail method
B. LIFO retail method assuming stable prices.
C. Dollar-value LIFO method assuming the price index was 100 at the beginning of the year and 120 at year end.

SOLUTIONS TO REVIEW QUESTIONS AND EXERCISES

True-False

1. (T)
2. (T)
3. (F) Net realizable value is defined as selling price less the estimated cost of completion and disposal. When the normal profit margin is subtracted from net realizable value the resulting amount is referred to as net realizable value less a normal profit margin.
4. (T)
5. (F) The loss resulting from the write-down of inventory to market is shown as a separate item in the income statement but not as an extraordinary item.
6. (T)
7. (T)
8. (T)
9. (F) The cost or market rule may be applied directly to each item or to the total of the inventory. When the cost or market rule is applied to the inventory as a whole, increases in the market prices of some items offset decreases in the market prices in other items to some extent. Thus, the application of the cost or market rule to individual inventory items gives the most conservative valuation for balance sheet purposes.
10. (F) If the contracted price of a purchase commitment is in excess of market price and it is expected that losses will occur when the purhase is effected, a loss should be recognized and an Accrued Loss on Purchase Commitments should be credited. The loss is reported on the income statement under other expenses and losses, and the Accrued Loss is reported in the liability section of the balance sheet.
11. (T)
12. (T)

13. (F)   When the relative sales value method is used, it is used because the items being valued vary in terms of such characteristics as shape, size, attractiveness, and so on. Because of these types of differences, the amount of gross profit generated by each item will be different.

14. (T)

15. (F)   Because selling price is greater than cost and the gross margin amount is the same for both, gross margin on selling price will always be less than the related percentage based on cost.

16. (T)

17. (F)   The conventional retail inventory method is designed to approximate the lower of average cost or market. Thus, the cost percentage computation includes markups but not markdowns. When a company has an additional markup, it normally indicates that the market value of that item had increased. If the company has a net markdown, it means that a decline in the utility of that item has occurred. Therefore, if the attempt is to approximate lower of cost or market, markdowns are considered a current loss and are not involved in the calculation of the cost to retail ratio.

18. (T)

19. (T)

20. (T)

Multiple Choice

1. (B)   Net Realizable Value $16
         NRV Minus Profit $11
         Replacement Cost $12

   Market is defined in this case as replacement cost because the replacement cost is between the upper limit (NRV) and the lower limit (NRV minus profit). Thus, when the replacement cost ($12) is compared to cost ($15), the inventory is valued at $12.

2. (B)   Increases in the market prices of some inventory items tend to offset decreases in other inventory items when the cost or market rule is applied to the inventory as a whole. Thus, the inventory valuation that results from applying the cost or market method to individual items in inventory (alternative A) will always be equal to or less than the inventory valuation that results from applying the cost or market rule to the inventory as a whole (alternative B).

3. (C)   If replacement cost is less than net realizable value less a normal profit margin, then replacement cost is below the lower limit for market value. When this occurs market is defined as the lower limit (NRV minus a normal profit margin).

4. (B)   The conservatism concept is based on the assumption that in accounting we provide for all losses and anticipate no gains. This is the basis for recognizing decreases in inventory prior to the point of sale, but not increases.

5. (D)   The gross profit method assumes a constant gross profit percentage, but makes no assumptions about the total amount of sales or purchases. Alternatively (A), (B), and (C) are basic assumptions of the gross profit method.

6. (A)   A 25% markup on cost is equivalent to a 20% markup on selling price:

   $$\text{GP on selling price} = \frac{\%\text{ markup on cost}}{100\% + \%\text{ markup on cost}}$$

   $$\text{GP on selling price} = \frac{.25}{1.25}$$

   $$\text{GP on selling price} = .20$$

   Sales $60,000
   GP ($60,000 x .20) 12,000

Cost of goods sold...	$48,000
Goods available for sale	65,000
Inventory loss	$17,000

7. (A)   See explanation of True-False question No. 17.

8. (C)   Markdown cancellations represent the cancellation of previous markdowns applied to a product. Therefore, markdown cancellations are limited to the total amount of markdowns previously recorded. Thus, for any entity, markdowns will be greater than or equal to markdown cancellations.

9. (B)

	Cost	Retail
Inventory 1/1/90	$14,200	$20,100
Purchase	32,600	50,000
	$46,800	$70,100
Additional Markups		1,900
Totals	$46,800	$72,000

(Cost ratio: $46,800 ÷ 72,000 = 65%)

Deduct Markdowns		2,200
Sales Price of Goods Available		$69,800
Deduct Sales		60,000
Ending Inventory at Retail		$9,800

Ending Inventory at LCM: $9,800 x .65 = $6,370

10. (C)   When the attempt is to approximate lower of cost or market, under the retail inventory method, markdowns are considered a current loss and are not involved in the calculation of the cost to retail ratio.

Review Exercises

1.   A. $51   B. $41   C. $40   D. $78

2.

Inventory, January	$ 30,000
Purchases	100,000
Freight-in	3,000
Purchase returns	(2,000)
Goods available (at cost)	$131,000
Sales	$120,000
Sales returns	4,000
Net sales	$116,000
Less gross profit (30% of 116,000)	34,800
Cost of goods sold	81,200
Inventory, January 31 (at cost)	$ 49,800

3.

	Cost	Retail
Inventory, April 1	$ 8,400	$12,000
Purchases	48,810	80,000
Freight-in	2,000	
Net markups		3,500
Goods available	$59,210	$95,500

Cost to retail ratio 59,210/95,500 = 62.0%

Less:

Sales	72,600	
Net markdowns	6,400	
		79,000

Inventory, April 30, at retail		$16,500

Inventory, April 30, at lower of cost or market
   (16,500 x .62) $10,230

4. A. **Conventional Retail**

	Cost		Retail
Beginning inventory	$ 46,000		$ 65,000
Purchases (net)	374,000		535,000
Totals	420,000		600,000
Add net markups			
Markups		35,000	
Markup cancellations		10,000	25,000
	$420,000		625,000
Deduct net markdowns			
Markdowns		26,000	
Markdown cancellations		16,000	10,000
Sales price of goods available			615,000
Deduct sales			520,000
Ending inventory at retail			$ 95,000

Cost-to-retail ratio $= \dfrac{420,000}{625,000} = 67.2\%$

Ending inventory at lower of cost or market:
$95,000 X .672 = $63,840

B. **LIFO Retail Method (Stable Prices)**

	Cost	Retail
Beginning inventory	$ 46,000	$ 65,000
Purchases (net)	374,000	535,000
Net markups		25,000
Net markdowns		(10,000)
Total excluding beginning inventory	374,000	550,000
Total including beginning inventory	$420,000	615,000
Net sales		$520,000
Ending inventory at retail		$ 95,000

Establishment of cost to retail percentage
  under assumption of LIFO retail 374,000 ÷ 550,000 = 68%

Ending inventory at cost:		
Beginning inventory (65,000 x .7077*)		$46,000
Additional increment	$95,000	
Ending inventory	65,000	
Beginning inventory	30,000	
Cost to retail percentage	x .68	20,400
Ending inventory at LIFO cost (stable prices)		$66,400

*($46,000 ÷ 65,000)

C. Dollar-value LIFO (Fluctuating Prices)

	Cost	Retail
Beginning inventory	$ 46,000	$ 65,000
Purchases (net)	374,000	535,000
Net markups		25,000
Net markdowns		(10,000)
Total excluding beginning inventory	374,000	550,000
Total including beginning inventory	$420,000	615,000
Net sales		$520,000
Ending inventory at retail		$ 95,000

Establishment of cost to retail percentage

assumption of LIFO retail 374,000 ÷ 550,000 = 68%

A.	Ending inventory at retail prices deflated to base-year prices $95,000 x 100/120 =	$79,167
B.	Beginning inventory at base-year prices	65,000
C.	Inventory increase from beginning of period	$14,167
D.	Increment priced in terms of end-of-year prices $14,167 x 100/120 =	$17,000

Ending inventory at cost:

First layer	$46,000
Second layer (increase at new price level times cost to retail percentage) $17,000 x .68 =	11,560
Ending inventory at LIFO cost (fluctuating prices)	$57,560

10

Acquisition and disposition of property, plant, and equipment

Chapter Synopsis

Chapter 10 presents the accounting issues related to the initial recording and ultimate disposal of property, plant, and equipment. Included is a discussion of the relevant costs related to the acquisition of property, plant, and equipment and the accounting methods used to retire these costs.

Chapter Review

1. **Property, plant, and equipment** possess certain characteristics that distinguish them from other assets owned by a business enterprise. These characteristics may be expressed as follows: (a) acquired for use in operations and not for resale, (b) long-term in nature and usually subject to depreciation, and (c) physical existence.

2. Property, plant and equipment are valued in the accounts at their **historical cost**. This includes all costs associated with obtaining the asset and preparing it for its intended use. The process of allocating the historical cost of property, plant, and equipment to the period benefited by that asset is known as **depreciation**. The topic of depreciation is presented in Chapter 11.

3. With minor exceptions, use of a method other than historical cost in valuing property, plant, and equipment represents a departure from generally accepted accounting principles. This position is justified on the grounds that: (a) cost reflects fair value on the date of acquisition, (b) cost is objective and verifiable, and (c) gains and losses should not be anticipated but should be recognized when assets are sold.

4. The assets normally classified on the balance sheet as property, plant, and equipment include land, buildings, and various kinds of machinery and equipment. The cost of each item includes the acquisition price plus those expenditures incurred in getting the asset ready for its intended use. In the case of **land**, cost typically includes (a) purchase price; (b) closing costs such as title, attorney, and recording fees; (c) cost of grading, filling, draining, and clearing the property; (d) assumption of any encumbrances on the property; and (e) any land improve-

ments that have an indefinite life. The cost of removing an old building from land purchased for the purpose of constructing a new building is properly charged to the land account.

5. **Building costs** include materials, labor, and overhead costs incurred during construction. Also, any fees such as those incurred for building permits or the services of an attorney or architect are included in acquisition cost. In general, all costs incurred from excavation of the site to completion of the building are considered part of the building costs.

6. With respect to **equipment**, cost includes purchase price plus all expenditures related to the purchase that occur subsequent to acquisition but prior to actual use.

7. When machinery and equipment to be used by an entity are constructed rather than purchased, a problem exists concerning the allocation of **overhead costs**. These costs may be handled in one of three ways: (a) assign no overhead to the cost of the constructed asset, (b) assign a portion of all overhead to the constructed asset, or (c) allocate overhead on the basis of lost production. The second method appears preferable because of its consistency with the historical cost principle. It should be noted that the costs of a constructed asset can never exceed the price charged by an outside producer.

8. Capitalization of interest cost incurred in connection with financing the construction or acquisition of property, plant, and equipment is addressed in **FASB Statement No. 34, "Capitalization of Interest Costs."** The profession generally follows the rule of **capitalizing only the actual interest costs incurred during construction.** While some modification to this general rule occurs, its adoption is consistent with the concept that the historical cost of acquiring an asset includes all costs incurred to bring the asset to the condition and location necessary for its intended use. Thus, interest capitalization is required by *FASB Statement No. 34.*

9. To qualify for interest capitalization, assets must require a period of time to get them ready for their intended use. Assets that qualify for interest cost

capitalization include assets under construction for an enterprise's own use (such as buildings, plants, and machinery) and assets intended for sale or lease that are constructed or otherwise produced as discrete projects (like ships or real estate developments). The period during which interest must be capitalized begins when three conditions are present: (a) expenditures for the asset have been made; (b) activities that are necessary to get the asset ready for its intended use are in progress; and (c) interest cost is being incurred.

10. The amount of interest that may be capitalized is limited to the **lower** of (a) actual interest cost incurred during the period, or (b) the amount of interest cost incurred during the period that theoretically could have been avoided if the expenditure for the asset had not been made (**avoidable interest**). The potential amount of interest that may be capitalized during an accounting period is determined by multiplying interest rate(s) by the **weighted-average amount of accumulated expenditures** for qualifying assets during the period.

11. When a **cash discount** is included in the terms of a plant-asset purchase, preferred treatment recognizes the discount as a reduction in the price of the asset. Failure to pay within the discount period does not alter this treatment.

12. Plant assets purchased on **long-term credit contracts** should be accounted for at the present value of the consideration exchanged on the date of purchase. When the obligation stipulates no interest rate, or the rate is unreasonable, an imputed rate of interest must be determined for use in calculating the present value.

13. **Nonmonetary assets** such as inventory or property, plant, and equipment are items whose price may change over time. Controversy exists in regard to the accounting for these assets when one nonmonetary asset is exchanged for another nonmonetary asset. A critical element in accounting for the exchange of nonmonetary assets is the type of assets involved. **If the transaction involves the exchange of dissimilar assets, the cost of the nonmonetary asset acquired is normally recorded at the fair value of the asset given up and a gain or loss is recognized.** The only time the fair value of the asset acquired is used to value the transaction is when its fair value is more clearly evident than the fair value of the asset given up.

14. **Similar nonmonetary assets** are assets that are of the same general type, that perform the same function, or that are employed in the same line of business. **When similar nonmonetary assets are exchanged and a loss results, the loss should be recognized immediately.** A loss is indicated when the fair value of the asset given up is less than its book value.

15. When **similar nonmonetary assets** are exchanged and a gain results, the presence or absence of cash (**boot**) as a part of the transaction must be considered before the transaction is recorded. If similar nonmonetary assets are exchanged and no cash is involved, no gain is recognized. When some cash is involved in the transaction, the entity giving the cash may not recognize a gain. However, when cash is **received,** a portion of the gain is recognized by the entity receiving the cash. The portion to be recognized is equal to the ratio of the cash received to the total consideration received times the total gain indicated.

16. To summarize these concepts, when a transaction involves an exchange of nonmonetary assets, losses are always recognized whether the exchange involves dissimilar or similar assets. Gains are recognized if the exchange involves dissimilar assets; gains are deferred (not immediately recognized) if the exchange involves similar assets, unless cash or some other form of monetary consideration is **received**, in which case a partial gain is recognized. Also, a gain or loss on the exchange on nonmonetary assets is computed by comparing the book value of the asset given up with the fair value of that same asset.

17. When a group of plant assets is purchased at a lump sum price, total cost must be allocated among the various assets on the basis of their relative fair market values. Plant assets acquired through the issuance of equity securities should be recorded at the fair market value of the securities issued. When market value of the securities is not readily determinable, the market value of the property should be used as the basis for recording the transaction. The basis used in recording donated plant assets is the fair market value of the asset received. The debit to plant assets can be offset by a credit to a stockholder's equity account entitled **Donated Capital.**

18. Costs related to plant assets that are incurred before the asset is placed in use are either added to the asset account (**capitalized**) or charged against operations (**expensed**) when incurred. For the costs to be capitalized, one of three conditions must be present: (a) the useful life of the asset must be increased, (b) the quantity of service produced from the asset must be increased, or (c) the quality of the units produced must be enhanced. In many instances, a considerable amount of judgment is required in deciding whether to capitalize or expense an item. However, consistent application of a capital/expense policy is normally more important than attempting to provide theoretical guidelines.

19. Generally, expenditures related to plant assets being used in a productive capacity may be classified as: (a) additions, (b) improvements and replacements, (c) reinstallation and rearrangement, and (d) repairs. Because **additions** result in the creation of new assets, they should be capitalized.

Demonstration Problem

Company A trades a used printing machine for a new improved model. The old machine has a book value of $12,000 (original cost $30,000 less $18,000 accumulated depreciation) and a fair value of $8,000. The new printing machine has a list price of $42,000, and Company A receives a $14,000 trade-in allowance on the old machine.· Compute (a) the cost to be recorded in the books of Company A for the new machine and (b) the amount of any gain or loss as a result of this transaction.

Solution:

(a)   Cost of new printing machine (similar assets)

List price of new machine	$42,000
Less trade-in allowance	14,000
Cash payment due	28,000
Fair value of old machine	8,000
Cost of new machine	$36,000*

*$36,000 represents the value given up by Company A to acquire the new machine.

(b)   Computation of loss

Book value of old machine	$12,000
Fair value of old machine	8,000
Loss on trade of old machine	$ 4,000

---

20.   **Improvements** and **replacements** are substitutions of one asset for another. Improvements substitute a better asset for the one currently used, whereas a replacement substitutes a similar asset. The major problem in accounting for improvements and replacements concerns differentiating these expenditures from normal repairs. If an improvement or replacement increases the future service potential of the asset, it should be capitalized. Capitalization may be accomplished by: (a) substituting the cost of the new asset for the cost of the asset replaced, (b) capitalizing the new cost without eliminating the cost of the asset replaced, or (c) debiting the expenditure to accumulated depreciation. The specific facts related to the situation will aid in determining the most appropriate method to use.

21.   **Reinstallation and rearrangement** costs are generally carried forward as a separate asset and amortized against future income.

22.   **Ordinary repairs** are expenditures made to maintain property, plant and equipment in operating condition. They are charged to an expense account in the period in which they are incurred.

23.   When a plant asset is disposed of, the accounting records should be relieved of the cost and accumulated depreciation associated with the asset. Depreciation should be recorded on the asset up to the date of disposal, and any resulting gains or losses should be reported in accordance with the provisions of *APB Opinion No. 30*. Plant assets may be retired voluntarily or disposed of by **sale, exchange, involuntary conversion,** or **abandonment.**

24.   Valuation of property, plant, and equipment on a basis other than historical cost has been widely discussed by those concerned with the financial reporting process. However, historical cost continues to be recognized as the accepted method for valuing these assets in the financial statements. Departures from historical cost include: (a) **constant dollar accounting,** (b) **current cost accounting,** (c) **net realizable value,** or (d) **a combination of constant dollar accounting and one of these other methods.** These valuation methods are discussed further in Chapter 27.

25.   **Appendix 10A** reviews the concept of casualty insurance. Included is a discussion of coinsurance, recovery from multiple policies, and accounting for casualty losses. Special situations related to interest capitalization include (a) non-interest bearing liabilities, (b) interim computations, and (c) interest compounding. These are discussed and illustrated in **Appendix 10-B.**

REVIEW QUESTIONS AND EXERCISES

True-False

Indicate whether each of the following is true (T) or false (F) in the space provided.

_____ 1. A building owned by a corporation is always classified as property, plant and equipment.

_____ 2. The cash or cash equivalent price of items classified as property, plant and equipment best measures the value of the asset on the date of acquisition.

_____ 3. Use of the current replacement cost method to account for property, plant and equipment would most likely result in the recognition of gains and losses prior to the time the asset is sold.

_____ 4. The cost of items classified as property, plant, and equipment should include all expenditures related to the asset incurred during the first three months of the asset's useful life.

_____ 5. When land has been purchased for the purpose of constructing a new building, all costs incurred in connection with preparing the land for excavation are considered building costs.

_____ 6. The interest costs on funds used to acquire an asset should not be capitalized even if a significant period of time is required to bring the asset to a condition or location necessary for its intended use.

_____ 7. If the allocation of overhead to self-constructed assets results in an asset cost that is greater than the cost that would be charged by an independent producer, the excess overhead should be recorded as a period loss.

_____ 8. An asset should be recorded at the fair market value of the consideration given up to acquire it or at its fair market value, whichever is higher.

_____ 9. Equipment purchased through the use of deferred payment contracts should be accounted for at the present value of the contract.

_____ 10. The purpose of imputed interest is to approximate the interest rate of a deferred purchase contract when one is not expressly stated.

_____ 11. In general, because the exchange of nonmonetary assets does not constitute a sale by either party involved in the transaction, the accounting should be based on the book value of the assets involved.

_____ 12. If an exchange of nonmonetary assets occurs and the assets are dissimilar, it is presumed that the earnings process related to these assets is completed.

_____ 13. If an exchange transaction involving similar nonmonetary assets results in a loss, the loss is recognized immediately, even when boot is included as a part of the transaction.

_____ 14. Gains and losses on the exchange of nonmonetary assets are computed by comparing the book value of the asset given up with the fair value of the asset given up.

_____ 15. When an exchange of similar nonmonetary assets results in a gain and boot is included as a part of the transaction, the gain to be recognized is limited to the amount of the boot received.

_____ 16. The recommended accounting treatment for donated property, plant, and equipment represents a departure from the cost principle.

_____ 17. Once an asset has been placed into productive use, the major criterion used to determine whether an expenditure should be capitalized or expensed is the significance of that expenditure in relation to the original cost.

_____ 18. By definition, any addition to a building or machine is capitalized because a new asset has been created.

_____ 19. If a capital expenditure related to a machine increases the useful life but does not improve its quality, the expenditure may be debited to accumulated depreciation rather than to the asset account.

_____ 20. According to *APB Opinion No. 30*, gains and losses on the retirement of property, plant, and equipment should be shown in the income statement as an extraordinary item.

Multiple Choice

Select the best answer for each of the following items and enter the corresponding letter in the space provided.

_____ 1. Which of the following is not a necessary characteristic for an item to be classified as property, plant, and equipment?
   A. Usually subject to depreciation.
   B. Characterized by physical substance.
   C. Can be used in operations for at least 5 years.
   D. Not acquired for resale.

_____ 2. Tech Theater Corporation recently purchased the State Theater and the land on which it is located. Tech plans to raze the building

immediately and build a new modern theater on the site. The cost of the State Theater should be:
A. written off as an extraordinary loss in the year the theater is razed.
B. capitalized as part of the cost of land.
C. depreciated over the period from the date of acquisition to the date the theater is to be razed.
D. capitalized as part of the cost of the new theater.

_____ 3. To be consistent with the historical cost principle, overhead costs incurred by an enterprise constructing its own building should be:
A. allocated on the basis of lost production.
B. eliminated completely from the cost of the asset.
C. allocated on an opportunity cost basis.
D. allocated on a pro rata basis between the asset and normal operation.

_____ 4. Which of the following nonmonetary exchange transactions represents a culmination of the earning process?
A. Exchange of similar productive assets.
B. Exchange of products by companies in the same line of business to facilitate sales to customers other than parties to the exchange.
C. Exchange of dissimilar productive assets.
D. Exchange of an equivalent interest in similar productive assets that causes the companies involved to remain in essentially the same economic position.

_____ 5. When boot is involved in an exchange of dissimilar assets:
A. gains or losses are recognized in their entirety.
B. gain or loss is computed by comparing the fair value of the asset received with the fair value of the asset given up.
C. only gains should be recognized.
D. only losses should be recognized.

_____ 6. Company A and Company B exchange similar productive assets. The asset given up by Company A has a book value of $12,000 and a fair market value of $15,000. The asset given up by Company B has a book value of $20,000 and a fair market value of $19,000. Boot of $4,000 is received by Company B. On the basis of the foregoing facts, what amount should Company A record for the asset received?

A. $15,000.
B. $16,000.
C. $19,000.
D. $20,000.

_____ 7. Assuming the same facts as those listed in question 6, what amount should Company B record for the asset received?
A. $15,000.
B. $16,000.
C. $19,000.
D. $20,000.

_____ 8. Would either company record a loss on the transaction explained in question 6?
A. Company A would record a loss.
B. Company B would record a loss.
C. Both companies would record a loss.
D. Neither company would record a loss.

_____ 9. An expenditure made in connection with a machine being used by an enterprise should be:
A. expensed immediately if it merely extends the useful life but does not improve the quality.
B. expensd immediately if it merely improves the quality but does not extend the useful life.
C. capitalized if it maintains the machine in normal operating condition.
D. capitalized if it increases the quantity of services produced by the machine.

_____ 10. Which of the following is not a condition that must be satisfied before interest capitalization can begin on a qualifying asset?
A. Interest cost is being incurred.
B. Expenditures for the assets have been made.
C. The interest rate is equal to or greater than the company's cost of capital.
D. Activities that are necessary to get the asset ready for its intended use are in progress.

Review Exercises

1. Russell Company acquired a group of plant assets at a cost of $150,000 from a company in financial difficulty. The fair market value of the assets acquired is estimated as follows:

Land..	$ 36,000
Buildings	108,000
Machinery..	72,000

What journal entry should Russell Company make to record this purchase?

2. Guy Corporation purchased a machine on January 1, 1990, for $25,000. Before the machine was utilized in a productive capacity, the following expenditures were made:

a.	Removal of a wall to accommodate the machine	$1,500
b.	Cost of training an operator	850
c.	Installation of a counting device	500
d.	Premium on a 3-year insurance policy	900

Depreciation on the machine was recorded at the end of each year. The depreciation rate is $3,000 per year. On October 1, 1996, the machine was sold for $8,000. Record the journal entries for the purchase and sale of the machine.

3. IBP Company and Zerix Company enter into an agreement for the trade of certain nonmonetary assets (machinery). The assets involved perform the same function and are employed in the same line of business. The reason for the exchange involves the size of the product produced by the machines. The machines exchanged by IBP Company have a book value of $245,000 (cost $325,000 less accumulated depreciation of $80,000) and a fair value of $275,000. The machines given up by Zerix Company have a book value of $260,000 (cost $350,000 less accumulated depreciation of $90,000) and a fair value of $290,000. In addition to the exchange of the machines, IBP Company agrees to pay Zerix Company $15,000 as part of the transaction. Record the exchange transaction on the books of both companies.

4. With respect to each of the following plant asset expenditures, indicate whether the item should be expensed or capitalized. Also, indicate whether the item is best classified as: (1) an addition, (2) an improvement, (3) a replacement, (4) a reinstallation or rearrangement, or (5) an ordinary repair.

		Expense	Capitalize	Classification
A.	A new wing on a factory building.			
B.	Steel beams in an old factory building substituted for wooden beams.			
C.	New tires placed on a delivery truck.			
D.	Fee of consulting firm for improvement of production flow by changing the placement of machinery in the factory.			
E.	A new tile floor in the office building substituted for an old tile floor.			
F.	Repainting the interior of the entire factory building.			
G.	New device attached to machinery that automatically sorts production. Such a device has not previously been available.			
H.	New motor installed in a machine. The old motor burned out unexpectedly.			

SOLUTIONS TO REVIEW QUESTIONS AND EXERCISES

True - False

1. (F) To be classified as property, plant, and equipment, the building (a) must be acquired for use in operations and not for resale, (b) be long-term in nature and generally subject to depreciation, and (c) possess physical substance. The second and third criteria would normally be met by any building owned by a company. However, a company could own a building that was not used in its operations and was held for sale. In this case the building would be classified as an other asset.

2. (T)

3. (T)

4. (F) Any costs related to an asset that are incurred after its acquisition such as additions, improvements, or replacements are added to the cost of the asset if they provide future service potential; otherwise, they are expensed in the period of incurrence.

5. (F)   When land has been purchased for the purpose of constructing a building, all costs incurred up to the excavation for the new building are considered land costs. Removal of old buildings, clearing, grading, and filling are considered costs of the land because these costs are necessary to get the land in condition for its intended purpose.

6. (F)   To qualify for interest capitalization, assets must require a period of time to get them ready for their intended use. *FASB Statement No. 34* specifies that the amount of interest to be capitalized for qualifying assets is that portion of total interest cost incurred during the period that theoretically could have been avoided if expenditures for the asset had not been made.

7. (T)

8. (F)   An asset should be recorded at the fair market value of what is given up to acquire it or at its own fair market value, whichever is more clearly evident.

9. (T)

10. (T)

11. (F)   The book value of assets can sometimes be misleading because of the variety of accounting methods that can be used to account for these items. Thus, when an exchange of nonmonetary assets is involved, the accounting should be based on the fair value of the asset given up or the fair value of the asset acquired, whichever is more clearly evident.

12. (T)

13. (T)

14. (T)

15. (F)   In this situation, part of the monetary asset is considered sold and part exchanged, therefore, only a portion of the gain is deferred. The formula to determine the amount of the gain recognized when boot is received is:

$$\frac{\text{Cash received}}{\text{Cash rec'd} + \text{fair value of asset rec'd}} \times \text{total gain} = \text{Gain recognized}$$

16. (T)

17. (F)   For an expenditure to be capitalized, one of three future benefit conditions must be present: (a) the useful life of the asset must be increased, (b) the quantity of units produced from the asset must be increased, or (c) the quality of the units produced must be enhanced.

18. (T)

19. (T)

20. (F)   Gains or losses on the retirement of property, plant, and equipment should be shown in the income statement along with other items that arise from customary business activities.

Multiple Choice

1. (C)   Items classified as property, plant, and equipment are characterized as items that are long-term in nature. The concept of long-term is generally considered to be in excess of one year, but no minimum number of years is required for this classification. Alternatives (A), (B), and (D) are appropriate characteristics for an item classified as property, plant, and equipment.

2. (B)   All expenditures made to acquire land and to ready it for use should be considered as part of the land cost. The purpose of the purchase was to acquire the land so a new theater could be constructed. The old theater has no economic use so that any portion of the purchase price attributable to the old theater is merely considered cost of the land acquired.

3. (D)   Based upon the historical cost principle, a portion of overhead cost should be assigned to a constructed asset to obtain that asset's total cost. The amount charged should be based upon a pro rata allocation between the asset and normal operations. The other allocation methods mentioned in alternatives A and C are difficult to measure and also are not consistent with the historical cost principle. Alternative B is not consistent with the historical cost principle.

4. (C) Similar nonmonetary assets are those that are of the same general type or that perform the same function or that are employed in the same line of business. If two entities exchange similar assets, the earnings process is not considered complete. Alternatives (A), (B), and (D) all represent exchanges of similar nonmonetary assets.

5. (A) A nonmonetary asset acquired in exchange for a dissimilar nonmonetary asset is usually recorded at the fair value of the asset given up, and a gain or loss is recognized.

6. (B)

Fair market value of Company A asset	$15,000
Book value of Company A asset	12,000
Total gain (unrecognized)	$ 3,000

Fair market value of Company B asset	$19,000
Less gain deferred	3,000
Basis of acquired asset to Company A	$16,000

7. (A) When similar monetary assets are exchanged and a loss results, the loss should be recognized immediately.

Bood value of Company B asset	$20,000
Fair market value of Company B asset	19,000
Loss on trade	$ 1,000

Company B--Journal Entry

New asset	15,000	
Cash	4,000	
Loss on trade	1,000	
Old asset		20,000

8. (B) See explanation in No. 7 above.

9. (D) Expenditures made in connection with assets being used by an entity should be capitalized if (a) the useful life of the asset is increased, (b) the quantity of units produced by the assets is increased, or (c) the quality of the units produced by the asset is enhanced. All other expenditures of this nature should be expensed when incurred. The only alternative that correctly completes the question is (D).

10. (C) Alternatives A, B, and D reflect the conditions that must exist before the interest capitalization can begin on a qualifying asset. These conditions come from *FASB Statement No. 34* which includes no requirements related to interest rates or an entity's cost of capital.

Review Exercises

1.	Fair Market Value	Percent of Fair Market Value	Apportionment of Cost
Land	$ 36,000	16-2/3%	$ 25,000
Building	108,000	50 %	75,000
Machinery	72,000	33-1/3%	50,000
Total	$216,000		$150,000

Journal Entry:

Land	25,000	
Building	75,000	
Machinery	50,000	
Cash......................................		150,000

2. Purchase Price = $25,000 + $1,500 + $850 + $500 = $27,850
   Book Value at 10-1-96 = $27,850 - (6 X $3,000) = $9,850 (before 1996 depreciation)
   Journal entries:

1-1-90	Machine...	27,850	
	Cash...		27,850
10-1-96	Depreciation Expense...	2,250	
	Accumulated Depreciation		2,250
10-1-96	Cash	8,000	
	Accumulated Depreciation	20,250	
	Machine...		27,850
	Gain on Sale		400

3. **Accounting by IBP Company**
   Computation of Gain:

Fair value of IBP machines	$275,000
Book value of IBP machines	245,000
Total gain (unrecognized)	$ 30,000

Basis of New Machines to IBP:

Fair value of			Book value of HBP	
Zerix machines	$290,000		machines	$245,000
Less gain deferred	(30,000)	OR	Cash paid	15,000
Basis of machines			Basis of machines	
received	$260,000		received	$260,000

Journal Entry:

Machines (from Zerix)	260,000	
Accumulated Depreciation	80,000	
Machines		325,000
Cash		15,000

Accounting by Zerix Company
   Computation of Total Gain:

Fair value of Zerix machines	290,000
Book value of Zerix machines	260,000
Total gain	$30,000

Portion of Gain Recognized by Zerix:

$$\frac{\$15,000}{\$15,000 + \$275,000} \times \$30,000 = \underline{\$1,551.00}$$

Basis of New Machines to Zerix:

Fair value of			Book value of	
IBP machines	$275,000		Zerix machines	$260,000
Less gain deferred			Add gain recognized	1,551
(30,000 - $1,551)	(28,449)	*OR*	Less cash received	(15,000)
Basis of machines			Basis of machines	
received	$246,551		received	$246,551

Journal Entry:

Cash	15,000	
Machines (from IBP)	246,551	
Accumulated Depreciation	90,000	
Machines		350,000
Cash		1,551

4. A. Capitalize--Addition   E. Capitalize--Replacement

     B. Capitalize--Improvement   F. Expense--Repair

     C. Expense--Repair   G. Capitalize--Addition

     D. Capitalize--Rearrangement   H. Capitalize--Replacement

11

Depreciation and depletion

Chapter Synopsis

Chapter 11 focuses on the concepts of depreciation and depletion. The various methods used in operationalizing each concept are presented along with a discussion of the accounting problems involved.

Chapter Review

1. **Depreciation**, as defined in accounting, is the systematic allocation of the cost of a plant asset to income. The **cost allocation approach** is justified because it matches costs with revenues and because fluctuation in market values is difficult to determine. An entry for depreciation is recorded during each year of the asset's useful life. The entry includes a debit to **depreciation expense** and a credit to **accumulated depreciation**. The latter account appears on the balance sheet as a direct deduction from the asset to which it applies.

2. To compute depreciation, an accountant must establish (a) the **depreciation base** to be used for the asset, (b) the asset's **useful life**, and (c) the depreciation **method** to be used. Determination of the first two factors requires the use of estimates.

3. Depreciation base is the difference between an asset's cost and its salvage value. **Salvage value** is the estimated amount that will be received at the time the asset is sold or removed from service.

4. The **useful life** (service life) of a plant asset refers to the number of years that asset is capable of economically providing the service it was purchased to perform. The service life of an asset should not be confused with its physical life. For example, a machine may no longer provide a useful service to an organization even though it remains physically functional. Thus, the estimate of an asset's service life is dependent upon both the economic factors and the physical factors related to its use. **Economic factors** are characterized by inadequacy, supersession, and obsolescence. **Physical factors** relate to wear and tear, decay, and casualties that prevent the asset from performing indefinitely.

5. The depreciation method selected for a particular asset should be **systematic and rational**. In other words, the method selected should, to the extent possible, match the probable pattern of decline in an asset's services.

6. Depreciation methods may be classified as:
A. Activity methods.
B. Straight-line methods.
C. Decreasing charge methods.
   a. Sum-of-the-years'-digits.
   b. double-declining balance.
D. Special depreciation methods.
   a. Inventory method.
   b. Retirement and replacement methods.
   c. Group and composite-life methods.
   d. Compound interest methods.

7. When the **activity method** (units of use or production) is used, depreciation is assumed to be a function of productive output rather than the passage of time. This method is most appropriate for assets such as machinery or automobiles where depreciation can be based on units produced or miles driven. One problem associated with the use of this method concerns a before-the-fact estimation of the total output the asset will achieve during its useful life.

8. Use of the **straight-line method** results in a uniform charge to depreciation expense during each year of an asset's service life. This method is based upon the assumption that the decline in an asset's usefulness is the same each year. Although the straight-line method is easy to use, it rests on an assumption that in most situations is not realistic.

9. The **decreasing charge methods** result in a higher depreciation charge during the early years of an asset's service life and lower charges in later years. This approach is justified on the basis that assets lose a greater amount of service potential in earlier years and thus depreciation should be higher.

10. The **sum-of-the-years'-digits** method and the **double-declining balance** method are the two most often used decreasing charge methods. The sum-of-the-years'-digits method requires multiplication of the **depreciation base** by a fraction that decreases during each year of an asset's service life. The double-declining balance method requires use of a constant percentage (twice the straight-line rate) applied to an **asset's cost less accumulated depreciation**. Salvage value is initially ignored under the double-declining balance method.

11. **Special depreciation systems** are appropriate when the assets involved possess certain unique characteristics. When it is impractical to depreciate assets on an individual basis (for example, hand tools or utensils), use of the **inventory method** is appropriate.

12. The **retirement and replacement methods** are used principally by public utilities and railroads that own many similar units of small value such as poles, ties, conductors, and telephones. The retirement method charges depreciation expense with the depreciable cost of units retired during the year. The replacement method maintains the cost of old units in the accounts and charges depreciation expense with the depreciable cost of replacement units purchased during the period.

13. **Group and composite methods** involve averaging the service life of many assets and applying depreciation as though a single unit existed. The composite approach refers to a collection of dissimilar assets, whereas the group approach refers to a collection of assets with similar characteristics.

14. In general, depreciation should be based on the number of months an asset is used during an accounting period. If a decreasing charge depreciation method is used for assets purchased during an accounting period, a slight modification is appropriate. When this situation occurs, determine depreciation expense for the full year and prorate the expense between the two periods involved. This process continues throughout the service life of the asset.

15. Depreciation expense reduces net income for the accounting period in which it is recorded even though a current cash outflow is not involved. However, depreciation should not be considered a source of cash. Cash is generated by revenues, not accounting procedures.

16. The estimates involved in the depreciation process are sometimes subject to revision as a result of unanticipated occurrences. Such revisions are classified as **changes in accounting estimates** and should be handled in the current and prospective periods rather than changing previously reported results. For tax purposes, companies are required to use an **accelerated cost recovery system (ACRS)** for depreciation purposes. Under the ACRS approach, capital expenditures use recovery periods ranging from three to twenty periods.

17. If the value of an asset is **permanently impaired** by a material amount it should be written down to its net realizable value. A permanent impairment in the value of property, plant, and equipment is recorded by recognizing a loss and reducing the book value of the asset through a credit to accumulated depreciation. If the asset is to continue in use, estimates of the remaining useful life and salvage value may be revised as well. If no future use of the asset is expected an entry should be made debiting a loss and crediting accumulated depreciation. This entry should reduce the book value of the asset to its salvage value.

18. **Financial statement disclosures** related to depreciation include:
    a. Depreciation expense for the period.
    b. Balances of major classes of depreciable assets, by nature and function.
    c. Accumulated depreciation, either by major classes of depreciable assets or in total.
    d. A general description of the method or methods used in computing depreciation with respect to major classes of depreciable assets.

19. **Depletion** refers to the process of recording the consumption of **natural resources** (wasting assets). The depletion base for natural resources includes **acquisition cost, exploration costs,** and **intangible development costs** reduced by any residual value related to the land. Tangible assets used in extracting natural resources are normally set up in a separate account and depreciated individually.

20. Depletion is normally based on the number of units extracted during the period, which corresponds to the activity depreciation method discussed earlier. A major problem one faces when computing depletion is **estimating recoverable reserves.**

21. Companies in the oil and gas industry may currently account for the costs using either the **successful efforts approach** or the **full costing approach.** Both successful efforts and full costing are historical cost approaches. The SEC once favored the development of a value-based accounting method for companies in the oil and gas industry known as Reserve Recognition Accounting (RRA). However, the development of RRA was abandoned and the SEC has asked the FASB to develop a comprehensive package of value-based disclosures for oil and gas procedures.

22. Unique problems, uncommon to most other types of assets, seem to exist in depletion accounting. Not infrequently, the **estimate of recoverable reserves** has to be changed either because new information has become available or because production processes have become more sophisticated. **Discovery value accounting** and **reserve recognition accounting** are essentially similar. If discovery value is recorded, an asset account would be debited and usually an Unrealized Appreciation account would be credited. Unrealized Appreciation would then be transferred to revenue as the natural resources are sold.

23. The tax law has long provided a deduction for the greater of **cost** or **percentage depletion** against income from oil, gas, and most minerals. The percentage or statutory depletion allows a write-off ranging from 5% to 22% (depending on the natural resource) as a percentage of gross revenue received instead of a percentage of cost. As a result, the amount of depletion may exceed the

investment cost that is assigned to a given natural resource.

24. Both publicly traded and privately held companies engaged in significant oil and gas producing activities are required to disclose (a) the basic method of accounting for those costs incurred in oil and gas producing activities, and (b) the manner of disposing of costs relating to oil and gas producing activities. Public companies must also disclose information about reserve quantities; capitalized costs; acquisition, exploration, and development activities; and a standardized measure of discounted future net cash flows related to proven oil and gas reserve quantities.

REVIEW QUESTIONS AND EXERCISES

True-False

Indicate whether each of the following is true (T) or false (F) in the space provided.

_____ 1. The accounting concept of depreciation reflects the decline in value associated with a plant asset.

_____ 2. An asset's cost less its salvage value is referred to as the depreciation base.

_____ 3. Physical factors such as wear and tear set the outside limit for the service life of an asset.

_____ 4. Whenever the economic nature of the asset is the primary determinant of service life, maintenance plays an extremely vital role in prolonging service life.

_____ 5. Estimation and judgment are the primary means through which the service life of an asset is determined

_____ 6. When selecting a depreciation method, the arbitrary assignment of cost to accounting periods without regard to the probable pattern of decline in an asset's services is not acceptable.

_____ 7. One problem associated with the activity method of depreciation concerns estimating the total units of output an asset will produce.

_____ 8. The straight-line depreciation method is used most often in actual practice. This is because the assumptions upon which it is based apply to most plant assets.

_____ 9. Accelerated depreciation methods accomplish the objective of writing an asset off over a shorter period of time than its useful life.

_____ 10. Under the double-declining balance depreciation method, salvage value is considered only in computing the amount of depreciation for the final year of an asset's service life.

_____ 11. The Internal Revenue Code allows the use of an accelerated depreciation method for tax purposes as long as the use of the method does not cause the company to report a net loss.

_____ 12. The replacement depreciation method is used when a new asset is purchased to replace an old asset.

_____ 13. Because depreciation expense does not require the use of cash, it is theoretically correct to consider depreciation as a source of funds to the enterprise.

_____ 14. If one of the estimates used in computing depreciation is subsequently found to require adjustments, no change in prior years' financial statements is required.

_____ 15. A permanent impairment in the value of property, plant, and equipment is recorded by recognizing a loss and reducing the book value of the asset through a credit to accumulated depreciation.

_____ 16. In recording depreciation for tax purposes, companies can use any method as long as the amount reported on the tax return exceeds the amount recorded for financial statement purposes.

_____ 17. Depletion is the systematic allocation of the cost of natural resources (wasting assets).

_____ 18. The full costing approach, related to accounting for exploration costs, requires that the full costs of exploration be charged against income in the year it is incurred.

_____ 19. The computation of depletion is essentially the same as the activity method of depreciation.

_____ 20. The percentage (statutory) depletion allowance has been repealed for most oil and gas companies and is of limited use in most other situations.

Multiple Choice

Select the best answer for each of the following items and enter the corresponding letter in the space provided.

_____ 1. The economic factors related to an asset's service life include:
A. obsolescence.
B. wear and tear.
C. decay.
D. unexpected casualties.

_____ 2. SL and YD Companies purchase identical equipment having an estimated service life of 5 years, with no salvage value. SL Company uses the straight-line depreciation method; YD Company uses the sum-of-the-years'-digits method. Assuming that the companies are identical in all other respects:

A. if both companies keep the asset for 5 years, YD Company's 5-year total for depreciation expense will be greater than SL Company's 5-year total.

B. if the asset is sold after 3 years, SL Company is more likely to report a gain on the transaction than YD Company.

C. SL Company's depreciation expense will be higher during the 1st year than YD's.

D. SL Company's net income will be lower during the 4th year than YD Company's.

_____ 3. Each year Guy Corporation sets aside an amount of cash equal to depreciation expense on its only machine. When the asset is completely depreciated, the cash fund will allow the corporation to buy a new machine if:

A. prices rise throughout the life of the property.

B. an accelerated depreciation method was used.

C. prices remain reasonably constant during the life of the property.

D. the retirement depreciation method is used.

_____ 4. The Apex Company purchased a tooling machine in 1980 for $30,000. The machine was being depreciated on the straight-line method over an estimated useful life of 20 years, with no salvage value. At the beginning of 1990, when the machine had been in use for 10 years, the company paid $5,000 to overhaul the machine. As a result of this improvement, the company estimated that the useful life of the machine would be extended an additional 5 years. What should be the depreciation expense recorded for this machine in 1990?

A. $1,000.

B. $1,333.

C. $1,500.

D. $1,833.

_____ 5. Sherman Company purchased a new machine on May 1, 1980, for $25,000. At the time of acquisition, the machine was estimated to have a useful life of 10 years and an estimated salvage value of $1,000. The company has recorded monthly depreciation using the straight-line method. On March 1, 1989, the machine was sold for $800. What should be the loss recognized from the sale of the machine?

A. $ 0.

B. $2,000.

C. $3,000.

D. $3,400.

_____ 6. The Exploitation Company acquired a tract of land containing an extractable natural resource. Exploitation Company is required by its purchase contract to restore the land to a condition suitable for recreational use after it extracts the natural resource. Geological surveys estimate that recoverable reserves will be 3 million tons and that the land will have a value of $600,000 after restoration. Relevant cost information follows:

Land	$6,000,000
Restoration	900,000
Geological surveys	300,000

If Exploitation Company maintains no inventories of extracted material, what should be the charge to depletion expense per ton of material extracted?

A. $1.80.

B. $1.90.

C. $2.00.

D. $2.20.

_____ 7. Each year a company has been investing an increasing amount in machinery. Because there are a large number of small items with relatively similar useful lives, the company has been applying straight-line depreciation method at a uniform rate to the machinery as a group. The ratio of this group's total accumulated depreciation to the total cost of the machinery has been steadily increasing and now stands at .75 to 1. The most likely explanation of this increasing ratio is that:

A. the estimated average useful life of the machinery is greater than the actual average useful life.

B. the estimated average useful life of the machinery is equal to the actual average useful life.

C. the estimated average useful life of the machinery is less than the actual average useful life.

D. the company has been retiring fully depreciated machinery that should have remained in service.

_____ 8. The estimated life of a building that has been depreciated for 30 of its originally estimated life of 50 years has been revised to a remaining life of 10 years. On the basis of this information and APBO, the accountant should:

A. continue to depreciate the building over the original 50-year life.
B. depreciate the remaining book value over the remaining life of the asset.
C. adjust accumulated depreciation to its appropriate balance, through net income, based on a 40-year life, and then depreciate the adjusted book value as though the estimated life had always been 40 years.
D. adjust accumulated depreciation to its appropriate balance, through retained earnings, based on a 40-year life, and then depreciate the adjusted book value as though the estimated life had always been 40 years.

____ 9. Composite or group depreciation is a depreciation system whereby:

A. the years of useful life of the various assets in the group are added together and the total divided by the number of items.
B. the cost of individual units within an asset group is charged to expense in the year a unit is retired from service.
C. a straight-line rate is computed by dividing the total of the annual depreciation expense for all assets in the group by the total cost of the assets.
D. the original cost of all items in a given group or class of assets is retained in the asset account and the cost of replacements is charged to expense when they are acquired.

____ 10. when depreciation is computed for partial periods under a decreasing charge depreciation method, it is necessary to:

A. charge a full year's depreciation to the year of acquisition.
B. determine depreciation expense for the full year and then prorate the expense between the two periods involved.
C. use the straight-line method for the year in which the asset is sold or otherwise disposed of.
D. use a salvage value equal to the first year's partial depreciation charge.

Review Exercises

1. Puttcamp Company acquired a machine on July 1, 1989, at a cost of $32,000. The machine has an estimated salvage value of $2,000 at the end of its 4-year useful life. Puttcamp Company uses the calendar year as its accounting period. Using the depreciation methods indicated, compute the depreciation expense for years 1989 and 1990, and the book value of the machine at December 31, 1990.

Depreciation Method	Depreciation Expense 1989	Depreciation Expense 1990	Book Value December 31, 1990
Straight-line	_____	_____	_____
Sum-of-the-years'-digits	_____	_____	_____
Double-declining balance	_____	_____	_____

2. Baxter Oil Company acquired the rights to explore for oil on a 2,000-acre plot of land in the Oklahoma Panhandle. The rights cost $80,000, and the exploration costs associated with the discovery of a major oil deposit amounted to $125,000. The company incurred $980,000 in developmental costs, of which $250,000 were for tangible equipment. This equipment has useful life of 10 years and should be of use in future exploration ventures. During the first year the company extracted 175,000 of the estimated 2.5 million barrels of oil related to the discovery. Prepare the journal entry for the first year's depletion and show how the above-mentioned assets would be reported in the balance sheet at the end of the first year.

3. For the following group of assets, compute the composite depreciation rate, the composite life, and the amount of depreciation recorded in the first year.

Asset	Original Cost	Salvage Value	Estimated Life (yr.)
A	$11,000	$ 500	5
B	7,000	200	4
C	12,500	800	3
D	16,000	1,000	6

If asset B is sold for $1,000 at the end of 3 years, what journal entry should be recorded?

4. Bernal Corporation purchased two separate pieces of equipment in March 1983. Facts related to the two items are noted below. Bernal Corporation follows a policy of recording a full-year's depreciation in the year of acquisition and no depreciation in the year of disposition.

Item	Cost	Salvage Value	Useful Life	Depreciation Method	Annual Repair Cost
A	$113,000	$ 5,000	8 yrs.	Sum-of-year's-digits	$1,500
B	$140,000	$10,000	10 yrs.	Double-declining balance	$2,500

Because of a lack of experience, the bookkeeper for the corporation made the following entry for the repair cost each year after depreciation was recorded.

Dr. Accumulated Depreciation
Cr. Cash

As a result, when item A was sold in July 1988 for $25,000, the bookkeeper recorded a loss on the sale. Also, when item B was sold in September 1990 for $40,000, the bookkeeper also recorded a loss. (Assume the bookkeeper ignored the debits to Accumulated Depreciation in computing annual depreciation expense on each asset.)

Required

(a) What journal entry did the bookkeeper record for each sale, assuming the only error was improperly charging the repair expense to accumulated depreciation. (b) What entry should have been made for each sale?

SOLUTIONS TO REVIEW QUESTIONS AND EXERCISES

True - False

1. (F) Depreciation is not a matter of valuation but a means of cost allocation in accounting. The concept is defined as the systematic allocation of the cost of an asset.

2. (T)

3. (T)

4. (F) When the economic nature of the asset is the primary determinant of service life, functional factors rather than physical factors (wear and tear) cause the asset to be retired. Thus, functional factors (inadequacy, supersession, and obsolescence) cannot be reversed by repairs and maintenance.

5. (T)

6. (T)

7. (T)

8. (F) The straight-line method is widely employed in practice because of its simplicity. The major objection to the straight-line method is that it rests on tenuous assumptions that in most situations are not realistic. The major assumptions are that (a) the asset's economic usefulness is the same each year and (b) the repair and maintenance expense is essentially the same each period.

9. (F) Accelerated depreciation methods provide for a higher depreciation cost in the earlier years and lower charges in later periods. The estimated useful life of an asset is unaffected by the depreciation method used.

10. (T)

11. (F) The IRS adopted an accelerated depreciation system known as the accelerated cost recovery system (ACRS). Under this method, the taxpayer determines the recovery deduction for an asset by applying a statutory percentage to the historical cost of the property. The use of ACRS is not affected by the reporting of a net loss.

12. (F) The retirement and replacement depreciation methods are used principally by public utilities and railroads that own many similar units of small value such as poles, ties, conductors, telephones, and so on. Under the replacement system, depreciation expense is charged with the cost of units purchased as replacements less salvage value from the units replaced.

13. (F)   Depreciation expense cannot be considered a source of funds because neither cash nor working capital is generated. Under the flow of funds concept, depreciation is an adjustment (addition to) to net income in arriving at funds or cash provided by operations.

14. (T)

15. (T)

16. (F)   For tax purposes companies are required to use an accelerated cost recovery system (ACRS) in computing depreciation. The rate of acceleration depends upon the useful life of the asset being depreciated. Congress enacted ACRS (a) to help companies achieve faster write-off of fixed assets in the hope of stimulating capital investment, and (b) to eliminate the controversy about useful lives of assets by adopting required recovery periods for most capital investments.

17. (T)

18. (F)   Under the full costing approach, all costs, whether related to successful or unsuccessful projects, are capitalized and charged against future operations.

19. (T)

20. (T)

Multiple Choice

1. (A)   The economic factors related to an asset's service life include: inadequacy, supersession, and obsolescence. The items listed in alternatives (B), (C), and (D) refer to the physical factors related to an asset's service life.

2. (D)   If both companies are identical in all respects other than depreciation, then the company using the straight-line depreciation method (SL) will have a higher depreciation expense in the 4th year of the asset's life than the company using the sum-of-the-year's-digits method (YD). Thus, SL company's net income will be lower during the 4th year.

3. (C)   Total depreciation on any asset is limited to the cost of that asset. If an amount of money equal to depreciation expense is set aside, the total accumulation will allow for the purchase of a new machine only if prices remain reasonably constant or decrease. The depreciation method employed has no impact on the total amount of depreciation.

4. (B)
Asset cost	$30,000
Depreciation at 1/1/90	15,000
Book value	15,000
Overhaul addition	5,000
Depreciation base	$20,000

Remaining useful life 10 + 5 = 15
Depreciation in 1990: $20,000 ÷ 15 = $1,333

5. (C)
Asset cost	$25,000
Depreciation 5/1/80 to 3/1/89 ($200/mo.)	21,200
Book value at 3/1/89	$ 3,800
Sales price	800
Loss on sale	$ 3,000

6. (D)
Land cost	$6,000,000
Restoration	900,000
Geological surveys	300,000
Total cost	$7,200,000
Land residual value	600,000
Depletion base	$6,600,000

Depletion expense per ton $6,600,000 ÷ 6,000,000 = $2.20.

7. (C) With a uniform rate of depreciation being charged, a steadily increasing ratio of total accumulated depreciation to total cost would indicate that the estimated average useful life of the machinery is less than the actual average useful life. If the estimated average useful life of the machinery was equal to the actual average useful life, the ratio would remain constant.

8. (B) Whenever the estimated useful life of an asset is changed, the undepreciated book value of the asset should be depreciated over the new estimated useful life. This change is merely a change in an estimate and does not require any special accounting treatment.

9. (C) Composite or group depreciation is defined as a system whereby a straight-line rate is computed by dividing the total of the annual depreciation expense for all assets in the group by the total cost of the assets.

10. (B) Under decreasing charge depreciation methods, depreciation expense is computed for each complete year of an asset's life. If the asset being depreciated under the decreasing charge method is purchased during a year, the depreciation for the entire year is computed and then a portion is allocated to depreciation expense based on the percentage of the year that the asset was used.

Review Exercises

1.

Depreciation Method	Depreciation Expense 1989	Depreciation Expense 1990	Book Value December 31, 1990
Straight Line	$ 3,750 (a)	$ 7,500 (b)	$ 20,750 (c)
Sum-of-the-years'-digits	6,000 (d)	10,500 (e)	15,500 (f)
Double-declining balance	8,000 (g)	12,000 (h)	12,000 (i)

(a) $30,000 x 1/4 X 1/2 = $3,750
(b) $30,000 x 1/4 = $7,500
(c) $32,000 - (a + b) = $20,750
(d) $30,000 x 4/10 x 1/2 = $6,000
(e) $6,000 + (9,000 x 1/2) = $10,500

(f) $32,000 - (d + e) = $15,500
(g) $32,000 x .5 x 1/2 = $8,000
(h) $8,000 + (8,000 x 1/2) = $12,000
(i) 32,000 - (g + h) = $12,000

2. Depletion base:

Land rights	$ 80,000
Exploration costs..	125,000
Intangible development costs ($980,000 - 250,000)....................	730,000
Depletion base..	$935,000

Depletion rate per barrel:
   $935,000 ÷ 2,500,000 = $.374
First year's depletion:
   175,000 x .374 = $65,450

Depletion expense	65,450	
Accumulated depletion of natural resource...............................		65,450

Balance sheet presentation:

Oil deposit (at cost)	$935,000	
Less accumulated depletion	65,450	$869,550

Tangible assets should be reported separately with a deduction for the related accumulated depreciation.

3.

Asset	Original Cost	Salvage Value	Depreciable Cost	Useful Life	Depreciation per year (straight-line)
A	$11,000	$ 500	$10,500	5	$2,100
B	7,000	200	6,800	4	1,700
C	12,500	800	11,700	3	3,900
D	16,000	1,000	15,000	6	2,500
	$46,500	$2,500	$44,000		$10,200

Composite rate = $\dfrac{\$10,200}{46,500}$ = 21.9 or 22%

Composite life (44,000 ÷ 10,200) = 4.31 years
   1st year's depreciation ($46,500 x .22) = $10,230
   Sale of asset B for $1,000 after 3 years:

Cash...	1,000	
Accumulated depreciation..........................	6,000	
Asset B		7,000

4.   (a) **Item A:**

Year	Computation	Depreciation Recorded
1983	$108,000 x 8/36	$24,000
1984	108,000 x 7/36	21,000
1985	108,000 x 6/36	18,000
1986	108,000 x 5/36	15,000
1987	108,000 x 4/36	12,000
	Total Depreciation	$90,000
	Repair Expense Charged to Depreciation (1,500 x 3)	(7,500)
	Depreciation Balance (1988)	$82,500

Entry by bookkeeper for sale of item A:

Cash	25,000	
Accumulated depreciation	82,500	
Loss on sale	5,500	
Item A		113,000

Correct entry for sale of item A:

Cash	25,000	
Accumulated depreciation	90,000	
Gain on sale		2,000
Item A		113,000

(b) **Item B:**	Year	Computation	Depreciation Recorded
	1983	$140,000 x .20	$ 28,000
	1984	112,000 x .20	22,400
	1985	89,600 x .20	17,920
	1986	71,680 x .20	14,336
	1987	57,344 x .20	11,469
	1988	45,875 x .20	9,175
	1989	36,700 x .20	7,340
		Total Depreciation	$110,640
		Repair Expense Charged to Depreciation (2,500 x 7)	(17,500)
		Depreciation Balance (1990)	$ 93,140

Entry by bookkeeper for sale of item B:

Cash	40,000	
Accumulated depreciation	93,140	
Loss on sale	6,860	
Item B		140,000

Correct entry for sale of item B:

Cash	40,000	
Accumulated Depreciation	110,640	
Gain on sale		10,640
Item B		140,000

12

Intangible assets

Chapter Synopsis

Chapter 12 discusses the identification, measurement, and disposition of intangible assets.

Chapter Review

1. **Intangible assets** are generally characterized by a lack of physical existence and a high degree of uncertainty concerning future benefits. These characteristics are rather broad and appear to be applicable to other assets not classified as intangible. Thus, accountants usually rely on tradition in classifying items as intangibles.

2. **Cost** is the appropriate basis for recording intangible assets. Like tangible assets, cost includes acquisition price and all other expenditures necessary in making the asset useful to the enterprise. When intangibles are acquired for consideration other than cash, the cost of the intangible is the fair market value of the consideration given or the intangible asset, whichever is more clearly evident.

3. The cost of an intangible asset is systematically charged to revenue through the process of **amortization**. The major problem involved in computing amortization is determination of the intangible's useful life. This problem stems from the high degree of uncertainty that surrounds the future usefulness of many intangible assets. The factors that might be considered in determining useful life include: (a) legal life, (b) economic conditions, and (c) actions of competitors.

4. When an intangible asset ceases to provide future service potential to an enterprise, its cost should be removed from the accounting records. In the case of intangible assets that are considered to have indeterminable useful lives, proper accounting requires amortization over a period not to exceed **40 years**. The entry for amortization includes a debit to an expense account and a credit to either the appropriate intangible asset account or a separate accumulated amortization account.

5. Intangible assets are **specifically identifiable** (cost of creating the intangible can be identified) or **goodwill-type intangibles**. Goodwill-type intangibles create a right or privilege that is not specifically identifiable; they have an indeterminate life; and their cost is inherent in a continuing business.

6. A **patent** gives the holder an exclusive right to use, manufacture, and sell a product or process for a period of 17 years. The two principal kinds of patents are **product patents**, which cover actual physical products, and **process patents**, which relate to the process by which products are made. **Amortization is recorded over the legal life or useful life, whichever is shorter.** Any legal costs incurred to defend a patent suit may be charged to the Patents account and amortized over the remaining useful life. However, **research and development** costs related to the development of a product, process, or idea that is subsequently patented must be expensed as incurred.

7. A **copyright** is a federally granted right that authors and other artists have in their creations. A copyright is granted for the life of the creator plus 50 years. During this time the owner or heirs have the exclusive right to reproduce and sell an artistic or published work. Normally, the useful life of a copyright is less than its legal life, but amortization should not exceed 40 years.

8. A **leasehold** is a contractual right to the use of specific property for a specified period of time. If rent is paid in advance, the amount is most appropriately included in the current or other asset category. Leases that are in substance purchases of assets should be recorded on the basis of substance rather than legal form. Detailed coverage of lease accounting is presented in Chapter 22.

9. Improvements made to leased property normally revert to the lessor at the end of the lease. Thus, the cost of **leasehold improvements** should be capitalized by the lessee and depreciated over the life of the lease or the useful life of the improvement, whichever is shorter.

10. Even though **trademarks and trade names** benefit the original user for an indefinite period of time, their cost must be amortized over a period not to exceed 40 years.

11. **Organization costs** are the costs incurred in the formation of a corporation. Such costs include legal fees, state incorporation fees, registration fees, and other costs involved in organizing a business. The minimum amortization period permitted by income tax regulations is 15 years.

12. A **franchise** provides an entity with the exclusive right to conduct a particular business or sell a particular product in a designated geographical area. Franchises may be for a definite period of time, for an indefinite period of time, or perpetual. Franchise costs that benefit future periods should be recorded in a Franchise account. These costs are amortized over the life of the franchise or 40 years, whichever is less.

13. **Goodwill** is recorded only when an entire business is **purchased** because **goodwill is a "going concern" valuation and cannot be separated from the business as a whole.** Goodwill is assumed to exist when a business enterprise demonstrates an ability to earn a profit on invested capital in excess of a rate considered to be normal. Goodwill can be measured in a business purchase by (a) discounting the extra earning potential of an enterprise and determining the present value of this extra inflow or (b) computing the difference between the fair market value of the net assets purchased and their bargained price.

14. Discounting the extra earning potential is, conceptually, the more appealing approach to the measurement of goodwill. However, this approach depends on a number of factors that are tenuous and subject to negotiation. The factors necessary to compute goodwill under this approach are: (a) the **normal rate of return** for the enterprise, (b) an estimate of the **future earnings** of the enterprise, (c) the **discount rate** that should be applied to excess profits, and (d) the **number of periods** over which excess profits should be discounted.

15. Goodwill, like other intangible assets, should be amortized over its useful life or 40 years, whichever is less. *APB Opinion No. 17* prohibits the complete write-off of goodwill against revenue in the period of purchase. The amortization of goodwill is not deductible for tax purposes.

16. **Negative goodwill** arises when the fair market value of the net assets acquired is higher than the purchase price of the asset. When negative goodwill exists, *APB Opinion No. 16* requires that it be applied to a reduction of the values assigned to noncurrent assets.

17. Intangible assets are normally shown in financial statements at cost less total amortization taken to date. The financial statements should disclose the method of amortization, but a separate Accumulated Amortization account need not be presented.

18. In general, *FASB Statement No. 2* requires that all **research and development** (R & D) costs be charged to expense when incurred. The following is a description of the recommended treatment of the costs associated with R & D activities:

a. **Materials, Equipment, and Facilities.** Expense the entire cost, unless the items have alternative future uses (in other R & D projects or otherwise), then carry as inventory and allocate as consumed or capitalize and depreciate as used.

b. **Personnel.** Salaries, wages, and other related costs of personnel engaged in R & D should be expensed as incurred.

c. **Purchased Intangibles.** Expense the entire cost, unless the items have alternative future uses (in other R & D projects or otherwise), then capitalize and amortize.

d. **Contract Services.** The cost of services performed by others in connection with the reporting company's R & D should be expensed as incurred.

e. **Indirect Costs.** A reasonable allocation of indirect costs should be included--except for general and administrative costs, which must be clearly related to be included and expensed.

19. Acceptable accounting practice requires that disclosure be made in the footnotes to the financial statements of the total R & D costs charged to expense in each period for which an income statement is presented. R & D costs for companies in the extractive industries may be (a) expensed as incurred, (b) capitalized and either depreciated or amortized over an appropriate period of time, or (c) accumulated as part of inventoriable costs. The method selected is guided by the degree of certainty of future benefits and the proper matching of revenues and expenses.

20. **Appendix 12A, Accounting for Computer Software Costs**, presents the diverse issues related to handling the costs involved in developing computer software. Coverage of the FASB position and answers to the key questions addressed in accounting for computer software are presented.

REVIEW QUESTIONS AND EXERCISES

True - False

Indicate whether each of the following is true (T) or false (F) in the space provided.

_____ 1. Lack of physical substance is the one characteristic of intangible assets that distinguishes them from all other assets reported on the balance sheet.

_____ 2. The same degree of uncertainty that exists in estimating the useful life of a machine is found in estimating the useful life of a patent.

____ 3. Cost is the basis for recording intangible assets, including acquisition price and all expenditures incurred to prepare the asset for its intended use.

____ 4. Amortization is the systematic charge to income of the cost of an intangible asset.

____ 5. Intangible assets are amortized over their useful life unless the intangible has the potential to remain in existence indefinitely.

____ 6. Immediate write-off of the cost of an intangible is not acceptable because the approach denies the existence of an asset that has just been purchased.

____ 7. A patent gives the holder the exclusive right to use a product or process for a period not to exceed 17 years.

____ 8. Long-term lease agreements ordinarily provide that any improvements made to the leased asset become the property of the party paying for the improvement at the termination of the lease.

____ 9. Coda Company secured a copyright on a unique literary work. All conservative estimates indicate that the copyright will be useful for its maximum useful life; thus, this is the period over which the copyright should be amortized.

____ 10. As a result of *FASB Statement No. 2*, all research and development (R & D) costs should normally be charged to expense when incurred.

____ 11. A marketing survey conducted for the purpose of determining a more efficient way to package a product is an example of R & D activities.

____ 12. The definition of R & D excludes the acquisition, development, or improvement of a product or process by an enterprise for use in its selling or administrative activities.

____ 13. The deferred charges classification on the balance sheet may include such items as long-term prepayments for insurance, rent, and other down payments.

____ 14. Goodwill is recorded only when an entire business is purchased or when the portion of a business purchased is responsible for all the goodwill accumulated by the enterprise.

____ 15. Conceptually, the best approach to use in measuring goodwill is to identify the individual attributes that comprise goodwill and value them individually. However, at the present time this approach is impossible.

____ 16. Use of the master valuation approach to measure goodwill requires an estimate of a firm's excess earning power.

____ 17. Determining the normal earning power of an enterprise requires an analysis of the earning power of similar companies.

____ 18. When a discount rate is applied to average excess earnings in the computation of goodwill, a higher discount rate will produce a higher value for goodwill.

____ 19. *APB Opinion No. 17* takes the position that goodwill should be written off over its useful life or 40 years, whichever is longer.

____ 20. Badwill arises when the fair market value of the asset acquired is higher than the purchase price of the asset.

Multiple Choice

Select the best response for each of the following items and enter the corresponding letter in the space provided.

____ 1. Sheets Company incurred the following cost related to the organization of the business:

Attorney's fee	$10,000
Underwriter's fee	15,000
State incorporation fee	7,000
	$32,000

The company wishes to amortize these costs over the maximum period allowed under generally accepted accounting principles. Assuming that Sheet Company began operation on January 1, 1990, what amount of organization costs should be amortized in 1990?
A. $4,400.
B. $2,200.
C. $1,000.
D. $ 800.

____ 2. Under current accounting practice, intangible assets are classified as:
A. amortizable or unamortizable
B. type A or type B
C. specifically identifiable or goodwill-type.
D. legally restricted or goodwill-type.

____ 3. One factor that is not considered in determining the useful life of an intangible asset is:
A. legal life.
B. expected actions of competitors.
C. salvage value
D. provisions for renewal or extension.

____ 4. On January 15, 1981, Pending Corporation was granted a patent on a product. On January 2, 1990, to protect its patent, Pending

purchased a patent on a competing product that originally was issued on January 10, 1986. Because of its unique plant, Pending does not feel that the competing patent can be used in producing a product. The cost of acquiring the competing patent should be:
- A. amortized over a maximum period of 8 years.
- B. amortized over a maximum period of 13 years.
- C. Amortized over a maximum period of 17 years.
- D. expensed in 1990.

____ 5. How should research and development costs be accounted for according to *FASB Statement No. 2*, "Accounting for Research and Development Costs"?
- A. Must be capitalized when incurred and then amortized over their estimated useful lives.
- B. Must be expensed in the period incurred unless contractually reimbursable.
- C. May be either capitalized or expensed when incurred.
- D. Must be expensed in the period incurred unless it can be clearly demonstrated that the expenditure will result in the discovery of a profitable product.

____ 6. A large publicly held company has developed and registered a trademark during 1988. How should the cost of developing and registering the trademark be accounted for?
- A. Charged to an asset account that should not be amortized.
- B. Amortized over 25 years if in accordance with management's evaluation.
- C. Expensed as incurred.
- D. Amortized over its useful life or 40 years, whichever is shorter.

____ 7. In 1990, Testit Corporation incurred R & D costs as follows:

Materials and facilities	$ 80,000
Personnel	110,000
Indirect costs	25,000
	$215,000

These costs relate to a product that will be marketed in 1991. It is estimated that these costs will be recovered by the end of 1993. What amount of R & D costs should be charged against 1990 income?
- A. $ 0.
- B. $ 25,000.
- C. $190,000.
- D. $215,000.

____ 8. Which of the following would not be considered an R & D activity?
- A. Adaptation of an existing capability to a particular requirement or customer's need.
- B. Searching for applications of new research findings.
- C. Laboratory research aimed at discovery of new knowledge.
- D. Conceptual formulation and design of possible product or process alternatives.

____ 9. Goodwill:
- A. generated internally should not be capitalized unless it is measured by an individual independent of the enterprise involved.
- B. is easily computed by assigning a value to the individual attributes that comprise its existence.
- C. represents a unique asset in that its value can be identified only with the business as a whole.
- D. exists in any company that has earnings that differ from those of a competitor.

____ 10. The amortization of goodwill:
- A. is dependent upon the number of years a company expects to use the benefits it provides.
- B. can be used for tax purposes only if the number of years involved exceeds five.
- C. represents as acceptable an accounting practice as does the immediate write-off method.
- D. should be computed using the straight-line method unless another method is deemed more appropriate.

Review Exercises

1. A patent was acquired by Williams Corporation on January 1, 1982, at a cost of $72,000. The useful life of the patent was estimated to be 10 years. At the beginning of 1986, Williams spent $9,000 in successfully prosecuting an attempted infringement of the patent. At the beginning of 1987, Williams purchased a patent for $25,000 that was expected to prolong the life of its original patent for 5 additional years. On July 1, 1990, a competitor obtained rights to a patent that made the company's patent obsolete. In the spaces provided, indicate the amounts requested. (Assume that amortization is credited directly to the Patent account when recorded.)
- a. Amortization expense for 1982: $_____.
- b. Balance in the Patent account at the beginning of 1986, immediately after the infringement suit: $_____.

c. Amortization expense for 1986: $_____.
d. Balance in the Patent account at the beginning of 1987, after purchase of the additional patent: $_____.
e. Amortization expense for 1987: $_____.
f. Amount of loss recorded on 7-1-90: $_____.

2. Holder Company is considering the acquisition of Koester Company on December 31, 1990. The current value of Koester's assets (excluding goodwill) is $300,000. Koester has obligations of $100,000 that would be assumed by Holder. Earnings during the past 5 years have remained rather stable at an average of $30,000 per year. For each of the following assumptions calculate (A) the amount to be paid for goodwill and (B) the total amount to be paid for Koester Company.

a. Earnings are to be capitalized at 10% in arriving at the business worth.
(A): $_____ (B): $_____
b. A return of 8% is considered normal on net identifiable assets at their appraised value; excess earnings are to be capitalized at 10% in arriving at the value of goodwill.
(A): $_____ (B): $_____

c. A return of 8% is considered normal on net identifiable assets at their appraised value. Excess earnings are expected to continue for 8 years. Goodwill is to be valued by the present value method using a rate of 10%. (The present value of 8 annual payments of $1 providing a return of 10% is 5.335.)
(A): $____ (B): $____

3. Buehlmann Company has a net worth of $480,000 excluding goodwill at December 31, 1990. During the past five years, earnings of the company have totaled $278,000. Included in these earnings figures is a nonrecurring loss of $26,000; amortization of intangibles totaling $32,000; and an extraordinary gain of $43,000. The industry within which Buehlmann operates considers a return of 10% on net worth to be normal for the industry. If average annual excess earnings are to be capitalized at 14% in arriving at goodwill, how much should Buehlmann be willing to accept from a prospective purchaser for the company?

SOLUTIONS TO REVIEW QUESTIONS AND EXERCISES

True-False

1. (F) In addition to lack of physical existence, intangible assets are characterized by a high degree of uncertainty concerning future benefits.

2. (F) A higher degree of uncertainty exists in estimating the useful life of an intangible asset than in estimating the useful life of a tangible asset such as a machine. This is due to the many factors that exist that might be considered in determining the useful life of an intangible asset. *APB Opinion No. 17* enumerates the factors that might be considered in determining useful life. In estimating the useful life of a tangible asset, an accountant generally considers only physical and/or economic factors.

3. (T)

4. (T)

5. (F) According to *APB Opinion No. 17*, intangible assets must be amortized over a period not exceeding 40 years.

6. (T)

7. (T)

8. (F) Long-term leases ordinarily provide that any improvements made to the leased property revert to the lessor at the end of the life of the lease. The lessee can make use of any improvements during the life of the lease, but they become the property of the lessor when the lease expires.

9. (F) A copyright is granted for the life of the creator plus 50 years and gives the owner, or heirs, the exclusive right to reproduce and sell an artistic or published work. However, the maximum period over which the cost of a copyright can be amortized is 40 years.

10. (T)

11. (F) In distinguishing R & D costs from selling and administrative activities, the FASB excluded costs associated with acquisition, development, or improvement of a product from the definition of R & D activities. Performing a market survey for the purpose of improving product packaging is clearly a selling and administrative activity.

12. (T)

13. (T)

14. (F) Goodwill is recorded only when an entire business is purchased because goodwill is a going-concern valuation and cannot be separated from the business as a whole.

15. (T)

16. (F) When the master valuation approach is used to measure goodwill, it is considered to be the excess of the cost over the fair value of the identifiable net assets acquired. Under this approach, goodwill is an excess net asset approach rather than an excess earning power approach.

17. (T)

18. (F) The lower the discount rate, the higher the value of the goodwill. For example, excess earnings of $20,000 capitalized at a rate of 10% yields a goodwill valuation of $200,000 ($20,000 ÷ .10). If the same $20,000 is capitalized at a rate of 20%, the goodwill valuation is $100,000 ($20,000 ÷ .20).

19. (F) Goodwill should never be written off at the date of acquisition and the period of amortization should not exceed 40 years. Thus, goodwill should be written off over its useful life or 40 years, whichever is shorter.

20. (T)

Multiple Choice

1. (D) The maximum amortization period for intangible assets allowed under generally accepted accounting principles is 40 years. If the $32,000 cost is amortized over a 40 year period the 1988 amortization amount is $800 ($32,000 ÷ 40).

2. (C) The current classification of intangibles is either specifically identifiable or of the goodwill-type. Specifically identifiable means that costs associated with obtaining a given intangible asset can be identified as a part of the cost of that intangible asset.

3. (C) Intangible assets are amortized over their legal life or their useful life, whichever is shorter. Actions of competitors as well as renewal or extension provisions affect the useful life of an intangible asset. Salvage value is a concept related to the computation of depreciation on tangible fixed assets. Salvage value is not a factor used in determining useful life of an intangible.

4. (A) The reason for acquiring the patent on the competing product is to protect the original patent acquired on 1/15/81. The original patent will expire during 1998. Thus, the cost of the patent on the competing product should be amortized over 8 years, the time between its acquisition (1990) and the expiration of the original patent's useful life (1998).

5. (B) *FASB Statement No. 2* has standardized and simplified accounting practice in the area of R & D expenditures by requiring that all research and development costs be charged to expense when incurred. The obvious exception to this rule is when the R & D costs are contractually reimbursed.

6. (D) A trademark is no different than any other intangible asset. The costs associated with the acquisition of a trademark are amortized over its useful life or 40 years, whichever is shorter.

7. (D) All R & D costs are charged to expense when incurred. Thus, the 1990 expenditures of $215,000 should be charged against 1990 income.

8. (A) R & D costs are expenditures made to develop new products or processes, to improve present products, and to discover new knowledge that may be valuable at some future date. The only alternative that does not fit the general classification of R & D expenditures is alternative A. Adapting existing capabilities to a specific requirement or need does not involve R & D.

9. (C) Goodwill is recorded only when an entire business is purchased because goodwill is a going-concern valuation and cannot be separated from the business as a whole. Goodwill generated internally should not be capitalized in the accounts because measuring the components of goodwill is simply too complex and associating any costs with future benefits is too difficult.

10. (D) Goodwill is an intangible asset that is amortized over a maximum of 40 years. The method used to compute the annual amortization charge is normally the straight-line method. However, another method may be selected if it is considered to provide a more relevant pattern in the write-off of goodwill.

Review Exercises

1.   PATENT ACCOUNT

	1-1-82	$72,000	7,200	Amortization 12-31-82 (a)
			7,200	Amortization 12-31-83
			7,200	Amortization 12-31-84
			7,200	Amortization 12-31-85
Infringement Suit	1-86	9,000		
(b) Balance	1-86	$52,200	8,700	Amortization 12-31-86 (c)
Patent Purchased		25,000		
(d) Balance	1-87	$68,500	6,850	Amortization 12-31-87 (e)
			6,850	Amortization 12-31-88
			6,850	Amortization 12-31-89
			3,425	Amortization 12-31-90
		$44,525	44,525	Loss on 7-1-90 (f)

(a) $72,000 ÷ 10 = $7,200
(c) $52,200 ÷ 6 = $8,700
(e) $68,500 ÷ 10 = $6,850

2. a. (A) $30,000 ÷ .10 = $300,000 - $200,000 = $100,000
        (B) $30,000 ÷ .10 = $300,000

    b. (A) Normal earnings: $200,000 x .08 = $16,000
             Excess earnings: $ 30,000 - $16,000 = $14,000
             $14,000 ÷ .10 = $140,000
        (B) $200,000 + $140,000 = $340,000

    c. (A) Excess earnings: $14,000
             Present value: 5,335
             Goodwill: $74,690
        (B) $200,000 + $74,690 = $274,690

3.   Earnings past 5 years... $278,000
      Less Extraordinary gains.................................   43,000
        235,000
      Plus nonrecurring loss   26,000
      Adjusted 5-year earnings................................ $261,000
      Average earnings ($261,000 ÷ 5).................... $ 52,200
      Normal earnings ($480,000 ÷ .10) .... $ 48,000
      Excess annual earnings................................... $ 4,200
      Excess earnings capitalized at 14%:
          $4,200 ÷ .14 = $30,000 (Goodwill)
      Selling price of business: $480,000 + $30,000 = $510,000

13

Current liabilities
and contingencies

Chapter Synopsis

Chapter 13 presents a discussion of the nature and measurement of items classified on the balance sheet as current liabilities. Attention is focused on the mechanics involved in recording current liabilities and financial statement disclosure requirements. Also included is a discussion concerning the identification and reporting of contingent liabilities.

Chapter Review

1. In general, liabilities involve future disbursements of assets or services. According to the FASB, a liability has three essential characteristics: (a) a present obligation that entails settlement by probable future transfer or use of cash, goods, or services; (b) an unavoidable obligation of a particular enterprise; and (c) the transaction or other event obligating the enterprise must have already happened. Liabilities are classified on the balance sheet as **current** obligations or **long-term** obligations. **Current liabilities** are those obligations whose liquidation is reasonably expected to require use of existing resources **classified as current assets** or the creation of other current liabilities.

2. The relationship between current assets and current liabilities is an important factor in the analysis of a company's financial condition. Thus, the definition of current liabilities for a particular industry will depend upon the time period (**operating cycle or one year, whichever is longer**) used in defining current assets in that industry.

3. Current liabilities are reported in the financial statements at their maturity value. Present value techniques are not normally used in measuring current liabilities because of the short time periods involved.

4. Current liabilities may be susceptible to precise measurement (**determinable**) or may contain a certain element of uncertainty (**contingent**). Determinable current liabilities are those obligations with no uncertainty concerning their **existence** or **amount**. The major problem surrounding determinable current liabilities concerns their possible omission from the financial statements. This possibility exists because current liabilities often result from unwritten extensions of credit or unrecorded accruals. However, where adequate record keeping exists, these liabilities are easily identified and recorded in the financial statements.

5. A wide variety of items are considered to be determinable current liabilities. These items are briefly reviewed in paragraphs 6 through 17.

6. **Accounts payable** represents obligations owed to others for goods, supplies, and services purchased on open account. These obligations, commonly known as **trade accounts payable**, should be recorded to coincide with the receipt of the goods or at the time title passes to the purchaser.

7. **Notes payable** classified as current liabilities arise when a promissory note is given in a trade purchase or for a short-term loan. Also, the currently maturing portion of long-term debts may be classified as a current liability. When a portion of long-term debt is so classified, it is assumed that the amount will be paid within the next 12 months out of funds classified as current assets.

8. Certain short-term obligations expected to be refinanced on a long-term basis should be **excluded** from current liabilities. Under *FASB Statement No. 6*, a short-term obligation is excluded from current liabilities if (a) it is intended to be refinanced on a long-term basis and (b) the ability to accomplish the refinancing is reasonably demonstrated. Both conditions must exist before the item can be excluded from current liabilities. Evidence as to the **intent** and **ability** to refinance usually comes from **actually refinancing** or **existing refinancing agreements.**

9. Short-term obligations expected to be refinanced may be shown on the balance sheet in captions distinct from both current liabilities and long-term debt such as Interim Debt, Short-term Debt Expected to be Refinanced, and Intermediate Debt. If a short-term obligation is excluded from current liabilities because of refinancing, a footnote to the financial statements is provided that includes: (a) a general description of the financing agreement; (b) the items of any new obligation incurred

or to be incurred; and (c) the terms of any equity security issued or to be issued.

10.   **Cash Dividends payable** are classified as current liabilities during the period subsequent to declaration and prior to payment. Once declared, a cash dividend is a binding obligation of a corporate entity payable to its stockholders. Stock dividends distributable are reported in the stockholders' equity section when declared.

11.   When **returnable deposits** are received from customers or employees, a liability corresponding to the asset received is recorded. The classification of these items as current or noncurrent liabilities is dependent on the time involved between the date of the deposit and the termination of the relationship that required the deposit.

12.   A company sometimes receives cash in advance of the performance of services or issuance of merchandise. Such transactions result in a credit to a deferred or unearned revenue account classified as a current liability on the balance sheet. As claims of this nature are redeemed, the liability is reduced and a revenue account is credited.

13.   Current tax laws require most business enterprises to collect taxes from customers and employees during the year and periodically remit these collections to the appropriate governmental unit. In such instances the enterprise is acting as a collection agency for a third party. If tax amounts due to governmental units are on hand at the financial statement data, they are reported as current liabilities. Items that generally fall into this classification include **sales taxes, use taxes, social security taxes,** and **income tax withholding**.

14.   **Accrued liabilities** represent unpaid obligations recognized at the balance sheet date. These generally result from past contractual commitments, past services received, or the operation of a tax law. The necessity of recording these obligations prior to actual payment stems from application of the matching principle in accrual basis accounting. Examples of unpaid expenses normally accrued at year end include **wages, interest, property taxes, payroll taxes, bonuses,** and **income taxes**.

15.   **Compensated absences** are absences from employment such as vacation, illness, and holidays for which it is expected that employees will be paid. In connection with compensated absences, **vested rights** exist when an employer has an obligation to make payment to an employee even if that employee terminates. **Accumulated rights** are those rights that can be carried forward to future periods if not used in the period in which earned.

16.   *FASB No. 43* requires that a liability be accrued for the cost of compensation for future absences if **all of** the following conditions are met: (a) the employer's obligation relating to employees' rights to receive compensation for future absences is attributable to employees' services already rendered; (b) the obligation relates to rights that vest or accumulate; (c) payment of the compensation is probable; and (d) the amount can be reasonably estimated. If an employer fails to accrue a liability because of a failure to meet only condition (d), that fact should be disclosed.

17.   The actual amount recorded for some liabilities depends upon the annual income of an enterprise. Because annual income cannot be known with certainty prior to year end, items such as income taxes, bonuses, and profit-sharing payments must be estimated when included in monthly or quarterly financial statements.

18.   A **contingent liability** is a potential obligation that is dependent upon the occurrence or nonoccurrence of one or more future events to resolve its status. A **loss contingency,** as defined in *FASB Statement No. 5*, is the basis for the existence of certain contingent liabilities. When a loss contingency exists, the likelihood that the future event or events will confirm the incurrence of a liability is characterized as **probable, reasonably possible,** or **remote**.

19.   When a company is threatened by legal action **(litigation, claims and assessments),** the recording of a liability will depend upon certain factors. Among the more prevalent are: (a) the period in which the underlying cause for action occurred, (b) the degree of probability of an unfavorable outcome, and (c) the ability to make a reasonable estimate of the amount of loss.

20.   If the realization of a loss contingency that could result in a liability is **probable** (likely to occur) and the amount of the loss can be **reasonably estimated**, a liability exists. This liability should be recorded along with a charge to income in the period in which the determination was made. It is important to note that **both** conditions listed above must be met before a liability can be recorded. If a loss is either probable **or** estimatible, **but not both,** or if there is at least a reasonable possibility that a liability may have been incurred then the financial statements should include the following footnote disclosures (a) the nature of the contingency; and (b) an estimate of the possible loss, range of loss, or indication that an estimate cannot be made.

21.   Product warranty costs may be accounted for using the **modified cash basis method** or the **accrual method**. The modified cash basis method must be used for income tax purposes and for financial accounting purposes when a reasonable estimate of warranty costs cannot be made at the time of sale. The accrual method includes two different accounting treatments: (a) **expense warranty treatment** and (b) **sales warranty treatment**. The expense warranty treatment is the generally accepted method for financial accounting purposes and should be used whenever the warranty is an integral and inseparable

part of the sale and is viewed as a loss contingency. The sales warranty treatment defers a certain percentage of the original sales price until some future time when actual costs are incurred or the warranty expires.

22. If a company offers premiums to customers in return for coupons, a liability should normally be recognized at year end for outstanding premium offers expected to be redeemed. The liability should be recorded along with a charge to a premium expense account.

23. Frequent-flier travel award programs have resulted in accounting problems for domestic airlines which offer such programs. Essentially, these travel awards represent a potential liability because those who hold these awards may displace paying passengers. In accounting for free travel awards, two methods may be used. These methods are **cost accrual** or **revenue accrual**. Under the cost accrual method the incremental costs to be incurred when free transportation is provided are accrued by a debit to an expense and a credit to an accrued liability. This entry is made at the time a free travel award is reached. Under the revenue deferral method a portion of the fares collected for tickets sold, and used by frequent fliers is deferred by a credit to unearned transportation revenue (a liability account).

24. Current liabilities are normally listed at the beginning of the **liabilities and stockholders' equity** section of the balance sheet. They may be listed in order of maturity, according to amount, or in order of liquidation preference. All disclosures necessary in fairly presenting current liabilities should be included in the financial statements. Examples of areas where **additional disclosure is usually warranted** include: (a) assets pledged as collateral for secured liabilities, (b) purchase commitments, (c) short-term obligations expected to be refinanced, and (d) loss contingencies for which a liability has not been recorded.

REVIEW QUESTIONS AND EXERCISES

True-False

Indicate whether each of the following is true (T) or false (F) in the space provided.

_____ 1. With the exception of leasehold contracts, all legal liabilities are accounting liabilities; but not all accounting liabilities are legal ones.

_____ 2. The only requirement for an obligation to be classified as a current liability is that it be liquidated within the operating cycle or one year, whichever is longer.

_____ 3. Because current liabilities tend to be liquidated within a short period of time, present value techniques are not normally applied.

_____ 4. If any uncertainty exists concerning a future obligation, it must not be recorded in the accounts as a liability.

_____ 5. When a company discounts its own note at a bank or loan company, the difference between the face amount of the note and the cash proceeds is most appropriately recorded as a discount on notes payable.

_____ 6. The currently maturing portion of a serial bond should not be classified as a current liability if it will be paid out of a sinking fund.

_____ 7. A short-term obligation expected to be refinanced must be excluded from current liabilities if the two conditions specified in *FASB Statement No. 6* are met.

_____ 8. The two conditions referred to in question 7 are: (a) an intent to refinance the obligation on a long-term basis and (b) an inability to pay the obligation out of current assets.

_____ 9. A stock dividend distributable is classified as a long-term liability because it will not be liquidated using current assets.

_____ 10. A current liability results when a company collects taxes from customers and employees.

_____ 11. *FASB No. 43* requires that a liability always be accrued for the cost of compensation for future absences of full-time employees.

_____ 12. The matching principle requires that incurred but unpaid expenses and the related liabilities be estimated in advance, recorded in the accounts, and reported in the financial statements on an accrual basis.

_____ 13. At year end, conditional payments such as income taxes, bonuses, and profit-sharing payments should be estimated and reported in the financial statements.

_____ 14. The term "contingency," as used in accounting, refers to situations that result in a liability after the passage of a specified period of time.

_____ 15. If a loss contingency is likely to occur and its amount can be reasonably estimated, it should be recorded in the accounts.

_____ 16. The risk of loss from catastrophes assumed by property and casualty insurance companies should not be accrued under the criteria established for loss contingencies.

_____ 17. Use of the modified cash basis method in accounting for product warranty costs is required when a company is unable to make a reasonable estimate of the amount of warranty obligations at the time of sale.

____ 18. When a company offers premiums to its customers in return for coupons, the cost of the premiums should be charged to expense when the premiums are distributed to customers.

____ 19. One factor to consider in determining whether a liability should be recorded with respect to threatened litigation is the effect such a liability will have on reported financial condition.

____ 20. If a short-term obligation is excluded from current liabilities because of refinancing, a footnote to the financial statements should be included disclosing the particulars of the refinancing arrangement.

Multiple Choice

Select the best answer for each of the following items and enter the corresponding letter in the space provided.

____ 1. Current liabilities are:
   A. liabilities that are due and payable on the balance sheet date.
   B. liabilities that may be paid out of any asset pool accumulated by the enterprise as long as payment is due within one year.
   C. due within one year or one operating cycle, whichever is longer.
   D. void of notes payable, as notes are always long-term.

____ 2. When the work "accrued" is used in connection with a current liability, it means:
   A. an expense has been incurred, but is unpaid at the financial statement date.
   B. an expense has been incurred for which cash has been paid.
   C. the liability will not come due in the subsequent accounting period.
   D. the liability is being contested and may not be paid.

____ 3. The currently maturing portion of long-term debt should be classified as a current liability if:
   A. the debt is to be converted into capital stock.
   B. the debt is to be refinanced on a long-term basis.
   C. the funds used to liquidate it are currently classified as an investment on the balance sheet.
   D. the portion so classified will be liquidated within one year using current assets.

____ 4. Which of the following would not constitute evidence concerning the ability to consum-

mate the refinancing of a short-term obligation?
   A. Actual refinancing after the balance sheet date by issuance of a long-term obligation.
   B. A statement by the board of directors that refinancing is inevitable.
   C. Entering into a financing agreement that clearly permits refinancing on a long-term basis with terms that are readily determinable.
   D. Actual refinancing after the balance sheet date by issuance of equity securities.

____ 5. Mann Corporation has $1,500,000 of short-term debt it expects to retire with proceeds from the sale of 50,000 shares of common stock. If the stock is sold for $20 per share subsequent to the balance sheet date, but before the balance sheet is issued, what amount of short-term debt could be excluded from current liabilities?
   A. $1,000,000.
   B. $1,500,000.
   C. $ 500,000.
   D. $ 0.

____ 6. The controller of Marcelle Corporation is entitled to a bonus of 10% of net income after bonus and tax deductions. If net income before tax and bonus amounts to $80,000 and the tax rate is 40%, what amount of bonus can the controller expect to receive?
   A. $3,000.
   B. $4,528.
   C. $5,106.
   D. $8,000.

____ 7. Which of the following loss contingencies is normally accrued?
   A. Pending or threatened litigation.
   B. General or unspecified business risk.
   C. Obligations related to product warranties.
   D. Risk of property loss due to fire.

____ 8. Drab Company becomes aware of a lawsuit after the date of the financial statements, but before they are issued. A loss and related liability should be reported in the financial statements if the amount can be reasonably estimated, and unfavorable outcome is highly probable, and:
   A. the Drab Company admits guilt.
   B. the court will decide the case within one year.
   C. the damages appear to be material.
   D. the cause for action occurred during the prior accounting period covered by the financial statements.

_____ 9. Use of the accrual method in accounting for product warranty costs:
A. is required for federal income tax purposes.
B. is frequently justified on the basis of expediency when warranty costs are immaterial.
C. finds the expense account being charged when the seller performs in compliance with the warranty.
D. represents accepted practice and should be used whenever the warranty is an integral and inseparable part of the sale.

_____ 10. Which of the following is not acceptable treatment for the presentation of current liabilities?
A. Listing current liabilities in order of maturity.
B. Listing current liabilities according to amount.
C. Offsetting current liabilities against assets that are to be applied to their liquidation.
D. Showing current liabilities immediately below current assets to obtain a presentation of working capital.

Review Exercises

1. Flakeo Company included a coupon in each box of its cereal. For every 10 coupons returned by a customer, Flakeo offered a silver spoon. Each spoon costs Flakeo 75 cents. During the first year of the offer, Flakeo sold 500,000 boxes of cereal. They estimated that 80% of the coupons would be redeemed. Flakeo distributed 28,000 spoons during the year. What was the premium expense for the first year? What amount of estimated liability should Flakeo Company show on its year-end balance sheet for unredeemed coupons?

2. Rose Corporation has a bonus agreement with its sales staff. Salespersons with more than 5 years of service share a bonus of 20% of net income after deducting income taxes but before deducting the bonus. Salespersons with less than 5 years of service share a bonus of 10% of net income after deducting income taxes and bonus. Net income before taxes and bonus is $250,000; Rose Corporation has an income tax rate of 40%. Compute the amount of bonus to be shared by (a) the salespersons with more than 5 years of service and (b) the salespersons with less than 5 years of service.

3. Jeff and Jason Corporation manufactures CB radios. Each radio is sold with a two-year unconditional warranty against defects. During 1990, 280 radios were sold for $150 each. The company estimates that the warranty cost will average $20 per unit. The actual warranty costs incurred in 1990 amounted to $2,350. Prepare journal entries for the sale of CBs, the estimated warranty cost, and the actual warranty cost incurred.

4. On August 1, Billingsley Company discounted its own $150,000, one-year, noninterest-bearing note at the Douglas National Bank. A discount rate of 14.5% was applied to the transaction.
(a) Prepare the journal entries for the initial transaction and the accrual of interest on September 1.
(b) Show how the note would be presented in the December 31 balance sheet.
(c) Calculate the effective interest rate incurred by Billingsley Company.

SOLUTIONS TO REVIEW QUESTIONS AND EXERCISES

True-False

1. (T)
2. (F) In addition to the "operating cycle or one year, whichever is longer" criteria, one other criteria is necessary for an obligation to be classified as current. Current liabilities are obligations whose liquidation is reasonably expected to require use of existing resources properly classified as current assets or the creation of other current liabilities.
3. (T)
4. (F) All liabilities, because they are probable future sacrifices, involve an element of uncertainty. Determinable current liabilities have little uncertainty associated with them. However, contingent liabilities, which are often recorded in the accounts, can have a certain degree of uncertainty associated with them until they are paid.

5. (T)
6. (T)
7. (T)
8. (F)   The two conditions required to exclude a short-term obligation from current liabilities are: (a) there must be intent to refinance the obligation on a long-term basis and (b) the company must demonstrate an ability to consummate the refinancing.
9. (F)   A stock dividend distributable is liquidated using capital stock rather than assets. Thus, a stock dividend distributable should be classified in an entity's equity section.
10. (T)
11. (F)   A liability for the cost of compensation for future absences is required if the four following conditions are met: (a) the employee's services have already been rendered, (b) the obligation relates to rights that vest or accumulate, (c) payment is probable, and (d) the amount can be reasonably estimated.
12. (T)
13. (F)   At year end, conditional payments need not be estimated as they can be readily measured. This is because conditional payments depend on the results of operations that are available at year end. During interim periods, conditional payments need to be estimated because results of operations (annual income) is not yet determined.
14. (F)   Contingencies result in liabilities if it is probable that a liability has been incurred and the amount of the loss can be reasonably estimated. The mere passage of time is not a criteria in determining whether a loss contingency should be recorded as a liability.
15. (T)
16. (T)
17. (T)
18. (F)   The cost of premiums should be charged to expense during the period in which the sale that gave rise to the premium is made. This method will find some of the premium cost being charged to expense when the premiums are distributed to customers. However, any portion of the estimated premium expense not charged to expense during the period of sale must be accrued at year end so that a proper matching of revenues and expense takes place.
19. (F)   Threatened litigation is a loss contingency that should be recorded as a liability if it is probable that a liability has been incurred and the amount of the loss is reasonably estimated.
20. (T)

Multiple Choice

1. (C)   Current liabilities are obligations that mature within one year or the operating cycle, whichever is longer, and they are reasonably expected to require the use of current assets for their liquidation.
2. (A)   An accrued expense is a debt incurred by a company that remains unpaid at the date of financial statements. For example, a company that pays its employees on Friday of each week would have an accrued liability for four days of salaries expense if the year-end financial statements were prepared on a Thursday.
3. (D)   The item would be classified as a current liability as long as it met the relevant criteria. The criteria include payment within one year or the operating cycle, whichever is longer, and payment made using assets classified as current.
4. (B)   The ability to consummate refinancing of a short-term obligation is best demonstrated by actual refinancing after the financial statement date but before the financial statements are issued. A mere statement by the board of directors that they can accomplish refinancing is not sufficient to classify the short-term debt as long-term debt.

5. (A) The maximum amount of short-term debt that can be excluded from current liabilities is limited to the amount secured through the refinancing arrangement. In this case the amount is $1,000,000 (50,000 x $20).

6. (B)
$$B = .10 (\$80,000 - B - T)$$
$$T = .40 (\$80,000 - B)$$

$$B = .10 (\$80,000 - B - .40[\$80,000 - B])$$
$$B = .10 (\$80,000 - B - \$32,000 - .4B)$$
$$B = .10 (\$48,000 - .6B)$$
$$B = \$4,800 - .06B$$
$$1.06\ B = \$4,800$$
$$B = \$4,528$$

7. (C) To accrue a loss contingency, it must be probable that a liability has been incurred and the amount must be reasonably estimated. Alternatives B and D might in some cases be considered probable, but the amount of any loss could not be predicted with any accuracy. Alternative A is incorrect because threatened litigation might not be probable and the amount would be difficult to estimate. Obligations related to product warranties are definitely probable, and the amount is normally estimable because of the past experience of the company.

8. (D) The liability must be related to the period covered by the financial statements. The other alternatives (A, B, and C) are inconsequential to recording the liability.

9. (D) Accounting for product warranty costs by accruing an expense is accepted practice that should be used whenever the warranty is an integral and inseparable part of the sale.

10. (C) Offsetting current liabilities against assets that are to be applied to their liquidation would be inappropriate. Such a presentation would cause working capital and current ratio-type analyses to be difficult to perform. Also, readers of the financial statements could be misled by such a presentation.

Review Exercises

1.
Estimate of coupons to be redeemed (500,000 x .8)	400,000
Coupons redeemed (28,000 x 10)	280,000
Estimated coupons redeemable	120,000
First year's premium expense:	
Coupons redeemed (28,000 x .75)	$21,000
Additional redemptions expected	
[(120,000 ÷ 10) x .75]	9,000
Total premium expense	$30,000
Estimated year-end premium liability (12,000 x .75)	$9,000

2. (a) **Greater than 5 years of service**

$$B = .20 (\$250,000 - T)$$
$$T = .40 (\$250,000 - B)$$
$$B = .20 [\$250,000 - .40(\$250,000 - B)]$$
$$B = .20 (\$250,000 - \$100,000 + .4B)$$
$$B = (\$30,000 + .08B)$$
$$.92\ B = \$30,000$$
$$B = \$32,608.69$$

(b) **Less than 5 years of service**

$$B = .10 (\$250,000 - B - T)$$
$$T = .40 (\$250,000 - B)$$
$$B = .10 [\$250,000 - B - .40(\$250,000 - B)]$$
$$B = .10 (\$250,000 - B - \$100,000 + .4B)$$
$$B = .10 (\$150,000 - .6B)$$
$$1.06\ B = \$15,000$$
$$B = \$14,150.94$$

3.   Journal Entries:

Sale of CBs (280 x $150):

Cash or Accounts Receivable	42,000	
Sales		42,000

Estimated warranty cost (280 X $20):

Warranty expense	5,600	
Estimated liability under warranty		5,600

Actual warranty cost:

Estimated liability under warranty	2,350	
Cash		2,350

4.   (a)

August 1	Cash	128,250	
	Discount on Notes Payable	21,750	
	Notes Payable		150,000
Sept. 1	Interest Expense	1,812.50	
	Discount on Notes Payable		1,812.50

(b)   Current Liabilities

Notes Payable	$150,000.00	
Discount on Notes Payable	12,687.50*	
		$137,312.50

*Discount Balance ($21,750 - (1,812.50 x 5) = $12,687.50)

(c) $21,750 ÷ $128,250 = 17% effective interest rate

14

Long-term liabilities

Chapter Synopsis

Chapter 14 presents a discussion of the issues related to long-term liabilities. A major portion of the chapter is concerned with accounting issues related to bonds payable transactions.

Chapter Review

1.   Long-term liabilities are obligations that are **not** payable within the operating cycle or one year, whichever is longer. These obligations normally require a **formal agreement** between the parties involved that often includes certain **covenants and restrictions** for the protection of the lender.

2.   Generally, long-term liabilities are incurred to finance operations and the acquisition of plant assets. In return for the funds received from these obligations, the borrower agrees to pay a stipulated rate of interest in addition to the principal. Interest is paid to the lender during each period that the obligation is outstanding.

3.   Long-term liabilities include **bonds payable, mortgage notes payable, long-term notes payable, lease obligations, pension obligations,** and **long-term contracts for the purchase of plants assets.** Pension and lease obligations are discussed in Chapters 21 and 22, respectively.

4.   **Bonds payable** represents an obligation of the issuing corporation to pay a sum of money at a designated maturity date plus periodic interest at a specified rate on the face value. The following terms are commonly used in discussing the various aspects of corporate bond issues:

Indenture. Describes the contractual agreement between the corporation issuing the bonds and the bondholders.

Face Value. Amount stated on the face of the bond that serves as the basis for periodic interest computations and represents the amount due at maturity (also known as maturity value).

Term Bonds. Issues that mature on a single date.

Serial Bonds. Issues that mature in periodic installments.

Mortgage Bonds. Secured bonds having a claim on real estate.

Junk Bonds. Term used to describe bonds that pay a high rate of interest because of the high credit risk associated with the bonds.

Debenture Bonds. Unsecured bonds.

Convertible Bonds. Bonds that may be exchanged for other securities of the corporation.

Commodity-Backed Bonds. Bonds that are redeemable in measures of a commodity such as barrels of oil, tons of coal, or ounces of a rare metal (also called asset-linked bonds).

Deep Discount Bonds. Bonds sold at a discount that provides the buyer's total interest payoff at maturity (also called zero interest bonds).

Income Bonds. Interest payments depend on the existence of operating income.

Callable Bonds. Issuer reserves the right to call and retire the bonds prior to maturity.

Registered Bonds. Bonds issued in the name of the owner.

Bearer or Coupon Bonds. Bonds not recorded in the name of the owner, transferred by mere delivery.

5.   **Bonds** are debt instruments of the issuing corporation used by that corporation to borrow funds from the general public or institutional investors. The use of bonds provides the issuer an opportunity to divide a large amount of long-term indebtedness among many small investing units. Bonds may be sold through an **underwriter** who either (a) guarantees a certain sum to the corporation and assumes the risk of sale or (b) agrees to sell the bond issue on the basis of a commission. Alternatively, a corporation may sell the bonds directly to a large financial institution without the aid of an underwriter.

6.   If an entire bond issue is not sold at one time, both the amount of the **bonds authorized** and the **bonds issued** should be disclosed on the balance sheet or in a footnote. This discloses the potential indebtedness represented by the unissued bonds.

7. When bonds are issued between interest dates, the purchase price is increased by an amount equal to the interest earned on the bonds since the last interest payment date. On the next interest payment date, the bondholder receives the entire semiannual interest payment. However, the amount of interest expense to the issuing corporation is the difference between the semi-annual interest payment and the amount of interest prepaid by the purchaser.

8. Bonds are issued with a **stated rate** of interest expressed as a percentage of the **par value** of the bonds. When bonds are sold for more than par value (at a **premium**) or less than par value (at a **discount**), the interest rate actually earned by the bondholder is different from the stated rate. This is known as the **effective rate** of interest and is set by economic conditions in the investment market. The effective rate exceeds the stated rate when the bonds sell at a discount, and the effective rate is less than the stated rate when the bonds sell at a premium.

9. Premiums and discounts resulting from a bond issue are recorded at the time the bonds are sold. The amounts recorded as discounts or premiums are amortized each time bond interest is paid. The time period over which discounts and premiums are amortized is equal to the period of time the bonds are outstanding (date of sale to maturity date). Amortization of bond premiums decreases the recorded amount of bond interest expense, whereas the amortization of bond discounts increases the recorded amount of bond interest expense. Unamortized premiums and discounts are reported with the **Bonds Payable** account in the liability section of the balance sheet. Premiums and discounts are not liability accounts, they are merely liability valuation accounts. Premiums are added to the Bonds Payable and discounts are deducted from the Bonds Payable.

10. Bond premiums and discounts may be amortized using the straight-line method. However, the profession's preferred procedure is the **effective interest method.** This method computes bond interest using the effective rate at which the bonds are issued. More specifically, **interest cost for each period is the effective interest rate multiplied by the carrying value (book value) of the bonds at the start of that period.**

11. Some of the costs associated with issuing bonds include engraving and printing costs, legal and accounting fees, commissions, and promotion expenses. *APB Opinion, No. 21*, "Interest on Receivables and Payables," indicates that these costs should be debited to a deferred charge account entitled, Unamortized Bond Issue Costs. These costs are then amortized over the life of the issue in a manner similar to that used for discount on bonds.

12. **Treasury bonds** are a corporation's own bonds that have been reacquired but not canceled. They should be shown on the balance sheet at their par value as a deduction from the bonds payable -- issued to arrive at bonds payable -- outstanding.

13. The following terms are important to an understanding of the accounting for extinguishment of debt:

Early Extinguishment. The reacquisition of debt before its scheduled maturity, except through conversion by the holder.

Reacquisition Price. The amount paid on extinguishment or redemption of debt before maturity. Includes any call premium and expense of reacquisition.

Net Carrying Amount. Amount of debt payable at maturity, adjusted for unamortized premium, discount, and expense of issuance.

Gain of Loss from Extinguishment. Difference between reacquisition price and net carrying amount of debt, recognized in income of the period of redemption. If reacquisition price exceeds net carrying amount, a loss results.

Refunding. The replacement of an existing bond issue with a new issue. At the time of redemption, the un-amortized premium or discount and expenses applicable to the bonds canceled should be removed from the accounts and the liability for bonds reduced in the proper amount.

In-Substance Defeasance. An arrangement whereby a company provides for the future repayment of one or more of its long-term debt issues by placing purchased securities in an irrevocable trust, the principal and interest of which are pledged to pay off the principal and interest of its own debt securities as they mature.

14. Material gains or losses resulting from the following types of debt extinguishments should be classified as **extraordinary items** on the income statement:

   a. early extinguishment of debt at less than the net carrying amount.
   b. early extinguishment of debt at more than the net carrying amount.
   c. early extinguishment of debt by exchanging common or preferred stock.
   d. refinancing existing debt with the new debt.
   e. retirement of debt maturing serially.
   f. in-substance defeasance of previously outstanding debt.

15. Interest is an inherent and natural ingredient of long-term debt. When the amount of interest stated on long-term debt is unrealistic in light of prevailing market conditions, the accountant must evaluate the entire arrangement to determine the appropriate amounts involved for properly recording the exchange and the

related interest. Use of present value techniques is recommended when attempting to reflect the true economic substance of such obligations.

16. An *APB Opinion No. 21* applies to all payables that represent commitments to pay money at a determinable future date. Specifically excluded from the requirements of *Opinion No. 21* are obligations settled in property or services and obligations payable at some indeterminable date.

17. When a long-term note is issued **solely for cash,** the **interest factor** is assumed to be the stated or coupon rate plus or minus the amortization of the discount or premium. In situations where a note is exchanged for **cash and some additional privilege,** the difference between the present value of the payable and the amount of cash loaned should be recorded as a discount on the note and as unearned revenue. This discount should be amortized by a charge to interest expense over the term of the note using the effective interest method. The unearned revenue is prorated on the same basis as the privilege that gave rise to the unearned revenue is realized by the lender/customer. For example, the privilege may be a favorable merchandise purchase agreement. In this case, the unearned revenue is prorated on the basis of the ratio between each period's sales to the lender/customer and the total sales to that customer for the term of the note.

18. When a debt instrument is exchanged for **noncash consideration** in a bargained transaction, the stated rate of interest is presumed fair unless; **(a)** no interest rate is stated; **(b)** the stated rate is unreasonable; or **(c)** the face amount of the debt is materially different from the current cash price of the consideration or the current market value of the debt. If the stated rate is determined to be inappropriate, an **imputed interest rate** must be used to establish the present value of the debt instrument. The imputed interest rate is used to establish the present value of the debt instrument by discounting, at that rate, all future payments on the debt instrument.

19. The imputed interest rate used for valuation purpose will normally be at least equal to the rate at which the debtor can obtain financing of a similar nature from other sources at the date of the transaction. The object is to approximate the rate that would have resulted if an independent borrower and an independent lender had negotiated a similar transaction under comparable terms and conditions.

20. **Mortgage notes** are a common means of financing the acquisition of property, plant, and equipment in a proprietorship or partnership form of business organization. Normally, the title to specific property is pledged as security for a mortgage note. If a mortgage note is paid on an installment basis, the current installment should be classified as a current liability.

21. Because of unusually high, unstable interest rates and a tight money supply, the traditional **fixed-rate mortgage** has been partially supplanted with new and unique mortgage arrangements. **Variable-rate mortgages** feature interest rates tied to changes in the fluctuating market rate of interest. Generally, variable-rate lenders adjust the interest rate at either one-or three-year intervals. Another mortgage innovation is the **shared appreciation mortgage** in which the lender grants a reduction in the interest rate in return for a share of the appreciation in the pledged real estate's value.

22. A significant issue in accounting today is the question of off-balance sheet financing. **Off-balance sheet financing** is an attempt to borrow monies in such a way that the obligations are not recorded. Included in this chapter is a discussion of two off-balance sheet financing arrangements: (a) research and development arrangements, and (b) project financing arrangements.

23. **Project financing arrangements** arise when the following three conditions are present: (a) two or more entities form another entity to construct an operating plant that will be used by both parties; (b) the new entity borrows funds to construct the project and repays the debt from the proceeds received from the project; and (c) payment of the debt is guaranteed by the companies that formed the new entity. The advantage of such an arrangement to the companies that form the new entity is that neither company reports the liability on their books.

24. Many project financing arrangements are further formalized through the use of **take-or-pay contracts** or **through-put contracts.** In take-or-pay contracts, a purchaser of goods signs an agreement with the seller to pay specified amounts periodically in return for products or services. The purchaser must make specified minimum payments even if delivery of the contracted products or services is not taken. Through-put contracts are similar to take-or-pay contracts, except that a service instead of a product is provided by the asset under construction.

25. Companies that have large amounts and numerous issues of long-term debt frequently report only one amount in the balance sheet and support this with comments and schedules in the accompanying notes to the financial statements. These foot-note disclosures generally indicate the nature of the liabilities, maturity dates, interest rates, call provisions, conversion privileges, restrictions imposed by the borrower, and assets pledged as security. Long-term debt that matures within one year should be reported as a current liability unless retirement is to be accomplished with other than current assets.

26. When a debtor experiences financial difficulty, a creditor may grant some concession to the debtor related to the debt obligation that exists between the two parties. When such a concession is granted, it is referred to as a **troubled debt restructuring.** The proper accounting for

these transactions is the subject of *FASB Statement No. 15*, "Accounting by Debtors and Creditors for Troubled Debt Restructurings." **Appendix 14A** presents a complete discussion of the concept of troubled debt restructurings as defined in *FASB Statement No. 15*.

27.   As noted in paragraph No 4(d) above, **serial bonds** are bonds that mature in periodic installments. A serial bond issue may be sold as though each series is a separate bond issue or it may be sold as a package. A comprehensive illustration that demonstrates the amortization of premium or discount on serial bonds and the accounting for the redemption of serial bonds before maturity is presented in **Appendix 14B.**

Demonstration Problems

1.   Sloan Company issued $250,000 of 10% bonds on January 1, 1988, due on January 1, 1998, with interest payable each July1 and January 1. If investors desire to earn an effective interest rate of 12%, how much should they pay for the bonds?

Solution:

Maturity value of bonds	$250,000
Present value of $25,000 due in ten years at 12% interest payable seimiannually (Table 6-2, 6% for 20 periods)	
.31180 X $250,000	$77,950
Present value of $12,500 interest payable semiannually for 10 years at 12% (Table 6-4, 6% for 20 periods	
11.46992 X $12,500	143,374
Proceeds from sale of bonds	221,324
Discount on bonds	$28,676

(If investors pay $221,324 for this bond issue, the effective interest rate on these 10% bonds would be 12%.)

2.   Using the facts in the problem above, prepare a schedule showing the amounts that would be used in recording the first two semiannual interest payments (July 1, 1988 and January 1, 1989).

Solution:

Date	Cash Credit	Interest Expense Debt	Bond Discount Credit	Carrying Value of Bonds
1/1/88				221,324
7/1/88	$12,500(a)	13,279(b)	779(c)	222,103(d)
1/1/89	12,500(e)	13,266(f)	766(g)	222,869(h)

(a) $250,000 X .10 X 6/12   (e) same as (a)
(b) $221,324 X .12 X 6/12   (f) $221,103 x .12 x 6/12
(c) $13,279 - $12,500   (g) $13,266 - $12,500
(d) $221,324 + 779   (h) $222,103 + 766

REVIEW QUESTIONS AND EXERCISES

True-False

Indicate whether each of the following is true (T) or false (F) in the space provided.

_____ 1. Long-term debt is ordinarily used by an enterprise as a more or less permanent means of financing to increase the earnings available to stockholders.

_____ 2. Generally, long-term debt, in whatever form, is issued subject to various covenants or restrictions for the protection of corporate stockholders.

_____ 3. Commodity-backed bonds are redeemable in measures of a commodity such as barrels of oil, tons of coal, or ounces of a rare metal.

_____ 4. Revenue bonds are bonds whose interest rate is a function of the revenue earned by the company issuing the bonds.

_____ 5. Bonds issued by a corporation represent a means of borrowing funds from the general public or institutional investors on a long-term basis.

_____ 6. When bonds are issued by a corporation, the AICPA requires that the issue be placed with an independent underwriter.

_____ 7. When bonds are issued between interest dates, the purchaser pays for interest accrued since the date the bonds were originally issued.

_____ 8. The stated rate of interest on bonds is the rate set by the party issuing the bonds.

_____ 9. If bonds are sold at a premium, the effective rate of interest is greater than the stated rate of interest.

_____ 10. *APB Opinion No. 21* requires that bond discount be reported in the balance sheet as a direct deduction from the face amount of the bond.

_____ 11. The amortization of a bond discount increases the amount of bond interest expense recorded each year.

_____ 12. Under the effective interest method semiannual interest expense is computed by multiplying the effective interest rate times a constant carrying value of the bonds.

_____ 13. If a company extinguishes debt through an in-substance defeasance, there is an immediate repurchase of the debt and the financial statements are relieved of the obligation.

_____ 14. Any gain or loss resulting from early extinguishment of a debt is not amortized to future periods.

_____ 15. In accordance with *FASB Statement No. 4*, gains and losses from extinguishment of debt should be aggregated and, if material, classified in the income statement as an extraordinary item.

_____ 16. The expenses associated with the issuance of bonds (printing costs, legal fees, etc.), should be added to the bond discount or subtracted from the bond premium on the date the bonds are issued.

_____ 17. When a noninterest-bearing note is given in return for property, the present value of the note is measured by the fair value of the property or by an amount that reasonably approximates the market value of the note.

_____ 18. An imputed interest rate used to determine the present value of a debt instrument may change during the life of the debt if a change occurs in the prevailing interest rate.

_____ 19. Two reasons often cited for off-balance sheet financing are: (a) keeping debt off the balance sheet enhances the quality of the balance sheet and permits credit to be obtained more easily and (b) loan covenants often impose a limitation on the amount of debt a company may have.

_____ 20. In a project financing arrangement, a single company sets up a second company for the purpose of financing a specific project that has a maximum life of five years.

Multiple Choice

Select the best response for each of the following items and enter the corresponding letter in the space provided.

_____ 1. Bonds with par value of $500,000 carrying a stated interest rate of 6% payable semi-annually on March 1 and September 1 were issued on July 1. The proceeds from the issue amounted to $510,000. The best explanation for the excess received over par value is:
   A. the bonds were sold at a premium.
   B. the bonds were sold at a higher effective interest rate.
   C. the bonds were issued at par plus accrued interest
   D. no explanation is possible without knowing the maturity date of the bond issue.

____ 2. If bonds are issued initially at a premium and the effective interest method of amortization is used, interest expense in the earlier years will be:
   A. greater than if the straight-line method were used.
   B. greater than the amount of the interest payments.
   C. the same as if the straight-line method were used.
   D. less than if the straight line method were used.

____ 3. ABP Opinion No. 21 requires that bond premium be reported in the balance sheet:
   A. at the present value of the future reduction in bond interest expense due to the premium.
   B. as a deferred credit.
   C. along with other premium accounts such as those resulting from stock transactions.
   D. as a direct addition to the face amount of the bond.

____ 4. The following information applies to both questions 4 and 5. On October 1, 1990 JMC Corporation issued 5%, 10-year bonds with a par value of $300,000 at 104. Interest is paid on October 1 and April 1, with any premiums or discounts amortized on a straight-line basis. The entry to record the issuance of the bonds would include:
   A. a credit of $7,500 to Accrued Interest Payable.
   B. a credit of $12,000 to Premium on Bonds Payable.
   C. a credit of $288,000 to Bonds Payable.
   D. a debit of $12,000 to Discount on Bonds Payable.

____ 5. See data in No. 4. The Bond Interest Expense reported on the 1990 income statement of JMC Corporation would be:
   A. $4,050.
   B. $6,900.
   C. $3,450.
   D. $3,750.

____ 6. When debt is extinguished before its maturity date through a refunding transaction, any difference between the reacquisition price of outstanding debt and its net carrying amount per books should be:
   A. amortized over the remaining original life of the extinguished issue.
   B. amortized over the life of the new issue.
   C. recognized currently in income as an extraordinary loss or gain.
   D. treated as a prior period adjustment.

____ 7. Which of the following is not a characteristic of a project financing arrangement?
   A. Two or more entities form another entity to construct an operating plant that will be used by both parties.
   B. The project must be one that neither entity could enter into on its own.
   C. The new entity borrows money to finance the project and repays the debt from the proceeds received from the project.
   D. Payment of the debt is guaranteed by the companies that formed the new entity.

____ 8. Stukel Corporation exchanged land with a fair market value of $150,000 for Cline Company's $226,000, noninterest-bearing, 4-year note. If the $150,000 amount represents the present value of the note at an appropriate rate of interest, Stukel Corporation should record the difference ($76,000) as:
   A. gain on the sale of land.
   B. premium on the sale of land.
   C. premium on notes receivable.
   D. discount on notes receivable.

____ 9. A debt instrument with no ready market is exchanged for property whose fair market value is currently indeterminable. When such a transaction takes place:
   A. the present value of the debt instrument must be approximated using an imputed interest rate.
   B. it should not be recorded on the books of either party until the fair market value of the property becomes evident.
   C. the board of directors of the entity receiving the property should estimate a value for the property that will serve as a basis for the transaction.
   D. the directors of both entities involved in the transaction should negotiate a value to be assigned to the property.

____ 10. Which of the following statements correctly depicts the nature of discounts or premiums as applied to a bond issue?
    A. When bonds are issued at a discount, the seller has an advantage in that interest payments are based upon an amount less than face value.
    B. The terms "discount" and "premium" are the same as loss and gain, respectively, to both buyer and seller.
    C. The difference between the effective rate of interest and the market rate of interest is the reason discounts and premiums arise.
    D. The net cash outflow (ignoring bond issue costs) to the seller of bonds issued at a premium will be less than the maturity value of the bonds plus total interest payments.

Review Exercises

1. Jeffrey Corporation issued $800,000 of 6% bonds at 97.5 plus accrued interest on August 1, 1990. The bonds are 9-year bonds dated December 1, 1989, and pay interest on June 1 and December 1, each year. The company's fiscal year coincides with the calendar year; straight-line amortization is used. Prepare the journal entries Jeffrey Corporation would make during 1990 relative to the bonds.

2. The following information relates to a $200,000, 4-year, 6% bond issue. The bonds, issued on 1-1-89, are due on 1-1-93 and pay interest on January 1 and July 1. The bonds are sold to yield 5%.

Maturity value of bonds payable	$200,000
Present value of $200,000 due in 4 years at 5%, semiannual interest (Table 6-2)	_____
Present value of $6,000 interest payable semi-annually for 4 years at 5% (Table 6-4)	_____
Proceeds from sale of bonds	_____
Premium on bonds	_____

Fill in the missing amounts and prepare an amortization schedule using the effective interest method.

3. On July 1, 1990, the Dresser Company issued $200,000 of 6%, 10-year bonds with interest dates of March 1 and September 1. The company received cash of $200,250, which included the interest accrued since the authorization date of March 1, 1990. The company maintains a policy of amortizing premiums and discounts on a straight-line basis.

    a. What amount of accrued interest did Dresser Company receive from investors on July 1, 1990?
    b. What was the amount of discount or premium? (Indicate which.) $____.
    c. What amount of cash will be paid to bondholders on September 1,1990? $____.
    d. What amount of accrued interest payable on bonds should appear on the 12-31-90 balance sheet? $____.
    e. What amount of bond interest expense should be reported on the income statement for 1990? $____.

4. The following transactions are taken from the records of the McCroden Corporation.

    a. Bonds payable with a par value of $800,000, carrying a stated interest rate of 9% payable semiannually on March 1 and September 1, were issued on June 1, 1987, at 102.5 plus accrued interest. The bonds are dated March 1, 1987 and mature on March 1, 1997.
    b. September 1 interest payment is made.
    c. Year-end (December 31) accrued interest on bonds payable is recorded and the bond premium is amortized using the straight-line method.
    d. March 1 interest payment is made.
    e. Bonds with a par value of $350,000 are purchased at 101 plus accrued interest on August 1, 1988, and retired. (Bond premium amortization is recorded only at year end.)
    f. September 1 interest payment is made.
    g. Year-end (December 31) accrued interest on bonds payable is recorded and the bond premium is amortized using the straight-line method.

Required:

Prepare journal entries for the transactions noted above.

SOLUTIONS TO REVIEW QUESTIONS AND EXERCISES

True-False

1. (T)
2. (F) Long-term debt is subject to various covenants or restrictions. However, these covenants and restrictions are for the protection of lenders not stockholders.

3. (T)
4. (F) Revenue bonds are bonds whose interest is paid from specified revenue sources. Such bonds are usually issued by airports, school districts, counties, tollroad authorities, and other governmental bodies.

5. (T)
6. (F) Companies issuing bonds may choose to place privately a bond issue by selling bonds directly to a large institution, financial or otherwise, without the aid of an underwriter. The AICPA has no rules about initial bond placements.

7. (F) When bonds are issued between interest dates, the purchaser pays for interest accrued from the last interest payment date to the date of the purchase. Thus, the maximum amount of accrued interest a purchaser can be required to pay is 6 months (assuming semiannual interest).

8. (T)
9. (F) If bonds sell for more than face value, they are said to have sold at a premium. Thus, the effective rate of interest (annual amount of interest divided by issue price of the bonds) is less than the stated rate of interest.

10. (T)
11. (T)
12. (F) Under the effective interest method, the interest expense for each interest period is computed by multiplying the effective interest rate times the carrying amount of the bonds at the start of the period. The carrying amount of the bonds either increases (for bonds issued at a discount) or decreases (for bonds issued at a premium) each period by the amount of the amortized discount or premium.

13. (F) In-substance defeasance is an arrangement whereby a company provides for the future payment of a long-term debt issue by placing purchased securities in an irrevocable trust, the principal and interest of which are pledged to pay off the principal and interest of the debt issue as they mature. The company is not legally released from being the primary obligor under the debt that is considered to be still outstanding.

14. (T)
15. (T)
16. (F) Bond issue costs are debited to a deferred charge account for Unamortized Bond Issue Costs and amortized over the life of the debt in a manner similar to that used for discount on bonds.

17. (T)
18. (F) An imputed interest rate is determined at the time a debt instrument is issued. Any subsequent changes in prevailing interest rates are ignored.

19. (T)
20. (F) Project financing arrangements arise when (a) two or more entities form another entity to construct an operating plant that will be used by both parties; (b) the new entity borrows funds to construct the project and repays the debt from the proceeds received from the project; and (c) payment of the debt is guaranteed by the entities that formed the new company.

Multiple Choice

1. (C) $500,000 x .06 = $30,000 annual interest

   $30,000 ÷ 12 = $2,500 interest per month
   March 1 to July 1 is 4 months accrued interest
   4 x $2,500 = $10,000 accrued interest
   $500,000 + $10,000 = $510,000 proceeds

2. (A) Interest expense is based on the carrying value of the bonds (face value plus unamortized premium). Early in the life of the bond issue, interest expense is higher under the effective interest method because the carrying amount of the bonds includes the total premium. Under the straight-line method, the bond premium is allocated equally to each bond interest period. Studying the bond premium amortization table in the text will help demonstrate this relationship.

3. (D) Premiums and discounts on bonds are liability valuation accounts. The accounting profession requires that discounts be shown as deductions from the face value of bonds and premiums must be added to the face value.

4. (B) Cash... 312,000

Bonds Payable		300,000
Premium on Bonds		12,000

   ($300,000 x 1.04 = $312,000)

5. (C) Annual Interest: $30,000 x .05 = $15,000/year

Interest October to December	$3,750
Amortization of Premium ($12,000 ÷ 120 = $100 x 3).....................	300
Interest Expense 1988...	$3,450

6. (C) According to *FASB Statement No. 4*, gains or losses from extinguishment of debt should be reported in the income statement as an extraordinary item, net of related income tax effect.

7. (B) A project financing arrangement has nothing to do with the ability of either entity involved to enter into the project on their own. The other three alternatives (A, C, and D) are relevant characteristics.

8. (D) The difference between the fair market value of the land and the face value of this noninterest-bearing note is considered a discount on the notes. The discount should be amortized over the life of the note.

9. (A) If the fair value of the property is not determinable and if the debt instrument has no ready market, the present value of the debt instrument must be estimated. The estimation involves approximating (imputing) an interest rate. The imputed interest rate is used to establish the present value of the debt instrument by discounting, at that rate, all future payments on the debt.

10. (D) For a $100,000, 10%, 5-year bond issued at a $12,000 premium, the following cash flow applies:

Bond Proceeds		$112,000
Bond Interest (5 years at $10,000)......................	$50,000	
Maturity Value..	100,000	150,000
Net Cash Outflow		$ 38,000

Review Exercises

1. 8-1-90   Cash.. 788,000
                Discount on Bonds Payable .... 20,000(a)
                    Bonds Payable..   800,000
                    Accrued Interest on Bonds...   8,000(b)
       (a) $800,000 - ($800,000 x .975) = $20,000
       (b) $800,000 x .06) x 2/12 = $8,000

    12-1-90   Bond Interest Expense 16,800

                Accrued Interest on Bonds.. 8,000

                Cash..   24,000

                Discount on Bonds Payable ....   800(a)

       (a) 9 years = 108 months. 108 - 8 = 100

          ($20,000 ÷ 100) x 4 = $800

    12-31-90   Bond Interest Expense 4,200
                    Accrued Interest on Bonds...   4,000
                    Discount on Bonds Payable   200

2. Maturity value of bonds payable..   200,000
    Present value of $200,000 due in 4 years at 5% semiannual
       interest (Table 6-2).. $164,150
    Present value of $6,000 interest payable semiannually for
       4 years at 5% (Table 6-4)   43,021
    Proceeds from sale of bonds   207,171
    Premium on bonds .... $ 7,171

Schedule of Interest Expense and
Bond Premium Amortization
Effective Interest Method
6% Bonds Sold to Yield 5%

Date	Credit Cash	Debit Interest Expense	Debit Bond Premium	Carrying Value of Bonds
1-1-89	$	$	$	$207,171
7-1-89	6,000(a)	5,179(b)	821(c)	206,350(d)
7-1-90	6,000	5,159	841	205,509
7-1-90	6,000	5,138	862	204,647
1-1-91	6,000	5,116	884	203,763
7-1-91	6,000	5,094	906	202,857
1-1-92	6,000	5,071	929	201,928
7-1-92	6,000	5,048	952	200,976
1-1-93	6,000	5,024	976	200,000
	$48,000	$40,829	$7,171	

   (a) $6,000 = $200,000 x .06 x 6/12
   (b) $5,179 = $207,171 x .05 x 6/12
   (c) $ 821 = $6,000 - $5,179
   (d) $206,350 = $207,171 - $821

3. a. $4,000: ($6,000 x 4/6).
    b. $3,750: discount [(200,000 + 4,000) - 200,250].
    c. $6,000: amount of semiannual interest payment.
    d. $4,000: accrual of 4 months' interest, Sept. 1- Dec. 31.
    e. $6,194: 6 months' interest plus discount amortization (3,750 x 6/116).

4. (a) Cash 838,000
            Bonds Payable   800,000
            Premium on Bonds Payable   20,000
            Interest Expense   18,000

    (b) Interest Expense 36,000
            Cash   36,000

    (c) Interest Expense 24,000
            Accrued Interest Payable   24,000
        Premium on Bonds Payable 1,196.58
            Interest Expense 1,196.58
              (($20,000 ÷ 117) X 7 = $1,196.58)

    (d) Interest Expense 12,000
        Accrued Interest Payable 24,000
            Cash   36,000

    (e) Bonds Payable 350,000
        Premium on Bonds Payable 7,703*
        Interest Expense ($350,000 X .09 X 5/12) 13,125
            Cash ($353,500 + $13,125)   366,625
            Gain on Retirement ($357,703 - $353,500)   4,203

    (f) Interest Expense 20,250
            Cash   20,250

    (g) Interest Expense 13,500**
            Accrued Interest Payable   13,500

        Premium on Bonds Payable 1,677.34***
            Interest Expense 1,677.34

---

   *   ($20,000 x 350/800 x 103/117 = $7,703)
   **   ($450,000 x .09 X 4/12)
   ***   Amortization per year on $450,000
           ($20,000 X 12/117 x 450/800) $1,153.84
        Amortization on $350,000 for 7 months
           ($20,000 x 7/117 x 350/800)   523.50
                                    $1,677.34

15

Stockholders' equity: contributed capital

Chapter Synopsis

Chapter 15 is the first of two chapters that focus on the stockholders' equity section of the corporate form of business organization. The issues discussed in this chapter relate to the securities used to reflect ownership of the corporate form of business organization.

Chapter Review

1. The corporate form of business organization begins with the issuance of a **corporate charter** by the state in which incorporation is desired. Once the charter is issued, the corporation is recognized as a legal entity subject to the laws of the state of incorporation. The laws of the state of incorporation that govern owners' equity transactions are normally set out in the state's business corporation act.

2. Within a given class of stock, each share is exactly equal to every other share. A person's percent of ownership in a corporation is determined by the number of shares he or she possesses in relation to the total number of shares owned by all stockholders. In the absence of restrictive provisions, each share carries the right to participate proportionately in: (a) **profits,** (b) **management,** (c) **corporate assets upon liquidation,** and (d) **any new issues of stock of the same class (preemptive right).**

3. The transfer of ownership between individuals in the corporate form of organization is accomplished by one individual's selling or transferring his or her shares to another individual. The only requirement in terms of the corporation involved is that it be made aware of the name of the individual owning the stock. A subsidiary ledger of stock-holders is maintained by the corporation for the purpose of dividend payments, issuance of stock rights, and voting proxies. Many corporations employ independent **registrars and transfer agents** who specialize in providing services for recording and transferring stock.

4. The basic ownership interest in a corporation is represented by **common stock.** Common stock is guaranteed neither dividends nor assets upon dissolution of the corporation. Thus, common stock-holders are considered to hold a residual interest in the corporation. However, common stockholders generally control the management of the corporation and tend to profit most if the company is successful. In the event that a corporation has only one authorized issue of capital stock, that issue is by definition common stock, whether or not it is so designated in the charter.

5. The amount an individual pays for shares of stock in a corporation represents the maximum amount that individuals can lose in the event of corporate liquidation. This is known as the concept of **limited liability.**

6. **Par value** is an amount printed on each stock certificate. This establishes the nominal value per share and is the minimum amount that must be paid by each stockholder if the stock is to be fully paid when issued. Stock issued for more than par value is said to be issued at a **premium.** Conversely, stock issued for less than par value is said to be issued at a **discount.** When stock is issued at a discount by the corporation, the holders of such stock are contingently liable to corporate creditors for the amount of the discount. This contingency is realized only in the event of liquidation when creditor claims remain unsatisfied.

7. Profits of a corporation distributed to stockholders are referred to as **dividends.** In general, dividends can be paid only out of accumulated profits in excess of accumulated losses. The determination of profits and losses must be based on generally accepted accounting principles or standards. Also, dividends must be formally approved by the board of directors and be in full agreement with capital stock contracts.

8. When **par value stock** is issued, the Capital Stock (common or preferred) account is credited for an amount equal to par value times the number of shares issued. Any amount received in excess of par value is credited to a **premium account** representing **additional paid-in capital.**

9. When **no-par stock** is issued, the Capital Stock account is credited for an amount equal to the value of the consideration received. If no-par stock has a **stated value,** it may be accounted for in the same way as true no-par stock. Alternatively, the stated value may be con-

sidered similar to par value with any excess above stated value being accounted for as additional paid-in capital.

10. When stock is sold on a **subscription** basis, the full price of the stock is not received initially. Normally only a partial payment is made originally, and the stock is not issued until the full subscription price is received. When an individual subscribes to a common stock issue, the corporation debits **Subscriptions Receivable** and credits **Common Stock Subscribed.** If the subscription price exceeds the stock's par value, additional paid-in capital would be credited for the excess.

11. More than one class of stock is sometimes issued for a single payment or lump sum amount. Such a transaction requires allocation of the proceeds between the classes of securities involved. The two methods of allocation used are (a) the **proportional method** and (b) the **incremental method.** The former method is used when the fair market value for each class of security is readily determinable.

12. Stock issued for consideration other than cash should be recorded by using the fair market value of the consideration or the fair market value of the stock issued, whichever is more clearly determinable. In cases where the fair market value of both items is not clearly determinable, the board of directors has the authority to establish a value for the transaction.

13. The costs associated with issuing capital stock may be written off against additional paid-in capital or capitalized as organization costs and amortized against future earnings. The SEC permits use of either method.

14. When accountants use the term **capital** they mean stockholders' equity or owners' equity. They then classify stockholders' or owners' equity into two further categories -- **contributed capital** (paid-in capital) and **earned capital.** Contributed capital is composed of amounts paid in on capital stock. Earned capital consists of undistributed income that remains invested in the business.

15. **Treasury stock** is a corporation's own stock that (a) was outstanding, (b) has been reacquired by the corporation, and (c) is not retired. Treasury stock is not an asset and should be shown in the balance sheet as a reduction in stockholders' equity. Treasury stock is essentially the same as unissued stock.

16. Two methods are used in accounting for treasury stock, the **cost method** and the **par value method.** Under the cost method, treasury stock is recorded in the accounts at acquisition cost. When the treasury stock is reissued, the Treasury Stock account is credited for the acquisition cost. If treasury stock is reissued for **more** than its acquisition cost, the excess amount is credited to **Paid-in Capital from Treasury Stock.** If treasury stock is reissued for **less** than its acquisition cost, the difference should be debited to any paid-in capital from previous

treasury stock transactions. If the balance in this account is insufficient, the remaining difference is charged to retained earnings.

17. Treasury stock accounted for under the par value method is debited to the Treasury Stock account at the stock's par value. Any original premium or discount related to the shares reacquired is removed from the accounts. Any excess of par value and related premium or discount over the acquisition cost is credited to Paid-in Capital from Treasury Stock. When acquisition cost exceeds par value and the related premium or discount, the difference is debited to Retained Earnings. If the treasury shares accounted for under the par value method are reissued, the accounting treatment is the same as that accorded any original issuance of stock.

18. Under the cost method, the cost of treasury stock is shown in the balance sheet as a deduction from the total of all owners' equity accounts. When the par value method is used, the total par value of treasury shares is shown as a deduction from the class of stock to which they relate.

19. **Preferred stock** is the term used to describe a class of stock that possesses certain preferences or features not possessed by the common stock. Preferred stock issues generally:
   a. Receive preference as to dividends.
   b. Receive preference as to assets in the event of liquidation.
   c. Are convertible into common stock.
   d. Are callable at the option of the corporation.

Some features used to distinguish preferred stock from common stock tend to be restrictive. For example, preferred stock may be **nonvoting, noncumulative,** and **nonparticipating.** A corporation may attach whatever preferences or restrictions in whatever combination it desires to a preferred stock issue so long as it does not specifically violate its state incorporation law.

20. Certain terms are used to describe various features of preferred stock. These terms are the following:
   a. **Cumulative.** Dividends not paid in any year must be made up in a later year before any profits can be distributed to common stockholders. Unpaid annual dividends on cumulative preferred stock are referred to as **dividends in arrears.**
   b. **Participating.** Preferred stock, that is participating, shares with the common stockholders in any profit distribution beyond a prescribed rate. This participation involves a pro rata distribution based on the total par value of the outstanding preferred and common stock.

c. **Convertible.** Preferred stockholders may, at their option, exchange their preferred shares for common stock on the basis of a predetermined ratio.

d. **Callable.** At the option of the issuing corporation, preferred shares can be redeemed at specified future dates and at stipulated prices.

21. Sometimes, because of the features attached to it, an issue of preferred stock is more characteristic of debt than of equity. However, despite the existence of creditorship characteristics, preferred stock is always accounted for as an equity security and is universally reported in the stockholders' equity section of the balance sheet.

REVIEW QUESTIONS AND EXERCISES

True-False

Indicate whether each of the following is true (T) or false (F) in the space provided.

_____ 1. Contributions by shareholders (paid-in capital) and income retained by the corporation represent the two primary sources from which corporate equity is derived.

_____ 2. Most corporations are granted their charters directly by the federal government.

_____ 3. Dividends in arrears on preferred stock should be classified on the balance sheet as a liability.

_____ 4. The preemptive right protects an existing stockholder from involuntary dilution of ownership interest.

_____ 5. The existence of a call price tends to set a ceiling on the market value of the preferred shares unless they are convertible into common stock.

_____ 6. Preferred stock does not have the voting right unless it possesses the participating feature.

_____ 7. The par value of a share of common stock usually is a good indication of what the stock is worth on the market.

_____ 8. In most states common stock subscribers who have signed a valid subscription contract have the same rights and privileges as stockholders who hold outstanding shares of common stock.

_____ 9. Common stock subscribed should be included in the liabilities section of the balance sheet.

_____ 10. Treasury shares are issued shares of the company's own stock that have been reacquired but not retired.

_____ 11. Treasury stock should be shown as a deduction from total stockholders' equity.

_____ 12. Treasury shares represent a reduction in the number of outstanding shares but not in the number of issued shares.

_____ 13. The gain on the sale of treasury stock should be included in income before extraordinary items on the income statement.

_____ 14. An investor who purchases treasury shares at less than the issuing company's cost may be held contingently liable to the company's creditors for this difference.

_____ 15. When capital stock is issued for noncash assets, the assets received should be recorded at the par value of the stock issued.

_____ 16. The acquisition of treasury shares at less than the original issue price of the shares increases total stockholders' equity.

_____ 17. Total stockholders' equity will be the same if the cost method is used to account for treasury stock as it will be if the par value method is used.

_____ 18. The dividend preference related to preferred stock is merely an assurance that the stated dividend rate or amount must be paid before any dividends can be paid on the common stock.

_____ 19. A convertible preferred stock issue normally will sell for a lower price than the same issue would without the conversion feature.

_____ 20. Under the cost method, the entire proceeds from reissuance of donated treasury shares is credited to Paid-in Capital from Treasury Stock or Donated Capital.

Multiple Choice

Select the best answer for each of the following items and enter the corresponding letter in the space provided.

_____ 1. In January 1990 Bell Corporation, a newly formed company, issued 10,000 shares of its $10 par common stock for $15 per share. On Julu 1, 1990, Bell Corporation reacquired 1,000 shares of its outstanding stock for $12 per share. The acquisition of these treasury shares:

A. decreased total stockholders' equity.
B. increased total stockholders' equity.
C. did not change total stockholders' equity.
D. decreased the number of issued shares.

_____ 2. Which of the following is **not** a legal restriction related to profit distributions by a corporation?

A. No amounts may be distributed among the owners unless the corporation capital is maintained intact.

B. The amount distributed in any one year can never exceed the net income reported for that year.

C. Profit distributions must be formally approved by the board of directors.

D. Dividends must be in full agreement with the capital stock contracts as to preferences and participation.

Answers to questions 3-6 are to be based on the following information.

At the opening of business January 1, 1990, Morris Corporation's records showed the following stockholders' equity information:

Preferred stock, 6%, $100 par
(1,000 shares) $100,000
Common stock, $100 par
(1,000 shares) 100,000
                                                                   200,000
Retained earnings 500,000
                                                                   $700,000

No dividends were paid to preferred stockholders in 1989, and none have yet been paid in 1990. On December 31, 1990, the directors of Morris Corporation declared a total cash dividend of $50,000.

_____ 3. If the preferred stockholders' share of the $50,000 total cash dividend is $6,000, the preferred stock must be:
A. cumulative and fully participating.
B. cumulative and nonparticipating.
C. noncumulative and fully participating.
D. noncumulative and nonparticipating.

_____ 4. If the preferred stockholders' share of the $50,000 total cash dividend is $12,000, the preferred stock must be:
A. cumulative and fully participating.
B. cumulative and nonparticipating.
C. noncumulative and fully participating.
D. noncumulative and nonparticipating.

_____ 5. If the preferred stockholders' share of the $50,000 total cash dividend is $28,000, the preferred stock must be:
A. cumulative and fully participating.
B. cumulative and partially participating.
C. noncumulative and fully participating.
D. noncumulative and partially participating.

_____ 6. If the preferred stockholders' share of the $50,000 total cash dividend is $15,000, the preferred stock must be:
A. cumulative and fully participating.
B. cumulative and partially participating.

C. noncumulative and fully participating.
D. noncumulative and partially participating.

_____ 7. An unacceptable method of reporting treasury stock transactions is:
A. to include losses on the sale of treasury stock as a direct charge against retained earnings.
B. to include losses on the sale of treasury stock as an extraordinary loss in the income statement.
C. to deduct the cost of treasury stock from total stockholders' equity in the balance sheet.
D. to deduct from retained earnings the excess of the amount paid for the treasury stock over the original issue price.

_____ 8. Treasury stock is:
A. canceled as soon as it is acquired.
B. a current asset.
C. the same as unissued stock.
D. included in issued shares.

_____ 9. Which of the following should not be included in the paid-in capital section of the balance sheet?
A. Retained earnings.
B. Premium on preferred stock.
C. Excess of sales price of no-par stock over its stated value.
D. Excess of sales price of treasury stock over its acquisition cost.

_____ 10. On the balance sheet common stock subscriptions receivable normally should be:
A. combined with trade receivables in the current asset section.
B. included in the stockholders' equity section as a deduction from common stock subscribed.
C. included in current assets as a separate item.
D. shown in the long-term investments section.

Review Exercises

1. Delta Corporation's stockholders' equity at December 31, 1989, is as follows:

Common stock, $10, par (10,000
shares) $100,000
Paid-in capital in excess of par 3,000
.... 103,000
Retained earnings 197,000
    Total stockholders' equity $300,000

The following treasury stock transactions occurred during 1990.

Jan. 2 -- Purchased at $12 per share, 1,000 shares of Delta Corporation common stock.

Feb. 4 -- Sold 500 shares of treasury stock at $13 per share.

May 10 -- Sold 500 shares of treasury stock at $8 per share.

Prepare journal entries to record the treasury stock transactions in 1990 under each of the following methods:
a. Cost method.
b. Par value method.

2. On January 6,1990, Ellis Corporation received a charter granting the right to issue 8,000 shares of $100 par value, 8% cumulative, nonparticipating preferred stock and 40,000 shares of $10 par value common stock. The following transactions were completed during 1990.
a. Received subscriptions to 25,000 shares of common stock at $15 per share. Down payments totaling 25% accompanied the subscriptions.
b. sold 5,000 shares of common stock for $13 per share.
c. Issued 4,000 shares of preferred stock to Karin Corporation for the following assets: equipment with a fair market value of $175,000; a factory building with a fair market value of $220,000; and land with an appraised value of $75,000.
d. Collected the balance of the subscription price on the common stock and issued the shares.
e. Declared the preferred dividend and a $.25 per share cash dividend on the common stock. (Net income for the year totaled $82,000.)

Required

A. Prepare the journal entries for the transactions listed above.
B. Prepare the stockholders' equity section of Ellis Corporation's balance sheet as of December 31,1990.

3. Staggs Corporation entered into the following stock transactions during the past year:
a. Received a charter allowing it to issue 15,000 shares of $100 par value preferred stock and 18,000 shares of $20 par value common stock.
b. Issued 11,000 shares of common stock to the corporate founders in exchange for land and a building valued by the board of directors at $70,000 and $215,000 respectively.
c. Sold 9,000 shares of preferred stock for $115 per share.
d. Sold 1,000 shares of preferred stock after value and 800 shares of common stock at $50 per share to an investor.
e. Purchased 500 shares of preferred stock for $108 per share.
f. Purchased 700 shares of common stock for $72 per share.
g. Sold 300 shares of the preferred stock held as treasury stock for $110 per share.
h. Resold 400 shares of common stock held as treasury stock for $65 per share.

Required

A. Prepare journal entries for the transactions noted above. No other transactions have affected the stock accounts. Record all treasury stock transactions using the cost method.
B. Assuming that Staggs Corporation had retained earnings of $187,000, prepare the stockholders' equity section of its balance sheet based on the above transaction.

SOLUTIONS TO REVIEW QUESTIONS AND EXERCISES

True-False

1. (T)

2. (F) Anyone who wishes to establish a corporation must submit articles of incorporation to the proper department of the government of the state in which incorporation is desired. The federal government does not become involved in the granting of corporate charters.

3. (F) No liability exists for preferred dividends in arrears. The only time a liability exists for dividends is after they are declared by the board of directors. Thus, any dividends in arrears on preferred stock should be disclosed in a footnote to the financial statements.

4. (T)

5. (T)

6. (F) The participating feature of preferred stock refers to the right of preferred shareholders to share ratably with the common stockholders in any profit distribution beyond the prescribed rate. Preferred stock is nonvoting stock.

7. (F) The par value of a stock issued has no relationship to the fair market value of the stock. Par value has but one real significance, it establishes the maximum responsibility of a stockholder in the event of corporate insolvency or other involuntary dissolution.

8. (T)

9. (F) Common stock subscribed is presented in the stockholders' equity section below common or preferred stock. This account indicates the corporation's obligation to issue shares of common stock upon payment of final subscription balances by those who have subscribed for stock. In order for an account to be included in the liability section of the balance sheet, the corporation has to intend to liquidate the item using corporate assets.

10. (T)

11. (T)

12. (T)

13. (F) If treasury stock is reissued at a price in excess of the acquisition cost, the excess is credited to an account titled Paid-in Capital from Treasury Stock. This account is shown in the equity section of the balance sheet. A corporation cannot report a "gain" or a "loss" from dealing in its own stock.

14. (F) Whether treasury stock is accounted for under the cost method or the par value method, no contingent liability exists for the reissuance of the treasury stock below its original acquisition price.

15. (F) The general rule to be applied when stock is issued for assets other than cash is that the noncash assets be recorded at either their fair market value or the fair market value of the stock issued, whichever is more clearly determinable.

16. (F) The amount debited to the Treasury Stock account at acquisition is deducted from total stockholders' equity. Thus, no matter what the reacquisition price, total stockholders' equity will decrease when treasury stock is acquired.

17. (T)

18. (T)

19. (F) The shareholder who owns convertible preferred stock not only enjoys the preferred claim on dividends, but also has the option of converting into a common shareholder. Because of the attractiveness of this feature, convertible preferred stock will normally sell for a higher price than the same issue would without the conversion feature.

20. (T)

Multiple Choice

1. (A) Total stockholders' equity is reduced by the carrying amount of treasury stock. Under the cost method, treasury stock is subtracted from the total of capital stock, additional paid-in capital, and retained earnings. When the par value method is used, treasury stock is reported in the balance sheet as a deduction from issued shares of the same class in order to show those outstanding. Under both methods, the total stockholders' equity is the same even though the components are different in amount.

2. (B) Alternatives A, C, and D represent legal restrictions related to profit distribution by a corporation. Alternative B is not a legal restriction. Even though corporations may not pay dividends in excess of total earnings, they can distribute a dividend in a particular year that exceeds the earnings for that year as long as they have undistributed earnings from prior years.

3. (D) If no dividends were paid in 1989 and the preferred stock does not receive a dividend for that year, they are not cumulative. The preferred stock is also not participating because the common shareholders received all the remaining dividends ($44,000) without any pro rata distribution to preferred shareholders.

4. (B) If preferred shareholders receive $12,000, they must be cumulative and nonparticipating. The $12,000 represents the current year's 6% dividend and last year's 6% dividend in arrears.

5. (A) The $28,000 dividend received by the preferred shareholders represents a cumulative and fully participating preferred stock. The $28,000 dividend includes:

One year's dividend in arrears	$6,000
Current year's dividends	6,000
Pro rata participation ($6,000 to common and the remainder divided based on total par values --	
$32,000 ÷ 2	16,000
	$28,000

6. (B) or (D) From the facts it is unclear whether the stock is cumulative or not. If the preferred is cumulative, or we know the preferred receives a $12,000 dividend ($6,000 from last year and $6,000 from this year). The fact that the preferred received $15,000 indicates that it could be cumulative and partially participating. However, the preferred could also be noncumulative and partially participating, which would mean they receive $6,000 for this year's dividend and $9,000 from the partially participating feature. If the preferred were noncumulative and fully participating, the dividend would be $25,000 ($6,000 + $19,000).

7. (B) When treasury stock is sold for less than the amount it was acquired for, the difference is debited to Paid-in-Capital from Treasury Stock or Retained Earnings under the cost method. Paid-in-Capital from Treasury Stock or Retained Earnings would also be debited under the par value method if treasury stock was reissued for less than par value.

8. (D) Treasury stock is a company's own stock that has been reacquired after having been issued and fully paid. In order for stock to be classified as treasury stock, it must remain uncanceled in the corporate treasury. Thus, treasury stock is considered to be issued but not outstanding.

9. (A) Paid-in-Capital refers to corporate capital that has been paid in by owners as a result of transactions involving the company's stock. Retained earnings is referred to as earned capital because it results from earnings retained in the business. Retained earnings is excluded from the paid-in-capital section of the balance sheet and is normally shown as the final item in the stockholders' equity section.

10. (C) Subscriptions receivable are normally collectible within one year, so they are properly classified as a current asset. However, they should be shown separately from trade receivables because subscriptions receivable do not result from the sale of goods and services in the normal course of business.

Review Exercises

1. a. **Cost Method**

Jan. 2	Treasury Stock (1,000 x 12)..	12,000	
	Cash..		12,000
Feb. 4	Cash (500 x 13)..	6,500	
	Treasury Stock (500 x 12)..		6,000
	Paid-in Capital from Treasury Stock..		500
May 10	Cash (500 x 8)...	4,000	
	Paid-in Capital from Treasury Stock..	500	
	Retained Earnings..	1,500	
	Treasury Stock..		6,000

   b. **Par value method**

Jan. 2	Treasury Stock (1,000 x 10)...	10,000	
	Paid-in Capital in Excess of Par (10% of 3,000)	300	
	Retained Earnings	1,700	
	Cash..		12,000
Feb. 4	Cash (500 x 13)..	6,500	
	Treasury Stock (500 x 10)...		5,000
	Paid-in Capital in Excess of Par..		1,500
May 10	Cash (500 x 8)...	4,000	
	Retained Earnings	1,000	
	Treasury Stock..		5,000

or

Cash...	4,000	
Paid-in Capital in Excess of Par..	1,000	
Treasury Stock...		5,000

2. (1) a.

Subscriptions receivable -- Common..	375,000	
Common Stock Subscribed..		250,000
Paid-in Capital in Excess of		
Par -- Common..		125,000
Cash	93,750	
Subscriptions Receivable -- Common		93,750

   b.

Cash	65,000	
Common Stock		50,000
Paid-in Capital in Excess of Par -- Common		15,000

   c.

Equipment...	175,000	
Building	220,000	
Land	75,000	
Preferred Stock...		400,000
Paid-in Capital in Excess of Par -- Preferred		70,000

   d.

Cash	281,250	
Subscriptions Receivable -- Common		281,250
Common Stock Subscribed..	250,000	
Common Stock		250,000

   e.

Retained Earnings	39,500	
Cash Dividend Payable -- Common		7,500*
Cash Dividend Payable -- Preferred...		32,000**

   *(30,000 shares of outstanding x .25 = $7,500)

   **(4,000 shares outstanding x $100 par value x .08 = $32,000)

(2)	**Stockholder's Equity:**

Preferred stock 8% -- par value $100 per share, cumulative, nonparticipating, 8,000 shares authorized, 4,000 shares issued and outstanding	$400,000
Common stock -- par value $10 per share, 40,000 shares authorized, 30,000 issued and outstanding	300,000
Paid-in Capital in Excess of Par -- Preferred	70,000
Paid-in Capital in Excess of Par -- Common	140,000
Total Paid-in Capital	910,000
Retained earnings	42,500***
Total stockholders' equity	$952,500

***($84,000 - $39,500)

3.	a.	Journal Entries:
1.	No entry necessary.

2. Land	70,000	
Building	215,000	
Common Stock		220,000
Paid-in-Capital in Excess of Par -- Common stock		65,000
3. Cash	1,035,000	
Preferred stock		900,000
Paid-in-Capital in Excess of Par -- Common Stock		135,000
4. Cash	140,000	
Common Stock		16,000
Paid-in-Capital in Excess of Par -- Common Stock		24,000
Preferred Stock		100,000
5. Treasury Stock -- Preferred	54,000	
Cash		54,000
6. Treasury Stock -- Common	50,400	
Cash		50,400
7. Cash	33,000	
Treasury Stock -- Preferred (108 x 300)		32,400
Paid-in-Capital from Treasury Stock-Preferred		600
8. Cash	26,000	
Paid-in-Capital in Excess of Par -- Common Stock	2,200	
Treasury Stock -- Common ($72 x 400)		28,800

B.

Staggs Corporation
Stockholders' Equity Section

Preferred Stock -- Par value $100 per share;		
Authorized 15,000 shares; issued 10,000 shares	$1,000,000	
Additional Paid-in Capital -- Preferred Stock	135,000	
		1,135,000
Common Stock -- Par value $30 per share;		
Authorized 18,000 shares; issued 11,800 shares	236,000	
Additional Paid-in Capital -- Common Stock	86,800	
		322,800
Additional Paid-in Capital from Treasury		
Stock -- Preferred		600
Total Paid-in Capital		1,458,400
Retained Earnings* (see note)		187,000
Total Paid-in Capital and Retained Earnings		$1,645,400
Less Cost of Treasury Stock (21, 600 Preferred +		
21,600 Common)		43,200
		$1,602,200

*Retained earnings are restricted for dividends in the amount of $43,200, the cost of treasury stock on hand.

16

Stockholders' equity:
retained earnings

Chapter Synopsis

Chapter 16 concludes the discussion of stockholders' equity. The focus in this chapter is on the accounts that appear in the stockholders' equity section in addition to capital stock.

Chapter Review

1. Stockholders' equity is composed of two concepts: (a) **contributed capital** and (b) **earned capital**. Capital stock and additional paid-in capital represent contributed capital, and retained earnings represents earned capital.

2. **Retained earnings** is a number that represents the excess of corporate net incomes over corporate net losses, less any dividends distributed to stockholders. Thus, retained earnings is increased by net income and prior period adjustments that result in gains. It is decreased by net losses, prior period adjustments that result in losses, dividends, and some treasury stock transactions.

3. The state incorporation laws normally provide information concerning the legal restrictions related to the payment of dividends. At any rate, corporations rarely pay dividends in an amount equal to the legal limit. That is due, in part, to the fact that assets represented by undistributed earnings are used to finance future operations of the business. If a company is considering declaring a dividend, two preliminary questions must be asked: (a) Is the condition of the corporation such that the dividend is **legally permissible**?, and (b) Is the condition of the corporation such that a dividend is **economically sound**?

4. A major reason for restricting dividend payments concerns the laws of some states that require that earnings equivalent to the cost of treasury shares purchased be restricted from dividend declarations. If the corporation buys its own outstanding stock, it has reduced its legal capital and distributed assets to stockholders. If this were permitted without restriction, the corporation could, by purchasing treasury stock at any price desired, return to stockholders their investments and leave creditors with little or no protection against loss.

5. Although the unencumbered credit balance in retained earnings is normally considered to provide the basis for dividend distributions, management must consider other financial conditions as well. If funds are unavailable for the payment of dividends, the extent of the credit balance in retained earnings is of little significance. Thus, before a dividend is declared, the question of availability of funds to pay the dividend must be considered.

6. The SEC encourages companies to disclose their dividend policy in their annual report. For example, companies that (a) have earnings but fail to pay dividends or (b) do not expect to pay dividends in the forseeable future are encouraged to report this information. In addition, companies that have had a consistent pattern of paying dividends are encouraged to indicate whether they intend to continue this practice in the future.

7. **Dividends** may be paid in cash (most common means), stock, scrip, or some other asset. Dividends other than a stock dividend reduce the stockholders' equity in a corporation through an immediate or promised distribution of assets. **Stock dividends** merely transfer a portion of the retained earnings account to contributed capital accounts in the stockholders' equity section.

8. The accounting for a **cash dividend** requires information concerning three dates: (a) **date of declaration**, (b) **date of record**, and (c) **date of payment**. A liability is established by a charge to retained earnings on the declaration date for the amount of the dividend declared. No accounting entry is required on the date of record. The liability is liquidated on the payment date through a distribution of cash.

9. **Property dividends** represent distributions of corporate assets other than cash. According to *APB Opinion No. 29*, a property dividend is a nonreciprocal transfer of nonmonetary assets between an enterprise and its owners. **Such transfers should be recorded at the fair value of the assets transferred.** Fair value is measured by the amount that would be realized in an outright sale near the time of distribution. When the property dividend is declared, fair market value should be recognized in the accounts with the appropriate gain or

loss recorded. The fair market value then serves as the basis used in accounting for the property dividend.

10. **Scrip dividends** are normally declared when the corporation has a sufficient credit balance in retained earnings but is short of cash. When a scrip dividend is declared, a special form of note is issued to stockholders, payable on some future date.

11. **Liquidating dividends** represent a return of the stockholders' investment rather than a distribution of profits. In a more general sense, any dividend not based on profits must be a reduction of corporate capital, and to that extent, it is a liquidating dividend.

12. A **stock dividend** can be defined as a **capitalization of retained earnings** that results in a reduction in retained earnings and a corresponding increase in certain contributed capital accounts. Total stockholders' equity remains unchanged when a stock dividend is distributed. Also, all stockholders retain their same proportionate share of ownership in the corporation.

13. Generally accepted accounting principles (GAAP) require that the accounting for stock dividends be based on the **fair market value of the stock issued**. When a stock dividend is declared, Retained Earnings is debited at the fair market value of the stock to be distributed. The entry includes a credit to **Common Stock Dividend Distributable** at par value times the number of shares, with any excess credited to **Paid-in Capital in Excess of Par**. Common Stock Dividend Distributable is reported in the stockholders' equity section between the declaration date and date of issuance.

14. A **stock split** results in an increase or decrease in the number of shares outstanding with a corresponding decrease or increase in the par or stated value per share. No accounting entry is required for a stock split as the total dollar amount of all stockholders' equity accounts remains unchanged. A stock split is usually intended to improve the marketability of the shares by reducing the market price of the stock being split. In general, the difference between a stock split and a stock dividend is based upon the size of the distribution. **If the number of shares issued exceeds 20 or 25% of the shares outstanding, treatment as a stock split is warranted.**

15. An **appropriation of retained earnings** serves to restrict retained earnings for a specific purpose. In general, the reasons for retained earnings appropriations concerns the corporation's desire to reduce the basis upon which dividends are declared (unappropriated credit balance in retained earnings). In an indirect manner, this process serves to limit the outflow of assets in the form of dividends.

16. To establish an appropriation of retained earnings, a corporation prepares a journal entry, **debiting** unappropriated retained earnings and **crediting** a specific appropriations account (for example, **Retained Earnings Appropriated for Sinking Fund**). Notice that the entry is confined to stockholders' equity accounts and does not directly affect corporate assets. The only way to dispose of an appropriation of retained earnings is to reverse the entry that created the appropriation.

17. **Self-insurance** refers to a situation where a business enterprise chooses to assume the risk of loss associated with certain casualties rather than transfer that risk to an insurance company. At the present time, two methods are acceptable in accounting for self-insurance. These methods are described as follows:

a. Make no entries in the accounts except for losses incurred as they arise.

b. Appropriate retained earnings annually; when losses occur, reverse the entry appropriating retained earnings and charge losses against revenues of the period in which the losses occur.

Prior to 1975 it was considered acceptable to accrue a portion of anticipated losses as an annual expense. This method is no longer acceptable for accounting or tax purposes.

18. A corporation that has accumulated a large debit balance (deficit) in retained earnings may, under the law of certain states, enter into a process known as a **quasi reorganization**. This procedure consists of the following steps:

a. All assets are revalued at appropriate current values so the company will not be burdened with excessive inventory or fixed asset valuations in following years. Any loss on revaluation increases the deficit.

b. Paid-in or other types of capital must be available or must be created, at least equal in amount to the deficit. If no such capital exists, it is created through donation of stock to the corporation by stockholders, by reduction of the par value of shares outstanding, or by some similar means.

c. The deficit is then eliminated by a charge against paid-in capital.

In addition to the steps above, a quasi reorganization requires (1) approval by stockholders, (2) fair and unbiased valuation of assets, (3) a zero balance in retained earnings at the conclusion of the reorganization, (4) the date of the quasi reorganization shown with retained earnings for the succeeding 10 years, and (5) that the amount of the deficit eliminated be disclosed in the balance sheet for three years.

REVIEW QUESTIONS AND EXERCISES

True - False

Indicate whether each of the following is true (T) or false (F) in the space provided.

____ 1. Capital stock and additional paid-in capital are considered donated capital, whereas retained earnings is considered earned capital.

____ 2. In general, the only owners' equity account that should ever have a debit balance is retained earnings.

____ 3. Extraordinary items do not affect retained earnings, as they are taken directly to the income statement.

____ 4. Very few companies pay dividends in amounts equal to their retained earnings legally available for dividends.

____ 5. The current cash position of a corporation is a prime consideration in deciding whether a cash dividend should be declared.

____ 6. Any dividend other than a stock dividend reduces the stockholders' equity in the corporation.

____ 7. All things being equal, growth companies tend to pay larger dividends than well-established companies, because growth companies have to provide an extra incentive for potential investors.

____ 8. A property dividend is a nonreciprocal transfer of nonmonetary assets between an enterprise and its owners.

____ 9. The distribution of a nonmonetary asset as an ordinary dividend may be regarded as equivalent to an exchange with owners and, therefore, recorded at the book value of the nonmonetary asset distributed.

____ 10. Any dividend not based on profits must be a reduction of corporate capital, and to that extent, it is a liquidating dividend.

____ 11. A stock dividend results in a capitalization of retained earnings with no corresponding decrease in stockholders' equity.

____ 12. One of the major distinctions between a stock split and a stock dividend is the fact that a stock split alters the par or stated value of the stock issue involved, while a stock dividend does not affect par or stated value.

____ 13. According to *FASB Statement No. 5*, the appropriation of retained earnings is acceptable practice as long as the assets set aside as a result of the appropriation are clearly disclosed in the financial statements.

____ 14. When an appropriation of retained earnings is established to cover the possibility of a specific loss, the subsequent incurrence of the loss may be charged directly to the appropriation because it will ultimately affect retained earnings.

____ 15. The concept of self-insurance is based on the belief that losses will be less over an extended period of time than the premiums that would be paid to insure against such losses.

____ 16. With respect to uninsured losses that may result from injury to others or damage to the property of others, accruing for such losses prior to their occurrence is acceptable only when such events are reasonably expected to occur.

____ 17. In most cases, a footnote to the financial statements can accomplish the same objectives as an appropriation of retained earnings in a more informative manner.

____ 18. *APB Opinion No. 12* indicated that disclosure of changes in the individual accounts comprising stockholders' equity is required to make the financial statements sufficiently informative.

____ 19. A quasi reorganization is a procedure whereby a corporation operating in a particular industry may discontinue operations in that industry and begin a new operation with essentially the same stockholders.

____ 20. A quasi reorganization results in an increase in the retained earnings account of the company entering into the process.

Multiple Choice

Select the best answer for each of the following items and enter the corresponding letter in the space provided.

____ 1. Two alternatives exist once a credit balance in retained earnings is recorded, it can be left intact and the offsetting assets used in the operations of the business or it can be:
A. reduced by a distribution of assets to the stockholders.
B. increased as a result of a sale of common stock above par value.
C. increased as a result of a sale of treasury stock at an amount in excess of par value.
D. reduced by a distribution of assets to creditors.

____ 2. G. F. Hanks Company declared a dividend which resulted in each stockholder receiving a special form of note payable, bearing a 3% interest rate and due in 6 months. This type of dividend is known as a (an):

A. equity dividend.
B. scrip dividend.
C. property dividend.
D. payable dividend.

____ 3. At the beginning of 1990, M.R. Ballard Company had retained earnings of $100,000. During the year Ballard reported net income of $50,000, sold treasury stock at a gain of $18,000, declared a cash dividend of $30,000, and declared and issued a stock dividend of 1,500 shares ($10 par value) when the market value of the stock was $20 per share. The amount of retained earnings available for dividends at the end of 1990 was:

A. $ 90,000.
B. $105,000.
C. $108,000.
D. $123,000.

____ 4. J. Talbot Cotton Company has 280,000 shares of $10 par value common stock outstanding. During the year Talbot declared a 5% stock dividend when the market price of the stock was $24 per share. Two months later Talbot declared a $.60 per share cash dividend. As a result of the dividends declared during the year, retained earnings decreased by:

A. $168,000.
B. $176,400.
C. $336,000.
D. $512,400.

____ 5. A feature common to both stock dividends and stock splits is:

A. a reduction in total stockholders' equity of a corporation.
B. a transfer from retained earnings to additional paid-in capital.
C. a reduction in market value per share.
D. a change in the number of shares of stock outstanding.

____ 6. When a corporation declares a property dividend, the corporation should:

A. divide the property equally among all stockholders.
B. record the dividend by debiting retained earnings for an amount equal to the fair value of the property to be distributed.
C. record the dividend by debiting retained earnings for an amount equal to the book value of the property to be distributed.
D. record the dividend on its books at the carrying value of the property distributed and inform stockholders as to the fair

value of the property so they may individually recognize a gain or loss.

____ 7. Which of the following specific appropriations of retained earnings does the FASB discourage a corporation from establishing?

A. Appropriation for Plant Expansion.
B. Appropriation for Bond Sinking Fund.
C. Appropriation for Future Losses.
D. Appropriation for Product Liability Suit Pending.

____ 8. Which of the following is not a requirement in accomplishing a quasi reorganization?

A. Approval should be received from corporate stockholders before the process is put into effect.
B. Retained earnings as of the date of a quasi reorganization must have a zero balance.
C. Retained earnings must be "dated" for a period of approximately 10 years to show the fact and the date of the quasi reorganization.
D. Assets should be written up by an amount that eliminates the deficit in retained earnings.

____ 9. A common justification for a corporation instituting a self-insurance program is:

A. the risk of loss can be spread over a large number of possible loss events that individually would be small in relation to the total potential loss.
B. insurance premiums reduce net income in periods when losses do not occur and thus the matching principle is violated.
C. a corporation with one major location should self-insure because insurance companies rarely provide a sufficient amount of funds to replace destroyed facilities.
D. over the long run, self-insurance is always the least costly method for insuring corporate property.

____ 10. Which of the following methods is unacceptable for accounting and tax purposes, as they pertain to self-insurance?

A. Make no entries in the accounts except for losses incurred as they arise.
B. Appropriate retained earnings annually and charge losses against revenues of the period in which the losses occur.
C. Accrue a portion of the anticipated losses annually as an expense.
D. All of the foregoing are acceptable for accounting purposes. However, item C is unacceptable for tax purposes.

Review Exercises

1. Coe Corporation has 100,000 shares of common stock outstanding. The corporation also owns 100,000 shares of Koch Company common stock purchased 5 years ago at $10 per share. Coe decided to distribute the Koch Company stock as a property dividend on the basis of one share of Koch stock for each share of Coe stock owned. The Koch stock has a current market value of $25 per share and has been accounted for using the cost method since the date of acquisition. Prepare the journal entries Coe Corporation would make for the declaration and payment of the dividend.

2. On January 1, 1990, the Hugh Hoyt Company burned to the ground, and all of the company's accounting records were destroyed. Because the company must pay income taxes for the year 1989, the board of directors has come to you for assistance in arriving at a reasonable estimate of the company's 1989 net income before income taxes. Though the company has no documents to substantiate the following, the company's bookkeeper does remember a few balances and transactions that took place during 1989. Using the pertinent data from below prepare a statement estimating Hugh Hoyt Company's 1989 net income before income taxes.

Unappropriated Retained Earnings balance, January 1, 1989	$65,900
Unappropriated Retained Earnings balance, December 31,1989	40,900
Established a reserve for plant expansion during June 1989	26,000
Cash in bank, December 31, 1989	7,965
Stock dividend declared and distributed during 1989	4,000
Issued 100 shares of $100 par value common stock at $103	10,300
Declared and paid a cash dividend during 1989	5,000
Accounts payable, December 31, 1989	8,000

3. The Merino Company has accumulated a large deficit in retained earnings over the past 10 years. The company has just developed a new product line, and prospects for future operations are quite good. The management of Merino Company is interested in effecting a quasi reorganization and has received appropriate approval from existing stockholders. Describe the accounting procedures required of a company effecting a quasi reorganization.

4. As of December 31, 1990, Coda Corporation had outstanding 1,000 shares of $100 par value 6% preferred stock and 5,000 shares of $10 par value common stock. Cash dividends were declared and paid during 1991-93 as follows:

$$1991-- \quad \$ 3,000$$
$$1992-- \quad \$11,000$$
$$1993-- \quad \$21,000$$

Assuming that there were no changes in the number of shares of stock outstanding, determine the amount of cash dividends paid to each class of stock under each of the following assumptions about the preferred stock.

a. Preferred stock is noncumulative and nonparticipating.

Year	Total Dividend	To Preferred	To Common
1991	$ 3,000		
1992	$11,000		
1993	$21,000		

b. Preferred stock is cumulative and nonparticipating.

Year	Total Dividend	To Preferred	To Common
1991	$ 3,000		
1992	$11,000		
1993	$21,000		

c.   Preferred stock is cumulative and fully participating.

Year	Total Dividend	To Preferred	To Common
1991	$ 3,000		
1992	$11,000		
1993	$21,000		

5.   The Frazier Corporation has the following accounts in its stockholders' equity section at the beginning of 1990:

Preferred Stock, $100 par value, 7% cumulative and nonparticipating, 5,000 shares authorized, 4,000 shares issued and outstanding (one year's dividends in arrears)	$400,000
Common Stock, $5 par value, 35,000 shares authorized, 15,000 shares issued and outstanding	75,000
Paid-in Capital in Excess of Par--Common	300,000
Retained Earnings	$1,080,000

During 1990, Frazier Corporation declared and distributed the following dividends in the order shown:

1.   The arrears dividend and the current dividend on preferred and a $3 per share common dividend.
2.   A 15% stock dividend on common stock, current market price is $28 per share.
3.   A $2 per share dividend on common stock outstanding.

Required:

A.   Prepare Journal entries for the declaration and distribution of each dividend. (Assume each dividend is distributed prior to the declaration of the subsequent dividend.)
B.   By what amount did these transactions change (increase or decrease) the total stockholders' equity section of Frazier Corporation?

SOLUTIONS TO REVIEW QUESTIONS AND EXERCISES

True - False

1.   (F)   Retained earnings does represent earned capital, but capital stock and additional paid-in capital are referred to as contributed capital. Investors contribute capital to the business in return for shares of stock that represent ownership in the corporation. These amounts are contributed to the company in the hopes that the entity will be successful in its operations and generate a positive return on contributed capital.

2.   (T)

3.   (F)   Even though extraordinary items are taken directly to the income statement they have an effect on retained earnings because the resulting net income or net loss is reflected in retained earnings through the closing process.

4.   (T)

5.   (T)

6.   (T)

7.   (F)   This statement is generally false. Growth companies need all the capital they can generate either through operations (net income) or outside financing (investors or creditors). People investing in such companies generally recognize this fact and hope they generate a positive increase in the value of their stock holdings.

8.   (T)

9.   (F)   A property dividend is a nonreciprocal transfer of nonmonetary assets between an enterprise and its owners. A transfer of a nonmonetary asset to a stockholder or to another entity in a nonreciprocal transfer should be recorded at the fair value of the asset transferred, and a gain or loss should be recognized on the disposition of the asset.

10. (T)
11. (T)
12. (T)
13. (F)   No assets are set aside in connection with an appropriation of retained earnings. Appropriations of retained earnings are nothing more than reclassifications of retained earnings.
14. (F)   An appropriation of retained earnings does not set aside any assets nor can it be used to charge losses against. When an appropriation is no longer necessary, either because the loss has occurred or because it no longer appears as a possibility, the appropriation should be returned to retained earnings.
15. (T)
16. (F)   At the present time this approach to recording self-insurance is not permitted under GAAP. A company that self-insures can either record losses as incurred or appropriate retained earnings and record losses as incurred.
17. (T)
18. (T)
19. (F)   A quasi reorganization is a procedure provided for in some state laws that eliminates an accumulated deficit and permits the company to proceed on much the same basis as if it had been legally reorganized, without the difficulty and expenses generally connected with a legal reorganization.
20. (T)

Multiple Choice

1. (A)   The credit balance in retained earnings serves as the basis for distributions of assets to stockholders (dividends). The sale of common stock or treasury stock would not result in an increase in retained earnings, and the payment to a creditor is merely a decrease in both assets and liabilities.

2. (B)   A scrip dividend is merely a special form of note payable. A dividend payable in scrip means that instead of paying the dividend now, the corporation has elected to pay it at a later date.

3. (A)

Retained Earnings			
Cash Dividend	30,000	100,000	Beginning Balance
Stock Dividend	30,000*	50,000	Net Income
		90,000	Ending Balance

*(1,500 X $20 =$30,000)

4. (D)   Stock dividend :
     280,000 x .05 = 14,000 x $24 .... $336,000
     Cash dividend:
     280,000 + 14,000 = 294,000 x $.60   176,400
     Decrease in retained earnings $512,400

5. (D)   The only feature listed that is common to both stock dividends and stock splits is the fact that the number of shares outstanding will change. Total stockholders' equity is not affected by a stock dividend or stock split. No transfer is made from retained earnings for a stock split and technically the market value of a stock issue is unaffected by a stock dividend. (The closer a stock dividend comes to a stock split, the greater the chance that the stock dividend will have an impact on market price.)

6. (B)   *APB Opinion No. 29* requires that property dividends be recorded at the fair value of the assets transferred with a gain or loss being recognized on the disposal by the company.

7. (C)   In general, a corporation can establish an appropriation for any contingency. However, the FASB does suggest that appropriations be designated with some contingency in mind. To establish an appropriation for "future losses" is most likely an attempt to reduce the amount of retained earnings apparently available for dividends without explaining to the stockholders exactly why. The FASB does not encourage the establishment of general or unspecified appropriations.

8. (D)   Alternatives A, B, and C represent requirements of a quasi reorganization. Arbitrarily to write up assets to eliminate a deficit in retained earnings would violate a requirement of a quasi reorganization that prohibits deliberately understating or overstating assets.

9. (A)   Self-insurance does allow the risk of loss to be spread over a large number of possible loss events that individually would be small in relation to the total potential loss. A corporation with only one location should not self-insure because it is unable to spread the risk among many locations. Alternative D could prove correct but not in all cases. A small company with no ability to spread the risk of loss over the long run might encounter a problem that could render them insolvent. Recording insurance premiums as expenses in the period the insurance is in effect is consistent with the matching principle.

10. (C)   Before 1975 the accrual of a liability for self-insurance was acceptable and widely used by many industries. However, at the present time this approach is not permitted under GAAP.

Review Exercises

1. Declaration of Dividend:

Investment in Securities	1,500,000	
Gain on Appreciation of Securities		1,500,000
Retained Earnings	2,500,000	
Property Dividend Payable		2,500,000

Payment of Dividend:

Property Dividend Payable	2,500,000	
Investment in Securities		2,500,000

2.

Unappropriated Retained Earnings, December 31, 1989		$40,900
Add:		
Reserve for Plant Expansion	$26,000	
Stock Dividend	4,000	
Cash Dividend	5,000	35,000
		$75,900
Less:		
Unappropriated Retained Earnings January 1, 1989		65,900
Estimated 1989 Net Income before Income Taxes		$10,000

3. To effect a quasi organization:

a. All assets are revalued at approximate current values so the company will not be burdened with excessive inventory or fixed assets valuations in following years. Any loss on revaluation increases the deficit.

b. Paid-in or other types of capital must be available or must be created, at least equal in amount to deficit. If no such capital exists, it is created through donation of stock to the corporation by stockholders, by reduction of the par value of shares outstanding, or by some similar means.

c. The deficit is then charged against the paid-in capital and thus eliminated.

d. The date of the quasi reorganization must be shown with retained earnings for approximately 10 years subsequent to the reorganization.

4.   a.   Noncumulative, nonparticipating

		Preferred	Common	TOTAL
1991	(1) Up to 6% of $100,000........................	$ 3,000		$ 3,000
1992	(1) 6% of $100,000.................................	6,000		6,000
	(2) Remainder..		$ 5,000	5,000
		6,000	5,000	11,000
1993	(1) 6% of $100,000.................................	6,000		6,000
	(2) Remainder.......................................		$ 15,000	15,000
		$ 6,000	$ 15,000	$21,000

b.   Cumulative, nonparticipating

		Preferred	Common	TOTAL	Arrearage
1991	(1) Up to 6% of $100,000........................	$ 3,000		$ 3,000	$3,000
1992	(1) Arrearage	3,000		3,000	-0-
	(2) 6% of $100,000.................................	6,000		6,000	
	(3) Remainder..		2,000	2,000	
		9,000	2,000	11,000	-0-
1993	(1) 6% of $100,000	6,000		6,000	
	(2) Remainder		15,000	15,000	
	....	$ 6,000	$ 15,000	$21,000	

c.   Cumulative, fully participating

		Preferred	Common	TOTAL	Arrearage
1991	(1) Up to 6% of $100,00........................	$ 3,000		$ 3,000	$3,000
1992	(1) Average..	3,000		3,000	-0-
	(2) 6% of $100,000.................................	6,000		6,000	
	(3) Up to 6% of $50,000........................		2,000	2,000	
		9,000	2,000	11,000	-0-
1993	(1) 6% of $100,000.................................	6,000		6,000	
	(2) 6% of $50,000.................................		3,000	3,000	
	(3) Participation (see below)	8,000	4,000	12,000	
		$ 14,000	$ 7,000	$ 21,000	

Participation - 1993: ....

Par value of preferred 100,000

Par value of common............................ 50,000

Total par value $150,000

Preferred $\frac{100,000}{150,000}$ x 12,000 8,000

Preferred $\frac{50,000}{150,000}$ x 12,000 4,000

Total available for participation $12,000

5. A. 1. Retained Earnings 101,000

             Dividend Payable - Preferred .... 56,000[a]
             Dividend Payable - Common 45,000

  [a](400,000 x .07 = 28,000 x 2 = \$56,000)

             Dividend Payable - Preferred 56,000
             Dividend Payable - Common 45,000
             Cash 101,000

    2. Retained Earnings 63,000

             Stock Dividend Distributable - Common.................. 11,250[b]
             Paid-in Capital in
             Excess of Par - Common 51,750

  [b](15,000 X .15 = 2,250 x \$5 = \$11,250)

             Stock Dividend Distributable - Common....................... 11,250
             Common Stock 11,250

    3. Retained Earnings 34,500

             Dividend Payable - Common .... 34,500[c]

  [c](15,000 + 2,250 = 17,250 x \$2 = \$34,500)

             Dividend Payable - Common 34,500
             Cash 34,500

  B. Decrease: <u>\$135,500</u> (\$101,000 + \$34,500 = \$135,500)

    A stock dividend has no effect on total stockholders' equity.

17

Dilutive securities and earnings per share calculations

Chapter Synopsis

Chapter 17 examines the issue related to accounting for dilutive securities at date of issuance and at time of conversion. Also, their impact of the computation of earnings per share is presented. The significance attached to the earnings per share figure by stockholders and potential investors has caused the accounting profession to direct a great deal of attention to the calculation and presentation of earnings per share.

Chapter Review

1. **Dilutive securities** are defined as securities that are not common stock in form but that enable their holders to obtain common stock upon exercise or conversion. The most notable examples include convertible bonds, convertible preferred stocks, warrants, and contingent shares.

2. In the case of **convertible bonds,** the conversion feature allows the corporation an opportunity to obtain common stock financing at cheaper rates. Also, the conversion feature entices the investor to accept a lower interest rate than he or she would normally accept on a straight debt issue. Accounting for convertible bonds on the date of issuance follows the procedures used to account for straight debt issues.

3. If bonds are converted into common stock, the issue price of the stock may be based upon (a) **the market price of the stock or bonds** (b) **the book value of the bonds.** The market price method, while theoretically sound, is subject to criticism because the corporation recognizes a gain or loss as a result of an equity investment in that corporation. Under the book value method, no gain or loss is recorded, as the issue price of the stock is recorded at the book value of the bonds. The book value method has received the most widespread acceptance among practitioners.

4. Convertible debt that is retired without exercise of the conversion feature should be accounted for as though it were a straight debt issue. Any difference between the cash acquisition price of the debt and its carrying amount should be reflected currently in income as a gain or loss.

5. **Convertible preferred stock** is accounted for in the same manner as nonconvertible preferred stock at date of issuance. When conversion takes place, the book value method is used. Preferred Stock, along with any related Additional Paid-in Capital, is debited; Common Stock and Additional Paid-in Capital, is debited; Common Stock and Additional Paid-in Capital (if an excess exists) are credited. If the par value of the common stock issued exceeds the book value of the preferred stock, Retained Earnings is debited for the difference.

6. **Stock warrants** are certificates entitling the holder to acquire shares of stock at a certain price within a stated time period. Warrants are potentially dilutive, as are convertible securities. However, when stock warrants are exercised, the holder must pay a certain amount of money to obtain the shares. Also, when stock warrants are attached to debt, the debt remains after the warrants are exercised.

7. When stock warrants are attached to debt, the proceeds from the sale should be allocated between the two securities. This treatment is in accordance with *APB Opinion No. 14*, and is based on the fact that the stock warrants can be traded separately from the debt. Allocation of the proceeds between the two securities is normally made on the basis of their fair market values at the date of issuance. The amount allocated to the warrants is credited to **Paid-in Capital - Stock Warrants.** The two methods of allocation available are (a) **the proportional method** and (b) **the incremental method.**

8. When detachable warrants are exercised, Cash is debited for the exercise price and Paid-in Capital - Stock Warrants is debited for the amount assigned to the warrants. The credit portion of the entry includes Common Stock and Additional Paid-in Capital. If detachable warrants are never exercised, Paid-in Capital - Stock Warrants is debited and Paid-in Capital from Expired Warrants is credited.

9. **Stock rights** are issued to existing stockholders when a corporation's directors decide to issue new shares of stock. Each share owned normally entitles the stockholders to one stock right. This privilege allows each stockholder the right to maintain his or her percentage ownership in the corporation. No entry is required **when rights are issued** to existing stockholders.

10. Employee **stock option plans** may be classified as **noncompensatory** or **compensatory.** According to *APB Opinion No. 25*, noncompensatory plans are plans that (a) include participation by all employees who meet limited employment qualifications, (b) are offered equally to all eligible employees, (c) limit the exercise time to a reasonable period, and (d) include a discount from market price no greater than one that might be offered to stockholders or others. Plans that do not possess **all** these characteristics are classified as compensatory.

11. Compensatory stock option plans involve unique accounting problems. **Compensation expense** is the difference between the market price of the stock and the option price on the **measurement date.** The measurement date is the first date on which both the number of shares involved and the option price are known. In many instances, the date on which the **option is granted** or **the stock is awarded** serves as the measurement date. Compensation expense is recognized in the period(s) in which the employee performs the services. In general, any method of allocation that is systematic and rational is appropriate, if the periods of service cannot be clearly defined.

12. Three basic types of plans used to compensate key executives and employees are: (1) **incentive or nonqualified stock options plans,** (2) **stock appreciation rights,** and (3) **performance-type plans.**

13. The major distinction between an incentive and a nonqualified option plan relates to the tax treatment afforded the plan. The incentive stock option plan provides the greater tax advantage to the recipient, while the nonqualified option plan provides a greater tax advantage to the issuing company. In an incentive stock option plan the market price of the stock and the option price at the date of grant must be equal. Thus, no compensation expense is recorded in such plans because no excess of market price over option price exists at the date of grant.

14. In a nonqualified stock option plan the difference between the market value and option price of the shares involved at the date of grant should be recorded as **deferred compensation expense** with an offsetting credit to **paid-in capital - stock options.** The deferred compensation expense is then allocated to a reduction of income over the period of service involved. Failure to exercise the options prior to their expiration date does not alter previous recognition of the compensation expense.

15. **Stock appreciation rights** are a form of employee compensation that avoids some of the cash flow problems recipients of nonqualified stock option plans face. Under a stock appreciation rights plan, an employee is given the right to receive **share appreciation**, which is defined as the excess of the market price of the stock at the date of exercise over a preestablished price. This share appreciation may be received in cash, shares of stock, or a combination of both. The accounting for stock appreciation rights is defined by *FASB Interpretation No. 28.* Compensation expense under this plan is the amount by which the quoted market value of the shares of the enterprise's stock covered by the grant exceeds the option price or value specified. The measurement date is the date of exercise.

16. *APB Opinion No. 15* requires that **earnings per share** be disclosed in the income statement. This requirement applies to entities classified as a public enterprise. A nonpublic enterprise is exempt from the requirement as a result of *FASB Statement No. 21.* The computation of earnings per share, as described by the APB, includes a complex set of rules that should be studied in detail for a complete understanding.

17. **In all computations of earnings per share, the weighted average of shares outstanding during the period constitutes the basis for the pershare amounts reported.** In computing the weighted average of shares outstanding, shares issued or retired during the period are weighted by the fraction of the period in which they were outstanding. These amounts are then added to the number of shares outstanding for the entire period. Stock dividends and stock splits that occur during the period require restatement of the shares outstanding prior to the stock dividend or split.

18. A **simple capital structure** is one that consists of common stock with no material amounts of potentially dilutive securities. Any corporation whose capital structure has potential dilution of less than 3% of earnings per common share outstanding is considered to have a simple capital structure. If a simple capital structure exists, the computation of earnings per share is merely the net income reported for the period (less any preferred dividends) divided by the weighted number of actual shares outstanding during the period.

19. A capital structure is said to be **complex** if it includes securities that could have a dilutive effect on earnings per common share. A complex capital structure require a **dual presentation** of earnings per share, each with equal prominence on the face of the income statement. This dual presentation consists of **primary earnings per share** and **fully diluted earnings per share.**

20. Primary earnings per share is based on the number of common shares outstanding plus the shares

referred to as **common stock equivalents.** A common stock equivalent is a security that, while not a common stock, gives its holder the right through conversion or exercise to acquire shares of common stock. **Convertible securities are common stock equivalents if, on the date of issue, the cash yield is less than 66-2/3% of the average Aa corporate bond yield.** Convertible securities are used in computing primary earnings per share if they meet the foregoing requirements, and the conversion feature must be exercisable within five years of the date of the financial statement.

21.   When convertible securities exist, the **"if converted" method** is used in computing both primary and fully diluted earnings per share. The "if converted" approach computes earnings per share by assuming **(a)** the conversion of convertible securities at the beginning of the period (or time of issuance of the security, if issued during the period), and **(b)** the elimination of the related interest charges or preferred dividends from net income available for common stockholders.

22.   Stock options and warrants are always considered to be common stock equivalents. However, their use in the computation of earnings per share is dependent upon their dilutive effect. In general, options and warrants are used in computing primary earnings per share **if the average market price during the period exceeds the exercise price of the options and warrants.** When the exercise price exceeds the market price, the options and warrants are said to be **antidilutive** and should not be used in computing either primary or fully diluted earnings per share. The **treasury stock method** is used in determining the dilutive effect of options and warrants. This method assumes that the proceeds from the exercise of options and warrants are used to purchase common stock for the treasury.

23.   For both options and warrants, exercise may not be assumed until the market price of the stock is above the exercise price for substantially all of three consecutive months, the latest of which is the last month of the period to which earnings per share data relate. Once this three-month criterion has been satisfied, the average market price of the common stock for the period should be used in computing primary earnings per share.

24.   **Fully diluted earnings per share** is based on the assumption that all potential common stock conversions that would have reduced earnings per share have taken place. In the case of stock options and warrants, the closing market price is used in computing the incremental shares if it is higher than the average market price.

25.   When the earnings of a period include earnings before extraordinary items, earnings per share amounts should be presented for both earnings before extraordinary items and net income, both for primary and fully diluted purposes. Presentation of per-share amounts for extraordinary items is optional. When earnings per share data include dual presentation, footnote disclosures should describe **(a)** the pertinent rights and privileges of the various securities outstanding, **(b)** the basis on which both primary and fully diluted earnings per share were computed, and **(c)** the effect of conversions subsequent to year end.

26.   **Appendix 17-A** includes a comprehensive illustration of the computation of earnings per share.

Demonstration Problem

Hutton Company issued $200,000 face value of bonds with a coupon rate of 9%. To make the bonds more attractive, the company issued detachable stock warrants at the rate of one warrant for each $100 bond sold. The bonds sold at issuance for 97.5. The value of the bonds without the warrants is considered to be $175,000, and the value of the warrants in the market is $35,000.

Required:

Prepare the journal entry for the issuance of the bonds and warrants.

Solution:

Value of bonds and warrants formulas:

(1) $$\frac{\text{Value of bonds without warrants}}{\text{Value of bonds without warrants + value of warrants}} \times \text{Purchase price} = \text{Value assigned to bonds}$$

(2) $$\frac{\text{Value of warrants}}{\text{Value of bonds without warrants + value of warrants}} \times \text{Purchase price} = \text{Value assigned to warrants}$$

(1) $$\frac{\$175,000}{\$175,000 + \$35,000} \times \$195,000* = \$162,500$$

(2) $$\frac{\$35,000}{\$175,000 + \$35,000} \times \$195,000 = \$32,500$$

Journal Entry:

Cash	195,000	
Discount on Bonds Payable	37,500	
Bonds Payable		200,000
Paid-in Capital Stock Warrants		32,500

*($200,000 X .975)

REVIEW QUESTIONS AND EXERCISES

True-False

Indicate whether each of the following is true (T) or false (F) in the space provided.

_____ 1. One of the primary reasons for issuing convertible securities is to obtain common stock financing at rates that are cheaper than those that would be necessary if either debt of common stock were issued.

_____ 2. Current authoritative pronouncements require that a portion of the proceeds received from the issuance of convertible debt be accounted for as being attributable to the conversion feature.

_____ 3. Compensation expense related to stock options granted to employees is the difference between the market price of the stock and the option price on the measurement date.

_____ 4. The measurement date for stock options granted to employees is the first date on which are known both (a) the number of shares that an individual employee is entitled to receive and (b) the market value of the stock.

_____ 5. A nonqualified stock option plan usually involves compensation expense because a spread exists between the market price and the option price of the stock involved at the date of grant.

_____ 6. In accounting for stock appreciation rights granted to key executives, compensation is measured at the date of grant as the difference between the market price and book value of the stock involved.

_____ 7. The major distinction between an incentive and a nonqualified option plan relates to the tax treatment afforded the plan.

____ 8. No compensation expense is recorded for an incentive stock option because no excess of market price over the option price exists at the date of grant.

____ 9. In computing earnings per share, if a stock dividend occurs after the end of the year, but before the financial statements are issued, the weighted-average number of shares outstanding for the prior year (and any other years presented in comparative form) must be restated.

____ 10. A corporation whose capital structure has potential dilution of less than 3% of earnings per common share outstanding is considered to have a simple capital structure.

____ 11. When the "if converted" method is employed, the conversion rate in effect during the period is used in computing primary earnings per share.

____ 12. Stock options and warrants are always included in the denominator shares in computing primary earnings per share.

____ 13. If shares are issuable upon the mere passage of time, they should enter into the computation of fully diluted earnings per share but not primary earnings per share.

____ 14. A corporation's capital structure cannot be simple if it includes convertible securities.

____ 15. A common stock equivalent gives its holder the right through conversion or exercise to acquire shares of common stock.

____ 16. The treasury stock method presumes that options can be exercised only if the company has sufficient treasury stock to issue upon the exercise of the warrants.

____ 17. If a security is considered to be a common stock equivalent at the time it is issued, it will continue to be classified as a common stock equivalent as long as it is outstanding.

____ 18. The treasury stock method will increase the number of shares outstanding whenever the exercise price of an option or warrant is below the market price of the common stock.

____ 19. A convertible debt security may be antidilutive even though its assumed exercise would increase the number of common shares outstanding.

____ 20. Earnings per share data are required for each of the following: (a) income from continuing operations; (b) income before extraordinary items; and (c) net income.

Multiple Choice

Select the best response for each of the following items and enter the corresponding letter in the space provided.

____ 1. When convertible debt is retired by the issuer, any difference between the cash acquisition price and the carrying amount of the debt should be:
A. reflected currently in income, but not as an extraordinary item.
B. reflected currently in income as an extraordinary item.
C. treated as a prior period adjustment.
D. treated as an adjustment of additional paid-in capital.

____ 2. The conversion of preferred stock into common requires that any excess of the par value of the common shares issued over the carrying amount of the preferred being converted should be:
A. reflected currently in income, but not as an extraordinary item.
B. reflected currently in income as an extraordinary item.
C. treated as a prior period adjustment.
D. treated as a direct reduction of retained earnings.

____ 3. On July 1, 1990, Custer Company granted John Jones, an employee, an option to buy 100 shares of Custer Co. stock for $20 per share, the option exercisable for 5 years from date of grant. Jones exercised his option on September 1, 1990, and sold his 100 shares on December 1, 1990. Quoted market prices of Custer Co. stock during 1990 were:

July 1 .... $20 per share
September 1 .... $24 per share
December 1 .... $27 per share

As a result of the option granted to Jones, Custer should recognize compensation expense on its books in the amount of:
A. $ 0.
B. $300.
C. $400.
D. $700.

____ 4. On June 30, 1988, Leaf Corporation granted compensatory stock options for 10,000 shares of its $24 par value common stock to certain of its key employees. The market price of the common stock on that date was $31 per share and the option price was $28. The options are exercisable beginning January 1, 1990, providing those key employees are still in the employ of the company at the time the options are exercised. The options expire on June 30, 1991.

On January 4, 1990, when the market price of the stock was $36 per share, all options for the 10,000 shares were exercised.

What should be the total amount of compensation expense recorded by Leaf Corporation for these options?
A. $ 0.
B. $ 7,500.
C. $12,000.
D. $30,000.

_____ 5. When a balance sheet account that had no previous balance is debited in connection with a compensatory stock option plan because the services relate to a future period, the balance of the account should be reported as a:
A. deferred charge.
B. prepaid expense.
C. reduction of stockholders' equity.
D. deferred credit.

_____ 6. Warrants exercisable at $20 each to obtain 10,000 shares of common stock were outstanding during a period when the average market price of the common stock was $25 and the ending market price was $24. Application of the treasury stock method for the assumed exercise of these warrants in computing fully diluted earnings per share will increase the weighted average number of outstanding common shares by:
A. 10,000.
B. 1,667.
C. 2,000.
D. 8,000.

_____ 7. In computing earnings per share, a convertible debt security is considered to be a common stock equivalent if at the time of issuance:
A. its cash yield is less than the effective interest rate on similar nonconvertible debt.
B. its cash yield is greater than two-thirds of its stated or coupon rate.
C. it is issued at a price above its face amount.
D. its cash yield is less than two-thirds of the average Aa corporate bond yield.

_____ 8. Options and warrants outstanding that are exercisable within 5 years are:
A. considered only when computing fully diluted earnings per share.

B. always classified as common stock equivalents.
C. classified as common stock equivalents only if their exercise would reduce earnings per share.
D. classified as common stock equivalents only if the market price of the stock has been in excess of the exercise price for substantially all of 3 months.

_____ 9. During 1990 Burch Company had a net income of $50,000 (no extraordinary items) and 50,000 shares of common stock and 10,000 shares of preferred stock outstanding. Burch declared and paid dividends of $.50 per share to common and $6.00 per share to preferred. Although the preferred stock is convertible into common stock on a share-for-share basis, it is not classified as a common stock equivalent. For 1990 Burch Company should report fully diluted earnings (loss) per share of:
A. $.83-1/3.
B. $1.00.
C. ($.20).
D. $.50.

_____ 10. King Corporation has net income for the year of $360,000 and a weighted average number of common shares outstanding during the period of 125,000 shares. The company has a convertible debenture bond issue outstanding. The bonds were issued two years ago at par ($1,500,000), carry a 7% interest rate, and are convertible into 25,000 shares of common stock. The average Aa corporate bond yield was 13% when these bonds were issued and the company has a 50% tax rate. Primary earnings per share are:
A. $2.88.
B. $2.75.
C. $2.40.
D. $2.05.

Review Exercises

1. Jamie Company issued 100 bonds, each with a face amount of $1,000, with detachable stock warrants at 101. Each warrant entitled its holder to acquire one share of $100 par common stock for $120 per share. Through discussion with investment bankers, it is determined that the bonds would sell for 97 without the warrants. The market value of each warrant is $50.
   a. Record the issuance of the bonds.
   b. Record the subsequent exercise of all of the warrants.
   c. Record the entry necessary if all of the warrants expire before being exercised.

2. Gerald Smith Company had 100,000 shares of common stock outstanding as of January 1, 1990. The following common stock transactions occurred during 1990.

    March 1 -- Issued 20,000 shares for cash.

    June 1 -- Issued a 10% stock dividend.

    September 1 -- Reacquired 10,000 shares as treasury shares.

    November 1 -- sold the 10,000 treasury shares for cash.

    Compute the weighted-average common shares for 1990.

3. The following information relates to Mann Company for 1990:

Common shares outstanding 1/1/90 100,000

Common shares issued 7/1/90 upon
  conversion of bonds having a face
  amount of $200,000...................................... 10,000

Net income -- 1990.. $200,000

Average Aa corporate bond yield:
  at 1/1/89.. 6%
  at 1/1/90.. 9%
  at 12/31/90... 10%
Income tax rate 50%

4%, 10-year convertible bonds issued 1/1/90 at 100:
  Face amount $200,000
  Conversion terms--50 shares of common for each $1,000 bond (all of the bonds were converted on 7/1/90.)

10%, $10 par, convertible, cumulative preferred stock issued 1/1/89 at 11:
  Par value $500,000
  Conversion terms--2 shares of common for each share of preferred

a. Compute the weighted-average common shares outstanding as if dual presentation of earnings per share is **not** required.

b. Do the convertible bonds qualify as common stock equivalents? Why or why not?

c. Does the preferred stock qualify as a common stock equivalent? Why or why not?

d. Assuming that dual presentation is required, compute the following for purposes of determining **primary** earnings per share:
    (1) Denominator shares.
    (2) Numerator earnings.

e. Assuming that dual presentation is required, compute the following for purposes of determining **fully diluted** earnings per share:
    (1) Denominator shares.
    (2) Numerator earnings.

SOLUTIONS TO REVIEW QUESTIONS AND EXERCISES

True-False

1. (T)

2. (F)   At the time of issuance, convertible debt is recorded like a straight debt issue. Any discount or premium that results from the issuance of convertible debt is amortized assuming the bonds will be held to maturity date because it is difficult to predict when, if at all, conversion will occur.

3. (T)

4. (F)   The measurement date is the first date on which are known both (1) the number of shares that an individual employee is entitled to receive and (2) the option or purchase price, if any.

5. (T)

6. (F)   With respect to stock appreciation rights, compensation is measured at the date of exercise rather than the date of grant. Also, the compensation is defined as the excess of the market price of the stock at the date of exercise over a preestablished price.

7. (T)

8. (T)

9. (T)

10. (T)

11. (T)

12. (F) Stock options and warrants outstanding and their equivalents (whether or not exercisable) are considered common stock equivalents and are included in primary earnings per share computations unless they are antidilutive or exercise cannot take place within five years.

13. (F) Shares that are issuable upon the mere passage of time should be considered outstanding for the computation of both primary and fully diluted earnings per share.

14. (F) A corporation's capital structure is regarded as simple if it consists only of common stock or includes no potentially dilutive convertible securities, options, warrants, or other rights that upon conversion or exercise could, in the aggregate, dilute earnings per share. Any corporation whose capital structure has potential dilution of less than 3% of earnings per common weighted averages shares outstanding is considered to have a simple capital structure.

15. (T)

16. (F) The treasury stock method assumes that options are exercised at the beginning of the year (or date of issue if later) and the proceeds from the exercise of options are issued to purchase common stock from the treasury.

17. (T)

18. (T)

19. (T)

20. (T)

Multiple Choice

1. (B) The method used to record the issuance of convertible debt follows that used in recording straight debt issues. Although theoretical objections can be raised to using straight debt accounting when convertible debt is retired, to be consistent, a gain or loss on retiring convertible debt needs to be recognized in the same way as a gain or loss on retiring debt that is not convertible. Also, material gains and losses on extinguishment of debt are considered extraordinary items.

2. (D) Convertible preferred stock is considered to be a part of stockholders' equity prior to the time it is converted. Thus, when convertible preferred stocks are exercised, there is no theoretical justification for recognition of a gain or loss. Therefore, any excess of the par value of common shares issued over the carrying amount of the preferred being converted is treated as a direct reduction of retained earnings. The rationale for this treatment is that the preferred shareholders are offered an additional return to facilitate the conversion of their shares to common stock.

3. (A) Compensation expense is measured by the difference between the market price and the option price of the stock at the date of grant. The option described in this question is an incentive stock option. An incentive stock option is characterized by the market price and option price of the stock being equal at the date of grant. Thus, no compensation expense is recorded for an incentive stock option.

4. (D) Total compensation expense is computed as the excess of the market price of the stock over the option price on the measurement date. The measurement date in this situation is June 30, because it's the first date on which we know both the number of shares employees are entitled to receive (10,000) and the option price ($28). The amount of compensation expense is computed as follows:

Market Price..............................	$31
Less: Option Price......................	28
Difference...................................	$ 3
Shares Offered	10,000
Compensation Expense...............	$30,000

5. (C) The following journal entry is made when the value of a compensatory stock option is recognized and employee services relate to future periods.

Deferred Compensation Expense
    Paid-in Capital -- Stock Options

The deferred compensation expense account is considered to be a contra stockholders' equity account. The balance in this account is amortized to expense over the period(s) in which the employee granted the option performs services.

6. (C)   Proceeds from exercise of options
         (10,000 x $20)............................. $200,000

         Shares issued upon exercise........   10,000
         Treasury shares purchased..........
         $200,000 ÷ $25)........................   (8,000)
         Incremental shares outstanding...   2,000

         Note: In computing fully diluted earnings per share, the closing market price is used in computing the incremental share if it is higher than the average market price.

7. (D)   A convertible security, whether bond or preferred stock, is a common stock equivalent if, at the time of issuance, it has an effective yield of less than 66 2/3% of the current average Aa corporate bond yield.

8. (B)   A common stock equivalent is a security that, although not a common stock, gives its holder the right through conversion or exercise to acquire shares of common stock. Options and warrants are considered common stock equivalents unless they are antidilutive or exercise cannot take place within five years.

9. (C)   Net Income $50,000
         Preferred Dividend......................   (60,000)
              Difference......................... ($10,000)
         ($10,000) ÷ 50,000 = ($.20) Net loss per share

         The preferred stock is antidilutive because conversion would create an increase in earnings per share. The increase would result from the fact that preferred dividends would be eliminated. The reduction of preferred dividends ($60,000) causes a percentage increase in income available to common shareholders (numerator) greater than the percentage increase in common stock and common equivalent shares caused by conversion of the preferred stock.

10. (B) Net income for the year.. $360,000
         Add: Adjustment for interest (net of tax) on 7% debentures   52,500
         Adjusted net income... $412,500

         Average number of shares outstanding 125,000
         Add: shares assumed to be issued upon conversion of bonds............................   25,000

         Average number of common & equivalent shares 150,000

         Primary Earnings Per Share: $412,500 ÷ 150,000 = $2.75

Review Exercises

1. a. Cash... 101,000
        Discount on Bonds Payable   3,951
            Bonds Payable...   100,000
            Paid-in Capital -- Stock Warrants   4,951

        Total proceeds = $100,000 x 1.01 = $101,000
        Market value of warrants = 100 warrants x $50 = $5,000
        Market value of bonds w/o warrants = $100,000 x .97 = $97,000

        Proceeds allocated to warrants:
              $5,000
         ─────────────── x $101,000 = $4,951
         $5,000 + $97,000

        Proceeds allocated to bonds:
              $97,000
         ─────────────── x $101,000 =   96,049
         $5,000 + $97,000
                                          $101,000

b. Cash 12,000
    Paid-in Capital -- Stock Warrants.. 4,951
      Common Stock 10,000
      Paid-in Capital in Excess of Par 6,951

c. Paid-in Capital -- Stock Warrants.. 4,951
    Paid-in Capital from Expired Warrants 4,951

2.

Shares Outstanding	Number of Months	Month-Shares
110,000[a]	2	220,000
132,000[b]	6	792,000
122,000	2	244,000
132,000	2	264,000

$$1,520,000 \div 12 = \underline{126,667} \text{ shares}$$

[a]Shares outstanding during January and February   100,000
  Retroactive application of June 1 stock dividend (10%)   10,000
    110,000

[b]Shares outstanding March 1 -- May 31   120,000
  Retroactive application of June 1 stock dividend (10%)   12,000
    132,000

3. a. $100,000 (1/2) + 110,000 (1/2) = \underline{105,000}$

    b. Yes.

        Cash yield $= \dfrac{\$40}{\$1000} = 4\%$

    2/3 of average Aa corporate bond yield = 2/3 of 9% = 6%
    Cash yield is less than 2/3 of average Aa corporate bond yield.

    c. No.

        Cash yield $= \dfrac{\$1}{\$11} = 9.1\%$

    2/3 of average Aa corporate bond yield = 2/3 of 6% = 4%
    Cash yield is not less than 2/3 of average Aa corporate bond yield.

    d. (1) Weighted-average common shares outstanding   105,000
           Common equivalent shares:
             From assumed conversion of bonds at 1/1/90
             (instead of their actual conversion at 7/1/90):

             200 bonds x 50 shares per bond x $\dfrac{6}{12}$ 5,000

             Denominator shares -- primary   110,000

      (2) Net income $200,000
           - Preferred dividends   (50,000)
          +   Interest (net of tax):

             Interest $\dfrac{4}{100}$ x 200,000 x $\dfrac{6}{12}$ = $4,000
               Tax effect (50%)   2,000   2,000
             Numerator earnings -- primary $152,000

    e. (1) Denominator shares for primary EPS   110,000
           Other potentially dilutive securities:
             From assumed conversion of preferred
              (50,000 shares of preferred x 2)   100,000
             Denominator shares -- fully diluted   210,000

      (2) Net Income $200,000
          + Interest for 6 months (net of tax)   2,000
          Numerator earnings -- fully diluted $202,000

18

Investments -- Temporary and long-term

Chapter Synopsis

Investments are classified in the financial statements as either temporary (current) or long term (noncurrent). Chapter 18 covers both temporary and long-term investments. The first section presents accounting for temporary investments (both equity and debt); the second section covers accounting for long-term investments (both equity and debt). The chapter also discusses the accounting for and reporting of the cash surrender value of life insurance and special-purpose funds.

Chapter Review

1. **Temporary investments** consist of marketable debt securities and marketable equity securities. To be classified as a temporary investment, an item must be **readily marketable** and **intended to be converted into cash within one year or the operating cycle, whichever is longer.**

2. *Statement of Financial Accounting Standards No. 12,* "Accounting for Certain Marketable Securities," addresses the issues related to the carrying value of marketable equity securities. Marketable equity securities are readily tradeable instruments representing ownership shares, or the right to acquire or dispose of ownership shares, in an enterprise at fixed or determinable prices.

3. Marketable equity securities are recorded at cost when acquired. When a balance sheet is prepared, the **marketable equity securities portfolio** is presented at the **lower of its aggregate cost or market value.** If the total cost of the portfolio exceeds the total market value of the portfolio, the difference is shown in a **valuation allowance account** in the current assets section of the balance sheet. Any change in the valuation allowance account must be taken into account in the determination of net income of the period in which the change occurs.

4. If the valuation allowance account increases, an **unrealized loss on valuation of marketable equity securities** will be included on the income statement. If the valuation allowance account decreases, the income statement will show a **recovery of an unrealized loss on valuation of marketable equity securities,** classified as

"other income." It is important to note that the recovery of loss on valuation of marketable equity securities can never exceed the amount included in the valuation allowance account. Thus, **the recovery is recognized only to the extent unrealized losses were previously recognized.** For example, assume the valuation allowance account has a credit balance of $25,000, representing past recognition of unrealized losses. If during the current year the marketable equity securities portfolio shows total market value exceeding total cost by $36,000, the "recovery" account would be credited for $25,000 and the "valuation allowance" account would be debited for $25,000.

5. When marketable equity securities are sold, cash is debited for the total proceeds less any selling costs incurred. The marketable equity securities account is credited for the **cost** of the securities, and any difference between net proceeds and cost is shown as a **realized** gain or loss. At the date of sale no regard is given to unrealized losses or recoveries or the amount accumulated in the valuation allowance account.

6. **Marketable debt securities** are generally accounted for at cost. However, application of the lower of costs or market approach to debt securities that are **readily marketable** and **classified as current assets** is acceptable.

7. **Balance sheet disclosures** related to marketable equity securities include: the aggregate cost, the aggregate market value, gross unrealized gains, and gross unrealized losses. For each period for which an **income statement** is prepared, **disclosures** should be made of: the net realized gain or loss, the basis on which cost was determined in computing realized gain or loss, and the change in valuation allowance included in net income.

8. Any temporary investments that do not conform to the criteria of marketable equity securities should be listed after marketable equity securities among the current assets under a separate classification. If temporary investments are less liquid than other current items, they should be listed after such items in the current asset section of the balance sheet.

9. An investment in **corporate bonds** normally represents a long-term commitment of funds by one

corporation in return for a promise by another corporation to pay a sum of money at a designated maturity date, plus periodic interest. The types and characteristics of bonds that may be purchased were discussed in **Chapter 14.** It would be wise to review that discussion in connection with the study of this chapter.

10. Investments in bonds are recorded at cost on the date of acquisition. When the stated rate of interest is less than the prevailing market rate of interest (yield rate), the bonds will sell at a **discount** (less than the maturity value). If the stated rate exceeds the market rate, the bonds will sell at a **premium** (more than the maturity value). Traditionally, discounts and premiums have not been recorded in separate accounts in the records of the purchaser. This is true even though *APB Opinion No. 21* recommends the disclosure of unamortized discount or premium on notes and bonds receivable.

11. The difference between the costs of bonds and their maturity value (that is, discount or premium) is amortized over the period of time from purchase date to maturity date. As was discussed in **Chapter 14,** the amortization of bond premiums or discounts can be accomplished using the **straight-line method** or the **effective interest method.** *APB Opinion No. 21* specifies a preference for the effective interest method and permits other methods only if the results obtained are not significantly different from those produced by the effective interest method. The amortization of bond premiums and discounts by the purchaser is taken directly to the Long-term Investments in Bonds account.

12. If bonds carried as long-term investments are sold before maturity date, entries should be made to amortize the discount or premium to the date of sale and to remove from the investments account the book value of bonds sold. Gain or loss on the sale of bonds represents the difference between the selling price and the book value of the bonds.

13. **Stock** of another corporation purchased as a long-term investment is recorded at the cash purchase price plus brokerage costs and other fees incidental to purchase. When stock is acquired for noncash consideration, it should be recorded at (a) the fair market value of the consideration given or (b) the fair market value of the stock received, whichever is more clearly determinable.

14. The extent of ownership held by one corporation in the common stock of another corporation generally determines the accounting treatment for the investment. The methods used in accounting for long-term investments in equity securities along with the criteria used in determining their applicability are identified below:

Method	Criteria
Equity	Investment in excess of a 50% equity interest.
Equity	Investment in excess of a 20% equity interest, except when evidence exists

of an inability to exercise significant influence.

Lower of Cost or Market	Investment of a less than 20% interest in the form of marketable equity securities, with no ability to exercise significant influence.
Cost	Investment in nonequity or non-marketable securities.

15. In general, investments accounted for under the **cost method** are maintained in the accounting records at acquisition cost until partially or entirely liquidated. Write-downs from cost are appropriate when (a) the dividends received represent a liquidating dividend and (b) operating losses of the investee significantly reduce the net assets and greatly impair its earning potential. Cash dividends received from the investee are recorded as investments revenue.

16. Under the **equity method,** the investment is originally recorded at cost and then subsequently adjusted by the investor's **proportionate share** of the investee's earnings and dividend payments. Income earned by the investee results in an increase in the investment account on the books of the investor. An investee's net loss or dividend payments reduce the investment account.

17. As mentioned in paragraph 14, the equity method is appropriate in a situation where an investor has the ability to exercise **significant influence** over the investee. According to *APB Opinion No. 18*, in the absence of evidence to the contrary, significant influence is presumed when an investor owns 20% or more of the voting stock of an investee. In an attempt to provide examples of circumstances where an investment of 20% or more might not enable an investor to exercise significant influence, the FASB issued *Interpretation No. 35*. The examples cited in this interpretation are not all-inclusive, but they do aid in determining when further analysis of a situation might be necessary.

18. When the equity method is not appropriate, investments in marketable equity securities must be accounted for using the **lower of cost or market method.** All noncurrent marketable equity securities account for under this method are grouped together for the purpose of comparing the aggregate cost and the aggregate market to determine the carrying amount at the balance sheet date. Any change in the **valuation allowance** (excess of aggregate cost over aggregate market) is shown separately in the equity section of the balance sheet.

19. A change in classification of a marketable equity security between current and noncurrent results in the individual security being transferred at its lower of cost or market valuation on the date of transfer. When cost exceeds market value, a realized loss is included in the determination of net income and the market value becomes the new cost basis.

20.   If an investor in equity securities receives a **stock dividend,** the carrying amount of the investment remains unchanged.   However, the additional shares serve to reduce the per share carrying amount as a result of the larger number of shares now held.

21.   **Stock rights** are issued to existing corporate stockholders when a corporation is about to sell additional shares of an issue already outstanding. By exercising the stock rights (purchasing the number of shares represented), investors maintain their proportionate share in the ownership of the corporation. If the holder of stock rights may purchase the additional shares at less than current market value, the rights have a value. In such instances, a portion of the carrying value of the original shares should be allocated to stock rights. This allocation is based on the respective market values of the original shares and stock rights at the time the rights are received.

22.   Three dates are important in understanding stock rights: (a) the date the rights offering is announced, (b) the date the rights are issued, and (c) the date the rights expire. From the date the rights offering is announced until its issue date, the right is inseparable from a share of stock. That is, each share of stock bought or sold during this period carries with it one right and the stock is said to be selling **rights-on.** After those holding the stock on the date the rights are issued receive their rights, the stock and the rights can be sold separately. During this period the stock is said to be selling **ex-rights.**

23.   The recipient of stock rights has the following three alternatives:
   a.   Purchase the additional shares and include the amount allocated to stock rights in the carrying amount of the new shares.
   b.   Sell the stock rights and include the amount allocated to the rights in determining the gain or loss on the sale.
   c.   Let the rights expire and record a loss equal to the amount allocated to stock rights.

24.   Assets set aside in **special purpose funds** are of two general types: (a) those in which cash is set aside for meeting specific current obligations and (b) those that are not directly related to current operations and therefore are in the nature of long-term investments. Examples of funds of the second type and the purpose of each are:

Fund	Purpose
Sinking Fund	Payment of long-term indebtedness
Plant Expansion Fund	Purchase or construction of additional plant
Stock Redemption Fund	Retirement of capital stock (usually preferred stock
Contingency Fund	Payment of unforeseen obligations

25.   The cash set aside in funds of a long-term nature is usually invested in securities so that an income may be earned on the assets included in the fund. The control of fund assets may be maintained by the corporation or placed in the hands of a trustee. If a trustee is appointed, that individual becomes the custodian of the assets and must make periodic reports to the company concerning the composition of the fund.

26.   Normally, a separate set of records is maintained to account for the assets, incomes, and expenses of the fund. If the fund is a administered by a trustee, the assets of the fund is administered by a trustee, the assets for the fund may be used to acquire the company's own securities (for example, stock or bonds). A problem arises concerning the accounting for dividends and interest on these securities if they are not immediately canceled.   The treasury stock should be deducted from common stock (or the stockholders' equity section); treasury bonds should be deducted from bonds payable. Dividend revenue or interest revenue should not be recorded for these securities.

27.   **Appendix 18A** demonstrates the accounting considerations involved when a company changes **from** the equity method or **to** the equity method when accounting for investments. If the investor's level of influence or ownership falls below that necessary for continued use of the equity method, a change must be made to either the **lower of cost or market method** or the **cost method,** whichever is appropriate. No retroactive restatement is necessary in adopting the new method. The earnings or losses that relate to the stock retained by the investor and that were previously recognized by the investor should remain as part of the carrying amount of the investment.

28.   A change to the equity method is appropriate when an investment accounted for by other than the equity method subsequently qualifies for use of the equity method. Such a change involves a retroactive adjustment in the carrying amount of the investment, results of operations, and retained earnings of the investor in a step-by-step acquisition manner as if the equity method had been in effect during all of the previous periods in which this investment was held.

Demonstration Problems

1. On February 1, Ahamo Company purchased 9% marketable bonds of Nlocnil Company having par a value of $300,000 at 99 plus accrued interest. Interest is payable on April 1 and October 1.

Required:

a. Compute the amount Ahamo Company will pay on February 1.
b. How much interest income will Ahamo Company record on April 1?

Solution:

a.

Face value	$300,000
% of par value	.99
Payment for face amount	297,000
Add interest accrued since last interest date	
(4 months): $300,000 x .09 x 1/2 x 4/6	9,000
Total amount paid	$306,000

b.

Interest payment received on April 1	
($300,000 x .09 x 1/2)	$13,500
Less interest accrued on February 1	9,000
Interest income recorded April 1	$4,500

2. Compute the price that should be paid for $25,000 of 9% bonds, interest payable semiannually, and maturing in eight years, if a 12% yield is desired.

Solution:

(Present value of maturity amount plus present value of interest)
($25,000 x PV of 1 to 16 periods @ 6% plus $1,125 x PV of an annuity of 1 for 16 periods at 6%)

$25,000 x .39365 (Table 6-2) + $1,125 x 10.10590 (Table 6-4)

$9,841	+	11,369
Price to yield 12% =		$21,210

3. On January 1, 1988, Arvis Company acquired $150,000 of Hurts Company 8% bonds at a price of $140,490. Interest is payable each December 31; the bonds mature on January 1, 1992. The investment is priced to yield a 10% return to the Arvis Company.

Required:

a. Prepare an amortization schedule applying the effective interest method.
b. What is the annual amount of discount amortized under the straight-line method?

Solution:

a.

Schedule of Interest Income and Bond Discount Amortization
Effective Interest Method
8% Bond Purchased to Yield 10%

Date	Debit Cash (a)	Credit Interest Income (b)	Debit Bond Investment (c)	Book Value of Bonds (d)
1/1/88				$140,490
1/1/89	12,000	14,049	2,049	$142,540
1/1/90	12,000	14,254	2,254	144,794
1/1/91	12,000	14,479	2,479	147,273
1/1/92	12,000	14,727	2,727	150,000

(a) Annual Interest.
(b) Previous balance of (d) x .10.
(c) (b) minus (a).
(d) Previous balance plus (c).

b. If the straight-line method of amortization was used, column (c) of the amortization schedule would have a constant amount of $2,377.50 ($9,510 [discount] ÷ 4); column (b) would have a constant amount of $14,377.50 ($12,000 + $2,377.50).

REVIEW QUESTIONS AND EXERCISES

True-False

Indicate whether each of the following is true (T) or false (F) in the space provided.

____ 1. According to *Statement of Financial Accounting Standards (SFAS) No. 12*, marketable equity securities should be reported on the balance sheet at the lower of aggregate cost or market.

____ 2. Under *SFAS No. 12*, the excess of aggregate market over cost (unrealized gains) of marketable equity securities classified as current assets is included in net income, but only to the extent of previously recognized unrealized losses.

____ 3. The account "Allowance for Excess of Cost of Temporary Investments Over Market Value" is classified in the balance sheet as a contra account to Temporary Investments.

____ 4. If a marketable equity security is transferred from the current to the noncurrent portfolio or vice versa, the security is transferred at its original cost.

____ 5. At the date of sale of a particular marketable equity security, the difference between the net proceeds from the sale of the security and its cost is recognized as a realized gain or loss without regard to any previously recognized unrealized gains or losses.

____ 6. Investment in bonds should be recorded on the date of acquisition at maturity value, as this is the amount recorded by the issuer in the bonds payable account.

____ 7. The amortization of a premium on bonds purchased as a long-term investment is recorded by debiting Interest Revenue on Bonds and crediting Long-term Investment in Bonds.

____ 8. Stock acquired in exchange for noncash consideration should be recorded at the fair market value of the consideration given.

____ 9. Investments by one corporation in the common stock of another corporation are classified as short-term or long-term investments, depending on the percentage ownership in the common stock.

____ 10. Use of the equity method in accounting for long-term stock investments requires consolidating a portion of the investee's equity in the investor's financial statements.

_____ 11. The equity method gives recognition to the fact that: investee earnings increase investee net assets that underlie the investment and investee losses and dividends decrease the net assets.

_____ 12. Once the equity method is adopted by an investor, the method must continue in use until the investment to which it has been applied is sold or liquidated by some other means.

_____ 13. Whenever an investment in marketable equity securities does not qualify for equity method treatment, the investor is required to use the lower of cost or market method in accounting for the investment.

_____ 14. Shares of stock received as a result of a stock dividend represent income to the recipient, whereas shares received as a result of stock split do not constitute income to the recipient.

_____ 15. From the date stock rights are issued until the date they expire, shares of stock of the issuing corporation are said to sell rights-on.

_____ 16. Stock rights received by an investor represent income to the investor at the time the rights are exercised, assuming that the exercise price is less than the market price of the stock.

_____ 17. Assets set aside in special funds are of two general types: (a) those in which cash is set aside for meeting specific current obligations and (b) those that are not directly related to current operations and therefore are in the nature of long-term investments.

_____ 18. When the company is the beneficiary and has the right to cancel the life insurance policy at its own option, the cash surrender value of the policy is an asset of the company.

_____ 19. A fund is always an asset and always has a debit balance; a reserve is an appropriation of retained earnings and always has a credit balance.

_____ 20. Funds administered by a trustee should be recorded as an account receivable and classified as long-term or current, depending on the timing of the use of the funds involved.

Multiple Choice

Select the best answer for each of the following items and place the corresponding letter in the space provided.

_____ 1. For marketable equity securities properly classified as current assets, the net unrealized loss associated with an increase in the valuation allowance should be:
A. included in net income as an extraordinary loss.
B. included in net income before extraordinary items.
C. ignored since a later market change may prevent the loss from being realized.
D. excluded from net income, but shown on the balance sheet as a reduction of stockholders' equity.

_____ 2. Use of the effective interest method in amortizing bond premiums and discounts results in:
A. a greater amount of interest income over the life of the bond issue than would result from use of the straight-line method.
B. a varying amount being recorded as interest income from period to period.
C. a variable rate of return on the book value of the investment.
D. a smaller amount of interest income over the life of the bond issue than would result from use of the straight-line method.

_____ 3. Doyle Corporation purchased 7,400 shares of Maynette Company's common stock. The purchase price was $362,600, which is equal to 50% of Maynette Company's retained earnings balance. Maynette Company's 46,000 shares of common stock are actively traded, and each share has a par value of $10. Doyle Corporation should account for this long-term investment using the:
A. cost method.
B. equity method.
C. lower of cost or market method.
D. market value method.

4. An investor using the equity method would be required to amortize the difference between his initial cost and his proportionate share of the underlying book value of the investee, if at date of acquisition the investor purchased 25% of the stock of the investee for $650,000 and the book value of the investee's total net worth was;
   A. $3,400,000.
   B. $3,000,000.
   C. $2,600,000.
   D. $2,000,000

5. Price Corporation used the equity method to account for its 30% investment in the common stock of Arthur Company. Price paid $300,000 over the book value in recognition of goodwill, which will be amortized over the maximum number of years allowable. During the first year after the investment, Arthur Company reported $250,000 of income and distributed a $150,000 cash dividend. The carrying amount of the investment would change by what amount during the first year?
   A. $20,000 increase.
   B. $22,500 increase.
   C. $30,000 increase.
   D. $60,000 decrease.

6. When the lower of cost or market method is used to account for long-term investments in marketable equity securities, a valuation allowance is used. Accumulated changes in the valuation allowance for long-term marketable equity securities should be:
   A. included in the determination of net income from operations.
   B. reported as an extraordinary item in the income statement.
   C. recorded as a prior period adjustment.
   D. included in the equity section of the balance sheet.

7. Reagan Company has decided to reclassify its investment in the marketable equity securities of D.C., Inc. from current to noncurrent. On the date of the decision, the D.C. securities, which originally cost $86,000, have a current market value of $71,000. Proper accounting treatment of this transfer requires:
   A. a cost basis of $71,000 with a realized loss of $15,000.
   B. a cost basis of $86,000 with a realized loss of $15,000.
   C. a cost basis of $71,000 with an unrealized loss of $15,000.
   D. a cost basis of $86,000 with an unrealized loss of $15,000.

8. Malloy Corporation owns 1,000 shares of common stock in Elaine Company. The stock is carried on Malloy's books at its original cost of $51,150, which is below current market. During August 1990, Elaine Company distributed a 10% stock dividend. On September 15, 1990, Malloy sold the shares acquired from the dividend for $50 per share. As a result of this transaction, Malloy should record:
   A. a gain of $350.
   B. a gain of $5,000.
   C. a loss of $115.
   D. neither a gain nor a loss.

9. Ross, Inc., owns 50 shares of the outstanding common stock of Goebel Company, which has several thousand shares publicly traded. These 50 shares were purchased by Ross in 1988 for $100 per share. On August 30, 1990, Goebel distributed 50 stock rights to Ross. Ross was entitled to buy one new share of Goebel common stock for $90 cash and two stock rights. On August 30, 1990 each share of stock had a market value of $132, ex-rights, and each right had a market value of $18. What is the cost basis of each new share that Ross acquires by exercising the rights?
   A. $90.
   B. $114.
   C. $132.
   D. $150.

10. Raman Company purchased a $250,000 life insurance policy on the life of one of its key employees. When is the cash surrender value of this policy an asset of the company?
   A. If the officer or his heirs are the beneficiaries.
   B. If the policy is either ordinary life or limited payment.
   C. If the company is the beneficiary and has the right to cancel the policy at its own option.
   D. If the premiums are paid by the company and, for income tax purposes, represent income to the officer.

Review Exercises

1. Bob Bazzetta Company made the following purchases of marketable equity securities as temporary investments during 1988.

June 2 --   Purchased 6,000 shares of Mary Jean Corporation common stock at a market price of $26 per share plus a brokerage commission of $2,500.

March 8 -- Purchased 12,000 shares of Sarah Company common stock at a market price of $32.50 per share plus brokerage commissions of $6,200.

Required:

A. Prepare the journal entries as of December 31, 1988 to value properly the Marketable Equity Securities account, assuming a market price of $27 per share for Mary Jean Corporation and $29 per share for Sarah Company.

B. Assume that Bob Bazzetta Company held these securities throughout 1989 and purchased no other marketable equity securities. Prepare the journal entry as of December 31, 1989 to value properly the Marketable Equity Securities account, assuming a market price of $28 per share for Mary Jean Corporation and $30 per share for Sarah Company.

C. On June 12, 1990, Bob Bazzetta Company sold 4,000 shares of Mary Jean Corporation for $28.50 per share, incurring $2,620 in brokerage commissions, taxes, and fees. Bob Bazzetta Company also sold 6,000 shares of Sarah Company on July 16, 1990, for $29 per share, incurring $4,580 in brokerage commissions, taxes, and fees. In addition to these sales, Bob Bazzetta Company purchased 5,000 shares of Kathleen Inc. on October 3, 1990 at a market price of $40 per share plus a brokerage commission of $2,800. On December 31,1990, the market price of each stock was: Mary Jean Corporation, $29; Sarah Company, $28; and Kathleen Inc., $36. Prepare journal entries for the sales of Mary Jean and Sarah stock and the purchase of the Kathleen stock. Also, prepare the journal entry as of December 31, 1990, to value properly the Marketable Equity Securities account.

2. The information presented below represents a portion of an amortization table prepared by a CPA for her client, Merino Corporation, to account for Merino's investment in $100,000 face value bonds issued by Coda Company that mature in 20 years. On the basis of the information in the table, answer the questions that follow:

Year	Interest Received $	Interest Income $	Increase in Book Value $	Book Value of Bonds
0				$85,805.00
1	7,000.00	7,293.43	293.43	86,098.43
2	7,000.00	7,318.37	318.37	86,416.80
3	7,000.00	7,345.43	345.43	86,762.23

Required:

A. Which amortization method does Merino Corporation use?
B. What was the amount of the bond discount or premium? (Indicate which.)
C. What is the annual interest rate stated on the bonds?
D. What is the effective interest rate on the bonds?

3. Levis corporation purchased 180,000 shares of Knoblett Corporation's 600,000 shares of outstanding common stock for $1,620,000, on January 1, 1990. The book value of Knoblett Corporation's net worth was $5,000,000 on the date of the purchase. The excess of the purchase price of Levis' investment over the book value is attributable to depreciable assets undervalued on Knoblett's books by $400,000. The undervalued assets have a remaining life of 6 years. For the year 1990 Knoblett reported operating net income of 850,000 and an extraordinary gain of $80,000. Dividends paid by Knoblett during the year amounted to $300,000. Determine the carrying value of the investment at December 31, 1990, assuming that the foregoing events have been correctly recorded using the equity method of accounting for long-term investments.

4. Frank Corporation owns 250 shares of Drab Company, originally purchased at $30 per share. Frank recently received one stock right for each share of Drab Company owned. The rights allow the purchaser to buy one additional share of stock for $28 per share, plus 4 rights. On the date the rights were issued, the stock was

selling for $50 per share ex-rights. The market value of the rights is $5 per right. Subsequent to the receipt of the rights, Frank (a) sold 50 rights for $250, (b) exercised 160 rights, and (c) let 40 rights lapse. Calculate the cost allocated to the stock and rights and prepare a journal entry for each of the three events noted. (Round calculations to the nearest whole cent.)

5. On January 3, 1990, Elizabeth Corporation bought 5,250 shares of Sallad Company common stock for $15 per share. At the time of the purchase Sallad Company had total assets of $270,000, liabilities of $30,000, common stock ($12 par value) of $180,000, and retained earnings of $60,000. The difference between book value acquired and the purchase price is attributable to assets having a remaining life of 5 years.

At the end of 1990, Sallad Company reported net income of $28,000 and paid cash dividends of $9,000 on December 31, 1990. The market value of Sallad stock on December 31, 1990 was $16 per share.

Required:

A. Prepare journal entries for these transactions using the lower of cost or market method.
B. Prepare journal entries for these transactions using the equity method.
C. What amount of gain or loss would Elizabeth Corporation report if 1,000 shares of Salled Corporation were sold at $16 per share on January 2, 1991? (Assume equity method.)

SOLUTIONS TO REVIEW QUESTIONS AND EXERCISES

True-False

1. (T)
2. (T)
3. (T)
4. (F)   If a marketable equity security is transferred from the current to the noncurrent portfolio, or vice versa, the security must be transferred at the lower of its cost or market value at the date of transfer.
5. (T)
6. (F)   Investment in bonds should be recorded on the date of acquisition at cost, which includes brokerage fees and any other costs incidental to the purchase.
7. (T)
8. (F)   When stock is acquired in exchange for noncash consideration (property or services), it should be recorded at (1) the fair market value of the consideration given or (2) the fair market value of the stock received, whichever is more clearly determinable. The absence of clearly determinable values for the property or services or a market price for the security acquired may force the use of appraisals or estimates to arrive at a cost.
9. (F)   The determining factor in the classification of an investment by one corporation in the common stock of another corporation is the intent of management. Although it is true that large investments in the common stock of a corporation are normally undertaken for the purpose of exercising control on a long-term basis, the ultimate decision on the classification rests on management's intent. However, the extent to which one corporation acquires the common stock of another corporation generally determines the accounting treatment for the investment.
10. (F)   If an investor exercises significant influence over the operating and financial policies of an investee (generally assumed when holdings are between 20% and 50%), the investor is required to account for the investment using the equity method. Consolidation of a portion of the investee's equity in the investor's financial statements is not required under the equity method.
11. (T)
12. (F)   If an investor's level of influence or ownership falls below that necessary for continued use of the equity method, a change must be made to either the lower of cost or market method or the cost method, whichever is appropriate.
13. (T)

14. (F) Shares received as a result of a stock dividend or stock split-up do not constitute revenue to the recipients because their interest in the issuing corporation is unchanged and because the issuing corporation has not distributed any of its assets.

15. (F) From the date stock rights are announced until they are issued, the shares of stock and the rights are not separable; the share is described as rights-on. After the rights are received by shareholders and up to the time they expire, the share and the right can be sold separately. A share sold separately from an effective stock right is sold ex-rights.

16. (F) When a right is received, a stockholder actually receives nothing that he or she did not have before because the shares already owned brought the stockholder the right; the stockholder has received no distribution of the corporation's assets. If the stockholder buys additional stock (exercises the rights), the carrying amount of the original shares allocated to the rights become part of the carrying amount of the new shares purchased.

17. (T)

18. (T)

19. (T)

20. (F) Funds administered by a trustee are shown in the long-term investments section of the balance sheet or in a separate section if relatively large in amount.

Multiple Choice

1. (B) The unrealized loss account appears on the income statement in the Other Expenses and Losses section and, therefore, would be included in income before extraordinary items.

2. (B) When a premium or discount is amortized under the straight-line method, the interest received is constant from period to period, but the rate of return is not the same year after year. Although the effective interest method results in a varying amount being recorded as interest revenue from period to period, it produces a constant rate of return on the book value of the investment from period to period.

3. (C) To use the equity method, Doyle Corporation would have to hold an investment of between 20% and 50% of Maynette Company's voting stock. The 7,400 shares owned by Doyle represent a little more than 16% of the voting stock (46,000). Also, whenever the investment is in marketable equity securities and the equity method is not appropriate, the investor is required to use the lower of cost or market method in accounting for the investment.

4. (D) When the book value of the investee's net worth is $2,600,000 or greater (as it is in alternatives A, B, and C), there is no excess of the investor's cost over the investor's proportionate share of the underlying book value. Only where the net worth is $2,000,000 (alternative D) is the investor's cost ($650,000) greater than the share of the underlying book value ($2,000,000 x .25 = $500,000).

5. (B)

Increase due to income	($250,000 x .30	=	$75,000
Decrease due to dividend	($150,000 x .30)	=	(45,000)
Amortization of goodwill	($300,000 ÷ .40)	=	(7,500)
Increase in investment			$22,500

6. (D) Accumulated changes in the valuation allowance for a marketable equity securities portfolio included in noncurrent assets are included in the equity section of the balance sheet and shown separately. The profession requires at each reporting date that the aggregate of noncurrent marketable equity securities be written down or up to market, but not in excess of original cost. Also, unrealized losses and recoveries are reported in the equity section of the balance sheet as long as the decline in the market value is viewed as temporary.

7. (A) If there is a change in the classification of a marketable equity security between current and noncurrent, the individual security is transferred between the portfolios at the lower of its cost or market value at the date of transfer. If the market value is lower than cost, the market value becomes the new cost basis, and the difference is accounted for as a realized loss and is included in the determination of net income.

8. (A)   Original shares   1,000
          10% stock dividend   100
          Total shares   1,100

          Cost basis per share: $51,150 ÷ 1,100 = $46.50
          Proceeds from sale of 100 shares (100 x $50) $5,000
          Cost basis of shares sold (100 x $46.50)   4,650
            Gain on sale $ 350

9. (B)   Cost of shares owned: 50 x $100 = $5,000
              August 30:
                   Market value of stock: 50 x $132 = 6,600
                   Market value of rights: 50 x 18 =   900
                   Cost allocated to stock: $\frac{\$6,600}{\$7,500}$ x $5,000 = $4,400

                   Cost allocated to rights: $\frac{\$900}{\$7,500}$ x $5,000 = $600

                   Cost allocated to each share of stock: $\frac{\$4,400}{50}$ = $88

                   Cost allocated to each right: $\frac{\$600}{50}$ = $12

                   Cost of new shares acquired by exercising rights:
                   Cash expended $90
                   Value of 2 rights   24
                       Cost basis $114

10. (C)   If the company is the beneficiary of the policy and has the right to cancel the policy at its own option,
          the cash surrender value of the policy is an asset of the company. When the employee or his heirs is
          the beneficiary, the company does not have to claim to the cash surrender value.

Review Exercises

1.

		Cost	Market	December 31,1988 Unrealized Gain (Loss)
A.	Mary Jean Corporation	$158,500	$162,000	$ 3,500
	Sarah Company	396,200	348,000	(48,200)
	Total Portfolio	$554,700	$510,000	$(44,700)

Entry - December 31, 1988:
   Loss on Valuation of Marketable Equity Securities 44,700
      Allowance for Excess of Cost of Marketable
      Equity Securities Over Market Value   44,700

		Cost	Market	December 31, 1989 Unrealized Gain (Loss)
B.	Mary Jean Corporation	$158,500	$168,000	$9,500
	Sarah Company.....................................	396,200	360,000	(36,200)
	Total Portfolio....................................	$554,700	$528,000	($26,700)

Entry - December 31, 1989:
Allowance for Excess of Cost of Marketable
    Equity Securities Over Market Value... 18,000*
      Recovery of Loss of Valuation of
        Marketable Equity Securities... 18,000

*Previous Unrealized Loss (1988)..	$44,700
Current Unrealized Loss (1989)	26,700
Recovery	$18,000

C. Entry - Mary Jean Sale - June 12, 1990:
Cash 111,380
    Marketable Equity Securities... 105,667
    Realized Gain on Sale of
        Marketable Equity Securities 5,713

Selling price (4,000 @ $28.50)	$114,000
Less commissions, etc..	2,620
Net proceeds...	111,380
Cost of 4,000 shares ($158,500 x 2/3)	105,667
Gain on sale...	$ 5,713

Entry - Sarah Sale - July 16, 1990:
Cash 169,420
Realized Loss on sale of Marketable Equity Securities................................... 28,680
    Marketable Equity Securities 198,100

Selling price (6,000 @ $29.00)	$174,000
Less commissions, etc...	4,580
Net proceeds...	169,420
Cost of 6,000 shares ($396,200 ÷ 2)...	198,100
Loss on sale...	$ 28,680

Entry - Kathleen Purchase - October 3, 1990:
Marketable Equity Securities.. 202,800
    Cash 202,800

December 31,1990:

	Cost	Market	December 31, 1990 Unrealized Gain (Loss)
Mary Jean Corporation	$52,833	$58,000	$5,167
Sarah Company	198,100	168,000	(30,100)
Kathleen, Inc.	202,800	180,000	(22,800)
	$453,733	$406,000	$(47,733)

Entry - December 31, 1990:
Loss on Valuation of Marketable Equity Securities 21,033*
    Allowance for Excess of Cost of Marketable
      Equity Securities Over Market Value... 21,033

*Previous unrealized loss...	$26,700
Current unrealized loss	47,733
Addition to allowance	$21,033

2. A. Effective interest method.
    B. Discount of $14,195 ($100,000 - $85,805).
    C. Stated interest rate = 7% ($7,000 + $100,000).
    D. Effective interest rate = 8.5% ($7,293.43 + $85,805.00).

3. Acquisition cost $1,620,000
    Plus:
        Share of income ($85,000 x .30).. $255,000
        Share of extraordinary gain ($80,000 x .30)   24,000   279,000
                                                                                                             $1,899,000

    Less:
        Dividends ($300,000 x .30) $90,000
        Amortization of undervalued assets
            ($400,000 x .30) ÷ 6..   20,000   110,000
    Carrying Value 12-31-90.. $1,789,000

4. Cost allocation to stock and rights:
        Stock 12,500/13,750 x $7,500 = $6,818.18
        Rights 1,250/13,750 x $7,500 = $681.82
    Cost allocated to each right: $2.73 ($681.82 + 250)
    Cost allocated to each share: $27.27 (6,818.18 + 250)
A. Entry for sale of 50 rights:
        Cash...   250.00
            Investment in Stock 136.50
            Gain on Sale of Investment...   113.50
B. Entry for exercise of 160 rights: (160 ÷ 4 = 40 shares @ $28)
        Investment in Stock 1,120.00
        Cash...   1,120.00
C. Entry for lapse of 40 rights: (40 x $2.73)
        Loss on Expiration of Stock Rights 109.20
            Investment in Stocks...   109.20

5. A. Investment in Sallad Company
            (5,250 @ $15)...   78,750
            Cash   78,750
        Cash   3,150
            Revenue from Investment
                (.35 X $9,000)...   3,150
    B. Investment in Sallad Company...   78,750
            Cash   78,750
        Cash   3,150
            Investment in Sallad Company...   3,150
        Investment in Sallad Company...   9,800
            Revenue from Investment...   9,800
            [Amortization of excess of book
            value ($84,000*) over purchase price
            ($78,750)] ($5,250 ÷ 5 years)]

        *(Net assets times percentage purchased $240,000 x .35)

C.   Carrying value of investment:

Purchase Price..	78,750	
Add share of revenue		
(9,800 + 1,050)	10,850	
Less dividends received..	(3,150)	
Carrying value	86,450	
Selling price of shares sold		
(1,000 @ $16)...		$16,000
Carrying value of shares sold		
(1000/5000 x 86,450)...		17,290
Loss on sale of shares		($1,290)

19

Revenue recognition

Chapter Synopsis

Chapter 19 is devoted to a discussion and illustration of revenue transactions that result from the sale of products and rendering of services. Revenue transactions that result from leasing and the sale of assets other than inventory are discussed in other sections of the text.

Chapter Review

1. **Revenues** are gross increases in assets or gross decreases in liabilities resulting from the profit-directed activities of an enterprise. As an element of the income measurement process, the revenue for a period is generally determined independently of expenses by applying the **revenue recognition principle. The revenue recognition principle provides that revenue is recognized when (a)** the earning process is complete or virtually complete and **(b)** an exchange has taken place.

2. The conceptual nature of revenue as well as the basis of accounting for revenue transactions are described in the following four statements.
   - **(a)** Revenue from selling products is recognized at the date of sale, usually interpreted to mean the date of delivery to customers.
   - **(b)** Revenue from services rendered is recognized when services have been performed and are billable.
   - **(c)** Revenue from permitting others to use enterprise assets, such as interest, rent, and royalties, is recognized as time passes or as the assets are used.
   - **(d)** Revenue from disposing of assets other than products is recognized at the date of sale.

3. Sales transactions result in the exchange of products or services of an enterprise for other valuable assets, normally cash or a promise of cash in the future. Although most sales transactions are fundamentally similar, differences in the method or terms of sale lead to real differences in the transactions themselves and thus to differences in the appropriate accounting for them.

4. The discussion of sales transactions in the chapter is divided between **product sales transactions** and **service sales transactions**, which are covered in **Appendix 19B**. The coverage of product sales trans-actions is further divided into the following topics: (a) revenue recognition at point of sale (delivery), (b) revenue recognition before delivery, (c) revenue recognition after delivery, and (d) revenue recognition for special sales transactions (covered in **Appendix A**). The accounting principles and methods related to product sales transactions are fairly well developed in the accounting literature. Service sales transactions have recently received attention from **AcSEC** and the **FASB**. These efforts are an attempt to develop accounting theory and methodology related to service transactions as distinct from product transactions. Thus, the information presented in **Appendix 19B** dealing with service sales transactions is more illustrative than authoritative because the concepts and methods presented are not official **GAAP**.

ACCOUNTING FOR PRODUCT SALES TRANSACTIONS

5. In general, a contract to sell merchandise in the future is not recorded as a sale until the merchandise is delivered and the transaction is complete. In certain cases, however, revenue is recognized at the completion of production even though no sale has been made. Examples of such situations involve precious metals or agricultural products with assured prices.

6. In most business enterprises, a far greater proportion of total sales volume is handled on a credit basis than on an ordinary cash sale basis. In situations where the seller gives the buyer the right to return the product, the FASB concluded that the transactions should not be recognized currently as sales unless **all** of the following six conditions are met:
   - **a.** The seller's price to the buyer is substantially fixed or determinable at the date of exchange.
   - **b.** Payment from the buyer to the seller has been made or the buyer is obligated to pay and the obligation is not contingent on resale of the product.
   - **c.** The buyer's obligation to the seller would not be changed in the event of theft, damage, or destruction of the product.
   - **d.** The buyer has economic substance apart from that of the seller.

e.   The seller does not retain significant future performance obligations to bring about the resale of the product.

f.   The amount of future returns can be reasonably predicted.

7.   Another exception to the general rule is caused by long-term construction-type projects. The accounting measurements associated with long-term construction projects are difficult because events and amounts must be estimated for a period of years. Two basic methods of accounting for long-term construction contracts are recognized by the accounting profession: (a) **the percentage-of-completion method** and (b) **the completed-contract method.**

8.   Under the percentage-of-completion method, revenue on long-term construction contracts is recognized as construction progresses. The accounting profession has for many years considered the percentage-of-completion method preferable "when estimates of costs to complete and extent of progress toward completion of long-term contracts are reasonably dependable." Costs pertaining to the contract plus gross profit earned to date are accumulated in a **Construction in Process account.** The amount of revenue recognized in each accounting period is based on a percentage of the total revenue to be recognized on the contract. This percentage may be (a) **costs incurred on the contract to date divided by the most recent estimated total costs (cost to cost method)** or (b) **an estimate by qualified engineers and architects.** Income recognized before completion is recorded by debiting **Construction in Process** and crediting **Revenue from Long-term Contracts.** Use of this method is dependent upon the seller's ability to provide a reliable estimate of both the cost to complete and the percentage of contract performance completed. When such estimates are considered reasonably dependable, the accounting profession has considered the percentage-of-completion method preferable.

9.   Under the completed-contract method, revenue and gross profit are recognized when the contract is completed. The principal advantage of the completed-contract method is that reported revenue is based on final results rather than on estimates of unperformed work. Its major disadvantage is the distortion of earnings that may occur. The accounting entries made under the completed-contract method are the same as those made under the percentage-of-completion method, with the notable exception of periodic income recognition.

10.   The AICPA recommends that the percentage-of-completion method and the completed-contract method not be viewed as acceptable, interchangeable alternatives. The percentage-of-completion method should be used when estimates of progress toward completion, revenues, and costs are reasonably dependable and all the following

conditions exist:

a.   The contract clearly specifies the enforceable rights regarding goods or services to be provided and received by the parties, the consideration to be exchanged, and the manner and terms of settlement.

b.   The buyer can be expected to satisfy all obligations under the contract.

c.   The contractor can be expected to perform contractual obligations.

11.   The completed-contract method should be used only when (a) an entity has primarily short-term contracts, (b) the conditions for using the percentage-of-completion method cannot be met, or (c) there are inherent hazards in the contract beyond normal, recurring business risks. When the current estimates of total contract revenue and contract cost indicate a loss is expected, the loss must be recognized in the period in which it becomes evident under both the percentage-of-completion and the completed-contract-methods.

12.   In addition to normal financial statement disclosures, construction contractors should disclose (a) the method of recognizing revenue, (b) the basis used to classify assets and liabilities as current, (c) the basis for recording inventory, (d) the effects of any revisions of estimates, (e) the amount of backlog on incomplete contracts, and (f) the details about contract receivables.

13.   In some cases revenue is recognized after delivery of the product to the buyer. This is due to the fact that in certain sales situations the sales price is not reasonably assured and revenue recognition is deferred. The methods generally used to account for the deferral of revenue recognition until cash is received are (a) **the installment method** and (b) **the cost recovery method.**

14.   In 1966, *APB Opinion No. 10*, concluded that except in special circumstances, the installment method of recognizing revenue is not acceptable. Use of the installment method is justified in situations where receivables are collectible over an extended period of time and there is no reasonable basis for estimating the degree of collectibility. The method is used extensively in tax accounting and has relevance because of the increased emphasis on cash flows.

15.   The term **installment sale** describes any type of sale for which payment is required in periodic installments over an extended period of time. The accounting for installment sales places emphasis on collection, as installment sales lead to income realization in the period of collection rather than the period of sale. This does not mean that revenue is considered unrealized until the entire sale price has been collected but rather that income realization is proportionate to collection. This is due to the fact that the ultimate profit is more uncertain in installment sales than in ordinary sales because collection is more doubtful.

16.   Under the installment sales method of accounting, the gross profit (sales less cost of goods sold) on installment sales is deferred to those periods in which cash is collected. Operating expenses, such as selling and administrative expenses, are treated as expenses in the period incurred. For installment sales in any one year, the following procedures apply under the installment sales method:

a.   During the year, record both sales and cost of sales in the regular way, using separate installment sales accounts, and compute the rate of gross profit on installment sales transactions.

b.   At the end of the year, apply the rate of gross profit to the cash collections of the current year's installment sales to arrive at the realized gross profit.

c.   The gross profit not realized should be deferred to future years.

In any year in which collections from prior years' installment sales are received, the gross profit rate of each year's sales must be applied against cash collections of accounts receivable resulting from that year's sales to arrive at the realized gross profit.

17.   When interest is involved in installment sales, it should be accounted for separately as interest income in the period received. Uncollectible installment accounts receivable should be accounted for in a manner similar to that used for such losses on other credit sales if repossessions do not normally compensate for uncollectible balances.

18.   **Repossessed merchandise** should be recorded in Repossessed Merchandise Inventory account. The item repossessed should be recorded at its **fair value** with the related gross profit and installment account receivable removed from the accounting records. The objective should be to put any asset acquired on the books at its fair value or, when fair value is not ascertainable, at the best possible approximation of fair value. If installment sales transactions represent a significant part of total sales, full disclosure of installment sales, the cost of installment sales, and any expenses allocable to installment sales is desirable. **Deferred gross profit on installment sales** is generally treated as consisting entirely of unearned revenue and classified as a current liability.

19.   Under the **cost recovery method**, no profit is recognized until cash payments by the buyer exceed the seller's cost of the merchandise sold. After all the costs have been recovered, any additional cash collections are included in income. *APB Opinion No. 10* allows a seller to use the cost recovery method to account for sales in which "there is no reasonable basis for estimating collectibility." The cost recovery method is required under *FASB Statement No. 45 (franchises)* and *No. 66 (real estate)* where a high degree of uncertainty exists related to the collection of receivables. The cost recovery

method is more appropriate than the installment method when there is a greater degree of uncertainty.

ACCOUNTING FOR
SPECIAL SALES TRANSACTIONS

20.   **Appendix 19A** includes a presentation of franchise sales and consignment sales transactions. In **franchise operations** a franchisor grants business rights under a franchise agreement to a franchisee. Four types of franchise arrangements have evolved in practice: (a) manufacturer-retailer, (b) manufacturer-wholesaler, (c) service sponsor-retailer (McDonald's, Pizza Hut, etc.), and (d) wholesaler-retailer. Franchise companies derive their revenue from one or both of two sources: (a) the sale of initial franchises and related assets or services and (b) continuing fees based on the operations of franchises.

21.   In 1981 the FASB issued **Statement No. 45,** "Accounting for Franchise Fee Revenue." This Statement was designed to curb abuses in revenue recognition and to standardize the accounting and reporting practices in the franchise industry.   **Initial franchise fees** are to be recorded as revenue only when and as the franchisor makes substantial performance of the services it is obligated to perform and collection of the fee is reasonably assured.   **Continuing franchise fees** should be reported as revenue when they are earned and receivable from the franchisee, unless a portion of them has been designated for a particular purpose, such as providing a specified amount for building maintenance or local advertising. When a franchisee is given an option to purchase equipment or supplies by a franchisor at a bargain purchase price (lower than the normal selling price), a portion of the initial franchise fee should be deferred and accounted for as an adjustment to the selling price of equipment or supplies.   A franchisor should disclose all significant commitments and obligations resulting from franchise agreements, including a description of services that have not yet been substantially performed.

22.   In a **consignment sales arrangement,** merchandise is shipped by the **consignor** to the **consignee,** who acts as an agent for the consignor in selling the merchandise. The merchandise shipped to the consignee remains the **property of the consignor** until a sale is made. When a sale is made, the consignee remits the proceeds, less any related expenses plus a sales commission, to the consignor. When the consignor receives word that a sale has been made, revenue is recognized and inventory is appropriately reduced.

23.   In accounting for consignment sales arrangements, the consignor periodically receives from the consignee an **account sales** that shows the merchandise received, merchandise sold, expenses chargeable to the

consignment, and the cash remitted. Revenue is then recognized by the consignor.

24. **Appendix 19B** presents a discussion of accounting for **service sales transactions**. Service transactions are defined as transactions between a seller and a purchaser in which, for a mutually agreed price, the seller performs, agrees to perform at a later date or agrees to maintain readiness to perform an act or acts, including permitting others to use enterprise resources that do not alone produce tangible commodity or product as the principal intended result. A variety of businesses are involved in rendering services to customers. These entities face the major accounting questions of when to recognize revenue as being earned and when costs should be charged to income.

REVIEW QUESTIONS AND EXERCISES

True - False

Indicate whether each of the following is true (T) or false (F) in the space provided.

_____ 1. Inherent in any sales transaction is an element of gain or loss.

_____ 2. FASB Concepts Statement No. 5 provides that revenue is recognized when (a) it is collected and (b) the earning process is complete.

_____ 3. Transactions for which sales recognition is postponed because of a high ratio of returned merchandise should not be recognized as sales until the return privilege has substantially expired.

_____ 4. The account Customer Advances represents a liability, and any balance appearing in that account at the time financial statements are prepared should ordinarily be shown in the balance sheet as a current liability.

_____ 5. Accountants normally prepare a journal entry for a "contract of sale," while a "contract to sell" is not recorded in the accounts.

_____ 6. The AICPA indicates that the percentage-of-completion method is preferred in accounting for long-term construction contracts only when estimates of costs to complete and extent of progress toward completion are verified by an independent certified public accountant.

_____ 7. The principal advantage of the completed-contract method in accounting for long-term construction contracts is that reported income is based on final results rather than on estimates of unperformed work.

_____ 8. The major disadvantage of the completed-contract method as compared with the percentage-of-completion method is that total net income over the life of the construction contract is normally smaller under the completed-contract method.

_____ 9. Because payment for a product sold on an installment basis is spread over a relatively long period, the risk of loss resulting from uncollectible accounts is greater in installment sales transactions than in ordinary sales.

_____ 10. Under the installment sales method, emphasis is placed on collection rather than on sale, and revenue is considered unrealized until the entire sales price has been collected.

_____ 11. The difference between realized gross profit and deferred gross profit on installment sales is based on the cash collections related to the installment sales.

_____ 12. Repossessed merchandise as a result of a defaulted installment sales contract should be recorded at the best possible estimate of what the item can ultimately be resold for in the second-hand market.

_____ 13. Deferred gross profit on installment sales is generally treated as consisting entirely of unearned revenue and is classified as a current liability.

_____ 14. According to the APB, the installment method of recognizing revenue is restricted to those cases in which receivables are collectible over an extended period of time and there is no reasonable basis for estimating the degree of collectibility.

_____ 15. When interest is involved in installment sales, it should be accounted for as an addition to gross profit recognized on the installment sales collections during the period.

_____ 16. A franchisor must disclose all significant commitments and obligations resulting from franchise agreements, including a description of services that have not yet been substantially performed.

_____ 17. Franchise companies derive their income almost exclusively from the collection and amortization of initial franchise fees.

_____ 18. In consignment sales accounting, merchandise shipped on consignment remains the property of the consignor until sold.

_____ 19. Expenses paid by the consignor in a consignment arrangement are normally deducted from any commission earned by the consignee.

____ 20. Consignment arrangements represent a method of postponing the recognition of revenue until it is known that a sale to a third party has occurred.

Multiple Choice

Select the best answer for each of the following items and enter the corresponding letter in the space provided.

____ 1. Which of the following is not an accurate representation concerning revenue recognition?
A. Revenue from selling products is recognized at the date of sale, usually interpreted to mean the date of delivery to customers.
B. Revenue from services rendered is recognized when cash is received or when services have been performed.
C. Revenue from permitting others to use enterprise assets is recognized as time passes or as the assets are used.
D. Revenue from disposing of assets other than products is recognized at the date of sale.

____ 2. Hartman Corporation recently received a long-term contract to construct a luxury liner. The contract will take 3 years to complete at a cost of $3,500,000. The price of the liner is set at $5,000,000. If the cost estimates at the end of the first year are in line with original estimates, and $1,050,000 of costs were incurred during the first year, the amount of income recognized during the first year using the percentage-of-completion method is:
A. $1,500,000.
B. $1,050,000.
C. $735,000.
D. $450,000.

____ 3. Referring to the information presented in question 2, at the end of the first year which of the following entries would be made to recognize revenue on the contract?
A. Accounts Receivable - Construction Contract
     Revenue on Long-Term Contract
B. Billings on Construction Contract
     Revenue on Long-Term Contract
C. Construction in Process
     Revenue on Long-Term Contract
D. Billings on Construction Contract
     Construction in Process

____ 4. Some companies defer the recognition of revenue because the collection of the sales price is not reasonably assured. One method employed to defer revenue recognition is the cost recovery method. Under the cost recovery method profit is not recognized until:
A. the entire sales price is collected.
B. the seller is convinced that collection is assured beyond a reasonable doubt.
C. the buyer formally accepts delivery of the merchandise involved in the sale.
D. cash payments by the buyer exceed the seller's cost of the merchandise sold.

____ 5. The realization of income on installment sales transactions involves:
A. recognition of the difference between the cash collected on installment sales and the cash expenses incurred.
B. deferring the net income related to installment sales and recognizing the income as cash is collected.
C. deferring the sales and cost of goods sold, proportionally, while recognizing operating or financial expenses in the period incurred.
D. deferring gross profit and all additional expenses related to installment sales until cash is ultimately collected.

The following information relates to questions 6-8.
During 1990, Winters Corporation sold merchandise costing $500,000 on an installment basis for $800,000. The cash receipts related to these sales were collected as follows: 1990, $250,000; 1991, $450,000; 1992, $100,000.

____ 6. What is the rate of gross profit on the installment sales made by Winters Corporation during 1990?
A. 37.5%.
B. 50%.
C. 60%.
D. 62.5%.

____ 7. If expenses, other than the cost of the merchandise sold, related to the 1990 installment sales amounted to $60,000, by what amount would Winters' net income for 1990 increase as a result of installment sales?
A. $240,000.
B. $190,000.
C. $71,250.
D. $33,750.

____ 8. What amounts would be shown in the December 31, 1991, financial statements for realized gross profit on 1990 installment sales, and deferred gross profit on 1990 installment sales, respectively?
   A. $168,750 and $37,500.
   B. $262,500 and $37,500.
   C. $131,250 and $50,000.
   D. $0 and $0.

____ 9. Initial franchise fees are reordered as revenue only when and as the franchisor makes substantial performance of the services it is obligated to perform and:
   A. the franchise agreement will last for 5 years or more.
   B. the franchisee has the financial support of a local bank.
   C. collection of the fee is reasonably assured.
   D. the franchisee maintains a specified minimum profit level.

____ 10. Which of the following is not an accurate statement regarding consignment arrangements?
   A. The merchandise shipped on consignment remains the property of the consignor until sold.
   B. Since the merchandise shipped remains the property of the consignor, the consignee had no legal obligation regarding any damage to the merchandise.
   C. The consignee is entitled to reimbursement from the consignor for expenses paid in connection with selling the goods and is generally entitled to a commission at an agreed rate on sale actually made.
   D. The consignor accepts the risk that the goods on consignment might not sell and thus relieves the consignee of the need to commit working capital to inventory.

Review Exercises

1. Match the revenue transaction listed on the left with the point of revenue realization generally considered appropriate listed on the right.

Revenue Transaction	**Point of Realization**
____ 1. Cash sales of merchandise	A. When accounts receivable are collected
____ 2. Sales of merchandise on account	B. When the designated agent collects the purchase price
____ 3. Percentage-of-completion method on long-term construction project	C. Date of delivery to customer
____ 4. Completed-contract method on long-term construction project	D. When the designated agent submits an "account sales"
____ 5. Installment sales	E. As a completion of the agreement by the seller progresses
____ 6. Consignment sales	

2. Dynomite Construction Company entered into a contract to construct a building for O.U. Money. The contract called for a flat fee of $900,000, and specified that a progress report be given periodically as to percentage of completion. Construction activities for the first two years are summarized below:

1990: Construction costs incurred during the year amounted to $172,800; estimated cost to complete, $547,200.

1991: Construction costs incurred during the year amounted to $385,450; estimated cost to complete, $166,750.

Using the percentage-of-completion method, compute the amount of revenue Dynomite Company should recognize in 1990 and 1991 as a result of this contract.

3.   The following information was taken from the records of Brenner Corporation for the years indicated. The company's year end is December 31.

	1990	1991	1992
Sales (on installment)	$450,000	$500,000	$620,000
Cost of sales	342,000	360,000	434,000
Gross Profit	$108,000	$140,000	$186,000
Cash receipts:			
1990 sales	$125,000	$280,000	$ 45,000
1991 sales		210,000	230,000
1992 sales			250,000

Calculate the amount of Realized Gross Profit on Installment Sales and Deferred Gross Profit to be reported in the year-end financial statement of Brenner Corporation for the three years noted.

SOLUTIONS TO REVIEW QUESTIONS AND EXERCISES

True - False

1.   (T)

2.   (F)   The revenue recognition principle adopted by the FASB has revenue recognized when (1) it is realized and (2) it is earned. Revenues are realized when goods and services are exchanged for cash or claims to cash (receivables). Revenues are earned when the entity has substantially accomplished what it must do to be entitled to the benefits represented by the revenues.

3.   (T)

4.   (T)

5.   (T)

6.   (F)   The accounting profession considers the percentage-of-completion method preferable when estimates of cost to complete and extent of progress toward completion of long-term contracts are reasonably dependable. There is no necessity to have these estimates verified by an independent third party. In 1981, the AICPA recommended that the completed-contract method and the percentage-of-completion method be used in specified circumstances and that these two methods not be viewed as acceptable alternatives in the same circumstances.

7.   (T)

8.   (F)   The total net income or gross profit over the life of a construction contract is the same under both the percentage-of-completion method and the completed contract method. The major difference between the methods is the timing of the recognition of gross profit during the life of the contract.

9.   (T)

10.   (F)   This statement is false because each time a portion of the revenue from an installment sale is collected, it is recognized as revenue. The statement in this question reads "...until the entire sales price is collected" which makes it false.

11.   (T)

12.   (F)   The objective with respect to repossessed merchandise is to put it on the books at its fair value or, when fair value is not ascertainable, at the best possible approximation of fair value.

13.   (T)

14.   (T)

15.   (F)   When interest is involved in installment sales, it should be accounted for separately as interest revenue distinct from the gross profit recognized on the installment sales collections during the period.

16.   (T)

17. (F) Franchise companies derive their revenue from one or both of two sources: (1) from the sale of initial franchise and related assets or services and (2) from continuing fees based on the operations of franchises.

18. (T)

19. (F) The consignee acts as an agent for the consignor in selling merchandise. The consignee earns a commission upon the sale of the consigned merchandise. However, expenses incurred by the consignor are not deducted from the commissions earned by the consignee.

20. (T)

Multiple Choice

1. (B) Revenues from services rendered is recognized when services have been performed and are billable. The receipt of cash does not necessarily signal the recognition of revenue.

2. (D)

Total cost	$3,500,000
Cost incurred	$1,050,000

% of total cost incurred $1,050,000 ÷ $3,500,000 = .30

Estimated income: $5,000,000 - $3,500,000 = $1,500,000

Income recognized in the first year

$1,500,000 x .30 = $450,000

3. (C) Under the percentage-of-completion method, the Construction in Progress account is used to record revenue throughout the contract period.

4. (D) Under the cost recovery method, after all costs have been recovered, any additional cash collections are included in income. Thus, profit is not recognized until cash payments by the buyer exceed the seller's cost of merchandise sold. This method is used where a high degree of uncertainty exists related to collection of receivables.

5. (C) Under the installment method of accounting, income recognition is deferred until the period of cash collection. Both revenues and cost of sales are recognized in the period of sale, but the related gross profit is deferred to those periods in which cash is collected. Thus, instead of the sale being deferred to the future periods of anticipated collection and then related costs and expenses being deferred, only the proportional gross profit is deferred, which is equivalent to deferring both sales and cost of sales. Other expenses such as selling expense and administrative expense are not deferred.

6. (A) Rate of gross profit is computed by dividing the gross profit by the sales price.

G.P. ($800,000 - 500,000)	$300,000
Sales Price	800,000
Rate of G.P. ($300,000 ÷ $800,000	37.5%

7. (D)

Rate of gross profit	37.5%
Cash collected	$250,000
Realized gross profit ($250,000 x 37.5%)	93,750
Less expenses	60,000
Increase in net income	$33,750

8. (A)

Total gross profit ($800,000 - $500,000)	$300,000
Gross profit realized in:	

1990 ($250,000 x 37.5%)	$ 93,750
1991 ($450,000 x 37.5%)	168,750
1992 ($100,000 x 37.5%)	37,500

The December 31, 1991, financial statements will show realized gross profit of $168,750 and deferred gross profit of $37,500 resulting from 1990 installment sales.

9. (C) The initial franchise fee is considered for establishing the franchise relationship and providing some initial services. Such fees are recorded as revenue only upon substantial performance by the franchisor and when collection of the initial franchise fee is reasonably assured.

10. (B) When a consignee accepts merchandise on a consignment arrangement, he or she agrees to exercise due diligence in caring for and selling the merchandise. If the consignee does not exercise due diligence in caring for the merchandise, he or she will be liable for damages sustained.

Review Exercises

1. 1. C   4. C
   2. C   5. A
   3. E   6. D

2. 1990:

Contract price		$900,000
Less:		
Cost to date	$172,800	
Estimated cost to complete	547,200	
Estimated total cost		720,000
Estimated total income		$180,000

Income recognized in 1990:

($172,800 ÷ 720,000) x $180,000 = $43,200

1991:

Contract price		$900,000
Less:		
Cost to date	$558,250	
Estimated cost to complete	166,750	
Estimated total cost		725,000
Estimated total income		$175,000

Income recognized in 1991:

($558,250 ÷ 725,000) X $175,000 =	$134,750
Less 1990 recognized income	43,200
	$ 91,550

3.

	1990	1991	1992
Rate of Gross Profit on sales	24%	28%	30%
Realized Gross Profit:			
1990 sales	$30,000	$67,200	$10,800
1991 sales		58,800	64,400
1992 sales			75,000
Realized gross Profit 12-31	$30,000	$126,000	$150,200
Deferred Gross Profit:			
1990 sales	$78,000	$10,800	
1991 sales		81,200	$ 16,800
1992 sales			111,000
Deferred Gross Profit 12-31	$78,000	$92,000	$127,800

20

Accounting for Income Taxes

Chapter Synopsis

Chapter 20 addresses the issues related to accounting for income taxes. Taxable income is computed in accordance with prescribed tax regulations and rules, whereas accounting income is measured in accordance with generally accepted accounting principles. Unfortunately for accountants, tax regulations and accounting principles are not always in agreement.

Chapter Review

1. Due to the fact that tax regulations and generally accepted accounting principles differ in many ways, taxable income and financial income frequently differ. The following represent examples of events that can result in such differences: (a) depreciation computed on a straight-line basis for financial reporting purposes and on an accelerated basis for tax purposes, (b) income recognized on the accrual basis for financial reporting purposes and on the installment basis for tax purposes, and (c) warranty costs recognized in the period incurred for financial reporting purposes and when they are paid for tax purposes.

2. The items discussed in paragraph one above can result in temporary differences between the amounts reported for book purposes and those reported for tax purposes. A **temporary difference** is the difference between the tax basis of an asset or liability and its reported amount in the financial statements that will result in taxable amounts (increase in taxable income) or deductible amounts (decrease in taxable income) in future years when the reported amount of the asset is recovered or when the reported amount of the liability is settled. When the book amount of an asset or liability differs from the tax basis as a result of a temporary difference, the future tax effects on taxable income must be reported in the current financial statements.

3. A **deferred tax liability** is the amount of deferred tax consequence attributable to the temporary differences that will result in net taxable amounts (taxable amounts less deductible amounts) in future years. The liability is the amount of taxes payable on these net taxable amounts in future years based on existing provisions of the tax law.

4. The following example is presented to demonstrate the deferred tax liability concept. Assume that Hale Company earns $50,000 of net operating income before depreciation for each of five consecutive years. The company depreciates its fixed assets using the straight-line method for accounting purposes and an acceptable accelerated method for tax purposes over this five-year period. The following schedule shows taxable income, income tax payable, accounting income, and income tax expense for the five-year period assuming a 40% tax rate.

Year	Taxable Income	Income Tax Payable	Accounting Income	Income Tax Expense
1	$ 40,000	$16,000	$ 44,000	$ 17,600
2	42,000	16,800	44,000	17,600
3	44,000	17,600	44,000	17,600
4	46,000	18,400	44,000	17,600
5	48,000	19,200	44,000	17,600
Totals	$220,000	$88,000	$220,000	$ 88,000

5. At the end of year one the entry to recognize the tax expense and the tax liability is:

Income Tax Expense	17,600	
Income Tax Payable		16,000
Deferred Tax Liability		1,600

Each year (two through five) the entry is made debiting the tax expense account and crediting the tax liability for the amounts indicated. Note that the **Deferred Tax Liability** account will increase in years one and two, remain unchanged in year three, and then decrease in years four and five so that a zero balance results at the end of the five-year period which represents the assets' useful life.

6. If temporary differences cause pretax accounting income to be less than taxable income in the current period then a **deferred tax asset** may be recognized. However, the **Financial Accounting Standards Board** has taken the position that, in general, a deferred tax asset can only be recognized to the extent that deductible amounts will offset in future years taxable amounts from other temporary differences that already exist. This position recognizes the fact that there must be income generated in the future for temporary differences resulting in future net deductible amounts to be offset. The FASB is of the opinion that earning income in the future (a) has not occurred, and (b) should not be assumed in preparing

financial statements for the current year. This concept is further discussed in later paragraphs.

7.   Differences between taxable income and accounting income can be categorized as either **(a) temporary differences** or **(b) permanent differences.** Temporary differences arise when the tax basis of an asset or liability and its reported amount in the financial statements differ. This difference will reverse and result in taxable or deductible amounts in future years as the asset is recovered or the liability is settled at its reported amount.

8.   Temporary differences originate in one period and reverse or "turn around" in one or more subsequent periods. For example, when a company records a product warranty liability an expense is recognized for accounting purposes but not for tax purposes. In future years when the product warranty liability is settled, tax deductible amounts result which reverse the effect of the original timing differences.

9.   Two concepts related to temporary differences are, **originating differences** and **reversing differences.** An originating difference is the initial temporary difference between the book basis and the tax basis of an asset or liability regardless of whether the tax basis of the asset of liability exceeds or is exceeded by the book basis of the asset or liability. A reversing difference, on the other hand, occurs when a temporary difference that originated in a prior period is eliminated and the tax effect is removed from the deferred tax account. In the depreciation example presented in paragraph 4 above, the originating difference was $1,600 and $800 in the first two years, and the reversing difference was $800 and $1,600 in the final two years.

10.   Permanent differences are items that (a) enter into financial income but *never* into taxable income, or (b) enter into taxable income but *never* into financial income. Examples of permanent differences include interest received on state and municipal obligations, proceeds from life insurance on key executives, and amortization of goodwill. These items are not included in the computation of taxable income, and the profession has concluded that the tax consequences of these differences should not be recognized.

11.   When recording deferred income taxes consideration must be given to the tax rate in effect when the timing differences reverse. Normally, the current tax rate is used to compute deferred income taxes. However, future tax rates, other than the current rate **should be used** when such rates **have been enacted into law.** When an unexpected change in the tax rate has been enacted into law, its effect on deferred income tax and related tax expense should be recorded immediately. The effects are reported as an adjustment to tax expense in the period of the change.

12.   A **net operating loss** occurs for tax purposes in a year when tax-deductible expenses exceed taxable revenues. Under certain circumstances the federal tax laws permit taxpayers to use the losses of one year to offset the profits of other years. This income-averaging provision is accomplished through the **carryback** and **carryforward** of net operating losses. Under these rules, a company pays no income taxes for a year in which it incurs a net operating loss.

13.   A company may carry a net operating loss back three years and receive refunds for income taxes paid in those years. The loss must be applied to the earliest year first and then sequentially to the second and third year. Any loss remaining after the three year carryback may be carried forward up to 15 years to offset future taxable income. A company may elect the loss carryforward only, offsetting future taxable income for up to 15 years.

14.   Regarding the recognition of a net operating loss carryforward, a question arises as to whether the tax effect of a loss carryforward should be recognized in the loss year when the potential benefits arise or in future years when the benefits are actually realized. The **FASB** has taken the position that the occurrence of a past event is needed to warrant the recognition of an asset. Although a loss carryforward creates a right to a potential economic benefit, future taxable income which has not yet occurred is not a basis for current recognition of that benefit. Therefore, in most cases no journal entry is made in the loss year to record the tax benefit of loss carryforwards. **The benefits are recognized in the year they are realized.**

15.   Understanding carryback and carryforward rules is important because these rules are applied to the net future deductible amount as if it were a real operating loss for purposes of determining the recognition of a deferred tax asset. To determine the amount of deferred tax asset (if any) and the deferred tax liability (if any) to report, it is necessary to prepare a schedule of taxable amounts and deductible amounts as illustrated in the text. With respect to recognition of deferred tax assets it should be remembered that:

(a)   Income tax payable does not change because of the carryback or carryforward of net deductible amounts.

(b)   A deferred tax asset is recorded only when the tax benefit of net deductible amounts can be realized by loss carryback from future years to reduce taxes paid in the current or a prior period.

(c)   If net future deductible amounts are carried forward in the scheduling process, they can be used only to offset taxable amounts from existing temporary differences.

16. The FASB requires companies to use **tax planning strategies** when establishing the period in which temporary differences will reverse and how they will be taxed or deducted. In considering tax planning strategies, it is appropriate to consider not only historical events that have tax consequences but also future events that are projected or expected to occur. A tax planning strategy must meet two criteria: **(a)** it must be a prudent and feasible strategy over which management has discretion and control, and **(b)** it cannot involve significant cost to the enterprise.

17. A **tax credit** is a direct reduction of income taxes payable. The FASB takes the position that the same rules that apply for a net operating loss situation as it applies to deferred income taxes should also apply to unused tax credits.

18. Deferred income taxes are reported on the balance sheet as receivables and payables. Classification as current or noncurrent depends on when the temporary differences reverse. Temporary differences that reverse in the next year should be classified as current and all other temporary differences should be classified as noncurrent. Also, the nature or type of temporary difference that gave rise to significant portions of deferred tax assets or liabilities should be disclosed. The balance in the deferred income tax account should be analyzed into its components and classified on the balance sheet into two categories: **one for net current amount** and **one for net noncurrent (or long-term) amount.**

19. The amount of income tax expense (or benefit) should be allocated to continuing operations, discontinued operations, extraordinary items, the cumulative effect of accounting changes, and prior period adjustments. In addition, the significant components of income tax expense attributable to continuing operations should be disclosed. **FASB Statement No. 96, Accounting for Income Taxes**, also requires companies to reconcile income tax expense on continuing operations with the amount that results from applying domestic federal statutory tax rates to pretax income from continuing operations.

20. The amounts of any operating loss carryforwards not recognized in the loss period, along with the expiration of these loss carryforwards, should be disclosed. In disclosing tax carryforwards, both the amount of tax operating loss carryforwards and the amount of financial accounting tax operating loss carryforwards should be disclosed. The FASB believes that the asset-liability viewpoint (balance sheet approach) is the most convenient method for accounting for income taxes. Under this approach, the objective of accounting for income taxes is to recognize the amount of current and deferred taxes payable or refundable at the date of the financial statements (1) as a result of events that have been recognized in the financial statements and (2) as measured by the provisions of enacted tax laws.

21. **Appendix 20-A** includes a comprehensive illustration of a deferred income tax problem with several temporary and permanent differences. In **Appendix 20-B** the authors present a discussion of the conceptual aspects of interperiod tax allocation. The effect of temporary differences on net operating losses is discussed in **Appendix 20-C.**

REVIEW QUESTIONS AND EXERCISES

True-False
Indicate whether each of the following is true (T) or false (F) in the space provided.

_____ 1. A temporary difference is the difference between the tax basis of an asset or liability and its reported amount in the financial statements that will result in taxable amounts or deductible amounts in future years when the reported amount of the asset is recovered or when the reported amount of the liability is settled.

_____ 2. When the book amount of an asset or liability differs from the tax basis as a result of a temporary difference, the future tax effects on taxable income must be reported solely in the future financial statement that the difference effects.

_____ 3. A deferred tax liability is the amount of deferred tax consequences attributable to existing temporary differences that will result in net taxable amounts in future years.

_____ 4. The concept of a deferred tax liability meets the definition of a liability established in Statement of Financial Accounting Concepts No. 6 because it (a) results from past transactions, (b) is a present obligation, and (c) represents a future sacrifice.

_____ 5. The reason the FASB takes a strong position against recognition of deferred tax assets concerns the fact that taxes are an expense and should not be associated with assets which represent items of value.

_____ 6. An originating difference is the initial temporary difference that occurs when the book basis of an asset exceeds the tax basis of a liability.

_____ 7. A reversing difference occurs when temporary differences that originate in prior periods are eliminated and the tax effect is removed from the deferred tax account.

_____ 8. A permanent difference results when the tax laws cause an item reported on the income statement to be different from that same item reported on the balance sheet.

_____ 9. A corporation that has tax-free income has an effective tax rate that is less than the statutory (regular) tax rate.

_____ 10. In computing deferred income taxes a new tax rate should be used if (a) it is probable that a future tax rate change will occur, and (b) the rate is reasonably estimatable.

_____ 11. Under the carryback and carryforward provisions of the federal tax laws a company pays no tax in a year in which it incurs a net operating loss and can carry that loss back three years and forward 15 years in offsetting past and future taxable income.

_____ 12. In general, the tax benefits of loss carryforwards should not be recognized in the loss year when the benefits arise, but rather in the year they are realized.

_____ 13. The only way a tax loss carryforward can be recognized in the current year is when an entity has incurred net losses during the past three calendar years and has no ability to carry any of the loss back.

_____ 14. A deferred tax asset is recorded only when the tax benefit of net deductible amounts can be realized by loss carryback from future years to reduce taxes paid in the current or prior periods.

_____ 15. The FASB requires companies to use tax planning strategies when estimating the period in which temporary differences will reverse and how they will be taxed or deducted.

_____ 16. In considering tax planning strategies, it is appropriate to focus attention totally on future events that are projected or expected to occur.

_____ 17. Tax planning strategies that anticipate the tax consequences of earning financial income or incurring financial loss or expense in future years are prohibited for purposes of recognition or measurement of a deferred tax asset or liability.

_____ 18. The alternative minimum tax system is used by corporations that wish to pay a smaller amount of tax in an earlier year and defer larger tax payments to later years when income is greater.

_____ 19. In classifying deferred taxes on the balance sheet, an entity should net the current deferred tax asset and liability amount and the net noncurrent deferred tax asset and liability amount thus reporting only one current and one noncurrent deferred tax amount.

_____ 20. The asset-liability approach to accounting for income taxes requires a journal entry at the end of each year which either increases an asset or decreases a liability.

Multiple Choice

_____ 1. Because tax regulations and GAAP are different in many ways, taxable income and financial income frequently differ. Which of the following would not result in a difference between tax and financial income.
   A. Depreciation computed on a straight-line basis for financial reporting purposes, but an accelerated method for tax purposes.
   B. Warranty costs are recognized in the period incurred for financial reporting purposes, but are recognized when they are paid for tax purposes.
   C. Goodwill amortization taken directly to retained earnings for financial reporting purposes, and handled according to existing tax regulations for tax purposes.
   D. Income is recognized on the accrual basis for financial reporting purposes, but is recognized on the installment basis for tax purposes.

_____ 2. A deferred tax liability is classified on the balance sheet as either a current or a noncurrent liability. The current amount of a deferred tax liability should be
   A. the net deferred tax consequences of temporary differences that will result in net taxable amounts during the next year.
   B. totally eliminated from the financial statements if the amount is related to a noncurrent asset.
   C. less than the noncurrent portion of the deferred tax liability.
   D. the total of all deferred tax consequences that are not expected to reverse in the operating period or one year, whichever is greater.

_____ 3. In general, the FASB takes a conservative approach regarding the recognition of a deferred tax asset because
   A. the entity is liable to overstate its financial position due to the inability to compute an accurate amount.
   B. earning income in the future is not assured and should not be assumed in preparing financial statements.

C. it is consistent with the approach taken with respect to the recognition of a deferred tax liability.

D. deferred tax assets have no economic value.

_____ 4. A major distinction between temporary and permanent differences is:

A. permanent differences are not representative of acceptable accounting practice.

B. temporary differences occur frequently, whereas permanent differences occur only once.

C. once an item is determined to be a temporary difference, it maintains that status; however, a permanent difference can change in status with the passage of time.

D. temporary differences reverse themselves in subsequent accounting periods, whereas permanent differences do not reverse.

_____ 5. The use of accelerated depreciation for tax purposes and straight-line depreciation for accounting purposes results in

A. a larger amount of depreciation expense shown on the tax return than on the income statement, over the asset's useful life.

B. the asset being fully depreciated for tax purposes in half the time it takes to become fully depreciated for accounting purposes.

C. a larger amount of depreciation expense shown on the income statement than on the tax return in the last year of the asset's useful life.

D. a loss on the sale of the asset in question if it is sold for its book value before its useful life expires.

_____ 6. Hrebic Corporation reports income before taxes of $500,000 in its income statement, but because of timing differences taxable income is only $200,000. If the tax rate is 45%, the corporation should report what amount of net income.

A. $337,500.

B. $275,000.

C. $225,000.

D. $ 90,000.

_____ 7. When a change in the tax rate is enacted into law, its effect on deferred income taxes should be

A. handled retroactively in accordance with the guidance related to changes in accounting principles.

B. considered, but it should only be recorded in the accounts if it reduces a deferred tax liability or increases a deferred tax asset.

C. recorded immediately.

D. applied to all temporary or permanent differences that arise prior to the date of the enactment of the tax rate change, but not subsequent to the date of the change.

_____ 8. The following information is taken from the accounts of Zigmond Company after its first year of operations:

Income before taxes		$100,000
Federal income tax payable	$41,600	
Deferred income tax	(1,600)	
Income tax expense		40,000
Net income		$60,000

Zigmond estimates its annual warranty expense as a percentage of sales. The amount charged to warranty expense on its books was $38,000. No other differences existed between accounting and taxable income. Assuming a 40% income tax rate, what amount was actually paid this year on the Company's warranty?

A. $34,000.

B. $38,000.

C. $40,000.

D. $42,000.

_____ 9. B & D Ford Company sells its product on an installment basis, earning a $450 pretax gross profit on each installment sale. For accounting purposes the entire $450 is recognized in the year of sale, but for income tax purposes the installment method of accounting is used. Assume Ford makes one sale in 1988, another sale is in 1989, and a third sale in 1990. In each case, one-third of the gross sales price is collected in the year of sale, one-third in the next year, and the final installment in the third year. If the tax rate is 50%, what amount of deferred income taxes should Ford Company show on its December 31, 1990 balance sheet?

A. $150.

B. $225.

C. $300.

D. $450.

_____ 10. Which of the following is not a criteria for a tax planning strategy?

A. It must be a prudent and feasible strategy over which management has discretion and control.

B. Management must have both the ability and intent to implement the strategy.

C. The strategy should not result in significant expenses to implement the underlying transactions or significant losses as a result of changing the future years in which the asset is recovered or a liability is settled.

D. The strategy should anticipate the tax consequences of earning financial income or incurring financial losses or expenses in future years for purposes of recognition or measurement of a deferred tax liability or asset.

Review Exercises

1. Numerous items create differences between taxable income and pretax financial income. For purposes of accounting recognition, these differences are of two types: (1) temporary differences and (2) permanent differences. These two classifications are further divided into other categories. Four of those categories are:

   Temporary Differences:
   A. Expenses or losses that are tax deductible after they are recognized in financial income.
   B. Revenues or gains that are taxable before they are recognized in financial income.

   Permanent Differences:
   C. Items recognized for accounting purposes but not for tax purposes.
   D. Items recognized for tax purposes but not for accounting purposes.

For each of the items listed below, indicate by letter which of the four categories it represents.

____ 1. Litigation accruals.
____ 2. Fines and expenses resulting from a violation of law.
____ 3. Percentage depletion.
____ 4. Proceeds from life insurance carried by the company on a key officer.
____ 5. Advance rental receipts.
____ 6. Prepaid contract and royalties paid in advance.
____ 7. Product warranty liability.
____ 8. Net operating loss deduction.
____ 9. Estimated liabilities related to discontinued operations.
____ 10. Interest received on state and municipal obligations.

2. Jerry Company reported the following net income before taxes and depreciation for the years indicated.

   1988: $80,000   **1989:** $100,000   **1990:** $75,000

The Company purchased assets costing $90,000 on January 1, 1988. The assets have a three-year useful life and no salvage value. For tax purposes the Company used an acceptable accelerated depreciation method that resulted in depreciation expense of $45,000; $30,000; and $15,000 for the three years respectively. For financial reporting purposes the straight-line method was used. If a 30% tax rate was in effect for the three years, what journal entry did Jerry Company make at the end of each year to reflect appropriate accounting for income taxes?

3. Kevin Corporation recorded the following pretax accounting income and taxable income for the three years shown below:

Year	Pretax Financial Income	Taxable Income
1988	$250,000	$190,000
1989	340,000	265,000
1990	360,000	280,000

Pretax financial income includes $20,000 of interest received from an investment in municipal bonds. The tax rate was 40% in 1988, but the legislature increased the tax rate to 50% at the end of 1989 and it remained at 50% in 1990.

Prepare journal entries to record income tax expenses, deferred taxes, and the income taxes payable at the end of each year.

SOLUTIONS TO REVIEW QUESTIONS AND EXERCISES

True-False

1. (T)
2. (F) When the book amount of an asset or liability differs from the tax basis as a result of a temporary difference, the future tax effects on taxable income must be reported in the current financial statements.
3. (T)
4. (T)
5. (F) If the deferred tax consequences of temporary differences result in future net deductible amounts, there must be income in the future to offset this net deductible amount. The tax consequences of possibly earning income in the future should not be anticipated in the current year. As a result, the FASB concluded that a deferred tax asset should not be recognized for temporary differences that will result in net future deductible amounts.
6. (F) An originating difference is the initial temporary difference between the book basis and the tax basis of an asset or liability regardless of whether the tax basis of the asset or liability exceeds or is exceeded by the book basis of the asset or liability.
7. (T)
8. (F) Permanent differences are items that (1) enter into financial income but never into taxable income, or (2) enter into taxable income but never into financial income.
9. (T)
10. (F) Even if it is probable that future tax rate change will occur, if it is not yet enacted into law, the current rate should be used.
11. (T)
12. (T)
13. (F) In general a tax loss carryforward cannot be recognized in the year in which the loss occurs. One exception to the general rule is when existing temporary differences are expected to result in net taxable amounts in the carryforward period. In this case, the tax benefit can be realized to the extent of net taxable amounts because it is known that the company will have taxable income in the future (realization assured).
14. (T)
15. (T)
16. (F) In considering tax planning strategies, it is appropriate to consider both historical events that have tax consequences as well as future events that are projected or expected to occur.
17. (T)
18. (F) The current tax law requires a corporation to compute its potential tax liability using the regular tax system and an alternative minimum tax system. The alternative minimum tax system is used to insure that corporations do not avoid paying a fair share of income taxes through various tax avoidance approaches.
19. (T)
20. (F) Under the asset-liability approach, the objective of accounting for income taxes is to recognize the amount of current and deferred taxes payable or refundable at the date of the financial statements (1) as a result of events that have been recognized in the financial statements and (2) as measured by the provisions of enacted tax laws.

Multiple Choice

1. (C) Because the amortization of goodwill is not deductible for tax purposes, if it were taken directly to retained earnings for financial reporting purposes there would be no difference in income because of this item. Items A, B, and D would all result in differences between tax and financial income.

2. (A) The concept of a current liability as defined in financial accounting applies with equal relevance in the case of deferred taxes. Thus, if the tax consequences of temporary differences result in net taxable amounts during the next year then a current liability has been created.

3. (B) The FASB's position is that, in general, deferred tax assets can be recognized only to the extent that deductible amounts will offset in future years taxable amounts from the elimination of other temporary differences that already exist. The Board believes that earning income in the future (1) is never assured, and (2) should not be assumed in preparing financial statements. Therefore, the tax consequences of possibly earning income in the future should not be anticipated in the current year.

4. (D) The only correct alternative regarding temporary differences and permanent differences is alternative D. Temporary and permanent differences occur with the same general frequency. Also, permanent differences do not change in status with the passage of time.

5. (C) Depreciation expense under an accelerated depreciation method will be larger in the early years of an asset's life and smaller in the later years. When compared to depreciation expense calculated under the straight-line method, the expense calculated under the accelerated method will be greater in the early years and less in the later years of an asset's useful life.

6. (B)
Income	$500,000
Tax expense	225,000
Net income	$275,000

   The tax expense is $225,000, which is reported on the income statement. Due to the temporary difference the company's tax liability is only $90,000 ($200,000 x .45). Thus, Deferred Income Taxes would be credited for $135,000 ($225,000 - $90,000) due to the temporary difference.

7. (C) When a change in the tax rate is enacted into law, its effect on deferred income tax should be recorded immediately. The effects are reported as an adjustment to tax expense in the period of the change.

8. (A) The $1,600 difference between tax expense and tax liability is caused by the warranty expense. Because the tax liability is greater by $1,600, the amount of warranty expense charged on the tax return was smaller than the $38,000 charged against accounting income. We also know that 40% of the difference between warranty expense and the warranty payments actually made is $1,600. Thus, the total difference is $4,000 ($1,600 x .40). The amount actually paid this year on the Company's warranty was $34,000 ($38,000 - $4,000).

9. (B)
	1988	1989	1990
Tax Expense	$225	$225	$225
Tax Liability	75	150	225
Deferred Tax (decrease)/increase	150	75	-0-
Deferred Tax Balance	$150	$225	$225

10. (D) Tax planning strategies that anticipate the tax consequences of earning financial income or incurring financial losses or expenses in future years are prohibited for purposes of recognition or measurement of a deferred tax liability or asset. Alternatives A, B, and C represent appropriate criteria for tax planning strategies.

Review Exercises

1.
1.	A	6.	B
2.	C	7.	A
3.	D	8.	D
4.	C	9.	A
5.	B	10.	C

2.

	1988		1989		1990	
	Acct.	Tax	Acct.	Tax	Acct.	Tax
Income before tax and depreciation............................	$80,000	$80,000	$100,000	$100,000	$75,000	$75,000
Depreciation expense.................	(30,000)	(45,000)	(30,000)	(30,000)	(30,000)	(15,000)
	$50,000	$35,000	$70,000	$70,000	$45,000	$60,000
Income tax	(15,000)	(10,500)	(21,000)	(21,000)	(13,500)	(18,000)
	$35,000	$24,500	$49,000	$49,000	$31,500	$42,000

1988:

Income Tax Expense.............................	15,000	
Deferred Income Taxes......................		4,500
Income Taxes Payable		10,500

1989:

Income Tax Expense.............................	21,000	
Income Taxes Payable		21,000

1990:

Income Tax Expense.............................	13,500	
Deferred Income Taxes...........................	4,500	
Income Taxes Payable		18,000

3. **1988**

Income Tax Expense	92,000(a)	
Deferred Tax Liability		16,000
Income Tax Payable (190,000 x .40)		76,000

1989

Income Tax Expense	160,000(b)	
Deferred Tax Liability		27,500
Income Tax Payable		132,500

Income Tax Expense	4,000(c)	
Deferred Tax Liability		4,000

1990

Income Tax Expense	170,000(d)	
Deferred Tax Liability		30,000
Income Tax Payable		140,000

(a)

Financial Income	250,000
Nontaxable Income	(20,000)
Taxable Financial Income	$230,000
Tax Rate	.40
Income Tax Expense	$ 92,000

(b)

Financial Income	$340,000
Nontaxable Income	(20,000)
Taxable Financial Income	$320,000
Tax Rate	.50
Income Tax Expense	$160,000

(c) Increase in Tax Expense and Deferred Tax Liability due to change in tax rate.
Difference between 1988 and 1989 Financial and Taxable Income
($230,000 - 190,000 = $40,000)
Change in the tax rate (50% - 40% = 10%)
$40,000 x .10 = $4,000

(d)

Financial Income	$360,000
Nontaxable Income	(20,000)
Taxable Financial Income	$340,000
Tax Rate	.50
Income Tax Expense	$170,000

21

Accounting for pensions

Chapter Synopsis

Chapter 21 discusses the various aspects of accounting for the cost of pension plans. Accounting for pension costs is somewhat complicated because of the variety of social concepts, legal considerations, actuarial techniques, income tax regulations, and varying business philosophies that affect the development and maintenance of pension plans. This chapter relates these issues to the recommended accounting treatment for the costs associated with a pension plan as described in *FASB Statement No. 87*.

Chapter Review

1. A **pension plan** is an arrangement whereby an employer provides benefits (Payments) to employees after they retire. The most common types of pension arrangements are **defined contribution plans** and **defined benefit plans**. In a defined contribution plan, the employer agrees to contribute a certain sum each period based on a formula. The formula might consider such factors as age, length of service, employer's profits, and compensation level. A defined benefit plan defines the benefits that the employee will receive at the time of retirement. The formula that is typically used provides for the benefits to be a function of the level of compensation near retirement and of the number of years of service.

2. The accounting for a defined contribution plan is straightforward. In this type of plan, the benefit of gain or the risk of loss from the assets contributed to pension plans is borne by the employee. The accounting for a defined benefit plan is complex. Because the benefits are defined in terms of uncertain future variables, an appropriate funding pattern must be established to insure that enough monies will be available at retirement to meet the benefits promised.

3. In the accounting for a pension plan, consideration must be given to accounting for the employer and accounting for the pension plan itself. A pension plan is said to be **funded** when the employer sets funds aside for future pension benefits by making payments to a funding agency that is responsible for accumulating the assets of the pension fund and for making payment to the recipients as the benefits come due. In an unfunded plan, the funds are under the control of the company and pension payments are made directly by the company as they become due.

4. Pension plans can be **contributory** or **noncontributory**. In a contributory plan, the employee bears part of the cost of the stated benefits or voluntarily makes payment to increase the benefits. If the plan is noncontributory, the employer bears the entire cost. Because the problems associated with pension plans involve complicated actuarial considerations, actuaries are engaged to insure that the plan is appropriate for all employee groups covered. Actuaries make predictions (actuarial assumptions) of mortality rates, employee turnover, interest and earnings rates, early retirement frequency, future salaries, and other factors necessary to operate a pension plan. Thus, accounting for defined benefit pension plans is highly reliant upon information and measurements provided by actuaries.

5. Most accountants agree that an employer's **pension obligation** is the deferred compensation obligation it has to its employees for their services under the terms of the pension plan. However, there are three ways to measure this liability. One approach is to base the obligation on the **vested benefits** current employees are entitled to. The vested benefits pension obligation is computed using current salary levels and includes only vested benefits. A second approach to the measurement of the pension obligation is to base the computation on all years of service performed by employees under the plan--both vested and nonvested--using **current** salary levels. This measurement of the pension obligation is called the **accumulated benefit obligation**. A third measurement technique bases the computation on both vested and nonvested service using **future** salaries. Because future salaries are expected to be higher than current salaries, this approach known as the **projected benefit obligation**, results in the largest measurement of the pension obligation.

6. Regardless of the approach used, the estimated future benefits to be paid are discounted to present value. While the accumulated benefit obligation is used in certain situations, the profession generally has adopted the

projected benefits obligation to measure the liability for the pension obligation.

7. In accounting for pensions, three major issues are involved. These are:
   a. Allocating the cost of the pension plan to the proper accounting period.
   b. Measurement and reporting of the assets and obligations arising from a pension plan.
   c. Financial statement disclosure of the status and effects of the pension plan.

There is now broad agreement that pension cost should be accounted for on the accrual basis. Accounting for pension plans requires measurement of the cost and its identification with the appropriate time periods in the same manner as other costs and expenses.

8. The determination of pension cost is very complicated because it is a function of a number of factors. These factors are identified and described below.

Service Cost. Because a pension is viewed as a form of deferred compensation, it follows that the cost of the pension occurs over the period that the employee provides services to the employer. In *FASB Statement No. 87*, the Board indicated that the service cost component recognized in a period should be determined as the actuarial present value of benefits attributed by the pension benefit formula to employee service during that period.

Interest. A pension is a deferred compensation arrangement where wages are deferred and a liability is created. Given that the liability is not paid until maturity, it is recorded on a discounted basis and accrues interest due to the passage of time over the life of the employee. The assumed discount rate should reflect the rates at which pension benefits could be effectively settled. The FASB did indicate that it is appropriate to look to available information about rates implicit in current prices of annuity contracts that could be used to effect settlement of the obligation.

Return on Plan Assets. The pension plan liability for deferred compensation may be discharged by funding the liability as it occurs. When this takes place, the assets contributed to the fund plus earnings on those assets should be sufficient to pay the pension claimants. However, if the employer chooses to use a funding method that either overfunds or underfunds the liability, an adjustment to pension expense is needed. Pension expense is reduced if the plan is overfunded and increased if it is underfunded.

Prior Service Cost. Plan amendments (including initiation of a pension plan) often include provisions to increase benefits for service provided in prior years. Because plan amendments are granted with the expectation that the employer will realize economic

benefits in future periods, the cost of providing these retroactive benefits is generally considered to be allocated to pension expense in the future. Thus, the retroactive benefits should not be recognized as pension expense entirely in the year of amendment but should be recognized during the service periods of those employees who are expected to receive benefits under the plan. The cost of the retroactive benefits is the increase in the projected benefit obligation at the date of the amendment.

Gains and Losses. A set of assumptions is used to estimate the pension obligation and pension expense. If these assumptions are inaccurate, adjustments to the appropriate accounts are necessary. That is, gains and losses develop as a result of the difference between actual and expected experience which must be accounted for.

These factors have the following effect on pension cost:
   a. Service cost increases pension expense.
   b. Interest increases pension expense.
   c. Return on plan assets decreases pension expense.
   d. Prior service cost generally increases pension expense.
   e. Gains and losses increase or decrease pension expense.

Asset gains (occurring when actual return on plan assets is greater than expected return) and **asset losses** (occurring when actual return on plan assets is less than expected return) are recorded in an Unrecognized Net Gain of Loss account and combined with unexpected gains and losses accumulated in prior years. **Liability gains** (resulting from unexpected decreases in the liability balance) and **liability losses** (resulting from unexpected increases in the liability balance) are deferred and combined in the same Unrecognized Net Gain or Loss account used for asset gains or losses.

9. The Unrecognized Net Gain or Loss account can continue to grow if asset gains and losses are not offset by liability gains and losses. To limit this potential growth, the FASB invented the **corridor approach** for amortizing the accumulated balance in the Unrecognized Gain or Loss account when it gets too large. The unrecognized net gain or loss account balance gets too large and must be amortized when it exceeds the arbitrarily selected FASB criterion of **10% of the larger of the beginning balance of the projected benefit obligation or the market-related value of plan assets.** Any systematic method of amortizing the excess may be used but it cannot be less than the amount computed using straight-line amortization over the average remaining service-life of all active employees. Amortization of the excess

unrecognized net gain or loss should be included as a component of pension expense only if, as of the **beginning of the year**, the unrecognized net gain or loss exceeded the corridor.

10.   *FASB Statement No. 87* requires immediate recognition of a liability (called the **minimum liability**) when the accumulated benefit obligation exceeds the fair value of plan assets.   The purpose of this minimum liability requirement is to insure that if a significant plan amendment or actuarial loss occurs, the recognition of a liability is necessitated at least for the accumulated benefit obligation not funded.   The Board does not permit the recording of an asset if the fair value of the pension plan assets exceeds the accumulated benefit obligation.

11.   If the amount paid (credit to Cash) by the employer to the pension trust is less than the annual provision (debit to Pension Expense), a credit balance accrual in the amount of the difference arises.   This accrued pension cost usually appears in the long-term liability section and must be titled Accrued Pension Cost, Liability for Pension Expense Not Funded, or Due to Pension Fund.   Classification as a current liability occurs when the liability requires the disbursement of cash within the next year.   When the cash paid to the pension trust during the period is greater than the amount charged to expense, a deferred charge equal to the difference is created.   This deferral should be reported as Prepaid Pension Cost, Deferred Pension Expense, or Prepaid Pension Expense in the current assets section if it is current in nature and in the other assets section if it is long-term in nature.

12.   The current financial statement disclosure requirements for pension plans are as follows:
   a.   A description of the plan including employee groups covered, type of benefit formula, funding policy, and the nature and effect of significant matters affecting comparability of information for all periods presented.
   b.   The components of net periodic pension expense for the period.
   c.   A schedule reconciling the funded status of the plan with amounts reported in the employer's statement of financial position.
   d.   The weighted-average discount rate and rate of compensation increase used to measure the projected benefit obligation and the weighted-average expected long-run rate of return on plan assets.

13.   The **Pension Reform Act of 1974** (ERISA) set out specific requirements for companies providing a pension plan for their employees.   These requirements are designed to safeguard employees' pension rights, specifically in the areas of funding, participation, and vesting.   The Act also created the **Pension Benefit Guaranty Corporation** (PBGC) to administer terminated plans and to impose liens on the corporate assets for certain unfunded pension liabilities.

14.   **Multiemployer pension plans** are plans sponsored by two or more different employers.   They are often negotiated as part of workers' labor union contracts in the trucking, coal mining, construction, and entertainment industries.   ERISA created an incentive for financially troubled companies to withdraw without penalty from multiemployer plans and shift their liability for paying pension benefits to the federal PBGC.   **Postemployment benefits** (other than pensions) can be defined as all forms of benefits, such as health insurance, life insurance, and disability benefits provided to a former employee.

15.   **ERISA** prevents companies from recapturing excess assets (pension plan assets in excess of projected benefit obligations) unless they pay participants what is owed to them and then terminate the plan.   The accounting issues that arise from these terminations is whether a gain should be recognized by the corporation when these assets revert back to the company.   Up to this point the profession has required that these gains be reported if the companies switched from a defined benefit plan to a defined contribution plan.   Otherwise, the gain is deferred and amortized over at least 10 years in the future.

REVIEW QUESTIONS AND EXERCISES

True-False

Indicate whether each of the following is true (T) or false (F) in the space provided.

_____   1.   When a pension plan is funded, the company sets aside funds for future pension benefits by making payments to a funding agency that is responsible for accumulating the assets of the pension fund.

_____   2.   An unfunded pension plan provides the employees covered by such a plan with nonmonetary assets at the time of retirement.

_____   3.   A noncontributory pension plan and an unfunded pension plan refer to the same type of plan.

_____   4.   Measuring the amount of pension obligation resulting from a pension plan is a problem involving actuarial consideration.

_____   5.   The amount of money it would take today to pay for all retirement benefits for both active and retired employees is called the prospective benefit obligation.

_____   6.   Once the actuary has computed the amount of money it will take to pay for all retirement benefits for both active and retired employees, a company is best advised to fund this obligation immediately.

_____ 7. The accounting for defined benefit pension plans is highly reliant upon information and measurements provided by actuaries.

_____ 8. The difference between the vested benefit obligation and the accumulated benefit obligation concerns the use of current salaries versus future salaries in the measurement process.

_____ 9. The projected benefit obligation provides a more realistic measure on a going concern basis of the employer's obligation under the plan and, therefore, should be used as the basis for determining service cost.

_____ 10. Assuming salary increases for employees covered by a pension plan, the accumulated benefit obligation will be greater than the projected benefit obligation.

_____ 11. The service cost component of a pension plan recognized in a period should be determined as the actuarial present value of benefits attributed by the pension benefit formula to employee services during that period.

_____ 12. When considering the interest rate component used in the determination of pension cost the FASB concluded that the rate selected should reflect conservatism.

_____ 13. The interest rate used to compute the projected benefit obligation should also be used as the rate of return on plan assets.

_____ 14. When a defined benefit pension plan is amended the expense and related liability for the prior service costs should be fully reported in the year in which the amendment was adopted.

_____ 15. In pension accounting, an entity is required to recognize a liability when the accumulated benefit obligation exceeds the fair value of plan assets and recognize an asset if the fair value of pension plan assets exceeds the accumulated benefit obligation.

_____ 16. If the cash paid to the pension trust fund during a period is greater than the amount charged to expense, a loss on pension plan funding is shown on the statement of income.

_____ 17. An employer is required to disclose in its financial statements a description of the pension plan, including employee groups covered, type of benefit formula, funding policy, and the nature and effect of significant

matters affecting comparability of information for all periods presented.

_____ 18. An employer that sponsors two or more separate defined benefit pension plans is not permitted to net one against the other unless the assets of one may be used to provide for benefits for the other.

_____ 19. Annual funding of a pension plan cannot be discretionary; an employer must fund the plan in accordance with an actuarial funding method that over time will be sufficient to pay for all pension obligations.

_____ 20. The three major accounting issues related to pension are (a) allocating the pension costs to the proper accounting periods, (b) measurement and reporting of assets and obligations arising from a pension plan, and (c) disclosure of the status and effects of a pension plan in the financial statements.

Multiple Choice

Select the best answer for each of the following items and place the corresponding letter in the space provided.

_____ 1. Which of the following is not a characteristic of a defined contribution pension plan?
A. The employer's contribution each period is based on a formula.
B. The benefits to be received by employees are defined by the terms of the plan.
C. The accounting for a defined contribution plan is straightforward and uncomplicated.
D. The benefit of gain or the risk of loss from the assets contributed to the pension fund are borne by the employee.

_____ 2. In accounting for a defined benefit pension plan:
A. an appropriate funding pattern must be established to insure that enough monies will be available at retirement to meet the benefits promised.
B. the employer's responsibility is simply to make a contribution each year based on the formula established in the plan.
C. the expense recognized each period is equal to the cash contribution.
D. the liability is determined based upon known variables that reflect future salary levels promised to employees.

_____ 3. The difference between a contributory pension plan and a noncontributory pension plan is:

A. contributory plans tend to be fully funded, whereas noncontributory plans are based on "pay-as-you-go" funding.

B. in contributory plans employees bear part of the cost of stated benefits or voluntarily make payments to the plan, whereas the costs of noncontributory plans are borne by the employer.

C. noncontributory plans are dependent upon a company's ability to consistently earn a net income for pension payments, whereas contributory plans are not dependent upon operating results.

D. in a contributory plan contributions are made, but in a noncontributory plan no contributions are made.

____ 4. The present value of the pension plan benefits that will have to be paid to both active and retired employees covered by a pension plan is dependent on all of the following factors except:

A. the benefit provisions of the plan.

B. characteristics of the employee group.

C. actuarial assumptions.

D. the income level of the entity setting up the plan.

____ 5. Alternative methods exist for the measurement of the pension obligation (liability). Which measure requires the use of future salaries in its computation?

A. Vested benefit obligation.

B. Accumulated benefit obligation.

C. Projected beneft obligation.

D. Restructured benefit obligation.

____ 6. Pension cost should be accounted for on the:

A. cash basis of accounting, recognizing the amount paid as the pension expense for the period.

B. accrual basis, in a manner similar to other costs and expenses.

C. current value basis, because employees need to be aware of the value of the retirement benefits they will receive.

D. prospective basis, because even though the expense is a current period item, the benefits and the related liability belong to future periods.

____ 7. Which of the following is not a factor considered in the determination of pension cost?

A. Service cost.

B. Interest.

C. Prior service cost.

D. Inflation.

____ 8. When a defined plan is amended and credit is given to employees for years of service provided before the date of amendment:

A. both the accumulated benefit obligation and the projected benefit obligation are usually greater than before.

B. both the accumulated benefit obligation and the projected benefit obligation are usually less than before.

C. the expense and the liability should be recognized at the time of the plan change.

D. the expense should be recognized immediately, but the liability may be deferred until a reasonable basis for its determination has been identified.

____ 9. Hargrove Company has the following information at 12-31 related to its pension plan:

Projected benefit
  obligation $10,000,000
Accumulated benefit
  obligation 8,000,000
Plan assets
  (fair value)........................... 5,000,000
Accrual pension cost.............. 750,000

Indicate the amount of additional liability Hargrove Company would recognize at 12-31.

A. $0.

B. $3,000,000.

C. $2,250,000.

D. $750,000.

____ 10. Using the same facts in question 9 above, what amount of additional liability would be recognized if Hargrove Company had prepaid pension cost of $550,000 rather than accrued pension cost of $750,000?

A. $0.

B. $550,000.

C. $3,000,000.

D. $3,550,000.

Review Exercises

1. Listed below on the left are a number of terms related to pension accounting. Match the terms on the left with the appropriate definitions on the right.

A. Defined benefit plan.
B. Funded pension plan.
C. Market related asset value.
D. Projected benefit obligation.
E. Defined contribution plan.
F. Prior service cost.
G. Qualified pension plan.
H. Liability gains and losses.
I. Service cost.
J. Accumulated benefit obligation.

_____ 1. Unexpected changes in the projected benefit obligation.

_____ 2. Computation of the deferred compensation amount based on both vested and nonvested service using future salaries.

_____ 3. This arises when a defined benefit plan is amended and credit is given to employees for services provided before the amendment.

_____ 4. The employer sets funds aside for future pension benefits by making payments to an agency such as a financial institution.

_____ 5. Present value of benefits accrued to date based on current salary levels.

_____ 6. In this plan it is necessary to determine what the contribution should be today to meet the pension benefit commitments that will arise at retirement.

_____ 7. Portion of the cost of a pension plan based on the work an employee provides to the employer.

_____ 8. A calculated amount that recognizes changes in fair value in a systematic and rational manner over not more than five years.

_____ 9. The employer agrees to contribute a certain sum to the plan each period based on a formula.

_____ 10. Pension plans designed in accord with federal income tax requirements that permit deductibility of the employer's contributions to the pension fund and tax-free status of the earnings of the pension fund assets.

2. G.J. Previts Company has a defined benefit pension plan which covers 220 employees. Based upon negotiations with the employees, Previts Company amends its pension plan as of 1/1/90 and grants $111,600 of prior service cost to its employees. The following schedule reflects employee groups based on expected years of retirement.

Group	Number of Employees	Expected Retirement on 12/31
A	30	1990
B	40	1991
C	35	1992
D	70	1993
E	45	1994
	220	

Required: Compute the annual amortization of the prior service cost using the **(a)** years-of-service method, and **(b)** straight-line amortization over the average remaining service life of employees.

3. On January 1, 1990, Johnson Company adopted FASB **Statement No. 87** to account for its defined benefit pension plan. Data related to the pension plan is presented below.

Plan assets, 1/1/90	$150,000
Projected benefit obligation, 1/1/90	150,000
Annual service cost, 1990	17,000
Settlement rate, 1990	12%
Actual return on plan asset, 1990	15,000
Employer's contribution, 1990	16,000
Benefits paid to retirees, 1990	10,000

Required: Based upon the information presented above prepare a pension work sheet for Johnson Company for 1990, and record the journal entry to formally recognize pension expense for 1990.

4.   On January 1, 1991 Jackson Company amended its pension plan to provide greater benefits to its employees. The amendment to the plan resulted in prior service costs with a present value of $90,000. Also, the following facts relate to the pension plan for 1991.

Projected benefit obligation, 12/31/90	$175,000
Plan assets, 12/31/90	171,000
Prior service cost, 1/1/91	90,000
Annual service cost, 1991	18,000
Settlement rate, 1991	12%
Actual return on plan assets	18,500
Employer's contribution, 1991	42,000
Benefits paid to retirees, 1991	12,000
Balance in prepaid/accrued pension cost	4,000Cr
Amortization of prior service cost using the years-of-service method	23,800

Required: Based upon the information presented above prepare a pension worksheet for Jackson Company for 1991, and record the journal entry to formally recognize the pension expense for 1991.

SOLUTIONS TO REVIEW QUESTIONS AND EXERCISES

True-False

1.   (T)

2.   (F)   A pension plan that is unfunded refers to a plan that has the pension fund under the control of the company rather than an independent funding agency. In an unfunded plan, pension payments to retired employees are made directly by the company as they become due.

3.   (F)   A noncontributory pension plan is a plan wherein the employer bears the entire cost. This is different from contributory plans where the employees bear part of the cost of the stated benefits or voluntarily make payments to increase their benefits. A plan can be noncontributory and unfunded or funded. The contributory and funding features are not mutually exclusive.

4.   (T)

5.   (T)

6.   (F)   Funding the pension plan obligation immediately is not a wise decision. First, most companies would not find immediate funding an efficient use of their liquid resources. Secondly, the IRS has established certain minimum and maximum amounts that can be taken as tax deductions in any given year. If a company were to fund the plan immediately, a substantial portion of this deduction would usually be lost.

7.   (T)

8.   (F)   The major difference between the vested benefit obligation and the accumulated benefit obligation is that the accumulated benefit obligation includes benefits for vested and nonvested employees at current salaries, whereas, the vested benefit obligation includes benefits for vested employees at current salaries.

9.   (T)

10.   (F)   The accumulated benefit obligation does not consider future compensation levels as does the projected benefit obligation. Thus, if salaries are assumed to increase as a result of raises, the projected benefit obligation will yield the greater liability as it is based on the larger amount.

11.   (T)

12.   (F)   The Board requires companies to select their assumptions regarding the interest rate in an explicit fashion. That is, the interest rate assumption used should represent the best estimate of the plan's expert experience solely with respect to interest rates. The rates should reflect current market conditions.

13. (T)
14. (F) The FASB has taken the position that no expense and in some cases no liability should be recognized at the time of the plan change. Their rationale is that the employer would not provide credit for past years of service unless it expected to receive benefits in the future. The retroactive benefits should not be recognized as pension expense entirely in the year of amendment but should be recognized during the service periods of those employees who are expected to receive benefits under the plan.
15. (F) Recognition of the liability is acceptable practice. However, based solely on conservatism, the FASB does not permit the recognition of an asset when the fair value of the pension plan assets exceed the accumulated benefit obligation.
16. (F) When the cash paid exceeds the amount charged to expense, a deferred charge equal to the difference is recorded. This deferral should be reported in the current asset section of the balance sheet if it is current in nature and in the other assets section if it is long-term in nature.
17. (T)
18. (T)
19. (T)
20. (T)

Multiple Choice

1. (B) If the benefits that the employee will receive are defined by the plan, then it is a defined benefit plan rather than a defined contribution plan. The characteristics described in alternatives A, C, and D are representative of a defined contribution plan.
2. (A) The accounting for a defined benefit plan is complex. Because the benefits are defined in terms of uncertain future variables, an appropriate funding pattern must be established to insure that enough monies will be available at retirement to meet the benefits promised.
3. (B) In a contributory pension plan, the employees bear part of the cost of the benefits or make voluntary contributions. In a noncontributory plan, the employer bears the entire cost.
4. (D) The present value of pension plan benefits is not affected by the income of the entity setting up the plan. These benefits are, however, dependent upon the benefit provisions, the employee group covered, and the actuarial assumptions employed.
5. (C) As its name implies, the projected benefit obligation bases the computation of the deferred compensation amount on both vested and nonvested services using future salaries. Vested benefit obligation and accumulated benefit obligation use current salary levels in computing the deferred compensation amount. There is no such concept as the restructured benefit obligation.
6. (B) Pension should be accounted for on the accrual basis. Most accountants recognize that accounting for pension plans requires measurement of the cost and its identification with the appropriate time periods, which involves application of accrual, deferral, and estimation concepts in the same manner that they are applied in the measurement and the time-period identification of other costs and expenses.
7. (D) Inflation is not a component used in determining pension cost. One could argue that inflation does in fact have an impact on the other factors that go into the determination of pension cost, but it is not in and of itself a primary factor. The determination of pension cost is a function of (1) service cost, (2) interest, (3) return on plan assets, (4) prior service cost, and (5) gains and losses.
8. (A) When a plan is amended both the accumulated benefit obligation and the projected benefit obligation are usually greater because employees have been given more benefits. With respect to the expense and liability, the FASB has taken the position that no expense and in some cases no liability should be recognized at the time of the plan change. Its rationale is that the employer would not provide credit for past years of service unless it expected to receive benefits in the future.
9. (C)

Unfunded accumulated benefit obligation	$3,000,000
Accrued pension cost	750,000
Additional liability required	$2,250,000

10. (D)

     Unfunded accumulated benefit obligation $3,000,000

     Prepaid pension cost.. 550,000

     Additional liability required $3,550,000

Review Exercises

1.
1.	H	6.	A
2.	D	7.	I
3.	F	8.	C
4.	B	9.	E
5.	J	10.	G

2. a)

Computation of Service Years

Year	A	B	C	D	E	Total
1990	30	40	35	70	45	220
1991		40	35	70	45	190
1992			35	70	45	150
1993				70	45	115
1994					45	45
	30	80	105	280	225	720

Computation of Annual Prior Service Cost Amortization

Year	Total Service-Years	x	Cost Per Service Year	=	Annual Amortization
1990	220		155		$34,100
1991	190		155		29,450
1992	150		155		23,250
1993	115		155		17,825
1994	45		155		6,975
					$111,600

b) $720 \div 220 = 3.27$

        $111,600 \div 3.27 = $34,128.44$

        Straight-line amortization:

1990	-	$34,128.44
1991	-	34,128.44
1992	-	34,128.44
1993	-	9,214.68*
		$111,600.00

        *($34,128.44 x .27)

3.

Johnson Company
Pension Work Sheet - 1990

	General Journal Entries			Memo Report	
Items	Annual Pension Expense	Cash	Prepaid/ Accrued Cost	Projected Benefit Obligation	Plan Assets
Balance 1/1/90				$150,000Dr	$150,000Dr
Service cost	$17,000Dr			17,000Cr	
Interest cost	18,000Dr			18,000Cr	
Actual return	15,000Cr				15,000Dr
Contributions		$16,000Cr			16,000Dr
Benefits				10,000Dr	10,000Cr
Entry 12/31	20,000Dr	16,000Cr	4,000Cr		
Balance 12/31/90			4,000Cr	$175,000Cr	$171,000Dr

Journal Entry:
Pension Expense	20,000	
Cash		16,000
Prepaid/Accrued Pension Cost		4,000

4.

Jackson Company
Pension Work Sheet - 1991

	General Journal Entries				Memo Report	
Items	Annual Pension Expense	Cash	Prepaid/ Accrued Cost	Projected Benefit Obligation	Plan Assets	Unrecognized Prior Service Cost
Balance 12/31/90			$4,000Cr	$175,000Cr	$171,000Dr	
Prior service cost				90,000Cr		$90,000Dr
Balance 1/1/91			4,000Cr	265,000Cr	171,000Dr	90,000Dr
Service cost	$18,000Dr			18,000Cr		
Interest cost	31,800Dr			31,800Cr		
Actual return	18,500Cr				18,500Dr	
Amortization PSC	23,800Dr					23,800Cr
Contributions		$42,000Cr			42,000Dr	
Benefits				12,000Dr	12,000Cr	
Entry 12/31	55,100Dr	42,000Cr	13,100Cr			
Balance 12/31/90			$17,100Cr	$302,800Cr	$219,500Dr	$66,200Dr

Journal Entry:
Pension Expense	55,100	
Cash		42,000
Prepaid/Accrued Pension Cost		13,100

22

Accounting for leases

Chapter Synopsis

Chapter 22 presents a discussion of the accounting issues related to leasing arrangements from the point of view of both the lessee and the lessor. Among the issues discussed are: (1) the classification of leasing arrangements, (2) the various methods used in accounting for leases, and (3) the financial statement disclosure requirements when leases are present.

Chapter Review

1. A **lease** is a contractual agreement between a lessor and a **lessee** that conveys to the lessee the right to use specific property (real or personal), owned by the lessor, for a specified period of time. In return for this right, the lessee agrees to make periodic cash payments (**rents**) to the lessor. An essential element of the lease conveyance is that the lessor conveys less than his or her total interest in the property.

2. In discussing the advantages of leasing arrangements, advocates point out that leasing allows for: (a) **100% financing,** (b) **protection against obsolescence,** (c) **flexibility,** (d) **less costly financing,** and (e) **off-balance sheet financing.**

3. The particulars of a lease arrangement are dependent on the agreement entered into by the lessee and lessor. Most lease contracts include provisions related to: (a) the duration of the lease, (b) the amount of periodic rental payments, (c) the party required to pay taxes, insurance, and maintenance, (d) the restrictions imposed on parties to the lease, (e) the cancellation terms, (f) default provisions, and (g) the alternatives of the lessee at the time of lease termination. The manner in which these various provisions are used in the lease agreement aids in determining the accounting methods used to portray properly the substance of each situation.

4. A variety of opinions exists regarding the manner in which certain long-term lease arrangements should be accounted for. These opinions range from total capitalization of all long-term leases to the belief that leases represent executory contracts that should not be capitalized. The FASB *Statements* dealing with lease accounting can be characterized as advocating capitalization of lease arrangements that are similar to installment purchases. In short, lease arrangements that transfer substantially all of the risks and rewards of ownership of property should be capitalized by the lessee.

5. For accounting purposes of the **lessee,** all leases may be classified as **operating leases** or **capital leases.** The lessee should classify and account for an arrangement as a capital lease if **one or more** of the following criteria are met on the date of the lease agreement.

    a. The lease transfers ownership of the property to the lessee.

    b. The lease contains a bargain purchase option.

    c. The lease term is equal to 75% or more of the estimated economic life of the leased property.

    d. The present value of the minimum lease payments (excluding executory costs) equals or exceeds 90% of the fair value of the leased property.

All leases that fail to meet **any** of these four criteria are classified and accounted for by the lessee as operating leases.

6. Under the capital lease method the lessee treats the lease transaction as if an asset were being purchased on time (installment basis). For a capital lease, the lessee records an asset and a liability at the lower of (a) the present value of the minimum lease payments during the term of the lease or (b) the fair market value of the leased asset at the inception of the lease. In determining the present value of the minimum lease payments, three important concepts are involved: (a) minimum lease payments, (b) executory costs, and (c) the discount rate.

7. **Minimum lease payments** include (a) minimum rental payments, (b) any guaranteed residual value, and (c) penalty for failure to renew or extend the lease. **Executory costs** include the cost of insurance, maintenance, and tax expense related to the leased asset. When the lease agreement specifies that executory costs are assumed by the lessee, the rental payments can be used without adjustment in the present value computation. The lessee uses its **incremental borrowing rate** (discount rate) to compute the present value of the minimum lease payments. This rate, often determined by the exercise of professional judgment, is defined as the rate that, at the inception of the lease, the lessee would have incurred to borrow the funds necessary to buy the leased asset. There is one exception to use of the incremental borrowing rate

by the lessee in computing the present value of the minimum lease payments. If the lessee knows the **implicit rate computed by the lessor**, and that rate is **less** than the lessee's incremental borrowing rate, then the lessee must use the implicit rate.

8. When the lessee uses the capital lease method, each lease payment is allocated between a reduction of the lease obligation and interest expense applying the **effective interest method.** The lessee should amortize the leased asset by applying one of the conventional depreciation methods. During the term of the lease, assets recorded under capital leases are separately identified in the lessee's balance sheet. Likewise, the related obligations are separately identified with the portion due within one year or the operating cycle, whichever is longer, classified with current liabilities and the balance with noncurrent liabilities.

9. In accounting for an operating lease, the lessee would use the accounting method known as the **operating (noncapitalization) method.** If the lease is considered a capital lease, use of the **capital lease (financing) method** is appropriate. When the lessee uses the operating method, the periodic rent associated with the lease is recognized in the period benefited by the leased asset. Under this method, the commitment to make future rental payments is not recognized in the accounts. Only footnote recognition is given to the commitment to pay future rentals.

10. The FASB requires that specific information with respect to operating leases and capital leases be disclosed in the lessee's financial statements or in the footnotes as of the date of the latest balance sheet presented. The specific requirements are well documented in a special section near the end of Chapter 22. This section includes both a listing of lessee and lessor disclosure requirements and an actual disclosure illustration. The general information required to be disclosed by the lessee **for all leases** includes, but is not necessarily limited to, the following:

    a. The basis on which contingent rental payments are determined.

    b. The existence and terms of renewal or purchase options and escalation clauses.

    c. Restrictions imposed by lease agreements, such as those concerning dividends, additional debt, and future leasing.

11. For accounting purposes of the **lessor,** all leases may be classified as: (a) **operating leases,** (b) **direct financing leases,** or (c) **sales-type leases.** The lessor should classify and account for an arrangement as a direct financing lease or a sales-type lease if at the date of the lease agreement **one or more** of the following **Group I** criteria are met and **both** of the following **Group II** criteria are met.

Group I

    a. The lease transfers ownership of the property to the lessee.

    b. The lease contains a bargain purchase option.

    c. The lease term is equal to 75% or more of the estimated economic life of the lease property.

    d. The present value of the minimum lease payments (excluding executory costs) equals or exceeds 90% of the fair value of the leased property.

Group II

    a. Collectibility of the payments required from the lessee is reasonably predictable.

    b. No important uncertainties surround the amount of unreimbursable costs yet to be incurred by the lessor under the lease.

All leases that fail to meet the aforementioned criteria are classified and accounted for by the lessor as operating leases.

12. A lessor should account for an operating lease using the **operating method.** A direct financing lease or a sales-type lease is accounted for by use of the **direct financing method.** The distinction between a direct financing lease and a sales-type lease is that **a sales-type lease involves manufacturer's or dealer's profit (or loss) and a direct financing lease does not.** The primary difference between applying the financing method to a direct financing lease and applying it to a sales-type lease is the recognition of the manufacturer's or dealer's profit at the inception of the lease.

13. Under the operating method, each rental receipt of the lessor is recorded as rent revenue on the use of an item carried as a fixed asset. The fixed asset is depreciated in the normal manner, with the depreciation expense of the period being matched against the rental revenue.

14. Leases that are in substance the financing of an asset purchased by a lessee require the lessor to substitute a "lease payments reeivable" for the leased asset. The **gross investment in the lease** is equal to the sum of (a) the minimum lease payments, plus (b) the unguaranteed residual value accruing to the benefit of the lessor. Unearned revenue, represented by the difference between the gross investment in the lease recorded as the receivable and the cost or carrying value of the property, is amortized to revenue over the lease term by use of the effective interest method. Any **contingent rentals,** including rentals based on variables such as machine hours of use, or sales volume, are credited to income when they become receivable.

15. The specific disclosure requirements related to a lessor's involvement in lease agreements are described in detail in a special section near the end of Chapter 22. Specific information is required to be presented in the financial statements or in the footnotes for operating leases, sales-type leases, and direct financing leases. In addition, a general description of the lessor's leasing arrangements is required. However, lessor disclosure requirements are applicable only to enterprises whose predominant business activity is leasing.

16. Leases have certain characteristics that create unique accounting problems. These problems have been addressed in both FASB *Statements* and FASB *Interpretations* issued subsequent to *FASB Statement No. 13*, "**Accounting for Leases.**" The next four paragraphs review these characteristics.

17. The **residual value** of a leased asset is the **estimated fair value** of the asset at the end of the lease term. The residual value may be **guaranteed** or **unguaranteed** by the lessee. A guaranteed residual value is said to exist when the lessee agrees to make up any deficiency below a stated amount in the value of the asset at the end of the lease term. A guaranteed residual value affects the lessee's computation of the minimum lease payments and, therefore, the amounts capitalized as a leased asset and a lease obligation. The net investment to be recorded by the lessor is the same whether the residual value is guaranteed or unguaranteed.

18. A **bargain purchase option** is a provision allowing the lessee, at his or her option, to purchase the leased property at a price that is sufficiently lower than the expected fair value of the property at the date the option becomes exercisable. When a bargain purchase option exists, the lessee must increase the present value of the minimum lease payments by the present value of the option price. The only difference between accounting for a bargain purchase option and a guaranteed residual value of identical amounts is in the computation of the annual depreciation. In the case of a guaranteed residual value, the lessee depreciates the asset over the **lease life**. When a bargain purchase option is present, the lessee uses the **economic life** of the asset in computing depreciation.

19. **Initial direct costs** are the costs incurred by the lessor that are directly associated with negotiating and consummating a **completed** leasing transaction. There are two types of initial direct costs, **incremental direct costs**, and **internal direct costs**. Incremental direct costs are costs incurred in originating a lease arrangement that are paid to third parties. Internal direct costs are costs directly related to specified activities performed by the lessor on a given lease.

When an operating lease is present, the initial direct costs are deferred and amortized over the life of the lease in proportion to rental income. In a sales-type lease, these costs are expensed in the period that profit on the sale is recognized. For direct financing leases, initial direct costs are added to the net investment in the lease and amortized over the life of the lease as a yield adjustment.

20. A "**sale-leaseback**" transaction is one in which the owner of property sells it to another and simultaneously leases it back from the new owner. The lessee, in a sale-leaseback transaction, should apply the same criteria mentioned earlier in deciding whether to account for the lease as a capital lease or an operating lease. Likewise, the lessor should apply the criteria mentioned earlier in deciding whether the sale-leaseback transaction should be accounted for using the operating method or the financing method.

21. **Appendix 22-A** presents a discussion of the accounting for **real estate leases** and **leveraged leases**. A leveraged lease is a complex leasing arrangement including three parties: a lessee, a long-term creditor(s), and a lessor. The long-term creditor(s) finances a large percentage of the asset, yet the tax benefits of the transaction remains with the lessor.

REVIEW QUESTIONS AND EXERCISES

True-False
Indicate whether each of the following is true (T) or false (F) in the space provided.

_____ 1. A lease is a contractual agreement conveying ownership of certain property from one party to another party.

_____ 2. Under a leasing arrangement, it is possible to write off the full cost of a leased asset including land and residual values.

_____ 3. If a lease contains a bargain purchase option, the lessee shall classify and account for the arrangement as a capital lease.

_____ 4. An operating lease refers to a lease agreement for property used in the operations of the lessee's business.

_____ 5. One of the major distinctions between an operating lease and a capital lease is the fact that annual rental payments under a capital lease are higher than rental payments under an operating lease.

_____ 6. Under the operating method, the lessee assigns rent to the periods benefiting from the use of the asset and does not record the commitment to make future payments.

_____ 7. Under the capital lease method, the lessee treats the lease transaction as if an asset were being purchased on an installment payment basis.

____ 8. The lessee records a capital lease as an asset, using the fair market value of the leased asset on the date of the lease as the asset's cost.

____ 9. The rental payments paid to a lessor in a capital lease transaction constitute a payment of principal plus interest because of the financing-type nature of the transaction.

____ 10. When the lessee accounts for a capital lease, the amortization (depreciation) of the asset and the discharge of the lease obligation should be handled in a consistent manner over the same number of accounting periods.

____ 11. If the lessee has knowledge of the lessor's implicit interest rate and it is lower than the lessee's incremental borrowing rate, the implicit interest rate should be used in computing the present value of minimum rental payments.

____ 12. During the term of the lease, assets recorded under capital leases are separately identified in the lessee's balance sheet.

____ 13. Contingent rantal payments refer to rental payments whole amounts are dependent on some factor other than the passage of time.

____ 14. A lessor must be a manufacturer or dealer to realize a profit (or loss) at the inception of a lease that requires application of sales-type lease accounting.

____ 15. When the direct financing method is applied to a direct financing lease, the difference between the gross investment in the lease and the lease payments receivable is recorded as unearned interest revenue.

____ 16. The unearned revenue related to a lease transaction accounted for under the direct financing method should be amortized to income over the lease term by use of the effective interest method.

____ 17. Lease disclosure requirements on the part of the lessor apply only to lessors whose predominant business activity is leasing.

____ 18. Any profit or loss experienced by the seller-lessee in a sale-leaseback transaction must be included in income at the date of the lease agreement.

____ 19. The criteria a lessee uses to determine whether a lease is a capital lease or an operating lease apply in the case of a sale-leaseback transaction.

____ 20. Initial direct costs are those costs associated with negotiating and consummating completed lease transactions.

Multiple Choice

Select the best answer for each of the following items and place the corresponding letter in the space provided.

____ 1. An essential element of a lease conveyance is that the:
A. lessor conveys less than his or her total interest in the property.
B. lessee provides a sinking fund equal to one year's lease payments.
C. property that is the subject of the lease agreement must be held for sale by the lessor prior to the drafting of the lease agreement.
D. term of the lease is substantially equal to the economic life of the leased property.

____ 2. Which of the following is not one of the commonly discussed advantages of leasing?
A. Leasing permits 100% financing versus 60 to 80% when purchasing an asset.
B. Leasing permits rapid changes in equipment, thus reducing the risk of obsolescence.
C. Leasing improves financial ratios by increasing assets without a corresponding increase in debt.
D. Leasing permits write-off of the full cost of the asset.

____ 3. Which of the following lease arrangements would most likely be accounted for as an operating lease by the lessee?
A. The lease agreement runs for 15 years and the economic life of the leased property is 20 years.
B. The present value of the minimum lease payments is $55,600 and the fair value of the leased property is $60,000.
C. The lease agreement allows the lessee the right to purchase the leased asset for $1.00 when half of the asset's economic useful life has expired.
D. The lessee may renew the two-year lease for an additional two years at the same rental.

____ 4. Under the operating method, a rent expense accrues day by day to the lessee as the property is used. This amount of rent expense is:
A. capitalized in an asset account and charged against income as the asset depreciates.
B. capitalized in an asset account and netted against the corresponding lease liability each time a balance sheet is prepared.

C. charged against income in the periods benefiting from the use of the asset.

D. charged against income at the same rate as the reduction in the corresponding lease liability.

____ 5. In a capital lease transaction, the lessee is using the lease as a source of financing. Therefore, over the life of the lease:

A. the payments to the lessor are equal to the dollar amount that would have been expended had the lessee purchased the property on the date of the lease agreement.

B. the rental payments to the lessor constitute a payment of principal plus interest.

C. the asset is depreciated neither by the lessee nor the lessor.

D. no portion of the rental payments to the lessor may be charged to income.

____ 6. To classify a lease arrangement as a direct financing lease, a lessor must be reasonably able to predict collectibility of the payments required from the lessee and must:

A. have no important uncertainties surrounding the amount of unreimburseable costs yet to be incurred under the lease.

B. show that the lease transfers ownership of the property to the lessee.

C. be sure that the term of the lease and the economic life of the leased property are equal.

D. show that the lessee is responsible for all executory costs during the period of the lease agreement.

____ 7. The primary difference between applying the financing method to a direct financing lease and applying it to a sales-type lease is the:

A. manner in which rental receipts are recorded as rental income.

B. amount of the depreciation recorded each year by the lessor.

C. recognition of the manufacturer's or dealer's profit at the inception of the lease.

D. allocation of initial direct costs by the lessor to periods benefited by the lease arrangements.

____ 8. If the residual value of a leased asset is guaranteed by a third party:

A. it is treated by the lessor as an unguaranteed residual value.

B. the third party is also liable for any lease payments not paid by the lessee.

C. the net investment to be recovered by the lessor is reduced.

D. it is treated by the lessee as an unguaranteed residual value but by the lessor as a guaranteed residual value.

____ 9. Any gain or loss resulting from a sale-leaseback where the lease is an operating lease must be:

A. taken into income on the date of the sale-leaseback agreement.

B. deferred and amortized in proportion to the rental payments over the period of time the asset is expected to be used by the lessee.

C. deferred and amortized in proportion to the rental payments over the economic life of the asset.

D. deferred and not taken into income until the lease agreement has terminated.

____ 10. When both land and building are involved in a lease agreement and the lease does not transfer ownership or contain a bargain purchase option, the lessee and the lessor consider the land and the building as a single unit if:

A. the fair value of the land s 25% or more of the fair value of the leased property.

B. the fair value of the land is less than 25% of the fair value of the leased property.

C. the land and building are leased for the same period of time and are considered to have the same economic useful life.

D. the fair value of the land and the fair value of the building are approximately equal.

Review Exercises

1. List the criteria that must be met before a lease arrangement is accounted for:

a. As a capital lease by the lessee.

b. As a direct financing lease by the lessor.

2. The following is a lease amortization schedule for a direct financing lease of equipment by D & K Zeller Company (lessor).

D & K Zeller Company
Lease Amortization Schedule

Date	Annual Lease Payment	Interest	Change in Carrying Value	Carrying Value
1-1-87				$120,000.00
12-31-87	$ 36,230.79	$ 9,600.00	$ 26,630.79	93,369.21
12-31-88	36,230.79	7,469.54	28,761.25	64,607.96
12-31-89	36,230.79	5,168.64	31,062.15	33,545.81
12-31-90	36,230.79	2,684.98	33,545.81	
	$144,923.16	$24,923.16	$120,000.00	

Prepare journal entries for: (a) the initial recording of the lease by the lessor, (b) the receipt of the first year's lease payment, and (c) the interest income earned during the first year.

3. Using the lease amortization schedule presented in exercise 2 as a basis, prepare the journal entries the lessee would make (assuming the capital lease method) for: (a) the initial recording of the lease by the lessee, (b) the lease payment on 12/31/88, and (c) the purchase of the equipment by the lessee on 12-31-90, for $10,000 (accumulated depreciation equals $120,000).

4. Prepare a lease amortization schedule for the lease agreement signed by Molinar Company (lessee) on January 3, 1990. The agreement is for seven years, requiring annual rental payments of $42,000, payable at the beginning of each lease year (January 3). The executory costs associated with the lease are the responsibility of Molinar Company, which has an incremental borrowing rate of 12%. Molinar Company is unaware of the implicit rate computed by the lessor. At the conclusion of the lease Molinar Company has the option to buy the equipment for $1.00.

SOLUTIONS TO REVIEW QUESTIONS AND EXERCISES

True-False

1. (F) A lease is a contractual agreement conveying the rights to use property from one party to another. A lease does not by definition transfer ownership. Such arrangements can be written into a lease agreement, but the transfer of ownership is not a part of all lease agreements.

2. (T)

3. (T)

4. (F) An operating lease refers to a lease arrangement that has all the characteristics of a rental agreement. When a lease is an operating lease, rent expense accrues day by day to the lessee as the property is used. The lessee assigns rent to the periods benefiting from the use of the asset and ignores any commitments to make future payments. A lessor accounts for an operating lease by recording each rental receipt as rental revenue for the use of the item which is still carried on its books as an asset.

5. (F) The size of rental payments depends on a number of issues that are determined by the lessee and lessor. The fact that a lease is accounted for as a capital lease or as an operating lease does not have an impact on the size of the annual rental payments.

6.   (T)

7.   (T)

8.   (F)   The leased asset recorded on the books of a lessee is recorded at the lower of (a) the present value of the minimum lease payments excluding any executory cost, or (b) the fair market value of the leased asset at the inception of the lease.

9.   (T)

10. (F)   Although the amount capitalized as an asset and the amount recorded as an obligation at the inception of the lease are computed at the same present value, the amortization of the asset and the discharge of the obligation are independent accounting processes during the term of the lease. They need not be written off over the same number of accounting periods.

11. (T)

12. (T)

13. (T)

14. (F)   The distinction for the lessor between a direct financing lease and a sales-type lease is the presence or absence of a manufacturer's or dealer's profit (or loss). A sales-type lease involves manufacturer's or dealer's profit, and a direct financing lease does not. The lessor is not required to be a manufacturer or dealer to account for a lease as a sales-type lease.

15. (F)   Under the direct financing method, the gross investment and the lease payment receivable are the same. Unearned interest revenue is defined as the difference between the gross investment (the receivable) and the fair market value of the property.

16. (T)

17. (T)

18. (F)   Any profit or loss experienced by the seller-lessee from the sale of the assets that are leased back under a capital lease should be deferred and amortized over the lease term in proportion to the amortization of the leased asset.

19. (T)

20. (T)

Multiple Choice

1.   (A)   A lease is a contractual agreement between a lessor and a lessee that conveys to the lessee the right to use specific property (real or personal), owned by the lessor, for a specific period of time in return for stipulated and generally periodic cash payments. An essential element of the lease agreement is that the lessor conveys less than the total interest in the property. There are no sinking fund or lease term requirements that must be met for a lease to exist. Also, leased property need not be held for sale prior to the lease agreement.

2.   (C)   A lease arrangement does not improve financial ratios. In a capital lease no asset is recorded so the ratios remain the same. When a capital lease is involved an asset is recorded but so is a corresponding liability. This transaction will actually result in a negative impact on most ratios of the lessee.

3.   (D)   Alternative A meets the 75% of the economic life test. Alternative B meets the 90% of the fair value of the leased property test. Alternative C appears to be a bargain purchase option. Thus, these situations all describe a capital lease arrangement because they meet one of the four capital lease criteria. Alternative D has no relationship to the four capital lease criteria and is most likely an operation lease arrangement.

4.   (C)   The rent expense resulting from an operating lease is charged against income in a manner consistent with the matching concept. Thus, rent expense is charged against income in the period(s) benefiting from the use of the leased asset.

5.   (B)   When a lessee uses a lease transaction as a means of financing, the characteristics of a normal financing transaction occur. Thus, the lessor expects to receive a periodic payment that represents a payment of principal plus an amount for interest. If the lessee borrowed the money from a bank to buy the asset, the repayment of the loan would include amounts for both principal and interest.

6. (A) Alternative A is the second of the two group II criteria that a lease must meet to be classified as a direct financing lease or a sales-type lease by a lessor. Remember, to be classified and accounted for as a direct financing lease or a sales-type lease by a lessor the lease arrangement must meet at least one of the group I criteria and both of the group II criteria.

7. (C) The manner in which rental receipts are recorded, the amount of depreciation recorded, and the allocation of initial direct costs are not primary differences in applying the financing method to a direct financing lease or a sales-type lease. The primary difference is in recognition of the manufacturer's or dealer's profit at the inception of the lease.

8. (D) The residual value is the estimated fair market value of a leased asset at the end of the lease term. A guaranteed residual value occurs when a lessee or another third party agrees to make up any deficiency below a stated amount that the lessor realizes at the end of the lease term. If the residual value is guaranteed by a third party, it is treated by the lessee as an unguaranteed residual value but by the lessor as a guaranteed residual value.

9. (B) Profit or loss in a sale-leaseback situation should be deferred and amortized. If the lease is a capital lease the profit or loss should be deferred and amortized over the lease term in proportion to the amortization of the leased assets. In an operating lease, the profit or loss should be deferred and amortized in proportion to the rental payments over the period of time the assets are expected to be used by the lessee.

10. (B) When a lease involves real estate and a building and the agreement does not transfer ownership or contain a bargain purchase option, the accounting treatment is dependent on the proportion of land to the building. If the fair value of the land is less than 25% of the fair value of the lease property, both the lessee and the lessor consider the land and the building as a single unit.

Review Exercises

1. a. The lessee should account for a lease arrangement as a capital lease if at the date of the lease agreement the lease meets **one or more** of the following four criteria:

   (1) The lease transfers ownership of the property to the lessee.

   (2) The lease contains a bargain purchase option.

   (3) The lease term is equal to 75% or more of the estimated economic life of the lease property.

   (4) The present value of the minimum lease payments (excluding executory costs) equals or exceeds 90% of the fair value of the leased property.

   b. The lessor should account for a lease as a direct financing lease if it meets **one or more** of the criteria noted in "a" above and **both** of the following criteria:

   (1) Collectibility of the payments required from the lessee is reasonably predictable.

   (2) No important uncertainties surround the amount of unreimbursable costs yet to be incurred by the lessor under the lease.

2. a. Initial recording by lessor:

Lease Payments Receivable	144,923.16	
Equipment		120,000.00
Unearned Interest Income-Leases		24,923.16

   b. Receipt of first year's lease payment:

Cash	36,230.79	
Lease Payments Receivable		36,230.79

   c. Interest income earned during the first year:

Unearned Interest Income-Leases	9,600.00	
Interest Income-Leases		9,600.00

3.   a.   Initial recording by lessee:
              Leased Equipment Under Capital Leases....................   120,000.00
                 Obligations Under Capital Leases 120,000.00
     b.   Lease payment on 12-31-88
              Interest Expense 7,469.54
              Obligations Under Capital Leases...............................   28,761.25
                 Cash 36,230.79
     c.   Equipment purchase on 12-31-90
              Equipment 130,000.00
              Accumulated Depreciation-Capital Lease....................   120,000.00
                 Leased Equipment Under Capital Leases...........   120,000.00
                 Accumulated Depreciation-Equipment...............   120,000.00
                 Cash...   10,000.00

4.   Molinar Company
                       Lease Amortization Schedule
                          (Annuity Due Basis)

Date	Annual Lease Payment (a)	Interest (12%) on Unpaid Obligation (b)	Reduction of Lease Obligation (c)	Balance of Lease Obligation (d)
1-3-90	--	--	--	$214,679
1-3-91	$42,000	-0-	$42,000	172,679
1-3-92	42,000	20,721	21,279	151,400
1-3-93	42,000	18,168	23,832	127,568
1-3-94	42,000	15,308	26,692	100,876
1-3-95	42,000	12,105	29,895	79,981
1-3-96	42,000	8,518	33,482	37,499
1-3-97	42,000	4,501*	37,499	-0-

*Rounded by $1
(a) Annual rental payment.
(b) 12% of the preceding balance of (d) for 1-3-90; since this is an annuity due, no time has elapsed at the date of the first payment and no interest has accrued.
(c) (A) Minus (b).
(d) 1-3-90 amount is computed by multiplying $42,000 (annual lease payment) by 5.11141 (present value of annuity due of seven periods at 12% from Table 6-5). Remaining amounts in column (d) are computed by subtracting (c) from the previous amount in column (d).

23

Accounting changes and error analysis

Chapter Synopsis

Chapter 23 discusses the different procedures used to report accounting changes and error corrections. The use of estimates in accounting as well as the uncertainty that surrounds many of the events accountants attempt to measure may make adjustments to the financial reporting process necessary. The accurate reporting of these adjustments in a manner that facilitates analysis and understanding of financial statements is the focus of this chapter.

Chapter Review

1. *APB Opinion No. 20* has standardized the manner in which accounting changes are reported. *Opinion No. 20* classifies accounting changes as follows:
    a. **Change in Accounting Principle.** A change from one generally accepted accounting principle **(GAAP)** to another generally accepted accounting principle.
    b. **Change in Accounting Estimate.** A change that occurs as the result of new information or as additional experience is acquired. An example is a change in the estimate of the useful lives of depreciable assets.
    c. **Change in Reporting Entity.** A change from reporting as one type of entity to another type of entity, for example, changing specific subsidiaries comprising the group of companies for which consolidated financial statements are prepared.

2. **Correction of an error in previously issued financial statements** is not an accounting change. Such errors include mathematical mistakes, mistakes in the application of accounting principles, or oversight or misuse of facts that existed at the time financial statements were prepared.

3. A change in accounting principle is not considered to result from the adoption of a new principle in recognition of events that have occurred for the first time or that were previously immaterial. For example, implementing a credit sales policy when one had not previously existed is not considered a change in accounting principle. Also, a change from an accounting principle that is not acceptable (non-GAAP) to a principle that reflects GAAP is considered **a correction of an error.** Thus, only those changes from one GAAP to another GAAP are defined as a change in accounting principle. Also, an enterprise wishing to change from one GAAP to another GAAP must demonstrate that the new principle provides more useful financial information.

4. Three approaches are suggested for recording the effect of changes in accounting principles: (a) **retroactively,** (b) **currently,** and (c) **prospectively.** Retroactive treatment requires computing the cumulative effect of the new method on the financial statements at the beginning of the period. A retroactive adjustment of the financial statements is then made, recasting the financial statements of prior years on a basis consistent with the newly adopted principle. Advocates of this method support its use on the basis of comparability between financial statements of past and subsequent periods.

5. Treating a change in accounting principle currently again requires computation of the cumulative effect of the change on financial statements at the beginning of the period. However, the adjustment is reflected in the current year's income statement as a special item between the captions **"extraordinary items"** and **"net income."** Advocates of this method contend that investor confidence is lost by a retroactive adjustment of financial statements for prior periods.

6. Prospective treatment of a change in accounting principle requires no change in previously reported results. Opening balances are not adjusted and no attempt is made to compensate for prior events. Advocates of this method contend that financial statements based on acceptable accounting principles are final since management cannot change prior periods by subsequently adopting a new principle.

7. *APB Opinion No. 20* has established guidelines that are to be used in determining the appropriate treatment to be accorded a change in accounting principle. In general, *Opinion No. 20* recommends use of the **current** (also called catch-up) **treatment** to account for

changes in accounting principles. In addition to the requirements noted in paragraph 5 above, income before extraordinary items and net income computed on a **pro forma** (as if) basis should be shown on the face of the income statement for all prior periods presented as if the newly adopted principle has been applied during all periods affected. These pro forma amounts are presented only as supplementary information.

8. In special circumstances, a change in accounting principle is handled **retroactively.** The five situations that require retroactive treatment are:

   a. Change from LIFO inventory valuation method to another method.

   b. A change in the method of accounting for long-term construction-type contracts.

   c. A change from the "full-cost" method of accounting in the extractive industries.

   d. A company that is issuing its financial statements for the first time to obtain additional equity capital, effecting a business combination, or registering securities. (This procedure is limited to closely held companies and may be used only once.)

   e. A professional pronouncement recommends that a change in accounting principle be treated retroactively.

9. When a company changes to the LIFO method of inventory valuation, the base-year inventory for all subsequent LIFO calculations is the opening inventory in the year the method is adopted. There is no restatement of prior years' income. Disclosure of the change to LIFO is limited to showing the effect of the change on the results of operations in the period of change. Also, the reasons for omitting the computations of the cumulative effect and the pro forma amounts for prior years should be explained.

10. *APB Opinion No. 20* recommends that **changes in estimates** (for example, uncollectible receivables, useful lives, and salvage values of assets) should be handled prospectively. Opening balances are not adjusted and no attempt is made to "catch up" for prior periods. The effects of all changes in estimates are accounted for in **(a)** the period of change if the change affects that period only or **(b)** the period of change and future periods if the change affects both.

11. Reporting a **change in an entity** requires restating the financial statements of all prior periods presented to show the financial information for the new reporting entity for all periods. The financial statements of the year in which the change in reporting entity is made should describe the nature of the change and the reason for it.

12. *FASB Statement No. 16* reaffirmed the conclusions of *APB Opinion No. 20* by requiring that corrections of errors be **(a)** treated as prior period adjustments, **(b)** recorded in the year in which the error was discovered, and **(c)** reported in the financial statements as an adjustment to the beginning balance of retained earnings. If comparative statements are presented, the prior statements affected should be restated to correct for the error.

13. Errors in the accounting process can result from mathematical mistakes, improper estimates, misapplication of accounting principles as well as numerous other causes. Once an error is discovered, an accountant must analyze the error by answering three questions:

   a. What type of error is involved?

   b. What entries are needed to correct for the error?

   c. How are financial statements to be restated once the error is discovered?

An error can affect (1) **real accounts only** (balance sheet), (2) **nominal accounts only** (income statement), or (3) **both real and nominal accounts** (balance sheet and income statement).

14. **Counterbalancing errors** are errors that occur in one period and correct themselves in the next period. **Noncounterbalancing** errors take longer than two periods to correct themselves and sometimes may exist until the item in error is no longer a part of the entity's financial statements. In the case of counterbalancing errors found at the end of the first period, the necessity for preparing a correcting journal entry depends on whether or not the books have been closed. If the books have been closed, no correcting entry is needed. Noncounterbalancing errors should always be corrected if discovered before they correct themselves, even if the books have been closed.

15. Some examples of counterbalancing and noncounterbalancing errors are presented here:

Counterbalancing Errors

   a. Failure to record accrued revenues or expenses.

   b. Failure to record prepaid revenues or expenses.

   c. Overstatement or understatement of purchases.

   d. Overstatement or understatement of ending inventory.

Noncounterbalancing Errors

   a. Failure to record depreciation.

   b. Recording a depreciable asset as an expense.

   c. Recording the purchase of land as an expense.

   d. Recording the discount on bonds as interest expense in the year of issue.

16. In situations where a great many errors are encountered, use of a work sheet as demonstrated in the text can facilitate analysis and ultimate correction of account balances.

REVIEW QUESTIONS AND EXERCISES

True-False

Indicate whether each of the following is true (T) or false (F) in the space provided.

_____ 1. Prior to the issuance of *APB Opinion No. 20*, "Accounting Changes," only one method was acceptable for reporting changes in accounting.

_____ 2. Correction of an error in previously issued financial statements is not an accounting change as defined by *Opinion No. 20*.

_____ 3. A change in accounting principle results when a company changes from one GAAP to another GAAP.

_____ 4. Instituting a policy whereby customers can now purchase merchandise on account, when in the past only cash sales were accepted, is evidence that a change in accounting principle has occurred.

_____ 5. When a change in accounting principle is treated retroactively, an adjustment is made recasting financial statements of prior years.

_____ 6. Use of the current or catch-up method in reporting accounting changes requires showing the cumulative effect of such changes as an extraordinary item on the income statement.

_____ 7. In general, *APB Opinion No. 20* recommends use of the prospective method in reporting the effect of changes in accounting principles.

_____ 8. With respect to a cumulative effect-type accounting change, when pro forma financial statements are presented, they are considered to be supplementary and should not be presented in place of financial statements for prior periods.

_____ 9. The retroactive treatment may be applied to an accounting change only in the case of closely held companies and it may be used only once.

_____ 10. A change in the method of accounting for long-term construction-type contracts is an example of accounting change that is permitted to be handled retroactively.

_____ 11. When a company changes to the LIFO method of inventory valuation, the base-year inventory for all subsequent LIFO calculations is the opening inventory in the year the method is adopted.

_____ 12. A change in accounting principle is considered appropriate only when the enterprise demonstrates that the alternative GAAP that is adopted provides more useful financial information.

_____ 13. If a change in an accounting estimate affects current net income by an amount equal to or greater than 1% of net income, the change should be handled retroactively.

_____ 14. Whenever it is impossible to determine whether a change in principle or a change in estimate has occurred, the change should be considered a change in estimate.

_____ 15. *FASB Statement No. 16* requires that corrections of errors be handled prospectively and shown in the current operating section of the income statement in the year the correction is made.

_____ 16. Counterbalancing errors are two separate errors that offset one another in the same accounting period.

_____ 17. Recording the purchase of land as an expense is an example of a noncounterbalancing error.

_____ 18. If accrued wages are overlooked at the end of the accounting period, expenses and liabilities will be understated and net income will be overstated.

_____ 19. If a counterbalancing error is discovered after the books are closed, no correcting entry is needed.

_____ 20. An understatement in ending inventory will result in a corresponding understatement of net income.

Multiple Choice

Select the best answer for each of the following items and place the corresponding letter in the space provided.

_____ 1. A change in accounting principle is evidenced by:
   A. a change from the historical cost principle to current value accounting.
   B. adopting the allowance method in estimating bad debts expense when a credit sales policy is instituted.
   C. changing the basis of inventory pricing from weighted-average cost to LIFO.
   D. a change from current value accounting to the historical cost principle.

_____ 2. Those advocating retroactive treatment of an accounting change contend that:
   A. restating prior years' financial statements is necessary in providing comparable financial statements.

B. currents year's income should be adjusted for the cumulative effect of the change.

C. investors lose confidence in a company that adjusts previously issued financial statements.

D. once financial statements, prepared in accordance with GAAP, are issued, they are final.

3. Which of the following is not a requirement of the current or catch-up method used to account for changes in accounting principles?

A. Financial statements for prior periods included for comparative purposes should be presented as previously reported.

B. The cumulative effect of the use of the new method is computed at the end of the period.

C. The cumulative effect of the adjustment should be reflected in the income statement between the captions "extraordinary items" and "net income."

D. Income before extraordinary items and net income computed on a pro forma (as if) basis should be shown on the face of the income statement for all periods presented as if the newly adopted principle had been applied during all periods affected.

4. The major reason the profession allows retroactive treatment for certain changes in accounting principles stems from the fact that:

A. the cumulative adjustment in the period of change might have so great an effect on net income that the resulting amount would be misleading.

B. investors demand comparable financial statements.

C. accounting tradition has held that certain changes in accounting principles are always handled retroactively.

D. there were no other alternative methods available for handling these specific accounting changes.

5. The general rule for differentiating between a change in an estimate and a correction of an error is:

A. based on the materiality of the amounts involved. Material items are handled as a correction of an error, whereas immaterial amounts are considered a change in an estimate.

B. if a generally accepted accounting principle is involved, it's usually a change in an estimate.

C. if a generally accepted accounting principle is involved, it's usually a correction of an error.

D. a careful estimate that later proves to be incorrect should be considered a change in an estimate.

6. Raiderland Corporation has a change for which they employ the retroactive approach. Raiderland restates the financial statements of all prior periods presented and discloses in the year of change the effect on net income and earnings per share data for all prior periods presented. This change is most likely the result of a:

A. change in accounting principle.

B. change in accounting estimate.

C. change in reporting entity.

D. change due to an error.

Questions 7,8, and 9 are based on the following information:

Husky Badger, Inc., is a calendar-year corporation. Its financial statements for the years ended 12-31-89 and 12-31-90 contained the following errors:

	1989	1990
Ending inventory	$5,000 overstatement	$8,000 understatement
Depreciation expense	$2,000 understatement	$4,000 overstatement

7. Assume that the 1989 errors were not corrected and that no errors occurred in 1988. By what amount will 1989 income before income taxes be overstated or understated?

A. $7,000 overstatement.

B. $8,000 overstatement.

C. $3,000 understatement.

D. $10,000 understatement.

_____ 8. Assume that no correcting entries were made at 12-31-89, or 12-31-90. Ignoring income taxes, by how much will retained earnings at 12-31-90 be overstated or understated?
   A. $7,000 overstatement.
   B. $8,000 overstatement.
   C. $3,000 understatement.
   D. $10,000 understatement.

_____ 9. Assume that no correcting entries were made at 12-31-89 or 12-31-90 and that no additional errors occurred in 1991. By how much will 1991 income before income taxes be over-stated or understated?
   A. $7,000 overstatement.
   B. $8,000 overstatement.
   C. $3,000 understatement.
   D. $10,000 understatement.

_____ 10. The 12-31-90, physical inventory of Wildcat Company appropriately included $4,500 of merchandise that was not recorded as a purchase until January 1991. What effect will this error have on 12-31-90: assets, liabilities, retained earnings, and income for the year then ended, respectively?
   A. No effect; overstate; understate; understate.
   B. No effect; understate; understate; overstate.
   C. Understate; no effect; overstate; overstate.
   D. No effect; understate; overstate; overstate.

Review Exercises

1. The following two independent changes were made by Ann Den Corporation during 1990.
   a. A machine costing $45,000 (no residual value) was being depreciated over a 15-year estimated useful life. On the basis of new information, not available at the time of the original estimate, management decided to revise the useful life to 20 years. This revision occurred early in the 9th year (1990) of the asset's useful life. The straight-line depreciation method is used.
   b. A machine costing $42,000 has been depreciated on a straight-line basis (6-year useful life, no residual value). At the beginning of the 4th year (1990), it was decided to change to the sum-of-the-years'-digits method.

Required:

With respect to each change (1) indicate the type of change, (2) record any journal entry necessary to recognize the change, and (3) record annual depreciation for 1990. (Ignore any income tax effect.)

2.   Match the items listed on the left with the appropriate description listed on the right.

Item

_____   1.   Changing the companies included in combined financial statements

_____   2.   Change from the cash basis of accounting to the accrual basis

_____   3.   Change from LIFO to FIFO

_____   4.   Change from sum-of-the-years'- digits to straight-line depreciation

_____   5.   Change to consolidated financial statements from statements of individual companies

_____   6.   Change in the percentage applied in the determination of bad debts, resulting from new market research study

_____   7.   Change from the current value approach to the historical cost approach in accounting for plant assets

_____   8.   Change to the "full cost" method of accounting by an oil company

_____   9.   Change from FIFO to weighted-average cost

_____   10. Change in the salvage value of machinery due to an increase in the price of scrap metal

Description

A.   Cumulative effect-type accounting change

B.   Retroactive effect-type accounting change

C.   Change in an accounting estimate

D.   Change in a reporting entity

E.   Correction of an error

3.   Staggs Company failed to prepare adjusting entries for the items listed below. Indicate the effect each omission would have on reported net income for 1990 by placing a check mark in the appropriate box.

Omission

a.   Accrued expense, end of 1989
b.   Accrued expense, end of 1990
c.   Prepaid expense, end of 1989
d.   Prepaid expense, end of 1990
e.   Unearned income, end of 1989
f.   Unearned income, end of 1990
g.   Accrued income, end of 1989
h.   Accrued income, end of 1990

Overstate	Understate	No Effect

4.   A three-year fire insurance policy beginning on September 1, 1988, was erroneously debited to the Land account when the $720 premium was paid. During 1990 the company sold all its land, reducing the Land account to a zero balance. Using the amount recorded in the Land account, the company suffered a $400 loss on the sale.

Required

Prepare two correcting entries

A.   assuming that the books have not been closed in 1990 and

B.   assuming that the books have been closed for 1990.

SOLUTIONS TO REVIEW QUESTIONS AND EXERCISES

True-False

1. (F) Prior to the issuance of *APB Opinion No. 20*, companies had considerable flexibility in reporting changes affecting comparability in accounting reports and many alternative accounting treatments were used for essentially the same type of transaction.

2. (T)

3. (T)

4. (F) This is not a change in an accounting principle but rather a new transaction that results in the use of a principle not previously required.

5. (T)

6. (F) The cumulative effect of the adjustment should be reported in the income statement between the captions "extraordinary items" and "net income." The cumulative effect is not an extraordinary item but should be reported on a net-of-tax basis in a manner similar to that used for an extraordinary item.

7. (F) Before *APB Opinion No. 20* was issued, accounting changes were reported retroactively, currently, and prospectively. However, *APB Opinion No. 20* provided classification by establishing guidelines that are to be used depending on the type of change in the accounting principle involved. The method to be used in reporting a change in accounting principle depends on whether the change is classified as (1) cumulative effect, (2) retroactive effect, or (3) change to the LIFO method of inventory.

8. (T)

9. (F) Under the retroactive method, a retroactive adjustment of the financial statements presented is made by recasting the statements of prior years on a basis consistent with the newly adopted principle. Any part of the cumulative effect attributable to years prior to those presented is treated as an adjustment of beginning retained earnings of the earliest year presented. This treatment is not limited to companies of a certain size, and it can be used as often as required. Listed in the text material are six situations that require the restatement of all prior period financial statements.

10. (T)

11. (T)

12. (T)

13. (F) Changes in accounting estimates must be handled prospectively, that is, no changes should be made in previously reported results. Opening balances are not adjusted and no attempt is made to catch-up for prior periods.

14. (T)

15. (F) The profession requires that corrections of errors be treated as prior period adjustments, be recorded in the year in which the error was discovered, and be reported in the financial statements as an adjustment to the beginning balance of retained earnings. If comparative statements are presented, the prior statements affected should be restated to correct for the error.

16. (F) Counterbalancing errors are errors that will offset or correct themselves over two periods. For example, the failure to record accrued wages in period one will cause (1) net income to be overstated, (2) accrued wages payable to be understated, and (3) wages expense to be understated. If no attempt is made to correct this error, then in period two, net income will be understated, accrued wages payable will be correct, and wages expense will be overstated. The net effect of this error for the two years (at the end of period time) is that net income, accrued wages payable, and wages expense will be correct.

17. (T)

18. (T)

19. (T)

20. (T)

Multiple Choice

1. **(C)** Because current value accounting is not GAAP, alternatives A and D cannot be correct. A change in accounting principle is defined as a change from one GAAP to another GAAP. Alternative B is incorrect because adopting a principle for a new transaction does not constitute a change in accounting principle.

2. **(A)** Advocates of the retroactive method argue that only by restatement of prior periods can changes in accounting principles lead to comparable financial statements. If this approach is not used, the year previous to the change will be on the old method; the year of the change will report the entire cumulative adjustment in income; and the following year will present financial statements on the new basis without the cumulative effect of the change.

3. **(B)** When the current or catch-up method is used, the cumulative effect of the use of the new method is computed at the beginning of the period not at the end. Alternatives A, C, and D are requirements of the current or catch-up period.

4. **(A)** The major reason for allowing retroactive treatment is that reflecting the cumulative adjustment in the period of the change might have such a large effect on net income that the figure would be misleading.

5. **(D)** Distinguishing between a change in an estimate and a correction of an error is not necessarily determined by a GAAP being involved. Also, materiality is not one of the criteria to be used in differentiating between a change in an estimate and a correction of an error. The best basis for differentiating between a change in one estimate and a correction of an error is to follow the general rule that "careful estimates that later prove to be incorrect should be considered a change in an estimate."

6. **(C)** The question describes most closely the accounting and disclosure requirements necessary for a change in reporting entity. A change in accounting principle (alternative A) is a broad concept that must be further defined in order to describe the appropriate treatment. Alternatives B and D do not require the disclosures indicated in the question.

7. **(A)**

	Effect on 1989 Income	
Ending inventory $5,000 overstatement	$5,000 -	over
Depreciation expense $2,000 understatement	2,000 -	over
Net effect	$7,000 -	over

8. **(D)**

	Effect on 1990 Retained Earnings	
1989 Ending inventory $5,000 overstatment	-0 -*	
1990 Ending inventory $8,000 understatement	8,000 -	under
1989 Depreciation expense $2,000 understatement	2,000 -	over
1990 Depreciation expense $4,000 overstatement	4,000 -	under
Net effect	$10,000 -	under

*This is an example of a counterbalancing error. This error overstates income by $5,000 in 1989 and understates income by $5,000 in 1990. Thus, at the end of 1990, there is no effect on retained earnings. If the $8,000 inventory error is not corrected, it will correct itself at the end of 1991. The depreciation errors are noncounterbalancing and will cause retained earnings to be in error until specifically corrected.

9. **(B)**

	Effect on 1991 Net Income	
1989 Ending inventory $8,000 understatement	$8,000 -	over
Net effect	$8,000 -	over

The 1989 and 1990 depreciation expense errors do not effect 1991 net income.

10. (D) The merchandise was correctly counted in the physical inventory and thus ending inventory and total assets are properly stated. The fact that the purchase was not recorded understates liabilities because accounts payable was not credited. Also, with the purchase not being recorded, the amount of merchandise available for sale is understated and results in an understatement of cost of goods sold. The understatement of cost of goods sold causes both net income and retained earnings to be overstated.

Review Exercises

1. a.   (1) Change in accounting estimate
   (2) No entry necessary
   (3) Depreciation expense   1,750*
           Accumulated depreciation   1,750

   *Depreciation to date:
   ($45,000 ÷ 15) x 8 = $24,000
   Book value ($45,000 - $24,000) = $21,000
   Future depreciation ($21,000 ÷ 12) = $1,750 per year

   b.   (1) Change in accounting principle.
   (2) Cumulative effect of change in depreciation method 9,000*
       Accumulated depreciation 9,000

   *Depreciation to date (straight-line):
   ($42,000 ÷ 6) x 3 = $21,000
   Depreciation to date (sum-of-the-years'-digits):
   $42,000 x 15/21 = $30,000
   Adjustment: ($30,000 - $21,000) = $9,000

   (3) Depreciation expense 6,000*
       Accumulated depreciation 6,000

   *42,000 x 3/21 = $6,000

2. 1. D   6. C
   2. E   7. E
   3. B   8. B
   4. A   9. A
   5. D   10. C

3. a. Understate
   b. Overstate
   c. Overstate
   d. Understate
   e. Understate
   f. Overstate
   g. Overstate
   h. Understate

4. A. Prepaid Insurance* 160
   Insurance Expense 240
   Retained Earnings 320
       Loss on Sale of Land 400
       Gain on Sale of Land 320

   *Land account was overstated by $720, so the $400 loss is actually a $320 gain. As of 12-31-90, $560 (28/36) of the prepaid insurance has expired. $240 of this amount is an expense for 1990, with the remainder taken directly to Retained Earnings. The unexpired portion of the prepaid insurance is recorded as an asset (Prepaid Insurance, $160).

   B. Prepaid Insurance 160
       Retained Earnings 160

24

Statement of Cash Flows

Chapter Synopsis

Chapter 24 discusses the preparation and significance of the statement of cash flows. This statement supplements the data presented in the balance sheet, income statement, and statement of retained earnings. The primary purpose of the statement of cash flows is to provide information about the cash receipts and cash payments of an entity during a period.

Chapter Review

1. **FASB Statement No. 95, "Statement of Cash Flows,"** was issued in November, 1987, with an effective date of July 15, 1988. A major reason for requiring the statement of cash flows as a basic financial statement concerns the feelings on the part of investors and analysts that accrual accounting has become too far removed from the underlying cash flows of the enterprise. Also, because financial statements take no cognizance of inflation, many look for a more concrete standard like cash flow to evaluate operating success or failure. The working capital concept, used in preparing the statement of change in financial position, is thought to be lacking in its ability to provide information that is as useful about **liquidity** and **financial flexibility** as is the cash basis.

2. The primary purpose of the **statement of cash flows** is to provide information about the **cash receipts** and **cash payments** of an entity during a period. A secondary objective is to provide information about the investing and financing activities of the entity during the period. Reporting the net increase or decrease in cash is useful because investors, creditors, and other interested parties want to know and can generally comprehend what is happening to the entity's most liquid resource - its cash. In general, a statement of cash flows provides information useful in answering the following questions: **(a)** Where did the cash come from during the period; **(b)** What was the cash used for during the period; and **(c)** What was the change in the cash balance during the period.

3. The statement of cash flows classifies cash receipts and cash payments by **operating, investing,** and **financing** activities. **Operating activities** include all transactions and events that are not investing and financing activities. Operating activities include cash effects of **transactions that enter into the determination of net income,** such as cash receipts from the sales of goods and services and cash payments to suppliers and employees for acquisitions of inventory and expenses. **Investing activities** include **(a)** making and collecting loans, and **(b)** acquiring and disposing of investments and productive long-lived assets. **Financing activities** involve liability and owners' equity items and include **(a)** obtaining cash from creditors and repaying the amounts borrowed, and **(b)** obtaining capital from owners and providing them with a return on, and return of, their investment.

4. The typical cash receipts and cash payments of a business entity classified according to operating, investing, and financing activities are shown below.

Operating Activities
Cash inflows
   From sale of goods or services
   From returns on loans (interest) and on equity.
   Securities (dividends).
Cash outflows
   To suppliers for inventory.
   To employees for services.
   To government for taxes.
   To lender for interest.
   To others for expenses.
Investing Activities
Cash inflows
   From sale of property, plant, and equipment.
   From sale of debt or equity securities of other entities.
   From collection of principal on loans to other entities.
Cash outflows
   To purchase property, plant, and equipment.
   To purchase debt or equity securities of other entities.
   To make loans to other entities.
Financing Activities
Cash inflows
   From sale of equity securities.
   From issuance of debt (bonds and notes).

Cash outflows

> To shareholders as dividends.
>
> To redeem long-term debt or reacquire capital stock.

It should be noted that (1) operating activities involve income determination items, (2) investing activities involve cash flows generally resulting from changes in long-term asset items, and (3) financing activities involve cash flows generally resulting from changes in long-term liability and stockholders' equity items.

5.   Some cash flows relating to investing or financing activities are classified as operating activities. For example, receipts of investment income (interest and dividends) and payments of interest to lenders are classified as operating activities. Conversely, some cash flows relating to operating activities are classified as investing or financing activities. For example, the cash received from the sale of property, plant, and equipment at a gain, although reported in the income statement, is classified as an investing activity, and the effect of the related gain would not be included in net cash flow from operating activities. Likewise a gain or loss on the payment of debt would generally be part of the cash outflow related to the repayment of the amount borrowed and therefore is a financing activity.

6.   The information used to prepare the statement of cash flows generally comes from three major sources: (a) **comparative balance sheets;** (b) **the current income statement;** and (c) **selected transaction data.** Actual preparation of the statement of cash flows involves three steps:

(1)   **Determine the change in cash.** This procedure is straightforward because the difference between the beginning and ending cash balance can be easily computed from an examination of the comparative balance sheets.

(2)   **Determine the net flow from operating activities.** This procedure is complex; it involves analyzing not only the current years' income statement but also comparative balance sheets as well as selected transaction data.

(3)   **Determine cash flows from investing and financing activities.** All other changes in the balance sheet accounts must be analyzed to determine their effect on cash.

7.   To compute net cash flows from operating activities it is necessary to report revenues and expenses on a cash basis. This is done by eliminating the effects of income statement transactions that did not result in a corresponding increase or decrease in cash. The conversion of accrual-based net income to net cash flow from operating activities may be done through either the **direct method** or the **indirect method.**

8.   Under the **direct method** (also called the income statement method) cash revenues and expenses are determined. The difference between these two amounts represents net cash flows from operating activities. In essence, the direct method results in the presentation of a cash basis income statement. Under the **indirect method** (also called the reconciliation method), computation of net cash flows from operating activities begins with net income. This accrual based amount is then converted to net cash flow from operations by adding back noncash expenses and charges and deducting noncash revenues.

9.   While **FASB Statement No. 95** encourages the use of the direct method when preparing the statement of cash flows, use of the indirect method is also permitted. However, if the direct method is used the FASB requires that a reconciliation of net income to net cash flow from operating activities shall be provided in a separate schedule. Therefore, under either method the indirect (reconciliation) approach must be presented. The text book includes **three comprehensive illustrations** which provide a detailed explanation of the preparation and presentation of the statement of cash flows. Each illustration should be studied prior to attempting the assigned problem material.

10.   Both the direct method and the indirect method have distinct advantages which should be considered when deciding on the method to be used in presenting the statement of cash flows. The principal advantage of the direct method is that it shows operating cash receipts and payments. Supporters contend that this is useful in estimating future cash flows and in assessing an entity's ability to (a) generate sufficient cash flow from operations for the payment of debt, (b) reinvest in its operations, and (c) make distributions to owners. Proponents of the indirect method cite the fact that it focuses on the difference between net income and net cash flow from operations as its principal advantage. Also, supporters of the indirect method contend that users are more familiar with the method, and it is less costly to present the statement of cash flow using this method.

11.   Minimum disclosure requirements for companies which use the direct method include the following.

Receipts
a.   Cash collected from customers.
b.   Interest and dividends received.
c.   Other operating cash receipts, if any.

Payments
a.   Cash paid to suppliers and employees for goods and services.
b.   Interest paid.
c.   Income taxes paid.
d.   Other operating cash payments, if any.

Use of the indirect method requires separate disclosure of changes in inventory, receivables, and payables relating to operating activities. Such disclosures are required for the purpose of aiding users in approximating the direct method.

12. The schedule shown below presents the common types of adjustments that are made to net income to arrive at net cash flow for operating activities.

Additions to Net Income
Depreciation expense
Amortization of intangibles and deferred charges
Amortization of bond discount
Increase in deferred income tax liability or deferred investment credit
Loss on investment in common stock using equity method
Loss on sale of plant assets
Decrease in receivables
Decrease in inventories
Decrease in accounts payable
Increase in accounts payable
Increase in accrued liabilities

Deductions from Net Income
Amortization of bond premium
Decrease in deferred income tax liability or deferred investment credit.
Income on investment in common stock using equity method
Gain on sale of plant assets
Increase in receivables
Increase in inventories
Increase in prepaid payable
Decrease in accounts payable
Decrease in accrued liabilities

13. Nine items, described as special problems related to preparing the statement of cash flows are presented in the text material. These items relate to various aspects of the statement of cash flows and should be understood for accurate preparation of the statement.

(a) **Adjustments similar to depreciation** - depreciation expense is added back to net income to arrive at net cash flow from operating activities. Likewise, amortization of intangible assets and amortization of deferred costs are also added back to net income.

(b) **Accounts receivable (net)** - an increase in the Allowance for Doubtful Accounts should be added back to net income to arrive at net cash flow from operating activities. This is due to the fact that the increase in the allowance results in a charge to bad debts expense (a noncash expense).

(c) **Other working capital changes** - some changes in working capital, although they affect cash, do not affect net income. Generally, these are investing or financing activities of a current nature such as the purchase of short-term investments.

(d) **Net losses** - if an enterprise reports a net loss instead of net income, the net loss must be adjusted for those items that do not result in a cash inflow or outflow. As a result of such adjustments, the net loss may turn out to be a positive cash flow from operating activities.

(e) **Gains** - because a gain on the sale of plant assets is reported in the statement of cash flows as part of the cash proceeds from the sale of the assets under investing activities, the gain is deducted from net income to avoid double counting.

(f) **Stock options** - compensation expense is recorded during the period(s) in which an employee performs the service if a company has a stock option plan. This expense is recorded by debiting compensation expense and crediting a stockholders' equity account. Thus, net income has to be increased by the amount of compensation expense in computing cash flow from operating activities.

(g) **Pensions** - the difference between the pension expense recorded during the period and the amount of cash funded for the pension plan must be an adjustment to net income in arriving at cash flow from operating activities.

(h) **Extraordinary items** - cash flows from extraordinary transactions and other events whose affects are included in net income, but which are not related to operations, should be reported as either investing or financing activities.

(i) **Significant noncash transactions** - significant noncash investing and financing activities (such as purchasing and asset by assuming long-term debt), if material in amount, should be disclosed in a separate schedule or narrative disclosure. These items are not to be incorporated in the statement of cash flows.

14. Near the end of Chapter 24 a **comprehensive illustration** of the statement of cash flows is presented. This illustration includes an explanation of how a work sheet can be used in preparing the statement. **Appendix 24A, The T-Account Approach to Preparation of the Statement of Cash Flows,** presents an alternative approach to the accumulation of the data necessary for preparation of the statement of cash flows. The T-account approach provides a quick and systematic method of accumulating the necessary cash flow information. Its use is considered superior to the work sheet approach by many accountants.

REVIEW QUESTIONS AND EXERCISES

True - False

Indicate whether each of the following is true (T) or false (F) in the space provided.

____ 1. One major reason for requiring the presentation of a statement of cash flows is that investors and analysts are concerned that accrual accounting has become too far removed from the underlying cash flows of the enterprise.

____ 2. The primary purpose of the statement of cash flows is to provide information about cash receipts and cash payments that resulted from operations.

____ 3. Operating activities as defined in FASB Statement No. 95 involve the cash effects of transactions that enter into the determination of net income.

____ 4. Financing activities include (a) making and collecting loans, and (b) acquiring and disposing of investments and productive long-lived assets.

____ 5. The cash received from the sale of property, plant, and equipment at a gain, although reported in the income statement, is classified as an investing activity.

____ 6. Determining net cash flow from operating activities involves analysis of the income statement alone as it is the statement that reflects the amount of cash generated from operations as well as the amount of cash used to conduct the operations.

____ 7. If a cash inflow and a cash outflow result from similar type transactions, such as the purchase and sale of property, plant, and equipment or the issuance and repayment of debt, they may be shown as a net amount from the two transactions in the statement of cash flows.

____ 8. Unlike the other financial statements, the statement of cash flows is not prepared from the adjusted trial balance.

____ 9. The conversion of net income to net cash flow from operating activities may be accomplished using either the direct method or the indirect method.

____ 10. As its name implies, the indirect method is not directly involved with the computation of accrual based net income because it results in the presentation of a condensed cash basis income statement.

____ 11. When computing net cash flow from operating activities under the indirect method, an increase in accounts receivable (net) during the year must be added to accrual based net income because more sales were made then those reflected in the income statement.

____ 12. When the direct method is used in determining cash flow from operating activities, users of the statement of cash flows are unable to reconcile the net income to the net cash flows from operations because this is only provided when the indirect method is used.

____ 14. Because the payment of cash dividends reduces both cash and retained earnings by a similar amount, this transaction has no effect on the statement of cash flows.

____ 15. If a company records a loss on the sale of equipment, the amount of the loss must be added back to net income to determine the proper amount of net cash flow from operating activities.

____ 16. The amortization of a bond premium should be handled in the same manner as depreciation of a plant asset, that is, added to net income when determining cash flows from operating activities.

____ 17. When a repair to equipment is debited to accumulated depreciation because it extends the asset's useful life, the transaction is considered neither an increase nor a decrease in cash for the period.

____ 18. When accounts payable increase during a period, cost of goods sold on an accrual basis is lower than cost of goods sold on a cash basis.

____ 19. The direct method is more consistent with the objective of the statement of cash flows because it shows operating cash receipts and payments where the indirect method does not.

____ 20. The principal advantage of the indirect method is that it focuses on the difference between net income and net cash flow from operating activities, thus providing a useful link between the statement of cash flows, the income statement, and the balance sheet.

Multiple Choice

Select the best response for each of the following items and place the corresponding letter in the space provided.

_____ 1. Which of the following is not one of the benefits investors and creditors can expect as a result of the presentation of the statement of cash flows?
A. Assess the enterprise's ability to meet its obligations, its ability to pay dividends, and its need for external financing.
B. Assess the effects on an enterprise's financial position of both its cash and noncash investing, and financing transactions during a period.
C. Assess the enterprise's ability to expand its operating facilities through the issuance of long-term debt.
D. Assess the reasons for differences between net income and associated cash receipts and payments.

_____ 2. As used in the preparation of the statement of cash flows, financing activities involve
A. Liability and owners' equity items and include obtaining cash from creditors and repaying the amounts borrowed.
B. Solely the acquisition of capital from owners and providing them a return on, and a return of, their investment.
C. Making and collecting loans, and acquiring and disposing of investments and productive assets.
D. All the activities which are similar to the major transactions of a financial institution.

_____ 3. Which of the following activities is classified as an investing activity on the statement of cash flows?
A. Cash received from the sale of goods and services.
B. Cash paid to suppliers for inventory.
C. Cash paid to lenders for interest.
D. Cash received from the sale of property, plant, and equipment at a gain.

_____ 4. The basis recommended by the FASB for the statement of cash flows is "cash and cash equivalents." As described in FASB Statement No. 95, cash equivalents are
A. All current assets that have no realization problems associated with the.
B. Short-term, highly liquid investments that are both readily convertible to known amounts of cash, and so near their maturity that they present insignificant risk of changes in interest rates.

C. All cash and near cash items that will be turned into cash within one operating period or one year, whichever is shorter.
D. All cash and investments in short-term securities that have a maturity of three months or less from the date of the financial statements.

_____ 5. The method used to compute net cash flows from operating activities that adjusts net income for items that affected reported net income but did not affect cash is known as the
A. Indirect method.
B. Direct method.
C. Adjustment Method.
D. Income statement method.

_____ 6. During 1990, John Mathews Company earned net income of $128,000. In addition, the Company experienced the following changes in the account balances listed below

Increases

Accounts payable.......................	$15,000
Inventory.....................................	12,000
Depreciation expense..................	26,000

Decreases

Accounts Receivable....................	$ 4,000
Prepaid expenses.........................	11,000
Accrued liabilities.......................	8,000

Based upon this information what amount will be shown for cash flows from operating activities for 1990.
A. $ 89,000.
B. $ 95,000.
C. $155,000.
D. $164,000.

_____ 7. R. L. Turner Company reported net income after taxes of $85,000 for the year ended 12/31/90. Included in the computation of net income were: depreciation expense, $15,000; amortization of a patent, $8,000; income from an investment in common stock of Newman Smith Inc., accounted for under the equity method, $12,000; and amortization of a bond premium, $3,000. Turner also paid a $20,000 dividend during the year. The cash flow from operating activities would be reported at
A. $57,000.
B. $73,000.
C. $77,000.
D. $93,000.

_____ 8. Of the following questions, which one would not be answered by the statement of cash flows?

A. Where did the cash come from during the period?

B. What was the cash used for during the period?

C. Were all the cash expenditures of benefit to the company during period?

D. What was the change in the cash balance during the period.

_____ 9. In its first year of operations Aston Company reported net income of $257,000. Total sales, all on account, amounted to $486,000, and collections of receivables during the year totaled $396,500. Aston uses the allowance method in accounting for bad debts expense and during the year recorded bad debts expense of $21,000. Based on these facts alone, what is the cash flow from operating activities?

A. $146,500

B. $188,500

C. $236,000

D. $325,500

_____ 10. How should significant noncash transactions (purchase of equipment in exchange for common stock) be reported in the statement of cash flows according to FASB Statement No. 95?

A. They should be incorporated in the statement of cash flows in a section labeled, "Significant Noncash Transactions."

B. Such transactions should be incorporated in the section (operating, financing, or investing) that is most representative of the major component of the transaction.

C. These noncash transactions are not to be incorporated in the statement of cash flows. They may be summarized in a separate schedule at the bottom of the statement, or appear in a separate supplementary schedule to the financials.

D. They should be handled in a manner consistent with the transactions that affect cash flows.

Review Exercises

1. Presented below is the income statement for the year ended December 31, 1990 for the Bazzetta Bulldozer Company. Also presented are the changes in selected balance sheet accounts between 12/31/89 and 12/31/90. On the basis of the information presented, compute the cash flow from operating activities using the indirect method. None of the items included in the income statement meet the requirements for extraordinary items.

Bazzetta Bulldozer Company
Income Statement
For the Year Ended December 31, 1990

Sales		$850,000
Cost of Sales (includes depreciation expense of $82,000		420,000
Gross Profit		$430,000
Operating Expenses:		
Salaries	$105,000	
Depreciation	36,000	
Rent	48,000	
Utilities	7,000	
Amortization of intangibles	15,000	211,000
Operating Income		$219,000
Other Income:		
Gain on Sale of Machinery	$ 18,000	
Other Expenses:		
Interest on Bonds (net of $1,200 premium amortization)	4,800	
Loss on Sale of Building	2,000	
Net Other Income and Expenses		11,200
Income before Income Taxes		$207,800
Federal and State Income Taxes		75,000
Net Income		$132,800

Selected Balance Sheet Data

Increases		Decreases	
Inventory	$76,000	Accounts Receivable	$69,000
Prepaid Expenses	19,000	Accrued Liabilities	9,000
Accounts Payable	54,000		

2.   Comparative balance sheets of the Madden Corporation, along with an income statement, and additional information for the years ended December 31, 1990 and 1991, are presented below. On the basis of the information presented prepare a statement of cash flows using the **(a) indirect method**, and **(b) direct method.**

Balance Sheets

	1990	1991
Cash	$ 10,000	$ 15,000
Accounts Receivable	20,000	33,000
Inventory	40,000	50,000
Building	60,000	65,000
Accumulated Depreciation	(12,000)	(16,000)
Total Assets	$118,000	$147,000
Accounts Payable	$ 20,000	$ 25,000
Common Stock	80,000	100,000
Retained Earnings	18,000	22,000
Total Equities	$118,000	$147,000

Income Statement
for 1991

Sales		$100,000
Cost of Sales		65,000
Gross Profit		$ 35,000
Operating Expenses:		
Depreciation	$ 4,000	
Other	17,000	21,000
Net Income		$ 14,000

Additional Information:
  a. Net income and a cash dividend account for the change in retained earnings.
  b. Common stock was issued for cash during 1991.

3.   Comparative balance sheets at December 31, 1990 and 1991, for the J & M Pruitt Company are shown below.

Balance Sheets

	1990	1991
Cash	$ 62,000	$98,000
Accounts Receivable	74,000	79,000
Inventory	118,000	124,000
Prepaid Expenses	5,000	6,000
Land	---	86,000
Plant Assets	224,000	279,000
Accumulated Depreciation	(86,000)	(80,000)
Franchise	32,000	24,000
Total Assets	$429,000	$616,000
Accounts Payable	41,000	53,000
Notes Payable	63,000	58,000
Bonds Payable	---	129,000
Common Stock	250,000	275,000
Additional Paid-in Capital	46,000	56,000
Retained Earnings	29,000	45,000
Total Equities	$429,000	$616,000

Additional Information:

    a.   A fully depreciated plant asset, which originally cost $20,000 and had no salvage value, was sold for $1,000.

    b.   Bonds payable were issued at par value. Two-thirds of the bonds were exchanged for land; the remaining one-third was issued for cash.

    c.   Common stock was sold for cash.

    d.   The only entries in the Retained Earnings account are for dividends paid in the amount of $10,000 and for the net income for the year.

    e.   Normal depreciation expense was recorded during the year and the franchise was amortized.

    f.   The income statement for the year is as follows:

Sales	$186,000
Cost of sales	102,000
Gross Profit	84,000
Operating expenses	59,000
Income before gain	25,000
Gain on sale of plant asset	1,000
Net Income	$ 26,000

Required:

(a) Prepare a statement of cash flows using the indirect methods.

(b) Prepare a statement of cash flows using the direct methods.

    4.   Presented below are data taken from the records of LaStarge Company. Prepare a statement of cash flows for the year ended December 31, 1990. (Use the indirect method.)

	December 31, 1989	December 31 1990
Cash	$ 10,000	$ 17,000
Accounts Receivable (net)	36,000	41,000
Inventory	66,000	74,000
Prepaid Expenses	6,000	11,000
Land	124,000	72,000
Plant Assets	225,000	376,000
Accumulated Depreciation	(60,000)	(40,000)
	$407,000	$551,000
Accounts Payable	$ 43,000	44,000
Accrued Liabilities	5,000	12,000
Bonds Payable	-0-	100,000
Common Stock	300,000	300,000
Retained Earnings	59,000	95,000
	$407,000	$551,000

Additional Data:

    1.   Land carried at a cost of $52,000 on 12/31/89, was sold in 1990 for $39,000. The loss (not extraordinary) was incorrectly charged directory to retained earnings.

    2.   Plant assets with a cost of $50,000 that were 60% depreciated were sold during 1990 for $15,000. The loss (not extraordinary) was reported on the income statement.

    3.   Net income as reported on the income statement for 1990 amounted to $63,000.

    4.   Cash dividends were paid during 1990. The entry to record the dividend included a debit to retained earnings and a credit to cash.

    5.   Depreciation expense for the year was $10,000.

    6.   Plant assets were purchased during the year. The seller accepted $100,000 in bonds and the remainder in cash.

SOLUTIONS TO REVIEW QUESTIONS AND EXERCISES

True-False

1. (T)
2. (F) The primary purpose of the statement of cash flows is to provide information about the cash receipts and cash payments of an entity during a period. This includes cash receipts and cash payments from operating, investing, and financing activities.
3. (T)
4. (F) This is the definition of investing activities.
5. (T)
6. (F) Determining net cash flows from operating activities involves analyzing not only the current year's income statement but also comparative balance sheets as well as selected transaction data.
7. (F) Individual inflows and outflows from investing and financing activities are reported separately. Thus, cash outflow from the purchase of property, plant, and equipment is reported separately from the cash inflow from the sale of property, plant, and equipment.
8. (T)
9. (T)
10. (F) It is the direct method that results in the presentation of a condensed cash basis income statement.
11. (F) When accounts receivable increase during the year, revenues on an accrual basis are higher than revenues on a cash basis because goods sold on account are reported as revenues. In other words, sales for the period led to increased revenue, but not all of those sales resulted in an increase in cash.
12. (F) If the direct method of reporting net cash flows from operating activities is used, the FASB requires that the reconciliation of net income to net cash flow from operating activities be provided in a separate schedule.
13. (T)
14. (F) The payment of dividends obviously has an impact on the statement of cash flows as it is an outflow of cash. Dividends are reported as an outflow in the financing activities section of the statement of cash flows.
15. (T)
16. (F) The amortization of bond premium reduces the amount of interest expense reported on the income statement, but it does not reduce the amount of cash flowing out of the business. Thus, the amount of bond amortization must be deducted from net income to arrive at cash flows from operating activities.
17. (F) The debit to accumulated depreciation as a result of an equipment repair is most likely offset by a credit to cash. Thus, such a transaction would cause a decrease in cash and be shown as an outflow on the statement of cash flows.
18. (F) Cost of goods sold is the same under either basis. Even if items for which cash has not been expended are eliminated from the computation, the amount of cost of goods sold remains the same.
19. (T)
20. (T)

Multiple Choice

1. (C) Alternatives (A), (B), and (D) are examples of the information an investor or creditor derive from use of the statement of cash flows. Alternative (C) requires a greater amount of in-depth information that is not available in the statement of cash flows alone.
2. (A) Financing a business requires the securing and repayment of funds generated from both owners and creditors. These are the activities that are defined as financing activities in the statement of cash flows.
3. (D) Investing activities include (a) making and collecting loans, and (b) acquiring and disposing of investments and productive assets. Thus, the cash received from the sale of property, plant, and equipment represents the disposal of productive assets.

4. (B) Alternative (B) is the exact definition of "cash and cash equivalents" found in FASB Statement No. 95. The definition also includes the requirement that only investments with original maturities of three months or less qualify as cash equivalents.

5. (A) The question reflects the definition of the indirect method.

6. (D)
Net income	$128,000
Increase in accounts payable	15,000
Increase in inventory	(12,000)
Increase in depreciation expense	26,000
Decrease in accounts receivable	4,000
Decrease in prepaid expenses	11,000
Decrease in accrued liabilities	(8,000)
Cash flows from operating activities	$ 164,000

7. (D)
Net income	$85,000
Depreciation expense	15,000
Amortization of patent	8,000
Amortization of bond premium	(3,000)
Investment income	(12,000)
Cash flows operating activities	$ 93,000

8. (C) The statement of cash flows, like the balance sheet and income statement, reflect the results of transactions entered into by the entity during the preceding year. The statement of cash flows could include the results of some cash flow transactions that were of great benefit and some that were of little benefit. The purpose of the statement is to reflect cash in flows and cash outflows, not to evaluate of the benefits derived from the transactions. A great deal of additional information would have to be included in the statement of cash flows for a reader to evaluate the benefit of each cash receipt or expenditure recorded.

9. (B)
Increase in receivables (sales)	$486,000
Decrease in receivables (collections)	396,500
Net increase in receivables	$ 89,500

Net income	$257,000
Increase in receivables	(89,500)
Bad debts expense	21,000
Cash flow from operations	$188,500

10. (C) According to FASB Statement No. 95, significant noncash transactions are not included in the statement of cash flows. The FASB indicates that such transactions can be summarized at the bottom of the statement of cash flows or appear in a separate schedule as a part of the financial statements.

Review Exercises

1.

Bazzetta Bulldozer Company
Statement of Cash Flows
For the Year End December 31, 1990

Cash flows from operating activities		
Net income		$132,800
Adjustments to reconcile net income to		
net cash provided by operating activities:		
Depreciation expense	$36,000	
Amortization of premium	15,000	
Gain on sale of machinery	(18,000)	
Amortization of premium	(1,200)	
Loss on sale of building	2,000	
Increase in inventory	(76,000)	
Increase in prepaid expense	(19,000)	
Increase in accounts payable	54,000	
Increase in accounts receivable	69,000	
Decrease in accountants liability	(9,000)	52,800
Net cash provided by operating activities		$185,000

2a. **Indirect Method**

Madden Corporation
Statement of Cash Flows
For the Year Ended December 31, 1991

Cash flows from operating activities		
Net income		$14,000
Adjustments to reconcile net income to		
net cash provided by operating activities:		
Depreciation expense	$ 4,000	
Increase in receivables	(13,000)	
Increase in inventory	(10,000)	
Increase in payables	5,000	(14,000)
Net cash provided by operating activities		-0-
Cash flows from investing activities		
Purchase of building		(5,000)
Cash flows from financing activities		
Sale of common stock	20,000	
Payment of dividends	(10,000)	10,000
Net increase in cash		$5,000
Cash, January 1, 1991		10,000
Cash, December 31, 1991		$15,000

2b. Direct Method

Madden Corporation
Statement of Cash Flows
For the Year Ended December 31, 1991

Cash flows from operating activities		
Cash received from customers (a)		$87,000
Cash paid to suppliers (b)	$70,000	
Other expenses	17,000	
Cash disbursed for operations		87,000
Net cash provided by operating activities		-0-
Cash flows from investing activities		
Purchase of building		(5,000)
Cash flows from investing activities		
Sale of common stock	20,000	
Payment of dividends	(10,000)	10,000
Net increase in cash		$ 5,000
Cash, January 1, 1991		10,000
Cash, December 31, 1991		$15,000

(a) $100,000 - 13,000 = $87,000
(b) $65,000 + 10,000 - 5,000 = $70,000

3a. **Indirect Method**

J & M Pruitt Company
Statement of Cash Flows
For the Year Ended December 31, 1991

Cash flows from operating activities		
Net income		$26,000
Adjustments to reconcile net income to		
net cash provided by operating activities		
Depreciation expense (a)	$14,000	
Amortization of franchise	8,000	
Gain of sale of plant asset	(1,000)	
Increase in receivables	(5,000)	
Increase in inventory	(6,000)	
Increase in prepaid expenses	(1,000)	
Increase in accounts payable	12,000	21,000
Net cash flows from operating activities		47,000
Cash flows from investing activities		
Sale of plant asset	1,000	
Purchase of plant asset	(75,000)	
Net cash used by investing activities		(74,000)
Cash flows from financing activities		
Sale of common stock	35,000	
Sale of bonds (129,000 x 1/3)	43,000	
Payment of dividends	(10,000)	
Payment of notes payable	(5,000)	
Net cash provided by financing activities		63,000
Net increase in cash		$36,000
Cash, January 1, 1991		62,000
Cash, December 31, 1991		$98,000

(a) $86,000 - 20,000 + \underline{\textbf{14,000}} = \$80,000$

3b. **Direct Method**

J & M Pruitt Company
Statement of Cash Flows
For the Year Ended December, 31, 1991

Cash flows from operating activities		
Cash received from customers (a)		$181,000
Cash paid to suppliers (b)	$96,000	
Operating expenses (c)	38,000	134,000
Net cash flow from operating activities		47,000
Cash flows from investing activities		
Sale of plant assets	1,000	
Purchase of plant assets	(75,000)	
Net cash used by investing activities		(74,000)
Cash flows from financing activities		
Sale of common stock	35,000	
Sale of bonds (129,000 x 1/3)	43,000	
Payment of dividends	(10,000)	
Payment of note payable	(5,000)	
Net cash provided by financing activities		63,000
Net increase in cash		$36,000
Cash, January 1, 1991		62,000
Cash, December 31, 1991		$98,000

(a) $186,000 - 5,000 = $181,000
(b) $102,000 + 6,000 - 12,000 = $96,000
(c) $59,000 - 14,000 - 8,000 + 1,000 = $38,000

4.

LaStarge Company
Statement of Cash Flows
For the Year Ended December 31, 1990

Cash flow from operating activities		
Net income (a)		$50,000
Adjustments to reconcile net income to		
net cash provided by operating activities		
Depreciation expense	$10,000	
Loss on sale of land	13,000	
Loss on sale of assets	5,000	
Increase on receivables	(5,000)	
Increase in inventory	(8,000)	
Increase in prepaid expenses	(5,000)	
Increase in payables	1,000	
Increase in accruals	7,000	18,000
Net cash provided by operating activities		$68,000
Cash flows from investing activities		
Sale of land	39,000	
Sale of plant assets	15,000	
Purchase of plant assets	(101,000)	
Net cash used by investing activities		47,000
Cash flows from financing activities		
Payment of dividend		(14,000)
Net increase in cash		$7,000
Cash, January 1, 1990		10,000
Cash, December 31, 1990		$17,000

(a) $63,000 - 13,000 = $50,000

25

Basic financial statement analysis

Chapter Synopsis

Chapter 25 focuses on the methodology used in the interpretation and evaluation of the information presented in financial statements. The chapter discusses the computational aspects of the various techniques used in the analysis of financial statements as well as their meaning and significance.

Chapter Review

1. Thus far, the discussion presented in the text has been concerned with the measurement and reporting functions of accounting. Chapter 25 discusses the communication function of accounting that involves **analyzing** and **interpreting** the economic information presented in financial statements. The techniques used in the analysis of financial statement data include: (a) **ratio analysis**, (b) **comparative analysis**, (c) **percentage analysis**, and (d) **examination of related data.**

2. Effective financial statement analysis is a skill that requires knowledge of the available techniques and extensive experience. The techniques can be learned by studying a textbook presentation on the subject. However, effective financial statement analysis requires the ability to (a) select the appropriate technique and (b) interpret the significance of the results obtained.

3. Ratios can be classified as follow:
   a. **Liquidity Ratios.** Measures of the short-run ability of the enterprise to pay its maturing obligations.
   b. **Activity Ratios.** Measures of how effectively the enterprise is using the assets employed.
   c. **Profitability Ratios.** Measures of the degree of success or failure of a given enterprise or division for a given period of time.
   d. **Coverage Ratios.** Measures of the degree of protection for long-term creditors and investors.

4. In the following paragraphs, the individual ratios included in the four classifications will be presented. The method of presentation will include: (a) **identification of the ratio,** (b) **the manner in which the ratio is computed,** and (c) **the significance of the ratio.** It is important to note that the significance of ratio analysis is dependent on a complete understanding of the circumstances surrounding the computation. For example, there are no minimum or maximum amounts that can be identified with individual ratios that are considered to be always good or always bad. Thus, the interpretation of any one ratio cannot be accomplished in a vacuum. **The proper interpretation of ratios involves trend analysis, comparisons with other ratios or industry averages, and a thorough understanding of the environment within which the entity operates.**

LIQUIDITY RATIOS

5. The **current ratio** is the ratio of total current assets to total current liabilities. **It is computed by dividing current assets by current liabilities,** and is sometimes referred to as the working capital ratio. The significance of the current ratio concerns the company's ability to meet its maturing short-term obligations.

6. The **acid-test ratio** relates total current liabilities to the most liquid current assets (cash, marketable securities, and net receivables). **To compute the acid-test ratio, these current assets are divided by total current liabilities.** This ratio is significant in that it focuses on the ability of a company to meet its short-term debt immediately.

7. The **defensive-interval ratio is computed by dividing defensive assets (cash, marketable securities, and net receivables) by projected daily expenditures from operations.** This ratio measures the time span a firm can operate on present liquid assets without resorting to revenues from next year's income sources. It also establishes a safety factor or margin for the investor in determining the capability of the company to meet its basic operational costs.

ACTIVITY RATIOS

8. The **receivables turnover ratio is computed by dividing net sales by net average receivables** (beginning plus ending divided by 2) **outstanding during the year.** This ratio provides an indication of how successful a firm

is in collecting its outstanding receivables. As a general rule, the receivables turnover is acceptable if it does not exceed the time allowed for payment under the selling terms by more than 10 to 15 days.

9. The **inventory turnover ratio** is a function of average inventory (beginning plus ending divided by 2) and cost of goods sold. **This ratio is computed by dividing cost of goods sold by average inventory.** Normally, a high inventory turnover is sought by an enterprise along with a minimum of "stock-out costs."

10. The **asset turnover ratio is determined by dividing net sales for the period by average total assets.** This ratio indicates how efficiently the company utilizes its assets. If the turnover ratio is high, the implication is that the company is using its assets effectively to generate sales. If the asset turnover ratio is low, the company either has to use its assets more efficiently or dispose of them.

PROFITABILITY RATIOS

11. The **profit margin on sales is computed by dividing net income by net sales for the period.** The significance of this ratio is that it indicates that amount of profit, on a percentage basis, that results from each sales dollar earned by the company.

12. **Dividing net income by total average assets yields the rate of return on assets earned by a company.** In computing this ratio, companies sometimes use net income before the subtraction of interest charges because, they contend, interest represents a cost of securing additional assets and, therefore should not be considered as a deduction in arriving at the amount of return on assets.

13. The **rate of return on common stock equity is computed by dividing net income after interest, taxes, and preferred dividends by average common stock equity.** When the rate of return on total assets is lower than the rate of return on common stock equity, the enterprise is said to be trading on the equity at a gain. The term **"trading on the equity"** describes the practice of using borrowed money at fixed interest rates or issuing preferred stock with constant dividend rates in hopes of earning a higher rate of return on the money used than the interest or preferred dividends paid.

14. As mentioned earlier in the text, many investors consider **earnings per share** to be the most significant statistic presented by a business entity. A discussion of the significance of earnings per share and the manner in which it is computed is presented in **Chapter 17.** Basically, earnings per share is computed by dividing net income by the number of shares of common stock outstanding. However, a complex capital structure alters this computation significantly.

15. **Dividing the market price of a share of stock by the earnings per share yields the price-earnings (P/E) ratio.** The factors that affect the price-earnings ratio include relative risk, stability of earnings, trends in earnings, and the market's perception of the growth potential of the stock.

16. The **payout ratio is the ratio of cash dividends to net income.** This ratio gives investors an indication of the portion of net income a company distributes to its stockholders. If investors desire cash yield from an investment in stock, they should seek out entities with high payout ratios.

COVERAGE RATIOS

17. The extent to which creditors are protected in the event of an entity's insolvency may be determined by the **debt total assets ratio.** This information may also be gained from the ratio of long-term debt to stockholders' equity or the ratio of stockholders' equity to long-term debt.

18. The **times interest earned ratio is computed by dividing net income before interest charges and taxes by the interest charge.** This ratio focuses on the ability of a company to cover all its interest charges. In general, difficulty in meeting interest obligations is indicative of serious financial problems.

19. The **book value per share of stock** is the amount each share would receive if a company were liquidated and the amounts reported on the balance sheet were realized. **Book value per share is computed by allocating the stockholders' equity items among the various classes of stock and then dividing the total so allocated to each class of stock by the number of shares outstanding.** This calculation loses its significance when the amounts reported on the balance sheet do not reflect the fair market value of the items.

20. **Cash flow per share is computed by dividing net income adjusted for noncash items found on the income statement by the number of shares of common stock outstanding.** This calculation represents the cash flow per share from operations and should not be construed to represent the flow of cash through the enterprise.

21. Ratio analysis is not without its limitations. Before placing a great deal of reliance on ratios alone, an investor must be aware of the fact that any ratio is only as sound as the financial data upon which it is built. The great variety of accounting policies relating to the computation of net income provides a good example of the reasons for exercising caution when interpreting financial ratios.

22. The presentation of **comparative financial statements** affords an analyst the opportunity to determine trends and analyze the progress an entity has made over a specified period of time. The annual financial statement presentation in a corporate annual report normally includes detailed comparative financial statement for the current and preceding year along with a 5- or 10-year summary of pertinent financial data.

23. **Percentage** or **common-size** analysis is a method frequently used to evaluate a business enterprise. This type of analysis involves reducing all the dollar amounts to a percentage of a base amount in the financial statement. All items in an income statement are frequently expressed as a percentage of sales or sometimes as a percentage of cost of sales. The items in a balance sheet are often analyzed as a percentage of total assets. **Horizontal analysis** is a form of percentage analysis that is useful in evaluating trend situations. Another approach, called **vertical analysis**, involves expressing each number on a financial statement in a given period as a percentage of some base amount.

REVIEW QUESTIONS AND EXERCISES

True-False

Indicate whether each of the following is true (T) or false (F) in the space provided.

_____ 1. Financial statement analysis is related to an accountant's role as a communicator of economic information.

_____ 2. Ratios classified as coverage ratios are concerned with the ability of an enterprise to meet obligations classified as short-term.

_____ 3. The current ratio is sometimes referred to as the working capital ratio because it is based upon analysis of working capital accounts.

_____ 4. If a company has a low inventory turnover, the acid-test ratio would most likely be a better measure of current debt-paying ability than the current ratio.

_____ 5. For most companies, a current ratio of less than 2.0 to 1 is considered to represent an inability to meet currently maturing liabilities and expenses.

_____ 6. The defensive-interval ratio measures the time span a firm can operate on present liquid assets without resorting to revenues from next year's income sources.

_____ 7. An acceptable receivables turnover for a company with credit terms of 3/10, n/45 would be 5 times.

_____ 8. The inventory turnover for a jewelry store would normally be higher than the inventory turnover for a supermarket because of the higher profit margin on jewelry store inventory items.

_____ 9. The asset turnover ratio is used to determine the average number of years an entity uses its fixed assets in a revenue-producing capacity.

_____ 10. Profitability ratios are frequently used as the ultimate test of management effectiveness.

_____ 11. If Company A has an 8% profit margin on sales and Company B has a 10% profit margin on sales, Company B will earn a greater amount of profit for a given period of time.

_____ 12. The term "trading on the equity" refers to the practice of selling common stock on the open market when a firm needs capital and then buying the stock back when the capital needs no longer exist.

_____ 13. A common problem related to the emphasis placed on earnings per share analysis is that investors concentrate too much attention on the single share of stock rather than on the enterprise as a whole.

_____ 14. The price-earnings ratio is computed by dividing the market price of a share of common stock by the net income for the period.

_____ 15. Generally, growth companies are characterized by low payment ratios, since they reinvest most of their earnings in the future operations of the company.

_____ 16. All things being equal, creditors tend to favor a low debt to stockholders' equity ratio.

_____ 17. When book value per share exceeds market price per share, the common stock is said to be selling at a discount.

_____ 18. The relevance of conclusions drawn from an analysis of financial ratios is enhanced when the ratios are computed from comparative financial statements.

_____ 19. When percentage analysis is used in connection with an income statement, the items shown on the income statement are normally expressed as a percentage of sales.

_____ 20. In situations where the calculations of net income includes a significant amount of estimated items, profitability ratios lose some of their credibility.

Multiple Choice

Select the best answer for each of the following items and enter the corresponding letter in the space provided.

_____ 1. If the working capital of an enterprise increased from $15,000 to $20,000 during a one-year period, which of the following statements correctly depicts the effect on the current ratio?
A. The current ratio would increase.
B. The current ratio would remain unchanged.
C. The current ratio would decrease if the change resulted from a decrease in current liabilities of $5,000.
D. It is impossible to determine the exact effect on the current ratio without knowing the composition of current assets and current liabilities.

_____ 2. The ratio that establishes a safety factor or margin for the investor in determining the capability of a company to meet its basic operational expenditures is the:
A. current ratio.
B. acid-test ratio.
C. defensive-interval ratio.
D. liquidity trend ratio.

_____ 3. Sloan Company's income statement included the following information related to its gross profit on sales.

Sales		$2,560,000
Beginning		
Inventory	$ 826,000	
Purchases	1,250,000	
	$2,076,000	
Ending		
Inventory	904,000	
Cost of		
Goods Sold		1,172,000
Gross Profit		$1,388,000

Sloan Company's inventory turnover is:
A. 1.31.
B. 1.35.
C. 1.42.
D. 1.47.

_____ 4. Which of the following departments in a large department store would most likely have a low profit margin and a high inventory turnover?
A. Women's fur coats.
B. Major appliances.
C. Hand tools and hardware supplies.
D. Men's fashions.

_____ 5. Billa Company earns a 7.4% return on assets. If net income amounts to $275,000, total average assets must be:
A. $18,500.
B. $203,500.
C. $2,035,000.
D. $3,716,216.

_____ 6. A profitable company with a large amount of debt in its capital structure will normally:
A. go bankrupt.
B. show a fairly high rate of return on common stock equity.
C. pay a greater amount of dividends than a company with a small amount of debt.
D. show a lower net income than companies with little or no debt in their capital structure owing to the large amount of interest expense.

_____ 7. Burnett Company has 120,000 shares of common stock outstanding on December 31, 1990, selling at a current market price of $56 per share. If the price-earnings ratio at December 31, 1990 is 14, what amount of net income did Burnett Company earn in 1990?
A. $480,000.
B. $1,680,000.
C. $5,040,000.
D. $6,720,000.

_____ 8. Book value per share of stock for a company with only common stock outstanding is:
A. an important statistic used in determining the rate of return on invested capital.
B. normally higher than market value for a highly profitable company.
C. a figure that loses much of tis relevance if the valuations in the balance sheet do not approximate fair market value of the assets.
D. normally lower than book value per share for a company with both common stock and preferred stock in its capital structure.

_____ 9. Perhaps the most severe criticism aimed at ratio analysis is:
A. the difficulty involved in computing most ratios.
B. the extensive variety of ratios that must be computed in order to answer the same questions.
C. the additional financial data that must be prepared along with the financial statements so the various ratios can be computed.

D. the difficulty problem of achieving comparability among firms in a given industry.

_____ 10. Ratios included in which of the following classifications would measure how effectively an enterprise is using the assets employed?
   A. Liquidity ratios.
   B. Activity ratios.
   C. Profitability ratios.
   D. Coverage ratios.

Review Exercises

1. The following ratios were prepared from data included in the December 31, 1990, financial statements of Longfield Corporation.

Current Ratio:	3.0 to 1
Acid-test Ratio:	1.4 to 1
Current Assets to Total Assets:	.3 to 1
Owners' Equity to Total Assets:	.4 to 1
Owners' Equity to Total Debt:	.66667 to 1

If total owner's equity at December 31, 1990 amounts to $950,000, compute the following account balances (round to the nearest hundred):

a. Current
   Assets _____
b. Quick
   Assets _____
c. Current
   Liabilities _____
d. Working
   Capital _____
e. Fixed
   Assets _____
f. Long-Term
   Debt _____

2. Listed below are a series of transactions and financial events. Opposite each transaction a ratio is listed which is used in financial analysis.

Transaction	Ratio
a. Purchased merchandise inventory on account.	Current ratio
b. Paid two years' rent in advance.	Acid-test ratio
c. The allowance for uncollectible accounts was increased.	Receivables turnover
d. Net sales remained unchanged, while total cost of operations decreased.	Profit margin on sales
e. Net income and total cash dividends were both increased by 5%.	Payout rates
f. Issued 5% nonconvertible preferred stock. No dividends were paid in the first year of issue.	Earnings per share
g. Bonds payable with a face value of $500,000 were converted dollar for dollar for common stock.	Debt to equity ratio
h. Sold marketable securities at	Current ratio

a price in excess of original cost.
i. Purchased a building in exchange for a long-term mortgage.   Book value per share

Indicate the effect (increase, decrease, or no effect) the transaction would have on the ratio listed opposite the transaction.

3. The following data are taken from the accounts of Monteleone Company as of December 31, 1990.

Accounts and Notes Payable	$ 46,500
Accounts Receivable (net), beginning	58,000
Accounts Receivable (net,) ending	64,600
Cash	35,000
Prepaid Expenses	19,000
Purchases (net)	127,800
Inventories, beginning	81,500
Inventories, ending	92,000
Sales	388,000
Sales Returns and Allowances	20,000
Other expenses (all cash expenses)	165,800
Accrued Liabilities	9,600
Marketable Securities	15,900

On the basis of the information above determine the December 31, 1990:
a. Amount of working capital
b. Current ratio
c. Acid-test ratio
d. Defensive-interval ratio
e. Receivables turnover
f. Inventory turnover
g. Profit margin on sales

4. The following data are taken from the accounts of Neeley Company as of December 31, 1990.

Total Assets, 1-1-90	$1,860,000
Total Assets, 12-31-90	2,245,000
Common Shares Outstanding All Year (no potential dilution)	48,000
Sales	1,525,000
Cost of Goods Sold	778,000
Cash Expenses (including interest of $40,000 and taxes of $110,000)	327,000
Depreciation and Amortization	160,000
Market Price of Stock 12-31	45
Cash Dividends	96,000
Total Debt	1,415,000
Sales Returns	40,000

On the basis of the information shown above compute the following as of December 31, 1990.

a. Asset turnover
b. Rate of return assets
c. Earnings per share
d. Price-earnings ratio
e. Payout ratio
f. Debt to total assets
g. Times interest earned
h. Book value per share
i. Cash flow per share

SOLUTIONS TO REVIEW QUESTIONS AND EXERCISES

True-False

1. (T)

2. (F) Coverage ratios are computed to help in predicting the long-run solvency of the firm. These ratios are of interest primarily to bondholders and long-term creditors who need some measure of protection available to them.

3. (T)

4. (T)

5. (F) Normally, the adequacy of an entity's current ratio is determined based on a comparison with the current ratio of other firms within the same industry. If a firm has a current ratio of at least 1 to 1, there is a presumption that they can meet currently maturing liabilities and expenses. However, it is always dangerous to generalize about the adequacy of a firm's current ratio due to the many variables that can make such generalizations false. For example, if the accounts receivable lack collectability or the inventory is not salable during the current period, then the entity would be mislead by the information conveyed by a 1 to 1 current ratio.

6. (T)

7. (F) The receivables turnover indicates how successful a firm is in collecting its receivables. The situation in the question indicates that the credit terms allow the customers a maximum of 45 days to pay their receivables. Thus, an acceptable receivables turnover in this situation would be 8 times (356 + 45). A receivables turnover of 5 times would indicate that customers are taking an average of 73 days (365 + 5) to pay their receivables, which would be an average of 28 days more than the maximum payment period.

8. (F) The inventory turnover ratio measures how quickly inventory is sold or liquidated from the inventory account. The mere fact that a large portion of the inventory held by a supermarket is perishable would cause its turnover to be higher than the inventory turnover for a jewelry store.

9. (F) The asset turnover ratio indicates how efficiently a company utilizes its assets. If the turnover ratio is high, the implication is that the company is using its assets effectively to generate sales. If the turnover ratio is low, the company either has to use its assets more efficiently or dispose of them.

10. (T)

11. (F) Profit margin in sales is computed by dividing net income by net sales for the period. This ratio will indicate which company earns the most on each dollar of sales. However, just because Company B has a higher profit margin does not necessarily indicate that they will generate a greater dollar amount of profit. Variables such as turnover and volume must be considered in addition to profit margin in order to determine the largest amount of profit.

12. (F) Th term "trading on the equity" describes the practice of using borrowed money at fixed interest rates or issuing preferred stock with constant dividend rates in hopes of obtaining a higher rate of return on the money used than the interest or preferred dividends paid. Trading on the equity is profitable when the capital obtained from bondholders or preferred stockholders earns enough to pay the interest or preferred dividends and leave a margin for common stockholders.

13. (T)

14. (F) The price earnings ratio is computed by dividing the market price of the stock by its earnings per share.

15. (T)

16. (T)

17. (F) Common stock is sold at a discount when it is sold for less than its par value. When a company's book value per share exceeds its market value per share, it's a fairly good sign that the company is experiencing some problems that have caused investors to avoid purchasing its stock.

18. (T)

19. (T)

20. (T)

Multiple Choice

1. (A) Whether the increase in working capital is caused by an increase in current assets or a decrease in current liabilities, the current ratio will increase.

2. (C) Neither the current ratio nor the acid-test ratio gives a complete explanation of the current debt paying ability of the company. The matching of current assets with current liabilities assumes that the current assets will be employed to pay off the current liabilities. The defensive-interval ratio measures the time span a firm can operate on present liquid assets without resorting to revenues from next year's sources. This ratio establishes a safety factor or margin for the investor in determining the capability of the company to meet its basic operational costs.

3. (B)

$$\text{Inventory turnover: } \frac{\text{Cost of goods sold}}{\text{Average inventory}}$$

$$\frac{1,172,000}{\dfrac{826,000 + 904,000}{2}} = 1.35$$

4. (C) Both women's fur coats and major appliances represent high profit items that would reflect low turnover. Men's fashions may represent a medium to high turnover item, but it is not a low profit item. Hand tools and hardware supplies is the only alternative that can be characterized as a low profit, high turnover item.

5. (D)

$$\text{Return on assets: } \frac{\text{Net income}}{\text{Average total assets}}$$

$$\frac{\$275,000}{\text{Average total assets}} = 7.4\%$$

$$\text{Average total assets} = \frac{\$275,000}{.074}$$

$$\text{Average total assets} = \underline{\$3,716,216}$$

6. (B) Alternative B is the best response. A company with a large amount of debt will normally show a high rate of return on common stock because they have financed a large part of their operations with debt. The other three alternatives would not "normally" be expected of a profitable company with a large amount of debt.

7. (A)

$$\text{Price earnings ratio: } \frac{\text{Market price of stock}}{\text{Net income} \div \text{shares outstanding}}$$

$$\frac{\$56}{\text{Net Income} \div 120,000} = 14$$

$$\text{Net income} \div 120,000 = 4$$

$$\text{Net income} = \underline{\$480,000}$$

8. (C) Book value per share of stock is the amount of money each share would receive if the company were liquidated on the basis of amounts reported on the balance sheet. However, if the valuations on the balance sheet are not representative of current fair market valuations, then book value has no real significance. A stock's market value is the more important figure as it reflects the confidence investors have in an entity as a result of its operations.

9. (D) Ratio analysis is criticized because a problem does exist in achieving comparability among firms in a given industry. Achieving comparability among firms that apply different accounting procedures is difficult and requires that the analyst (a) identify basic differences existing in their accounting and (b) adjust the balances to achieve comparability.

10. (B) Activity ratios measure how effectively an enterprise is using the assets employed.

Review Exercises

1.
a.	Current Assets	$712,500	d.	Working Capital	$ 475,000
b.	Quick Assets	$332,500	e.	Fixed Assets	$1,662,500
c.	Current Liabilities	$237,500	f.	Long-Term Debt	$1,187,500

To solve this exercise, the ratios should be computed in the following order (solve for "x" in each case.):

1. Owners' equity to total debt:
$$\frac{\$950,000}{x} = .6667; x = \$1,425,000 \text{ (rounded from } \$1,424,992)$$

2. Owners' equity to total assets:
$$\frac{\$950,000}{x} = .4; x = \$2,375,000$$

3. Current assets to total assets:
$$\frac{x}{\$2,375,000} = .3; x = \$712,500$$

4. Current ratio:
$$\frac{\$712,000}{x} = 3.0; x = \$237,500$$

5. Acid-test ratio:
$$\frac{x}{\$237,500} = 1.4; x = \$332,500$$

6. Long-term debt:
$1,425,000 - $237,500 = $1,187,500

7. Working capital:
$712,500 - $237,500 = $475,000

8. Fixed assets:
$2,375,000 - $712,500 = $1,662,500

2.
a.	Decrease	f.	No effect
b.	Decrease	g.	Decrease
c.	Increase	h.	Increase
d.	Increase	i.	No effect
e.	No effect		

3.
a. Amount of Working Capital **$170,400** ($226,500 - $56,100)
b. Current ratio **4.04 to 1** (226,500 ÷ $56,100)
c. Acid test ratio **2.06 to 1** ($115,500 ÷ $56,100)
d. Defensive-interval ratio **149 days** {$115,500 ÷ [($117,300 + $165,800) ÷ 365]}
e. Receivables turnover **6 times** {$368,000 ÷ [(58,000 + $64,600) ÷ 2)}
f. Inventory turnover **1.35 times** {$117,300 ÷ [($81,500 + $92,000) ÷ 2]}
g. Profit margin on sales **23%** ($84,900 ÷ $368,000)

4.   a.   Asset turnover: **.72 times**
          {$1,485,000 + [($1,860,000 + $2,245,000) ÷ 2]}
     b.   Rate of return on assets: **10.7%**
          {$220,000 + [($1,860,000 + $2,245,000) ÷ 2] }
     c.   Earnings per share: **$4.58**
          ($220,000 ÷ 48,000)
     d.   Price earnings ratio: **9.83**
          ($45 ÷ $4.58)
     e.   Payout ratio: **43.6 %**
          ($96,000 ÷ $220,000)
     f.   Debt to toatl assets: **63%**
          ($1,415,000 ÷ $2,245,000)
     g.   Times interest earned: **9.25 times**
          ($370,000 ÷ $40,000)
     h.   Book value per share: **$17.29**
          ($830,000 ÷ 48,000)
     i.   Cash flow per share: **$7.92**
          [($220,000 + $160,000) ÷ 48,000]

26

Full disclosure in financial reporting

Chapter Synopsis

Chapter 26 addresses the topic of financial statement disclosure. Accountants and business executives are fully aware of the importance of full disclosure when presenting financial statements. However, determining what constitutes full disclosure in financial reporting is not an easy task. Thus, the purpose of this chapter is to review present disclosure requirements and gain insight into future trends in this area.

Chapter Review

1. Recent trends in financial reporting reflect an increase in the amount of disclosure found in financial statements. This increased disclosure is a result of the efforts of the SEC and the FASB. The pronouncements issued by these organizations include many disclosure requirements that are designed to improve the financial reporting process. Numerous reasons can be cited for this increased emphasis on disclosure requirements. Some of the more significant reasons include (a) the complexity of the business environment, (b) the necessity for timely financial information, and (c) the use of accounting as a control and monitoring device.

2. Footnotes are an integral part of the financial statements of a business enterprise. Although they are normally drafted in somewhat technical language, footnotes are the accountant's means of amplifying or explaining the items presented in the main body of the statements. Many of the footnote disclosures which are common in financial accounting are discussed and presented throughout the text. The more common footnote disclosures are as follows:

    a. **Significant Accounting Policies.** This information is designed to inform the statement reader of the accounting methods used in preparing the information included in the financial statements. Accounting policies of a given entity are the specific accounting principles and methods currently employed and considered most appropriate in the circumstances to present fairly the financial statements of the enterprise.

    b. **Inventory.** The basis upon which inventory amounts are stated (lower of cost or market) and the method used in determining cost (LIFO, FIFO, average cost, etc.) should also be reported.

    c. **Property, Plant and Equipment.** The basis of valuation for property, plant, and equipment should be stated (usually historical cost). Pledges, liens, and other commitments related to these assets should be disclosed.

    d. **Credit Claims.** A liability may have numerous covenants that are not conveniently disclosed in the liability section of the balance sheet. To avoid a cumbersome presentation in the body of the balance sheet, this additional information is disclosed in the footnotes.

    e. **Claims of Equity Holders.** The rights of various equity security issues along with certain unique features that may apply to certain issues are commonly disclosed in footnotes to the financial statements.

    f. **Gain or Loss Contingencies.** Because many contingent gains or losses are not properly included in the accounts, their disclosure in the footnotes provides relevant information to financial statement users. These contingencies may take a variety of forms such as litigation, debt and other guarantees, possible tax assessments, renegotiation of government contracts, sales of receivables with recourse and so on.

    g. **Deferred Taxes, Pensions, and Leases.** Extensive disclosures are required in these three areas. A careful reading of the notes to the financial statements provides information as to off-balance sheet commitments, future financing needs, and the quality of a company's earnings.

    h. **Changes in Accounting Principles.** Either in the summary of significant accounting policies or in the other notes, changes in accounting principles (as well as material changes in estimates and corrections of errors) are discussed.

i. **Subsequent Events.** Events or transactions which occur subsequent to the balance sheet date but prior to the issuance of the financial statements should be disclosed in the financial statements.

3. In some instances a corporation is faced with a sensitive issue that requires disclosure in the financial statements. Examples of items that can be characterized as sensitive have been identified in the *Statements on Auditing Standards* issued by the Auditing Standards Boards of the AICP. These include: **related party transactions, errors and irregularities,** and **illegal acts.** It is important for the accountant/auditor who must determine the adequacy of the disclosure to exercise care in balancing the rights of the company and the needs of the financial statement user.

4. With the increase in diversification within business entities, investors are seeking more information concerning the details of diversified (conglomerate) companies. Particularly, they have requested revenue and income information on the individual segments that comprise the total business income figure. Various arguments have been presented both for and against increased disclosure of segments information. In 1976 the FASB issued *Statement No. 14,* "Financial Reporting for Segments of a Business Enterprise." This statement requires the disclosure of the **enterprise's operations in different industries, its foreign operations, its major customers,** and **its export sales** in a complete set of financial statements. The information required by *FASB Statement No. 14* may be included in the body of the financial statements, in the notes to the financial statements, or in a separate schedule included as an integral part of the financial statements.

5. *FASB Statement No. 14* does require the use of some judgment in meeting its requirements. Issues such as (a) the definition of a segment, (b) allocation of common costs, and (c) transfer pricing decisions must be considered before the disclosure requirements can be satisfied. This exercise of judgment does provide some flexibility which allows management to determine the most meaningful breakdown of its divisional data.

6. Three factors should be considered by management in determining industry segments. These factors are: (a) the nature of the product, (b) the nature of the production process, and (c) markets or marketing methods. Whether a segment is significant enough to disclose depends upon whether it satisfies one of the following tests: (a) its revenue is 10% or more of the combined revenue of all the enterprise's industry segments, (b) the absolute amount of its operating profit or loss is 10% or more of the greater of the combined operating profit of all industry segments that did not incur a loss or the combined operating loss of all industry segments that did incur an operating loss, or (c) its identifiable assets are 10% or more of the combined identifiable assets of all industry segments.

7. Segment reporting remains a somewhat controversial topic from a number of perspectives. The following issues continue to be debated.

a. **Definition of a Segment.** This problem revolves around the subjectivity involved in selecting segments. While accountants generally feel that companies should be free to select segment breakdowns, this could lead to lack of comparability over a period of time.

b. **Allocation of Common Costs.** Many different bases for allocation have been suggested, such as sales, gross profit, assets employed, investment, and marginal income. The choice of a basis is important because it can materially influence the relative profitability of the segments.

c. **Transfer Pricing Problems.** At present, different approaches to transfer pricing are used. Some firms transfer the goods at market prices; others use costs plus a fixed fee; and some use variable cost.

8. **Interim reports** are financial reports issued by a business enterprise for a period of less than one year. The SEC requires certain companies coming under its control to file quarterly financial statements that are similar in form and content to their annual reports. Guidance in the area of accounting and reporting for interim periods is currently provided by *APB Opinion No. 28,* **"Interim Financial Reporting."** However, the FASB is now working on improvements in interim reporting standards.

9. *APB Opinion No. 28* indicates that the same accounting principles used for annual reports should be applied in preparing interim reports. However, the general approach used in preparing these reports is the subject of some debate. Two different approaches have been advocated in practice. One approach is referred to as the **discrete view** and the other is the **integral view.** Those advocating the discrete view believe that each interim period should be treated as a separate accounting period. Those who favor the integral view consider the interim report to be an integral part of the annual report. At present, many companies follow the discrete approach for certain types of expenses and the integral approach for others, because the standards employed at present are fairly flexible.

10. In *APB Opinion No. 28,* the Board indicated that it favored the integral approach in preparing interim reports. However, certain items do not lend themselves to strict application of the guideline. As a result, unique reporting problems are encountered for such items as (a) advertising and similar costs, (b) expenses subject to

year-end adjustments, (c) income taxes, (d) extraordinary items, (e) changes in accounting principles, (f) earnings per share, and (g) seasonality.

11. The fact that many business entities encounter seasonal variations in their operations poses a problem in the analysis of interim reports. The greater the degree of seasonality experienced by a company, the greater the possibility for distortion. For example, a seasonal business that earns 50% of its net income in one quarter may lead the analyst to spurious conclusions. In such a situation, the analyst would be misled if the results of any one of the quarters were interpreted as representing one-fourth of the year's operating results. Thus, caution should be exercised when attempting to draw generalizations from a single interim report.

12. Although some standards exist for interim reporting, the subject is in need of a thorough review and analysis. It is unclear as to whether the discrete, integral, or some combination of these two methods will be proposed. In addition to the problems noted in paragraphs 10 and 11, the profession continues to debate the extent of involvement an independent auditor should have with interim reports.

13. Information related to the social concerns of a business enterprise has received a great deal of attention in recent years. Many potential investors are interested in an entity's concern for protection of the environment. In response to this concern, the SEC requires that the following type of environmental information be disclosed in filings with that agency.

    a. The material effects that compliance with federal, state, and local environmental protection laws may have upon capital expenditures, earnings, and competitive position.

    b. Litigation commenced or known to be contemplated against registrants by a government authority pursuant to federal, state, and local environmental regulatory provisions.

    c. All other environmental information of which the average prudent investor ought reasonably to be informed.

14. An **audit report** is issued each time an **independent auditor** performs an audit of an entity's financial statements. An audit report is essentially the expression of an opinion, by the auditor, on the **fairness** with which the financial statements present the entity's **financial position** and **results of operations**. In the audit report, the auditor must state whether the financial statements were presented in accordance with generally accepted accounting principles and whether such principles were applied on a basis consistent with that used for the preceding year.

15. If an auditor arrives at the opinion that the financial statements are fairly presented, the audit report that is issued is known as an **unqualified opinion**. When an auditor is unable to express an unqualified opinion (normally as a result of scope limitation, financial statement inadequacies, or material uncertainties), he will issue either (a) **a qualified opinion,** (b) **an adverse opinion,** or (c) **a disclaimer of opinion**. Departures from an unqualified opinion put the financial statement reader on guard as to possible deficiencies in the presentation of the financial statements. When the auditor departs from the standard unqualified audit report, the reason for the departure must be clearly indicated in the audit report.

16. In 1985 the AICPA issued a statement on standards for the preparation of prospective financial statements. Prospective financial statements are financial statements based upon the entity's expectations about future operation. There are two types of prospective financial statements, (a) **financial forecasts,** and (b) **financial projections**. A financial forecast is composed of prospective financial statements that present, to the best of the company's knowledge and belief, its expected financial position, results of operations, and cash flows. A financial projection is composed of prospective financial statements that present, to the best of the company's knowledge and belief - **given one or more hypothetical assumptions** - its expected financial position, results of operations, and cash flows.

17. The **National Commission on Fraudulent Financial Reporting** defined fraudulent financial reporting as intentional or reckless conduct whether act or omission, that results in materially misleading financial statements. Situational pressures on the company as well as individual pressures on management personnel can result in fraudulent activities which lead to fraudulent financial reporting. A weak corporate climate contributes to these situations.

REVIEW QUESTIONS AND EXERCISES

True-False

Indicate whether each of the following is true (T) or false (F) in the space provided.

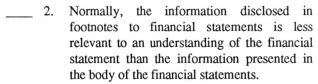

_____ 1. Footnotes are an integral part of the financial statements of a business enterprise.

_____ 2. Normally, the information disclosed in footnotes to financial statements is less relevant to an understanding of the financial statement than the information presented in the body of the financial statements.

_____ 3. When gain or loss contingencies exist, an enterprise will generally disclose them in footnotes to the balance sheet.

_____ 4. A careful reading of the notes to the financial statements provides information as to off-balance sheet commitments, future financing needs, and the quality of a company's earnings.

_____ 5. Footnotes related to the claims of equity holders are quite rare, as this kind of information is presented in the equity section of the balance sheet directly opposite the class of security to which the information applies.

_____ 6. An executory contract refers to a contract entered into by an enterprise that must be fulfilled by an executive of the company.

_____ 7. When consolidated financial statements are presented by a business enterprise, that enterprise is required to disclose the principles of consolidation in the notes to its financial statements.

_____ 8. Accounting policies of a given entity are normally the specific accounting principles recommended by the industry in which the entity operates.

_____ 9. When an auditor examines the financial statements of a business enterprise for the purpose of expressing an opinion thereon, he or she attempts to determine whether the statements are an accurate representation of the entity's financial position and results of operations.

_____ 10. An auditor is a professional who conducts an independent examination of the accounting data presented by the business enterprise for the purpose of expressing an opinion thereon.

_____ 11. An adverse auditor's opinion is an indication that the financial statements do not present fairly the financial position and results of operations.

_____ 12. A particular segment is not significant enough to disclose unless its revenues exceed 10% of the revenues earned by the other segments being reported.

_____ 13. When a company presents consolidated financial statements without segment information, there is no way to tell the extent to which the differing product lines contribute to the company's overall profitability.

_____ 14. Those who argue against the reporting of segment information contend that the wise variation among firms in the choice of segments, cost allocation, and other account-

ing problems limits the usefulness of segment information.

_____ 15. *FASB Statement No. 14* requires disclosure of an enterprise's operations in different industries, its foreign operations, its export sales, and its major customers.

_____ 16. Disclosure of segment information is required of all companies that operate in more than one industry.

_____ 17. Interim financial reports prepared by a business enterprise normally include a complete set of financial statements for a period of less than one year.

_____ 18. The required approach to handling extraordinary items in interim financial reports is to charge or credit the loss or gain in the interim period that it occurs instead of attempting some arbitrary multiple-period allocation.

_____ 19. For purposes of computing earnings per share and making the disclosures required by *APB Opinion No. 28*, each interim period should stand alone; that is, all applicable tests should be made for that single period.

_____ 20. According to *APB Opinion No. 28*, when a company issues a quarterly income statement, that statement should represent approximately one-fourth of the total net income for the year in which the quarter exists.

Multiple Choice

Select the best answer for each of the following items and enter the corresponding letter in the space provided.

_____ 1. Which of the following questions would an analyst be least likely to find addressed by the footnotes to the financial statements?
   A. What method of depreciation is used on plant assets?
   B. Over what period of time is the recorded goodwill being amortized?
   C. How many separate bank accounts does the company maintain?
   D. What restrictions are required by the new bond issue?

_____ 2. The focus of *APB Opinion No. 22* is on the disclosure of accounting policies. This information is important to financial statement readers in determining:
   A. net income for the year.
   B. whether accounting policies are consistently applied from year to year.
   C. the value of obsolete items included in ending inventory.
   D. whether the working capital position is adequate for future operations.

3. Which of the following best characterizes the difference between a financial forecast and a financial projection?
   A. Forecasts include a complete set of financial statements while projections include only summary financial data.
   B. A forecast is normally for a full year or more and a projection presents data for less than a year.
   C. A forecast attempts to provide information on what is expected to happen whereas a projection may provide information on what is not necessarily expected to happen.
   D. A forecast includes data which can be verified about future expectations while the data in a projection is not susceptible to verification.

4. If the financial statements examined by an auditor lead the auditor to issue an opinion that contains an exception that is not of sufficient magnitude to invalidate the statement as a whole, the opinion is said to be:
   A. unqualified.
   B. qualified.
   C. adverse.
   D. exceptional.

5. An industry segment is regarded as significant and therefore identified as a reportable segment if it satisfies one or more quantitative tests that deal with segment revenues, income, or assets. In addition to these quantitative tests the FASB believes entities should not report too many segments so as to overwhelm users with detailed information that may not be useful. The FASB also requires that
   A. segment results equal or exceed 75% of the combined sales to unaffiliated customers for the entire enterprise.
   B. a separate set of financial statements be shown for each identified segment.
   C. any segment reporting a net loss for two consecutive years be eliminated.
   D. the entity disclose in the notes to the financial statements each segment considered but not reported.

6. Which of the following view appears to be the prevailing one among accountants concerning the way in which operating segments of a business enterprise should be defined?
   A. The enterprise should be free to select the breakdown that best represents the underlying activities of a business.

B. Segments defined by a geographical location is the most appropriate basis because such information can be easily compared with other businesses operating in the same geographic location.
   C. Segments should be defined by product line because this basis is most appropriate for determining profit of the segment.
   D. The legal entity disclose in the notes to the financial statements each segment considered but not reported.

7. The practice of charging a price for goods "sold" between divisions or subsidiaries of a company is known as:
   A. common cost allocation.
   B. transfer pricing.
   C. intercompany pricing.
   D. intracompany pricing.

8. The publication of profit projections by a business enterprise is:
   A. required by the SEC on an annual basis.
   B. recommended for all companies whose primary source of revenue changes during any one fiscal period.
   C. prohibited by the AICPA because accounting is considered to be historical in nature rather than forward-looking.
   D. encouraged by the SEC, which has issued a safe harbor rule to protect entities that present this kind of information.

9. *FASB Statement No. 14* requires that all of the following information be presented for each reportable segment and in the aggregate for the remaining industry segments except:
   A. revenues.
   B. profitability.
   C. long-term debt.
   D. identifiable assets.

10. *APB Opinion No. 28* indicates that:
    A. all companies that issue an annual report should issue interim financial reports.
    B. the discrete view is the most appropriate approach to take in preparing interim financial reports.
    C. the three basic financial statements should be presented each time an interim period is reported upon.
    D. the same accounting principles used for the annual report should be employed for interim reports.

Review Exercise

1. Match the item on the left with the phrase on the right that most appropriately describes that item.

    A. Footnote information
    B. Accounting policy disclosure
    C. Auditor's report
    D. Reporting of segment information
    E. Interim financial reporting
    F. Social responsibility disclosures
    G. Financial forecast
    H. Financial projection
    I. Fraudulent financial reporting
    J. Management discussion and analysis

    _____ 1. A report useful to investors that indicates, among other things, the accounting basis used by an entity to prepare its financial statements.

    _____ 2. A report used to provide information on the profitability of a company for less than a one-year period.

    _____ 3. Information related to environmental and ecological issues addressed by the firm.

    _____ 4. Financial information based on a company's assumptions reflecting conditions it expects would exist in the future, given one or more hypothetical assumptions.

    _____ 5. Information that is an integral part of the financial statements that serves as a means of amplifying or explaining the items presented in the main body of the statements.

    _____ 6. A part of an entity's annual report that covers three aspects of the business -- liquidity, capital resources, and results of operations.

    _____ 7. Information related to the accounting methods used in the preparation of year-end financial statements.

    _____ 8. Information based on a company's assumptions reflecting conditions it expects to exist in the future and the course of action it expects to take.

    _____ 9. Intentional or reckless conduct, whether act or omission, that results in materially misleading financial statements.

    _____ 10. Information related to revenue and profit breakdowns by divisional lines.

SOLUTIONS TO REVIEW QUESTIONS AND EXERCISES

True-False

1. (T)
2. (F) The information in the footnotes to financial statements and the information in the body of the financial statements is equally relevant. The footnotes provide a means of amplifying on the data presented in the body of the financial statements. Because of the complexity of economic events reflected in the financial statements, footnotes are a necessary part of full disclosure in financial reporting.
3. (T)
4. (T)
5. (F) It is quite common to have equity footnotes related to contracts and senior securities outstanding that might affect the various claims of the residual equity holders. These footnotes are important and are by no means rare.
6. (F) When two parties commit themselves to some undertaking on the basis of a signed contract but neither party has yet performed, the contract is executory.
7. (T)
8. (F) The accounting policies of a given entity are the specific accounting principles and methods currently employed and considered appropriate to present fairly the financial statements of the enterprise. An entity is required, by *APB Opinion No. 22*, to include a footnote in its financial statements that provides information about the significant accounting policies it has adopted.
9. (F) This statement is made false by the use of the word *accurate*. An auditor expresses an opinion on whether the financial statements "present fairly" the financial position and results of operation. In the auditing literature the term *presents fairly* has a specific meaning.
10. (T)
11. (T)
12. (F) There are three quantitative tests that determine whether a segment is significant enough to disclose. To be disclosed, a segment must meet either a revenue test, a profit test, or an asset test. The revenue test requires the segment's revenue to be 10% or more of the combined revenue of all the enterprise's industry segments.
13. (T)
14. (T)
15. (T)
16. (F) For segment information to be reported, a particular segment must meet certain quantitative tests. Thus, an entity could operate in more than one industry but not have any particular segment, other than its major operation, that meets the segment tests.
17. (F) Interim financial reports normally show summarized information on revenues, expenses, assets, liabilities, and shareholder's equity. The profession encourages but does not require companies to publish a balance sheet and a statement of changes in financial position.
18. (T)
19. (T)
20. (F) The profession has not taken a definite position on the most appropriate method to use in recognizing revenues and expenses during an interim period. Entities currently use both the discrete and integral viewpoint in the preparation of interim financial statements. Because of the vague nature of the standards for interim financial reports, it is difficult to characterize the relationship of interim financial reports and annual financial reports.

Multiple Choice

1. (C)   Footnotes are the accountant's means of amplifying or explaining the items presented in the main body of the financial statements. The information in the footnotes is designed to increase the reader's ability to understand an entity's financial position, results of operations, and changes in financial position. Knowing the number of bank accounts a company maintains adds little if anything to one's ability to understand the financial statements.

2. (B)   Financial statement users are concerned with comparability between financial statements issued in different accounting periods. In an attempt to promote comparability, the accounting profession requires consistent application of accounting principles or an explanation in the financial statements about any changes that have taken place. The disclosure of accounting policies in each year's financial statements helps readers evaluate the consistent application of accounting principles.

3. (C)   Because a projection includes at least one hypothetical assumption, the data presented therein is not necessarily expected to happen. There is normally no difference in the type of information or the length of time covered by the data in forecasts or projections.

4. (B)   A qualified opinion is issued by an auditor when an item material to the financial statements or the audit examination requires mention in the financial statements. An adverse opinion is issued when the financial statements do not present fairly the financial position of the entity.

5. (A)   The reason the FASB requires the 75% rule is to prevent a company from providing limited information on only a few segments and lumping all the rest into one category.

6. (A)   The FASB concluded that no one method by itself is universally applicable in identifying segments and that management should exercise its judgment in determining industry segments. Thus, identified segments should be those that, in management's opinion, best represent the underlying activities of a business.

7. (B)   A transfer price system is used for several reasons, but the primary objective is to measure the performance and profitability of a given segment of the business in relation to other segments. In addition, a pricing system is needed to insure control over the flow of goods through the enterprise.

8. (D)   Profit projections are not required by the SEC nor are they prohibited by the AICPA. Also, there is no reason why a company whose primary source of revenue changes is any more likely to present profit projections. The SEC has encouraged management to present this type of information. The safe harbor rule provides protection to an enterprise that presents an erroneous projection as long as the projections were prepared on a reasonable basis and were disclosed in good faith.

9. (C)   *FASB Statement No. 14* does not require information on long-term debt. Segments do not incur debt separately; debt is the responsibility of the company, not of a particular segment.

10. (D)   *APB Opinion No. 28*, "Interim Financial Reporting," provides guidance on the presentation of financial information included in interim reports. This document makes no requirements about who would present interim reports nor does it express a preference for the discrete or integral view. Also, it does not require management to present any specific financial statements for an interim period. However, *APB Opinion No. 28* does require use of the same accounting principles in interim reports as in annual financial statements.

Review Exercises

1.
1. C	5. A	9. I	
2. E	6. J	10. D	
3. F	7. B		
4. H	8. G		

27

Financial reporting and changing prices

Chapter Synopsis

Chapter 27 discusses the alternative methods for disclosing the impact of inflation in financial statements. The current reporting model based on the use of the historical cost principle is being criticized because of its inability to produce meaningful financial statements. This chapter presents a detailed discussion of the valuation approaches that are being suggested as alternatives to the historical cost reporting model.

Chapter Review

1. Historical cost financial statements have been criticized for their failure to reflect the impact of the substantial inflation that has prevailed in the United States during recent years. In an effort to address this criticism, three different solutions have been offered.

   a. **Constant dollar accounting.** Change the measuring unit but retain the historical cost reporting model.

   b. **Current cost accounting.** Retain the measuring unit but change the historical cost reporting model.

   c. **Current cost/constant dollar accounting.** Change the measuring unit and change the historical cost reporting model.

2. Under **constant dollar accounting** (also known as **price-level accounting**) a dollar is valued in terms of its **purchasing power.** Purchasing power refers to the number of items in general that the dollar can be used to purchase. When inflation occurs, the dollar cannot buy as many items as it could in the past; thus purchasing power declines during periods of inflation. When constant dollar accounting is applied, historical cost data are adjusted for changes in purchasing power of the unit of measurement (the dollar).

3. **Current cost accounting** abandons historical cost as a basis for financial statement preparation and shifts to some measure of current value. This method is based upon the presumption that investors are interested in what the business is worth now, rather than the cost of various items incurred at some point in the past. The practical problems associated with determining present values are answered with the contention that any objective approximation of economic value is more useful to financial statement readers than are historical cost figures. Also, quoted market prices, second-hand market values, appraisals, or specific index numbers are advocated as meaningful indicators of economic value.

4. The **current cost/constant dollar accounting** approach advocates a change in both the unit of measurement and the historical cost mode. Those supporting this approach argue that the unit of measurement must be standardized and that after standardization some form of current value accounting should be employed. Some who support this method have indicated that it is the only way to determine real changes in enterprise wealth and earning power.

5. Inflation accounting has been widely discussed during the past decade. The **Accounting Principles Board,** the **Financial Accounting Standards Board,** and similar organizations in other countries have spent a great deal of time and effort searching for the best method to use in reflecting the impact of inflation in financial statements. Past efforts of the **APB** and **FASB** did not result in a required form of inflation accounting. However, in 1979 the **FASB** issued *Statement No. 33,* **"Financial Reporting and Changing Prices,"** which required certain large publicly held enterprises to disclose supplementary information on both a constant dollar basis and a current cost basis. In 1986 the **FASB** issued *Statement No. 89,* **"Financial Reporting and Changing Prices"** which eliminated the requirement to report changing price information. However, the board encouraged companies to continue reporting this information on a voluntary basis. Since the issuance of *Statement No. 89,* very few companies have opted for voluntary disclosure of changing price information.

6. Constant dollar accounting requires the use of a **price index** to measure the **price level** (aggregation of specific prices at any particular time). A price index is a weighted-average relation between money and a given set of goods and services. The **FASB** requires the use of **The Consumer Price Index for All Urban Consumers (CPI-U)** in constant dollar accounting.

7. The restatement (translation or conversion) of historical dollars into dollars of current purchasing power is accomplished by multiplying the amount to be restated by a fraction. The numerator of the fraction is the index number for current prices and the denominator is the index number in effect when the item originated. For example, assume that a building acquired in 1968 for $50,000 when the CPI-U was 105 is to be reported in the December 31, 1988 financial statements on a constant dollar basis. If the 12-31-88 CPI-U were 22·, the following amount would be reported:

$$\$50,000 \times \frac{225}{105} = \underline{\underline{\$107,142.85}}$$

8. When constant dollar financial statements are prepared using an end-of-the-year index, certain amounts require adjustment; others do not. Items requiring adjustment are known as **nonmonetary items,** and items not requiring adjustments are **monetary items.** **Monetary assets and liabilities** are items whose amounts are fixed by contract or otherwise and do not require restatement in constant dollar financial statements. Examples of monetary assets and liabilities include cash, accounts and notes receivable and payable, long-term liabilities, accruals, etc. **Nonmonetary items** are all the items reported on financial statements that are not considered to be monetary. These items require restatement when constant dollar statements are prepared.

9. Instead of using an index that reports end-of-the-year dollars, the use of an average index is frequently advocated. An average index restates historical cost numbers to average-for-the-year prices instead of end-of-the-year prices. One advantage of this approach is that many items on the income statement do not need adjustment because they are earned or incurred evenly throughout the year. For example, sales revenue and most expenses can often be considered to be earned or incurred evenly throughout the period. As a result, these elements need not be adjusted when converting from an historical cost to a constant dollar system. Ease of computation is therefore a real advantage of using an average-for-the-year index instead of an end-of-the-year index.

10. A disadvantage of the average-for-the-year approach is that monetary items that are stated in end-of-the-year dollars must be converted back to average-for-the-year dollars. To many, this conversion causes confusion because a monetary item such as cash is restated to average-for-the-year dollars and therefore is not reported at the same amount as the historical cost balance sheet. Despite the objections to the average-for-the-year index, the FASB decided that the average-for-the-year index should be used. Thus, the illustrations of constant dollar restatement shown in the text use the average-for-the-year approach.

11. A loss in purchasing power occurs when net monetary assets are held during a period of inflation, because the prices of various goods and services increase during such a period when the net amount of monetary assets remains unchanged. Thus, the net monetary assets command a smaller amount of goods and services in the marketplace. If an entity holds net monetary liabilities during a period of inflation, a gain occurs, because the debt can be liquidated using dollars with less purchasing power. These gains and losses are known as **purchasing power gains and losses on net monetary items.**

12. Monetary assets and liabilities are stated in dollars of current purchasing power in the historical dollar balance sheet; consequently, they will appear at the same amounts in constant dollar statements (remember, when an average-for-the-year index is used there is some difference in the monetary items). The fact that the end of the current-year amounts are similar in historical dollar and in constant dollar statements does not obscure the fact, however, that purchasing power gains or losses result from holding monetary times during a period of general price-level change. Conversely, the amounts shown for nonmonetary items in historical costs statements are adjusted in constant dollar statement for changes in the general price level.

13. The comprehensive example in the text material describing the preparation of constant dollar statements, including computations of the purchasing power gain or loss on net monetary items, should be reviewed in detail for a thorough understanding of the process.

14. The following advantages and disadvantages of constant dollar accounting have been advanced by members of the accounting profession and business community.

Advantages of Constant Dollar Accounting

a. Management is provided with an objectively determined quantification of the impact of inflation.

b. Comparability of financial statements between firms is preserved.

c. Comparability between the financial statements of a single firm is enhanced.

d. The historical cost-based accounting system is preserved.

e. The necessity of and the attraction to the piecemeal approaches used in combating the effects of inflation are eliminated.

Disadvantages of Constant Dollar Accounting

a. The cost of preparing these statements is not offset by the benefit of having them.
b. The statements can cause confusion and be misunderstood by users.
c. The shortcomings of the historical cost method are not eliminated.
d. Purchasing power gains from monetary items are misleading.
e. The impact of inflation is assumed to fall equally on all businesses.

CURRENT COST ACCOUNTING

15. **Current cost** is the cost of replacing the identical asset owned, that is, one of the same age and of the same operating capacity. Current cost is the most conceptually appealing surrogate for current value, and if presented, the FASB requires supplementary financial statement information to be presented on a current cost basis.

16. In a comprehensive current cost model, holding gains and losses are usually segregated between those that are realized and those that are unrealized. **Realized holding gains and losses** are the difference between the current cost and the historical cost of the assets sold or consumed during the period. **Unrealized holding gains and losses** relate to assets on hand at the end of the year. These gains and losses represent the difference between the current cost of an asset and its cost on the date it was acquired.

17. **Current cost income from continuing operations** reflects current cost margins - sales revenues less the current cost of inputs. **Realized income** measures the total income realized during the year and is the same as historical cost net income. **Current cost income** measures the total income of the enterprise for one period and takes into account both realized and unrealized holding gains and losses.

18. Current cost accounting is not without its advantages and disadvantages. The following arguments both for and against use of current cost accounting have been identified.

Arguments for Use of Current Cost

a. Current cost provides a better measure of efficiency.
b. Current cost is an approximation of the service potential of assets.
c. Current cost provides for the maintenance of physical capital.
d. Current cost provides for an assessment of future cash flows.

Arguments against Use of Current Cost

a. Method is subjective because it is difficult to determine the exact current cost of all items at any point in time.
b. Maintenance of physical capital is not the accountant's function.
c. Current cost is not always an approximation of the fair market value.

19. Constant dollar accounting and current cost accounting are both based upon the **theory of capital maintenance**. Essentially, this means that income is recognized only after capital is kept intact. However, these two methods differ in regard to the manner in which they view capital maintenance. The objective of constant dollar accounting is to maintain capital in terms of constant purchasing power as measured by a general index of the level of prices. The objective of current cost accounting is to maintain capital in terms of operating capacity or the ability to provide goods and services at the same level at the end of the period as at the beginning.

20. Other matters of importance to accounting for changes in current cost include: **(a)** recoverable amounts, **(b)** income taxes, and **(c)** determination of current cost. The term **recoverable** means the current value of the net amount of cash expected to be received from the use or sale of an asset. When the recoverable amount of an asset is **permanently lower** than its current cost amount, the recoverable amount should be used as the measure of the asset and the expense associated with the use or sale of the asset. Total income tax is based on historical cost and is charged as an expense in arriving at income from continuing operations in a current cost application. Also, when determining the current cost of inventory and property, plant, and equipment the following bases may be used: (a) **direct pricing**, (b) **indexation**, or (c) **standard cost**.

Demonstration Problem

Carrollton Company purchased a machine for $80,000 on January 1, 1988, when the price index was 130. The machine has an estimated useful life of 8 years and no salvage value. At December 31, 1988, the price index was 150 and December 31, 1989, it was 160.

Required:

a. At what amount would the equipment be carried on constant dollar balance sheets at 12-31-88 and 12-31-89?

b. What is the amount of depreciation expense (straight-line) that would be shown on constant dollar income statements for the years ended 12-31-88 and 12-31-89?

Solution:

a. Balance Sheet Amounts
    12-31-88: $80,000 x 150/130 = $92,308
    12-31-89: ($80,000 x 160/130) or ($92,308) x 160/150 = $98,462

b. Income Statement Amounts
    12-31-88: ($10,000 x 150/130) or ($92,308 x 12.5%**) = $11,538
    12-31-89: ($10,000* x 160/130) or ($98,462 x 12.5%) = $12,308

* ($80,000 - 8 years)
**(8-years useful life results in depreciation at a rate of 12.5% per year.)

REVIEW QUESTIONS AND EXERCISES

True - False

Indicate whether each of the following is true (T) or false (F) in the space provided.

_____ 1. The historical cost principle has been criticized for its failure to report the effects of inflation on financial statements.

_____ 2. Constant dollar accounting is a method that changes the measuring unit in financial statement presentations but retains the historical cost reporting model.

_____ 3. The purchasing power of the dollar increases during periods of inflation and decreases during periods of deflation.

_____ 4. A price index used in converting historical cost financial statements to constant dollar financial statements is a weighted-average relationship between money and a given set of goods and services.

_____ 5. The primary objective of adjusting historical costs for changes in the general price level is to reflect the current cost of assets purchased in prior years.

_____ 6. The concept of net monetary items in constant dollar financial statements is equivalent to the concept of working capital in historical cost financial statements.

_____ 7. Adjusting historical costs for price-level changes provides explicit information about "real" losses from holding monetary assets and "real" gains from holding monetary liabilities during a period of inflation.

_____ 8. All assets and liabilities not classified as monetary items are classified as nonmonetary items for constant dollar accounting purposes.

_____ 9. A long-term liability due in 10 years would be classified as a nonmonetary item because the purchasing power of the dollars to be used to liquidate that liability would change by the time it became due.

_____ 10. A purchasing power gain will result from the purchase of a fixed asset at less than its current market value.

_____ 11. Constant dollar accounting provides management with an objectively determined quantification of the impact of inflation on its business operations.

_____ 12. Current cost, as an approach to current value, is most often computed by applying a specific price index to the historical cost or book value of assets.

_____ 13. Realized holding gains and losses are the difference between the current cost and the selling price of assets sold or consumed during the period.

_____ 14. In a current cost accounting model, current cost income from continuing operations is the same as historical cost income from continuing operations.

_____ 15. If a current cost approach to the preparation of financial statements is used, the specific changes in individual financial statement items must be considered.

_____ 16. A major argument against current cost adjustments is that its use is subjective because it is difficult to determine the exact current cost of all items at any point in time.

_____ 17. When the recoverable amount of an asset is permanently lower than its current cost amount, the recoverable amount should be used as the measure of the asset and of the expense associated with the use or sale of the asset.

_____ 18. While FASB Statement No. 89 suggests voluntary disclosure of changing price information, it does require comprehensive financial statements when such data is voluntarily disclosed.

_____ 19. In determining current cost, indexation involves using either external or specific internal indexes to value both inventories and property, plant, and equipment.

_____ 20. When cost of goods sold is measured on a LIFO basis, it is assumed to provide an acceptable approximation of cost of goods sold on a current cost basis if the effect of any decrease in inventory layers is excluded.

Multiple Choice

Select the best response for each of the following items and place the corresponding letter in the space provided.

_____ 1. During a period of deflation an entity would have the greatest purchasing power gain by holding:
A. cash.
B. plant and equipment.
C. accounts payable.
D. inventory.

_____ 2. When the constant dollar approach is used, monetary items consist of:
A. cash items plus all receivables with a fixed maturity date.
B. cash, other assets expected to be converted into cash, and current liabilities.
C. assets and liabilities whose amounts are fixed by contract or otherwise in terms of dollars regardless of changes in the price level.
D. assets and liabilities classified as current on the balance sheet.

_____ 3. Raider Company began the month of June with $82,000 in monetary assets and $55,000 in monetary liabilities. During the month of June the price index rose from 110 to 115. If the company transacted no business during the month and ended with the same composition of monetary assets and monetary liabilities, what amount of net purchasing power gain or loss (rounding to the nearest whole dollar) did they incur?
A. $3,227 loss.
B. $2,500 gain.
C. $1,227 loss.
D. No gain or loss was incurred.

_____ 4. K. Shivley, Inc. acquired a building on June 1, 1974, when the price index was 120, and a machine on December 15, 1975, when the price index was 175. The cost of the building was $250,000, and the machine had a cost of $140,000. If constant dollar financial statements were prepared on December 31, 1988, when the price index was 220, these assets would be shown at what restated amounts? (Ignore depreciation, assume end-of-year dollars).
A. Building $136,363
   Machine $111,363
B. Building $250,000
   Machine $140,000
C. Building $300,000
   Machine $245,000
D. Building $458,333
   Machine $176,000

_____ 5. The FASB requires that the index used in constant dollar accounting be the:
A. Gross National Product Implicit Price Deflator (GNP Deflator).
B. Consumer Price Index for all Urban Consumers (CPI-U).
C. Wholesale Price Index.
D. Composite Construction Cost Index.

6. Which of the following is an advantage of constant dollar accounting?
   A. Constant dollar financial statements are easily understood by users.
   B. Constant dollar accounting eliminates the effects of price-level changes without having to develop a new structure of accounting.
   C. Constant dollar accounting assumes that the impact of inflation falls equally on all businesses and all classes of assets and costs.
   D. Purchasing power gains that result from constant dollar accounting represent successful management of the business.

7. Three different income numbers are reported on an income statement prepared using the current cost model. One of these numbers is always the same as historical cost net income. That number is called:
   A. realized income.
   B. current cost income from continuing operations.
   C. holding gain income.
   D. current cost net income.

8. Which of the following is not an argument in favor of the current cost model?
   A. Current cost provides a better measure of efficiency.
   B. Current cost provides for the maintenance of physical capital.

   C. Current cost is always an approximation of the fair market value.
   D. Current cost is an approximation of the service potential of the asset.

9. As a result of *FASB Statement No. 89*, companies:
   A. are free to select either the constant dollar or current cost approach in presenting required supplemental financial statements that reflect changing price information.
   B. must distinguish between realized and unrealized holding gains in all financial statements presented.
   C. should change the primary historical cost financial statements by restating certain nonmonetary items (inventory and fixed assets) for price-level changes.
   D. are no longer required to disclose supplementary changing price information, but are encouraged to disclose it on a voluntary basis.

10. If depreciation is based on current cost rather than historical cost:
   A. depreciation expense will be greater in the earlier years than in the later years.
   B. gains and losses on the sale of fixed assets can be eliminated.
   C. a fixed asset would never be fully depreciated.
   D. a better measure of operating efficiency is obtained by the company.

Review Exercises

1. P & K Weiss Company was organized in 1988. All of the capital stock was issued, land and buildings were acquired, and bonds were sold at the beginning of 1988 when the price index was 110. The index at the beginning of 1989 (the current year) was 120, and at the end of 1989 it is 130. Inventories are priced using the FIFO method;

they consist of goods acquired during the last three months at an average index for those months of 127. The December 31, 1989 balance sheet accounts presented below are based upon historical dollar amounts. You are asked to prepare the 12-31-89 constant dollar balance sheet. (Round all amounts to the nearest whole dollar, restate using end-of-year dollars.)

	12-31-89 Historical Dollars	Conversion Factor	12-31-89 Constant Dollar Amounts
Cash..	$40,000		
Accounts Receivable.............................	88,000		
Inventories...	125,000		
Building...	210,000		
Accumulated Depreciation.....................	(30,000)		
Land..	50,000		
	$483,000		
Accounts Payable.................................	$ 80,000		
Bonds Payable.....................................	110,000		
Common Stock.....................................	150,00		
Premium on Common Stock...................	105,00		
Retained Earnings	38,000		
	$483,000		

2. Sutton Company began operations on January 1, 1988, by issuing common stock at par value for inventory costing $125,000, a building valued at $50,000, and $25,000 cash. During the year Sutton Company sold 60% of its inventory for $120,000, incurring cash expenses of $20,000 and depreciation expenses of $5,000. The sales and cash expenses were incurred evenly throughout the year. The price index increased from 100 to 110 during 1988, with an average index of 105. Prepare a historical cost balance sheet and income statement and a constant dollar balance sheet and income statement at 12-31-88. Also, show the computation of any purchasing power gains or losses on net monetary items that may result. (Restate using end-of-year dollars.)

3. Rose Corporation decided to adopt a current cost system when it began operations in January 1990. At the beginning of the year, inventory was purchased at a cost of $34,000. During the year, Rose Corporation sold $18,000 of its inventory for $38,000. The inventory sold had a current cost of $22,000 on the date of sale. Ending inventory has a current cost of $26,000. Selling expenses for the year were $2,000 on both an historical and a current cost basis. Ignoring all tax effects, prepare a current cost income statement for Rose Corporation.

SOLUTIONS TO REVIEW QUESTIONS AND EXERCISES

True-False

1. (T)

2. (T)

3. (F) During periods of inflation the purchasing power of the dollar decreases because it takes a greater number of dollars to purchase a specified amount of goods and services. The opposite occurs in periods of deflation.

4. (T)

5. (F) The objective of constant dollar accounting is to maintain capital in terms of constant purchasing power as measured by a general index of the level of prices.

6. (F) Net monetary items are the net monetary assets minus monetary liabilities. This is not the same as working capital in historical cost financial statements. Although monetary assets are similar to current assets, monetary liabilities include long-term obligations. Thus, net monetary items are not the same as working capital.

7. (T)

8. (T)

9. (F) Long-term debt payable in a fixed sum is always a monetary item.

10. (F) Current market value of fixed assets has nothing to do with the computation of purchasing power gains. Purchasing power gains and losses are computed through an analysis of the effects of price-level changes on monetary items. The computation of the purchasing power gain or loss on net monetary items involves preparing a detailed statement of sources and uses of monetary items for the period under consideration, restated item by item.

11. (T)

12. (T)

13. (F) Realized holding gains and losses are the difference between the current cost and the historical cost of the assets sold or consumed during the period.

14. (F) In the current model, three different income numbers are reported. Current cost income from continuing operations reflects current cost margins - sales revenues less the current cost of inputs. Realized income measures the total income realized during the year. Realized income and historical cost income are always the same.

15. (T)

16. (T)

17. (T)

18. (F) Even when voluntarily presented, the FASB does not require the preparation of comprehensive financial statements on a current cost/constant dollar basis. Restatement is necessary only for inventory, property, plant, and equipment, cost of goods sold, and depreciation and depletion expense. Sales and other revenues and other expenses do not have to be adjusted.

19. (T)

20. (T)

Multiple Choice

1. (A) During a period of deflation the purchasing power of the dollar increases. Thus, the greatest purchasing power gain will result from holding cash in periods of deflation.

2. (C) Monetary items are items on a financial statement that are already stated in current dollars and thus require no restatement in constant dollar financial statements. They include assets and liabilities whose amounts are fixed by contract or otherwise in terms of dollars regardless of changes in the price level.

3. (C) Net monetary assets June 1 ($82,000 - $55,000) $27,000

    Amount needed at the end of June to maintain
       purchasing power [$27,000 x (115 + 110)].. 28,227
    Net monetary assets June 30 27,000
    Purchasing power loss... $ 1,227

4. (D) Building: $250,000 X (220 ÷ 120) = $458,333

    Machine: $140,000 X (220 ÷ 175) = $176,000

5. (B) The FASB requires use of the Consumer Price Index for All Urban Consumers (CPI-U)

6. (B) Constant dollar accounting preserves the historical cost-based accounting system that is currently used and understood. Thus, the impact of price-level changes are recorded without having to develop a new structure of accounting. The other three alternatives (A, C, and D) represent disadvantages said to be associated with constant dollar financial statements.

7. (A) Realized income measures the total income realized during the year. Realized income and historical cost income are always the same. Current cost net income measures the total income of the enterprise for one period and takes into account both realized and unrealized holding gains.

8. (C) Current cost is not always an approximation of the fair market value. An asset's value is a function of the future cash flows generated by it. Current cost, however, does not necessarily measure an increase in the service potential of that asset.

9. (D) *FASB Statement No. 89* was issued in 1986 for the purpose of removing the requirement to disclose changing price information. When the FASB issued *Statement No. 89* they encouraged companies to continue to disclose changing price information on a voluntary basis. However, since the issuance of the statement very few companies have chosen to present the information voluntarily.

10. (D) Using current cost rather than historical cost results in a better measure of operating efficiency. This is due to the fact that depreciation is based on a more relevant amount (current cost) and the resulting net income provides a more reliable assessment of the efficient use of assets in generating a relevant return on the assets employed. The other alternatives would not be considered appropriate.

Review Exercises

1.

	12-31-89 Historical Dollars	Conversion Factor	12-31-89 Constant Dollar Amounts
Cash	$40,000		$40,000
Accounts Receivable	88,000		88,000
Inventories	125,000	130/127	127,953
Building	210,000	130/110	248,182
Accumulated Depreciation	(30,000)	130/110	(35,455)
Land	50,000	130/110	59,091
	$483,000		$527,771
Accounts Payable	$ 80,000		$ 80,000
Bonds Payable	110,000		110,000
Common Stock	150,000	130/110	177,273
Premium on Common Stock	105,000	130/110	124,091
Retained Earnings	38,000		36,407*
	$483,000		$527,771

*Determined by computing the amount needed to balance the balance sheet.

2.

Income statement	12-31-88 Historical	Conversion Factor	12-31-88 Constant Dollar
Sales	$120,000	110/105	$125,714
Cost of Goods Sold	75,000	110/100	82,500
Gross Profit	$ 45,000		$43,214
Cash Expenses	20,000	110/105	20,952
Depreciation	5,000	110/100	5,500
Net Income	$ 20,000		$ 16,762
Purchasing Power Loss on Net Monetary Items	--		7,262
Net Income	$ 20,000		$ 9,500

Balance Sheet	12-31-88 Historical	Conversion Factor	12-31-88 Constant Dollar
Cash	$125,000		$125,000
Inventory	50,000	110/100	55,000
Building	50,000	110/100	55,000
Accumulated Depreciation	(5,000)	110/100	(5,500)
	$220,000		$229,500
Common Stock	$200,000	110/100	$220,000
Retained Earnings	20,000		9,500
	$220,000		$229,500

Computation of Purchasing Power Loss:

	Amount	Conversion Factor	Restated Amount
Beginning Net Monetary Assets	$ 25,000	110/100	$ 27,500
Increase due to Sales	120,000	110/105	125,714
	$145,000		$153,214
Decrease due to Expenses	20,000	110/105	20,952
	$125,000		$132,262
Ending Net Monetary Assets			125,000
Purchasing Power Loss on Net Monetary Items			$ 7,262

3.

Rose Corporation
Statement of Income
For the Year Ended 12-31-90
(Current Cost Basis)

Sales	$38,000
Cost of Goods Sold	22,000
Gross Profit	$16,000
Selling Expenses	2,000
Current Cost Income from Continuing Operations	$14,000
Realized Holding Gain	4,000 [a]
Realized Income	$18,000
Unrealized Holding Gain	10,000 [b]
Current Cost Net Income	$28,000

[a] $22,000 - $18,000 = $4,000

[b] $26,000 - $16,000 = $10,000